sent

_to_ kill

SENT TO KILL

The shocking true story behind
a forgotten African colonial war

GRAHAM FYSH

Cover designed by Gavin Fysh

Published by LifeTime Creations, Seattle, Washington
http://www.lifetimecreations.com
Printed in the United States
ISBN: 9781-494-28698-9
Also available as an e-book on Kindle and other online stores.

To my wife
MARCIA
without whose loving patience,
understanding, support and advice
I could never have written this
book.

ACKNOWLEDGEMENTS

My thanks go to Bruce Ramsey for his excellent editing and counsel, to Letlatsa Moqalo, who guided me around Moorosi's mountain, to Ed Harowicz for drawing the maps, and to those countless dedicated people in universities, libraries, archives and bookstores around the world who helped me gather the material for this work. I am particularly grateful to the Western Cape Archives and Records Service, who graciously granted me permission to use many of the illustrations in this book; the Lesotho National Archives in Maseru; the Morija Museum and Archives in Lesotho; and the National Library of South Africa. All the sketches by Arthur Pattisson are courtesy of the Western Cape Archives and Records Service.

AUTHOR'S NOTES

• The currency used at the time of the events in this book was the British pound (£), which was divided into 20 shillings, with each shilling worth 12 pence. In today's money, one 1870s pound would be worth roughly R1000 (South African); US$100; or £60 sterling.

• For the most part, I have retained the names of places used by the colonial government at the time in which the events in this book take place. For example, I use the then-official colonial name of Basutoland even though many inhabitants referred to it as The Lesotho, the name it was given (without "The") when it gained independence in 1966. The Orange River, the name I use, was known by the Baphuthi and Basotho as the Senqu River.

But I have made changes to some of the names used in documents at the time — for example, I refer to the people as Baphuthi and Basotho, in line with today's spelling. Also, Moorosi was often spelled Morosi or Moirosi and Moorosi's son Lehana was referred to by the colonial authorities as Doda.

• This book is an illustrated and modified version of my earlier book *MOOROSI: A South African king's battle for survival*, published in 2012.

— Graham Fysh

PREFACE

The world map was redrawn by the European powers in the 17th, 18th and 19th centuries.

Equipped with ships that could encircle the globe and firearms that could kill from a distance, the Europeans determined they could take control of the rest of the world for themselves, and ignore any claims to the land that the original inhabitants might inherently possess.

In Africa, as in many other parts of the world, they "discovered" huge tracts of real estate, which they set about acquiring, often by force. They saw those who already occupied the territories that they invaded as barbarians and heathens who possessed no redeeming qualities. The original inhabitants' languages, culture and governmental systems were all deemed inferior and unworthy of use, adaptation or preservation. After all, a new superior culture had been graciously brought to enlighten them.

Of all the European powers, the greatest invader of Africa was Britain, a country that also came to dominate much of the rest of the world.

As they occupied the newly acquired land, and redrew the historical boundaries between peoples along their own lines, the European settlers exploited the land's agricultural and mineral wealth, taking possession of large areas for their farms and towns. To them, the native peoples were a ready source of cheap labour or, if they resisted the colonial takeover, hindrances to be eliminated in a form of what the world was later to call ethnic cleansing.

In so doing, the colonialists turned any rational concept of governance on its head. The newly arrived invaders were the rulers. The original occupiers of the land and rulers of the people were the rebels.

This book tells of one of those African adventures. In a riveting true story, it describes how British settlers sought to take control of the Southern African territory of Quthing (today part of Lesotho), ruled by King Moorosi, leader of the Baphuthi people, in the way they had already done in territories to the south. It tells, too, how the astute Moorosi was more than a match for his would-be rulers.

As you enter the world of 19th Century African colonialism:

• Watch as an aggressive newly arrived magistrate attempts to impose colonial rule on people who fear it will destroy the very essence of who they are as a people.
• Watch as seemingly small incidents lead to major clashes.
• Watch tensions rise as the stand-off becomes increasingly polarized.
• Watch as a French missionary attempts to secure peace through compromise.
• Watch hostilities increase to the point where war becomes inevitable.

And be prepared to be surprised when you learn how it all ends.

View bonus items, express your opinion, and learn more at www.sent-to-kill.com

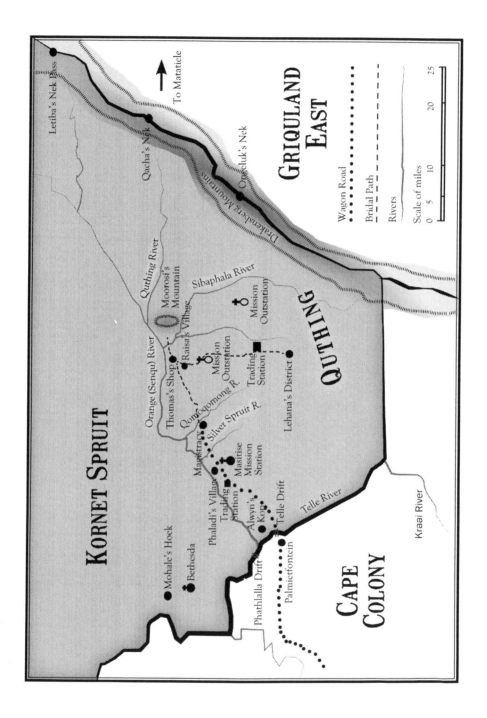

1

Quthing, Basutoland — Tuesday, May 22, 1877

Raisa crashes his axe alongside a healthy corn stalk, loosening its roots. He repeats the motion, digging into the ground on both sides of the stalk until he is able to pull up the plant and throw it to the side. Clearly, although harvest time in the lowlands along the Orange River is here, Raisa is not reaping this crop. He is ruining it.

Alerted by neighbours, a woman runs to the field, pleading with him to stop. "This is my field," MaLebenya screams. "These are my crops. What are you doing, Raisa?"

"You know what I'm doing and why I'm doing it," Raisa replies.

"I don't want you to do this," MaLebenya continues. "I tended to these plants. I weeded them. I watered them. I'm going to harvest them soon. Stop what you are doing. These crops are mine."

Raisa ignores her.

MaLebenya runs at him, screaming and pushing against his chest with one hand while trying to grab the axe with the other. Raisa shoves her aside.

He moves to the next plant, determined systematically to uproot each one in the field.

Realizing that, without help, she cannot stop Raisa from what he is doing, MaLebenya moves away. At 34, she is in her prime of life and, some among the Baphuthi would say, too young to be a widow. It was only a few weeks ago that they mourned the death of her husband from a fever; an unusual event in a largely healthy community. Now she is suffering a second loss.

Her screams attract others, many family members who, like her, live in Raisa's Village. "This man is destroying my cornfield," she shouts. "Help me stop him."

The crowd watches anxiously, some sympathizing with MaLebenya's plight. But no one dares interfere. For one thing, Raisa is MaLebenya's late husband's brother, making this a family quarrel. For another, Raisa is a Baphuthi sub-chief or headman. He holds sway over the people who live in his village, a collection of round mud huts with thatched cone-shaped roofs, which forms part of the territory ruled by King Moorosi, the leader of the Baphuthi people. Raisa's powers are subject only to the Baphuthi chiefs above him and to Moorosi himself.

MaLebenya recalls how her husband ploughed the field and sowed the corn seed. After that, as custom demanded, she had tended to it as it grew, and, now that he has died, had been planning to harvest and store the corn to see her through the approaching winter. Ground into meal and turned into porridge for herself and her children, it was to have been her subsistence.

Now her brother-in-law is taking away her means of survival.

⚜

As the afternoon sun reaches its zenith across the African sky and starts its journey back toward the mountaintops, MaLebenya grows weary of protest. She slumps among tall grass near the field. Angry and disillusioned, she sobs quietly. Her crop is destroyed. It cannot be replaced. She is furious at Raisa.

But she believes a white man who recently arrived in Quthing might help her get back at him for what he has done.

Quthing — Friday, May 25, 1877

The Baphuthi people have been lining up outside the semi-completed stone-built magistracy since dawn. Most have travelled for some hours on horseback, although a few have walked for hours and even days.

They have come to this compound alongside the Qomoqomong River to seek travel passes or to pay their hut taxes to Hamilton Hope, who three weeks ago became the first — and only — white colonial magistrate in Quthing.

Today the line-up to see Hope is interrupted by a 20-strong group approaching from the direction of the river. At its head is MaLebenya, talking loudly and waving her hands in the air.

It has been three days since Raisa destroyed her cornfield, but MaLebenya's anger has not dissipated. Now she has walked 15 miles to bring her complaint against Raisa to the new white official.

Hope, representative of whites who first settled in Cape Town more than 200 years ago, at first fears the interruption might be some sort of protest against his presence. He cannot understand what they are saying, but stares at the group through his piercing blue eyes, which

Hamilton Hope

reinforce his authoritative bearing and air of confidence, making him appear older than 38.

When MaLebenya tells him, through a translator, that she has a complaint against a headman, Hope's demeanour changes. Aha. A complaint not against him, but against a headman. Now that's what he wants to hear.

Since he arrived three weeks ago, he has done little more than collect hut taxes. Yet his appointment as "resident magistrate for the district of Quthing in the territory of British Basutoland" involves considerably more than collecting taxes.

His task is to bring British colonial rule to Quthing and to the Baphuthi people who live here under King Moorosi. Although Quthing was included by the British in the territory they called Basutoland, the 5,000-strong Baphuthi people speak their

Magistrate's offices

own language and have remained independent, although they have always lived as friendly neighbours alongside the Basotho.

Their independence has continued even as the rest of Basutoland has come increasingly under colonial control, largely because the Orange River dividing Quthing from the rest of Basutoland often is impassable, making it almost impossible to govern the territory effectively from Mohale's Hoek, the seat of government for neighbouring Kornet Spruit, under which it fell. Until now. Until Hope's arrival.

The idea for the Quthing post originated with Charles D. Griffith, the Cape Colony's Basutoland administrator stationed in Maseru, the Basutoland capital, who chose Hope for the post. "Moorosi is about the wildest and most uncivilized of any of the chiefs in Basutoland," he told the government in Cape Town. "We need to bring him to his senses."

Now, Hope reasons, this woman could help him toward doing just that.

Five hundred feet above Hope, on the slopes of a rock-crested hill, an 80-year-old man mounted on a horse holds the reins with one hand and a long-barrelled gun with the other. A blanket helps to ward off the cool morning wind.

King Moorosi is remarkably lithe, even though he has fought several battles. Although he walks with an awkward gait as a result of an ankle injury 10 years ago,

King Moorosi, sketched by Arthur Pattisson

he has aged well, helped by the brisk mountain air, constant exercise and, for the most part, a plentiful supply of nutritious food. He sits erect on his horse, making full use of his 5-foot-7-inch height.

His skin is fairer than that of most Africans, resembling that of the Arab people, those Europeans who meet him say. Around his neck is a leather necklace. From it hang beads, bones, small goat horns, baboon's fingers, claws of wild birds, porcupine quills and other totems that he has collected over the years. Each has a meaning and a purpose, for Moorosi is revered not only as king, but also as a rain maker and diviner among his people. His long earrings — which his people jokingly call "rings of governing" — are a trademark, their jingling announcing him as he approaches.

Moorosi's intellect matches his physical ability. As is the case with most Baphuthi people, he shows no sign of losing his mental skills with age. He is self-confident, speaks eloquently and thinks quickly. Intensely independent, he is proud of his people, the land they occupy, his ancestors and their way of life. He is a strong leader, a good shot and a shrewd fighter.

Bushman bowman, as portrayed in a sketch by Fred Christol. [*The Mountain Bushmen of Basutoland* by Marion Walsham How, 1958]

So strong is his leadership that others — Khoisan people, whom many call Bushmen, and some members of the Xhosa-speaking Thembu people from the south — have been absorbed into the Baphuthi nation. Moorosi himself has two Khoisan women among his dozen wives, a gesture of respect to the mountain people who first lived here back in the mists of time.

Indeed, the Khoisan gave him his first two horses, some 50 years ago, which they stole in a raid on a white farm in the Cape Colony to the south. Later his people acquired hundreds of horses, from which today's smaller Basotho ponies, adept at negotiating the narrow mountain paths of the area, were bred.

Moorosi wonders how his ancestors would have viewed this white government official come to live in their midst. He thinks of his ancestors, his father Mokuoane, the son of Mokhoebi, the son of Thibela, the son of Khanyane, the son of Tsele, the son of Kobo, the son of Titi, the son of Langa.

For 40 years, since the death of his father, these ancestors all have watched over him as he has led his people. Now he looks to them for wisdom as Hope's arrival marks the beginning of a new era for the Baphuthi, one through which he must lead them to ensure their survival as a people.

He will welcome Hope because Baphuthi custom demands they welcome strangers. He will respect Hope. He will learn from him.

But he will watch Hope's actions carefully, particularly should they impinge on his realm.

⁂

With Abraham Sighata — the chief constable employed by Hope — translating, MaLebenya describes what Raisa did to her cornfield.

Hope feels a shot of adrenalin move through his body. He is confident her complaint will provide him with a start on his mission aimed at ensuring that colonial law, standards and order are imposed on the Baphuthi people. Here, unlike his previous position as an assistant magistrate in Mafeteng, he will be solely in charge. It will not be easy, but he will make his mark on the territory, which stretches 40 miles at its widest point from east to west and 120 miles from south to north. He will do so with a tough approach that will brook no opposition, bringing the "untamed" Moorosi to his senses in no uncertain way.

He will do so without his wife of 13 years, Emma Cecile, whom he calls Mimmie. Absent, too, will be his mother-in-law, Elizabeth Rolland, 74, who lived with the couple after the death of Elizabeth's French-born missionary husband four years ago. They live in Burghersdorp, 60 miles to the south, in the Cape Colony. For now, they will not join him.

As Moorosi watches the movement in the valley below, he recalls that over many years, he fought those who wanted to take away their country. He protected their land. He kept his people together. He maintained their right to rule themselves. He retained their freedom.

He remembers how nine years ago he reluctantly placed his people and their land under the protection of the British, who had safeguarded the Basotho people from the Boers — white farmers in the adjoining Free State who had steadily been seizing more and more Basotho territory. He followed the lead of the now-departed great Basotho leader Moshoeshoe, whom he respected as a father and who had asked the British to protect him.

But then, Moorosi recalls, the British handed over Basutoland, including the Baphuthi land, to the Cape Colony.

At first, he had thought the Cape Colony people would be like the British who let them run their own country. But he hears stories from his neighbours that the people from the Cape are interfering more than the British government. It seems they do not want only to protect them; they want to govern them.

And now, he ponders, the colonial government is putting a white magistrate on Baphuthi land, among his people. Why does he need to be here?

True, other whites have settled on their land.

The first white man who came to live among them was the missionary Ellenberger. He is a good man. He teaches their people and their children well. He is away now, and his work is being done by the men he trained. But he said he would return.

Then came Thomas, the trader and the white men who help him run his three stores. Moorosi and the Baphuthi people are content for them to be here. The traders give them money in return for their eggs, wool and corn and sell them goods they can use, such as blankets and saddles.

But now here is a man from the white government to the south. He is not sure about him.

Ellenberger the preacher and Thomas the trader have been joined by Hope the administrator. A new religion, a new economy, and now a new government, all from outside.

He told Griffith, the head of the white magistrates who lives in Maseru, he did not want Hope to come here. He recalls asking him, "What is wrong with the way I govern my people? My people love me and respect me. They are happy. Their crops are good. Their cattle are fat. Why do you want to send this man here?"

Griffith told him this man Hope would help him to run the country, but Moorosi would still govern his people. He reluctantly accepted Griffith's reassurance, but Moorosi is fearful that might not be the case. You cannot have two kings in one country.

Moorosi tugs on the reins of his horse, directing it toward a path that leads down the mountainside. His earrings swing from side to side and his necklace bounces up and down in time with the horse's lope.

He realizes he is facing the biggest challenge of his life.

Cape Town — The same day

Some 600 miles south of Basutoland, Sir Henry Bartle Frere is making his first public appearance as the new British-appointed governor-general of the Colony of the Cape of Good Hope in its capital, Cape Town, at the tip of the African continent.

Frere, 61, speaking today at the opening of Parliament, introduces himself to the people of the colony. First settled by the Dutch in 1652 and established as a British colony in 1814, it is now home to 828,000 people, a third of them white, and the rest made up of aborigines called Hottentots (98,000), mixed-race people (120,000), Malay (10,000) and 365,000 black people, mostly Xhosa-speaking, who live in the north-eastern part of the colony, south of Basutoland, on the colony's frontier.

The colony was granted a degree of self-rule almost six years ago, but the ultimate power still lies in Britain, where Queen Victoria reigns over the most powerful nation in the world, which has colonized large parts of the globe.

British Colonial Secretary Lord Carnarvon has sent Frere — knighted for his achievements in British India — to South Africa not just to govern the colony, but primarily to establish a confederation of the disparate and often antagonistic white-run colonies and self-proclaimed states. Instead of the Transvaal, Orange Free State, Natal, Griqualand West, Griqualand East and the Cape Colony each governing themselves, they would be one unit, with each having a degree of self-rule, in one parliament under British supervision. It will be called the South African Dominion.

As for Basutoland, Frere knows only that it exists and little more.

Paris — The same day

David Frederic Ellenberger and his wife Emma have been in Europe for more than two years, recuperating from 15 years of spreading the Gospel among the Basotho and most recently the Baphuthi people — work that left them exhausted.

They have sought to regain their strength for their return early next year, when they would have been away from Africa for three years. They are as eager to get back to their work as they believe the Baphuthi people and King Moorosi himself are for them to return.

Those acquainted with the couple were not surprised to find that they needed time off. Ellenberger filled every day of his time among the Baphuthi trying to cope with the demands of two passions.

One was to spread the Gospel. He ran schools and churches, visiting people in the far-flung areas of the mission field, counselling those who wished to become Christians, encouraging those who had converted to the faith, and preparing for Sunday services.

If a moment passed when he had nothing to do, he would create a new task to ensure his time did not pass unused.

His other driving force was to record the history and customs of the people.

He would sit down to his recording duties after dinner until 1 a.m. and waken at 6 a.m. to get in study time before mission work demanded all his attention. Those long hours, lack of sleep and incessant work are why, people always assume, he looks so frail. His face, framed between a full beard and a sharply receding hairline, is drawn; his eyes look tired. He appears frail and weak, but, driven by his overriding desire and determination to spread the Christian message, he never allowed tiredness or physical pain to be an excuse.

Even here in Paris, he finds it difficult to relax. He has supervised the printing of thousands of copies of the New Testament and Christian works he helped translate.

Ellenberger also has spent many hours at the offices of the Paris Evangelical Missionary Society, which he joined at age 21. There, after studying medicine for a year, he studied theology for four years. He and Emma left for Basutoland soon after his ordination. Now, at 42, Ellenberger is determined he will continue to pursue his life's mission and return to Quthing within a year.

Today Ellenberger is visiting with Georges Steinheil, a 19-year-old Swiss studying theology at the Maison des Missions in Paris who plans one day to work in Basutoland as a missionary.

"I have heard that you are Swiss, also studied at the Maison des Mission in Paris

Frederic Ellenberger

Emma Ellenberger

and are a member of the Paris Evangelical Missionary Society," Steinheil says.

Ellenberger nods in agreement, adding, "Not only that. Your name is Georges and my wife and I named our youngest son Georges. He was born here in Paris just a year ago, on June 6th."

Steinheil laughs. "A good name. But, seriously, I am told that if anyone under-stands the Baphuthi and Basotho people and how to reach them with the Gospel, that person is you. I want you to tell me all about it. Do not spare any details."

Ellenberger is delighted at the company of someone who intends to follow the same path he took nearly two decades ago. He will be pleased to share the knowledge of 16 years in Basutoland and in particular the last 11 years in Quthing.

Soft-spoken and erudite, Ellenberger tells how when he arrived in Quthing, he received a warm welcome from Moorosi, who had asked him to start a mission sta-tion there and presented him with an ox, a traditional gift to someone you respect.

"The Baphuthi king told me I could choose anywhere I liked for the mission station.

"After a week I came across an area called Masitise. The place was ideal. Not only was there sufficient land and water to establish a village for the Christians, but, being hidden above the valley on the slopes of a hill, it was particularly good from a defensive point of view.

"Three weeks later Moorosi met me there and we agreed on the bounda-ries of the station. We also resolved questions relating to springs, land for fields, grazing ground and so on."

Ellenberger says he took his wife and children to settle with him at Masitise in January 1867. "I built a two-roomed house, but I

Two-roomed house built by Ellenberger.

realized that it would soon be too small for the needs of my family, as Emma was pregnant.

Then one day I made the most amazing find."

Emma enters the room to tell him a donor is waiting in the parlour.

"I'm afraid I must go," Ellenberger says. "Let's meet again next week."

Quthing — Tuesday, May 29, 1877

Hope, who has picked up only a smattering of the local languages, listens intently as Sighata translates MaLebenya's complaint against headman Raisa.

Clearly, Hope reasons, the case is open and shut. Raisa is not only guilty of tres-passing and destruction, he is also guilty of treating a woman like a piece of property.

"I will issue a summons against Raisa," Hope tells MaLebenya. "It will instruct him to appear before me to answer the charges you have levelled against him. Return here on Monday. I will then give you the summons to take to him."

Hope is confident he will pronounce Raisa guilty — what possible defence could he have? — and sentence him. Of course, the principles of British justice demand he give him a hearing.

Above all, he will be firm and authoritative.

Hope learned firmness and discipline from his father, William Hope, a graduate of England's Sandhurst military college and major in the British Seventh Fusiliers. Major Hope emigrated with his family to Cape Town in June 1846 when Hope was 7.

After a stint as a government clerk, his father was appointed Auditor-General of the Cape, a post he held until his death in 1858, almost 20 years ago, at the age of 51.

Although Hope was only 19 when his father died, he still remembers the emphasis his father put on serving one's country and doing what was right under the law.

He is convinced his father, a strict disciplinarian, would have been proud were he to see him now, conducting this hearing, which will serve two purposes: Hope will show his superiors in the colonial office that he is taking control in spite of his relatively short experience; and the people will realize his will is strong and his justice swift.

No longer, he believes, will they be able to continue their barbaric, uncivilized and unproductive way of living or to practice their heathen customs. The rule of colonial law has arrived.

Paris — Thursday, May 31, 1877

Steinheil reminds Ellenberger that when they were interrupted he mentioned an amazing find he had made in the early days at the Masitise mission station.

"Yes, it was amazing," Ellenberger replies. "I climbed up the hill on the west of the flat slope I had chosen for the mission station and, in an area I had not explored before, I saw a cave under an enormous rock. The people told me that, years before, Bushmen had lived there. Later porcupines had burrowed into it. As I examined it, I realized that this cave could be turned into a home. The front was about 80 feet long and I reasoned I could safely dig back into it for at least 15 feet. I could dig down so that the ceiling would be about 6 feet high.

"At the back of the cave, on the left, in a corner, a small spring provided fresh water. I could incorporate that in our kitchen-pantry area."

Ellenberger tells Steinheil how he used bricks to fill in the 60-foot-wide front of the cave, including a front door in the centre and two windows on each side. He also closed in both sides on the left and right with walls and, in each fitted a window. On the inside, he covered the bricks with mud, which he whitewashed.

"You built it yourself?"

"Yes, I did. I divided the house into four rooms, each 15 feet square. The first room on the left, that closest to the kitchen, was the dining room. Alongside was the living room, to which the front door gave access. The main bedroom, which included a big steel bed with a mattress made of dried corn leaves and a baby's cradle for the child who was soon to be born, lay alongside the living room and, at the end was the

Ellenberger's cave house; the kitchen is the building on the left.

Plan of cave house as recalled by Victor Ellenberger, Fred's son.

children's room.

"I had my own mission station. My own house. My own people, the Baphuthi, among whom I would work."

"You must have been pleased."

"I felt fulfilled, doing what I was called to do, all those years before here in Paris. God was giving me the greatest oppor-tunity of my life to serve him.

"Today the cave house and my original two-roomed house are sufficient to accom-modate our eight children, who range in age from one to 15, and who will all soon be there with me and Emma again."

Ellenberger adds that six years ago, the British government handed its administration of Basutoland to the Cape Colony, which has been more vigorous in asserting control over the territory, which it sees as a prosperous agricultural area it can exploit and whose people can form a ready supply of labour.

"When I left, the Cape administration had exerted little direct control over Moorosi and the Baphuthi people, although I believe that is now changing."

"How did you preach to the people?"

"I went out among them. I did not wait for them to come to me. I spread the word among them and, after people became Christians, I established two outstations, run by Baphuthi converts.

"I also built schools where we taught them the Bible and how they should live, as well as school subjects. Emma helped me in teaching at the school and preparing services. She also led sewing groups for the women."

"How many of the people have become Christians?"

"At the time I left, a few hundred were living active Christian lives. Indeed, two great Baphuthi Christians are now helping to run the mission station while we are away. The Missionary Conference estimates the number of Christian adults in all of Basutoland has grown above 5,000."

"And the total population of Basutoland is...?"

"Around 150,000."

Ellenberger describes how he added a building in which to work, where he stored all his books on mission work among the Basotho. In that room, too, he operated a printing press for several years.

Steinheil nods. "Has Moorosi been receptive to the Gospel?"

"He shows some interest, and he and I talk often about the Gospel, but his heart remains in his ancient customs.

Typical Baphuthi hut

It is difficult for him and others to discard those ways. I think he will become a Christian when I return. He is an intelligent man, speaks well and is self-confident.

"These people love proverbs and folklore and storytelling," Ellenberger continues. "Especially humorous stories. The listeners roar with laughter even though they might have heard the story many times.

"It is probable that this love of story telling is partly responsible for the purity of their languages. Debased, ungrammatical speech as among the Europeans is unknown among the Basotho and the Baphuthi. "

A necklace, probably of a traditional doctor, consisting of horns, shells, beads, wood, porcupine quills, bird claws and even the foot of a tortoise. [*Morija Museum and Archives*]

"Interesting," Steinheil says. "Sloppy language causes sloppy thoughts. I hope we do not influence the Baphuthi that way. Talking of adopting our ways, have the people's customs changed since you arrived there?"

"Yes, in some ways. Those who have become Christians are increasingly adopting European customs and clothing, but most continue to follow the old customs and traditions while paying respect to the British and now the Cape Colony's authorities."

Ellenberger explains that the men build the huts. Almost all Basotho work in the fields. They plant corn, millet and sorghum, beans, sugar cane, watermelon, pumpkin, gourds, calabashes, tobacco and hemp. Now and then they eat meat, which is cooked on a stick, stuck in the ground near a fire. A major part of their diet is thick milk, kept in a skin bag. Most of their food is eaten cold.

"Owing to their simple diet and healthy way of life, the Basotho live to a great age," Ellenberger says. "It is said that years ago people who lived to be 100 to 120 years were not uncommon; and that their health and intelligence remained unimpaired to the end of their days."

Most of their time is spent in the open air, the missionary continues. The Baphuthi are well-built people who can last for days without food and recover well from most injuries. They also can go without sleep for days.

"Even as I hope to teach these people, I think I will learn something from them," Steinheil comments, with a smile.

"I think we all can. Yet I don't want to give the impression that they are never ill," Ellenberger adds. "The people do become sick and they have doctors who treat them. Some of these doctors are impostors. Some have knowledge only of certain diseases. Others have studied and have a considerable knowledge of diseases and the medicinal properties of plants.

"This knowledge often has to be bought and those who have it guard it," he continues.

Several head of cattle is not too high a price to pay for a secret remedy. Sometimes charlatans combine witchcraft and medicine. They throw divining bones, condemn a fellow tribesman as carrying an evil spirit and order him to be cast out and sometimes thrown over a cliff and killed.

"Yet, apart from such occasional incidents, you find little crime among the Baphuthi," Ellenberger adds. "Violence is rare. It is all the more remarkable because there is little police supervision. The people seem to have a natural love of order and respect for authority. They show an almost superstitious respect for their king. He runs the judicial and political systems and he is the guardian of the land and all its natural resources."

"Sounds like the divine right of kings," says Steinheil.

"It is. Here's another thing," Ellenberger continues. "Family is even more important to them than to us. The Basotho and the Baphuthi look to the family for support, friendship and sustenance. When you have no food, no house or no cattle, your family will ensure you do not sleep in the cold and you do not starve. If someone in your family dies, the rest of the family will take you in and care for you. It is considered bad to break the family bonds.

This scene, captured for a postcard in the early 1900s, is typical of a *khotla*, a hearing usually held outside a chief's hut and which often involved family matters.

"Their custom, or law, holds the head of the family responsible for the conduct of its members, the village for that of its households and the tribe for the behaviour of its village communes. The tribe is a big family that extends outward. Individual rights, such as we have here in France are unknown to the Basotho. No one owns the land; it belongs to the people.

"Morality is so dependent on the social order that any breakdown in this order is likely to be followed by degeneracy and anarchy.

"The family and tribal bonds extend even beyond the grave. You have to know who you are descended from. You have to have regard for your ancestors."

He explains that he has traced Basotho and Baphuthi family history back a long way. He has drawn up an extensive genealogy of the people.

"How long ago did this all happen?" Steinheil asks. "I have heard they have been in that part of Africa for only a few generations."

"My studies have shown these people have lived in and around that part of Africa for much longer than a few generations," Ellenberger replies. "Their memories, passed on from generation to generation, are amazing. I have been able to trace some families back 30 generations."

"Let's see," Steinheil responds. "If you take a generation as 30 years, that means you have traced their genealogy back 900 — almost a thousand — years?"

"Indeed."

"But how can that be? They have no written records. Do you mean to tell me they have remembered their genealogy?"

"They have passed it on. Just as the Bible records who begat whom, so do these people. The only difference is that the genealogies in the Bible are today written and those of the Basotho and Baphuthi remain oral. And just as it was important to the

Jewish people to know who was in the royal line of descent, so it is important to the Basotho, too. The reasoning is the same. If you can trace your ancestry to a line of kings, you are considered to be royalty, too. Indeed, it is the same with the kings and queens of Europe and England.

"Because the lines of descent are unwritten, unravelling their history and separating truth from the tangle of tradition is not an easy task. But I have been able to verify ancestors by comparing the oral history of one clan with that of another. When I find the same ancestor occurring in a number of them, I have to accept that person as real."

"Yes, that makes sense," comments Steinheil, intrigued by what he is hearing. "What else do you know about their history?"

"The Baphuthi moved to the region now known as Basutoland from the north after a dispute with a clan in Tugela, which is now home to the Zulu people," Ellenberger says. "They arrived around 1720 when they settled among the Bafokeng in the area that is now north-western Basutoland. The Bafokeng introduced them to iron hoes. Later the Baphuthi migrated south, to where they live today.

"There, they came across the Bushmen, who lived in caves in the winter and in huts made from branches, or under skins spread on poles during the summer. They were hunters. They lived off wild animals, many of which have now disappeared from the land.

"By contrast, the Baphuthi were, and still are, farmers. They build huts, plant their fields and raise cattle. Boys are taught by their fathers to herd stock, to cultivate the ground and to use weapons. Girls are taught by the matrons obedience, courtesy, housekeeping and cooking and also to assist in the work of the fields. Some of the Bushmen moved away. Others were absorbed into the Baphuthi people.

"There is much more," Ellenberger says. "I need to stop now, but next time we meet I'll have things to tell you about the Baphuthi people that will astound you."

2

Quthing — Monday, June 4, 1877

The summons is ready. It has been drawn up by Hope and translated by Charles Maitin, Hope's new clerk and translator, who arrived in Quthing yesterday. His arrival brings to two the number of white administrators in the Baphuthi territory.

The son of French missionaries who settled among the Basotho 34 years ago, Maitin, 31, was born and bred in Basutoland. As a result, he has a thorough knowledge of the Sesotho language, which most of the Baphuthi can speak.

The summons orders Raisa to present himself in court on Thursday, June 14 to answer charges that he destroyed a cornfield belonging to MaLebenya.

"Take this summons to him," Hope instructs MaLebenya, "it tells him to come here on June 14th — in 10 days — and present himself to this court. If we find him guilty, we will punish him."

Quthing — Friday, June 8, 1877

The widow MaLebenya makes her way to Raisa's hut to present Hope's summons to him. She sees that the mat over the doorway is rolled down, indicating he does not want to be disturbed. MaLebenya stops short at entering the hut as that would be breaking a strict Baphuthi moral code. But Raisa has seen his late brother's wife approaching. He emerges from his hut and walks forward to meet her.

MaLebenya thrusts the summons toward him.

"What's this?" Raisa asks, grabbing the piece of paper.

"It says you must go to the magistrate because you destroyed my crop," replies MaLebenya. "He says it was wrong and you must be punished."

The words are inflammatory to Raisa. Who is this new magistrate to accuse him of doing wrong? What does he know about right and wrong?

"This man Hope is interfering in matters on which he has no authority. I will ignore this meaningless paper," he says, thrusting the summons back in MaLebenya's hands.

"It says you must be there in six days," responds MaLebenya.

Raisa curls his upper lip in a sneer. "That might be what it says," he shouts. "But does that mean it is what I will do?"

Paris — The same day

"You were going to tell me something about the Basotho people that would surprise me," says Georges Steinheil. "I think you used the phrase, 'astound you' if I recall."

Ellenberger smiles and leans back in his chair. "You will recall I said that, through a combination of tradition, language and customs, we can trace the Basotho people — including the Baphuthi — farther back than I have described so far," he says. "We have found out, for example, that the Bafokeng, who introduced the Baphuthi to iron hoes and

15

whom I mentioned earlier, migrated from Egypt or Ethiopia to the south of Africa. It must have taken centuries.

"But we can go back even farther, back even before the time of Christ. I believe — and I am not alone in this belief — that today's Basotho and Baphuthi people are descendants of Semitic people who lived in the Middle East thousands of years ago. We have found a strong link between their customs and those of the ancient Hebrews."

Steinheil's eyes light up. "Now that you mention it, I have heard that Europeans who first arrived in the country said the Basotho varied in colour from light brown to dark black, even in the same families."

"Indeed," Ellenberger responds. "The reason, we believe, is that they reflect the original people from whom they sprang. Their lighter skin colour and Arabian-like features represent their Middle Eastern origin; their blackness reflects their intermarriage as they made their way down through Africa.

"My fellow missionaries have described some of the Basotho people as almost Arab or Persian in their appearance. As one put it, 'they are tall, beautifully built, with aquiline noses, upright foreheads and lips almost as thin as those of Europeans.'

"Of course, I noticed those characteristics myself when I first arrived there. The missionary Eugene Casalis records his initial observations in his book, which I have here, 'Their skin was soft, bronze rather than black, their limbs robust and well modelled.' He also says that in the case of the Basotho aristocracy, their eyes are more prominent, their noses less flattened and their lips thinner, more like those of Europeans than Africans.

"These people also carry the culture of the people from whom they originally sprang. In short, these people are not barbaric. They are not savages, as the white colonial authorities often say. Nor can they be described as truly heathen, another epithet often thrown their way by the Europeans. We believe these people among whom I have been preaching the Gospel are descendants of a Middle Eastern people whose beliefs and customs are recorded in the Old Testament."

Steinheil sits up straight.

"Recorded in the Old Testament?"

Ellenberger nods. He explains that the theory of links between the Basotho people and the ancient Hebrews is strongly held by the missionary Casalis, who recorded his thoughts in the book from which he earlier quoted and which Casalis wrote 15 years ago, in 1862.

Steinheil notes that Casalis is now director of the Maison des Missions in Paris.

Among Casalis's evidence, Ellenberger continues, is the similarity of words in Setswana — closely related to the Basotho language Sesotho — and other languages spoken in Africa, such as those in the Congo, the Comoro Islands and Delagoa, as well as Swahili. Casalis also identified a number of words in languages of the Batswana and Basotho people that appeared to be of Hebrew origin.

Ellenberger takes out Casalis's book, *The Basotho*, flips through the pages to one containing a chart that Casalis drew up.

"Look here, the Hebrew word for children, *bene*, is *bana* in Setswana. It is the same in Sesotho. To repent — a term associated with religious beliefs and likely to be retained if the beliefs are similar — is *bakah* in Hebrew and *baka* in Setswana and Sesotho. The Hebrew for to swear, or attest, is *anah*; in Sesotho it is *ana*."

He flips through a few pages and reads to Steinheil from Casalis' book: "We might further notice, as bearing resemblance to the Hebrew, the forms of the verbs, the suffixing pronouns, the frequent use of the noun as adjective, and of the verb as adverb, the manner in which the comparative and superlative are formed, and several interesting idioms."

ENGLISH.	SECHUANA.	HEBREW. ENGLISH PRONUNCIATION.
Antelope.	Tsepe.	צבי Tsebi.
Truth.	Amanite.	אמן Amen.
Children.	Bana.	בני Bene.
Father.	Hara.	הורה (*Genitor*) Horeh.
Voice.	Kolou.	קול Kol.
Marrow.	Mokho.	מח Moach.
Wool.	Romo.	רמה Romah.
To execrate.	Rora.	ארר Arar.
Who.	Mang.	מי Man.
To swear, to attest.	Ana.	ענה Anah.
To see.	Bona.	בן (*Cernere*) Boun.
To shut.	Kuala.	כלא Kala.
Serpent.	Noha	נחש Nahash.
To weep, to cry.	Lela	ילל Jalal.
To cook.	Apea.	אפא Apa.
To repent.	Baka.	בכה (*Flere de*) Bakah.
To fall.	Oua.	הוה (*Casus*) Ouah.
High place.	Pahama.	במה Bamah.
Riches, abundance.	Nala.	נלה (*Acquirere*) Nalah.
To cross.	Tsela.	צלה Tsalah.
To hope.	Tsepa.	צפה Tsapah.
To flow.	Palala.	בלל (*Fudit*) Balal.
To return, to come in.	Boea.	בוא (*Intrare domum*) Bo.
To withdraw.	Suta.	שט Sout.
To laugh.	Tseha.	צחק Tsahak.

Table in *The Basutos* by Eugene Casalis.
[Morija Museum & Archives]

Ellenberger reads on, "We find nothing of a savage nature when we seek the reflection of their thoughts and feeling in the vocabulary and grammar of their respective idioms, which, if they do not display a degree of civilization similar to our own, may, without hesitation, be said to reproduce that of the patriarchal era."

Ellenberger adds an observation of his own. The women who adorn themselves with the traditional Basotho dress wear round their loins a girdle of twisted grass called the *thethana*, which word, he explains, may be derived from the Hebrew *thanah*, meaning a fig tree, the leaves of which Adam and Eve are said to have made themselves aprons. "So," he laughingly adds, "you see, their language goes right back to the origin of mankind.

"Here's another example. The Baphuthi, like the Basotho, begin their month on the new moon. So did the ancient Babylonians, Hebrews and Romans. They also begin the civil day at sunset, and count days from evening to evening, which the Jewish people still do."

Ellenberger adds that the Baphuthi common law also appears to have been passed on from thousands of years ago. The system of land tenure, in which the land belongs to the nation under the chief, excludes any concept of private land ownership. That system and the major principles of the Basotho common law are largely identical with those of the patriarchal dispensation of the Old Testament.

"Being in Basutoland is like living among the patriarchs of old," says Ellenberger.

Although their customs appear to have remained the same over the ages, the missionary adds, belief in one powerful God like that of the Hebrews appears to have waned. Instead they worship their ancestors and attribute to them a divine power for good and evil. But the concept of God appears occasionally. Some missionaries, say by using the word *Molimo* the Basotho designate the Great Lord Creator of their several tribes.

"There is an ancient prayer that means 'New gods, pray for us to the God of old,' in which the Basotho invoke the Deity through the mediation of the spirits. You could argue that this points to the necessity of mediation between God and man. We, too, believe in Jesus as a mediator."

Steinheil leans forward, fascinated. "Why, then, do the people name themselves after animals? I understand the Baphuthi, for example, are named after a variety of antelope called the *phuthi* or duiker."

"Yes," replies Ellenberger. "Duikers used to abound in that area, but they have almost all gone now, as a result of hunting. I believe that these emblems are, to the Baphuthi and other Basotho clans, symbols of the Divine Being, just as the Ark of the Covenant was the symbol of God for the Israelites of old.

"They wanted more than just to rely on the mediation of their ancestors, who were invisible. They wanted something tangible to symbolize the God of old to which they could pray and from whom they could seek aid.

"But to return to the law," Ellenberger continues. "It is, of course, not written down, but is passed down from generation to generation. It is accepted among the people. They do not question it; they do not seek to alter it. And that law, as I mentioned, is strikingly similar to that of the Hebrews."

Ellenberger opens his Bible and turns to Deuteronomy 25:5.

"Here's an example of Baphuthi custom being the same as that of the ancient Hebrew people," he tells Steinheil. "Let me read it to you. 'When brothers reside together, and one of them dies and has no son, the wife of the deceased shall not be married outside the family to a stranger. Her husband's brother shall go in to her, taking her in marriage, and performing the duty of a husband's brother to her.'

"The ancient Hebrews took this system seriously. As we read in verses 7 to 10: However, if a man does not want to marry his brother's wife, she shall go to the elders at the town gate and say, 'My husband's brother refuses to carry on his brother's name in Israel. He will not fulfil the duty of a brother-in-law to me.' Then his brother's wife shall go up to him in the presence of the elders and pull his sandal off his foot and spit in his face. And she shall answer and say, 'So shall it be done to the man who does not build up his brother's house.' And the name of his house shall be called in Israel, 'The house of him who had his sandal pulled off.'

"The Bible also has other references to the system, known as the levirate, going back as far as Genesis," Ellenberger adds, "In that book, chapter 38, we read that Er, Judah's first born, was put to death by the Lord. Then, in verse 8, we read: 'then Judah said to Onan, 'Lie with your brother's wife and fulfil your duty to her as a brother-in-law to produce offspring for your brother.'

"This same approach, followed by the Hebrews so long ago, is reflected in the evidence given to the Commission on Laws and Customs of the Basotho, which sat in Cape Town four years ago. I have a copy of it." Ellenberger searches among his papers for the commission report.

"Ah, here it is. Listen to the evidence given to the commission by George Tladi Moshesh, son of the late Chief Moshoeshoe: 'If the husband dies, his wife, or wives, belong to his eldest surviving brother who is to raise up seed to his deceased brother by taking them to wife himself or giving them to other men as wives. If the deceased has left any children, the son of the first wife will be his heir, and can claim all the children born to his deceased father's wives, and all cattle given for any of these children belong to him.'

"You may be struck by the similarity between how the Bible describes the Hebrew law and how George Moshesh describes the Basotho law 2,500 years later. If anything the law is stricter than it was among the Hebrews. The purpose is to preserve the family line. The Bible is filled with references to family lines. You'll recall Jesus' ancestry was traced back to David, giving him legitimacy among the Jewish people. And so it is today among the Baphuthi. If you can trace your history back to the

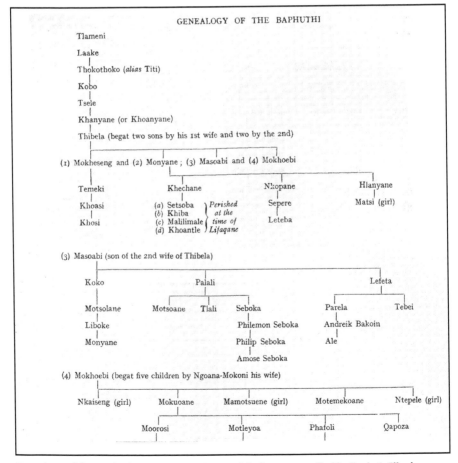

Genealogy of the Baphuthi, as set out in *History of the Basuto* compiled by Frederic Ellenberger [1912]. Moorosi's sons included Letuka (by his first wife MaSakale), Lehana and Lemena.

family line of a famous chief or king, your people hold you in high esteem.

"As I have told you, I have been able to trace the history of these people back a thousand years," Ellenberger adds. "To them, the lines of descent are just as important as they were to the Hebrew people. Moorosi, the Baphuthi king, can trace his ancestry back over 10 generations.

"It is also a way of preserving the family's property. Women are granted access to land through their husbands. But when a woman's husband dies her land can be taken away from her for any reason. She holds the land by virtue of being a man's wife, not in her own right. Although action might not be taken against a woman who refuses to marry her brother-in-law, her land can be taken away.

"The widow also must often leave her male children behind with her deceased husband's family. The emphasis is on the family, its heritage and its land rather than on the individual.

"Major clashes occur with the colonial government and the missionaries on three major aspects of their customs. They involve the *lebollo*, or circumcision, and sometimes cruel and merciless initiation rites that young men undergo under seclusion to mark their transition to manhood, the *sethepu*, or polygamy, and

Book of Genesis translated and printed by Ellenberger.

the *bohadi*, or the practice of giving cattle to a father for the privilege of marrying his daughter.

"As Casalis notes, we see evidence of these three practices, too, among the ancient peoples of the Middle East. For example, the age of the administration of the initiation rite is about the same as that of Ishmael, when he and his father Abraham received the sign of the covenant. Many Hebrew kings had multiple wives. King Solomon had 700.

"Also, Baphuthi marriages are conducted in the same way as among the Etruscans, the ancient Romans and the Arabs. The parents of the man pay a value, often called a dowry, to the parents of the woman he is to marry.

"Casalis points out that it is a curious coincidence that, at the rate of remuneration awarded to young shepherds in the southern part of Africa, a Basotho man, in order to acquire sufficient means to procure a wife, would be obliged to serve for the same number of years as Jacob did to the father of Rachel and Leah."

"The practice of sacrifice is familiar to the Baphuthi and Basotho, too. Some offer victims as a method of averting domestic or public calamities. It is therefore an easy transition for them to understand that Jesus died for their sins."

Ellenberger rises from his chair. "Are there any issues that I have not discussed?"

"I wonder what you think of the new magistrate. You mentioned him, but did not elaborate. Do you think he will do some good for the Baphuthi and help them to follow the Christian way?"

Ellenberger pauses, tugs at his beard, looks away from Steinheil, and stares toward the wall. "Let me think about that. I will try to answer the question when we talk again later, perhaps in a day or two."

Steinheil is intrigued. He judges from Ellenberger's reaction that this question is not easy for him to answer.

Quthing — Wednesday, June 13, 1877

Having been ordered twice by the new government official to appear before him tomorrow, Raisa realizes that the time has come to speak with his king. Raisa is reluctant to obey the magistrate's order, but is nervous about the implications of defying the magistrate, who represents the powerful white government to the south.

Raisa is convinced he acted correctly in destroying MaLebenya's cornfield. After all, she had refused to become his wife, as she should have done when her husband died. She also had refused to let him become the father to her children.

Clearly she had been influenced by the white people's thinking. Why else would she disobey? Why else would she go against everything that was right and just? He was doing the right thing, but she rebelled and did the wrong thing.

So he had taken away the cornfield. She no longer had any right to it. The field would have become his if she had become his wife. But now the field belongs to the people and must be returned to them — without its crop.

Leaving his village, he rides on horseback along the Orange River for several miles until he reaches Moorosi's stronghold, a flat-topped mountain that the Baphuthi chief over the last decade has turned into a fortress.

Moorosi's mountain, from a contemporary photograph.

The 1,500-foot mountain appears similar to many around it. Three sides consist of sheer rock cliff faces. On the fourth, facing south, the less-sheer rock face drops from the summit to a 150-foot-long plateau before dropping off farther to level ground.

What sets the mountain apart is the size and nature of its flat top. The summit stretches for 600 yards from north to south and is about 300 yards wide. Here Moorosi has established a self-sustaining village, including two stone houses where he has accumulated a stockpile of rifles and ammunition, many given to him by his

people and others purchased with cattle and corn from those who have worked in
the diamond fields and brought back weapons. Never-failing springs provide fresh
water and caves and openings in rocky outcrops on the edges of the mountaintop
furnish shelter for hundreds.

Moorosi has emulated Moshoeshoe, the man he so much admired, who set up
his headquarters on a flat-topped mountain called Thaba Bosigo, near Maseru, from
where he defended himself when attacked. Moorosi has made his mountain even
more impregnable than Thaba Bosigo.

At the base of Moorosi's Mountain, Raisa dismounts and sets out to climb to the
top of the mountain where he will meet his king. With large strides, he ascends a
series of rocky ledges, along a path that leads to the top.

As he climbs, he notes that Moorosi is building up his defences. His people have
built a series of six-foot-high stone-and-earth walls, that, along with natural rock
formations, serve not only to block the path of unwanted intruders, but to create
protection for armed men to fire on them.

Told by lookouts who is approaching, Moorosi walks a short way down the path
to greet Raisa. Together they make their way around stone fences at the top of the
mountain to Moorosi's hut, outside which the chief takes a seat.

The view from here is commanding. To the northeast, the land flattens out for
a distance and crosses the Quthing river before rising to the bush-covered slopes
of the next mountain, beyond which lie more mountains. To the southwest, the
land drops sharply to the Orange River before climbing mountains and dipping
into valleys across many miles as far as the eye can see. To the south stands a rocky
outcrop about half the height of Moorosi's Mountain, keeping watch as a sort of
sentinel. The scene imbues the viewer with a sense of supremacy.

Before they discuss the issues surrounding the cornfield and custody of MaLebenya's children, Moorosi and Raisa talk of the magistrate and what his presence
here means for the Baphuthi people.

"You have already asked these people to come here," Raisa reminds Moorosi. "You
asked for their protection and you let us become British citizens. You accept money
from the government to collect the hut tax for them."

"You are right," Moorosi replies. "I have already accepted a degree of colonial rule
and I am not opposed to some of the things the white government has brought. If
they spend the hut tax to improve the conditions of our people, as they have said they
will, I will not object. Also, I do not object to sending our children to the missionary
schools. It is good that our people learn to read and to write."

"Does that mean I must do what the magistrate tells me to do?" Raisa asks.

"Not necessarily. We do not want the government telling us how we should live
on our land," Moorosi replies. "We did not give the land to them. It it is our land.
I cannot give it away. You cannot give it away. Not even my cheeky son Lemena,
with the white man's ways that he learned working for many years on the diamond
fields, can give it away. It belongs to our people, to all of us. Without our land, we
are nothing. It provides us with our food. It is where we graze our cattle. It is where

Views from mountain top: Looking northeast (above) southwest (below, top) and south.

we walk and run and sleep and where our children grow up. We welcome strangers, but they must respect our land. It is our land. It is not their land."

Raisa stands. He thrusts his hands forward to emphasize his words.

"The magistrate says I'm wrong to have taken away MaLebenya's field."

"MaLebenya was wrong to have gone to the magistrate," Moorosi replies. "I did not tell her she could go to the magistrate. If she was unhappy with your actions, she should have come to me. I am thinking what action we should take about MaLebenya going to the magistrate and about the magistrate listening to MaLebenya without referring the matter to me. We are discussing it at our *khotla*."

"MaLebenya must marry me," Raisa adds. "She must obey me. Her sons will be my sons. She and her family belong to me now and I will see to her needs. But the field is no longer hers. It belongs to the people. She can keep her husband's cattle, which now also become my cattle. But she cannot keep my brother's plot of land."

Moorosi remains seated. He looks up, into Raisa's eyes.

"What you say about the plot is right. But it also is true that in each case we should look in fairness at the people involved and at the obligations of support.

"It is true that MaLebenya is a rebellious person who refuses to accept your decision. She listens to the missionaries and the government with their new ideas, ideas that are not our ideas. Their ideas will break up our families. They will leave young widows like MaLebenya alone, unable to care for themselves.

"MaLebenya should have come to me. I would have held counsel and decided whether you acted in the right way."

"What then should I say to the magistrate? He has instructed me to appear before him. Should I stay away? Or should I go before him?"

Moorosi stands up, indicating the discussion is at an end. "This matter is one that I must judge, not the magistrate. MaLebenya must come to me. You must come to me. I will be the judge."

Raisa is unsure what to do. He will obey Moorosi because he is king of all the Baphuthi. He does not trust Hope or accept his authority. Hope has no say over MaLebenya.

But he has heard that the white government is powerful. It has policemen and soldiers. Raisa fears what Hope will do to him if he fails to appear before him.

Paris — Friday, June 15, 1877

Ellenberger leans back in his chair, tugs at his beard and coughs nervously.

"Your question — what I think of the new magisterial presence — is a complex one to answer," he says. For the first time since he met him, Steinheil senses Ellenberger seems unsure of himself.

"I know that some of the missionaries have aligned themselves with the British and Cape Colonial administrations. Some, like Emile Rolland, have switched from being missionaries to becoming administrators. Other missionaries have advised the Basotho to obey the laws imposed by the British, and now the colonial administration.

"These missionaries believe that the administration's laws are closer to the way the Basotho should live than are the Basotho customs. They believe it is a Christian administration and is promoting a Christian way of life. They see themselves and the administration as working together. I understand that approach. But I also believe it is not as easy as that. And a few missionaries support my view.

"I believe that administrators and missionaries are following different paths.

"Ours is the path of persuasion.

"I did not go to Masitise to force anyone to become a Christian. That would be fruitless. People do not become Christians out of fear. They become Christians because they decide that is the way of life they should follow. In the eyes of God, of what value is belief arrived at through fear?

"The administration, on the other hand, is following the path of power. Being a magistrate means you are representing a legal system being imposed on the people. You sit in judgment and you have the power to sentence people to long terms of imprisonment. You have no jury. You are the sole judge of right and wrong and what punishments need to be imposed. If you impose the law firmly you are only doing your job well. I'm sure Hope will impose his will — the will of the government — on the people. It doesn't matter whether they are persuaded that he is right. He'll impose his will on them anyway.

"There is another path," he continues. "That is the path of profit.

"It is found among the people who have set up trading stations on the Baphuthi land, such as a man named Joseph Thomas who has set up three trading stations in Quthing. It goes without saying that they are not there to spread Christianity. Neither are they there to impose laws. They are there to make money.

"Because that is their goal, they tend not to interfere with others whose goals are different. Yet, the paths cross. If exposure to the white man's way through the magistrates or the missionaries means the people buy more European goods, the traders are happy."

Steinheil adds: "I would imagine there are times, too, when the traders try to influence the administration so they will have good conditions under which to trade."

Ellenberger nods.

"That is true. That is another way the paths cross. At times, they run parallel. At other times they cross."

"And now the path of persuasion, which you represent, is about to cross with the path of power, " Steinheil continues. "Is there not the chance that they will join together? Surely you should welcome the presence of the administration. If they impose their standards and their justice on the people, you will benefit because it is in essence a Christian justice."

"Perhaps," Ellenberger responds. "But I have been working among the Baphuthi for six years without the direct presence of the administration. I have worked in peace. There has been no conflict. The people, if I may say so myself, respect and even love me. Those who disagree with me and do not want to become Christians often tell me so and simply stay away. They do not try to drive me out. Now, with the arrival of Hope I am told trouble is stirring.

"We missionaries have not always seen eye to eye with the authorities. Because we understand the people and see much through their eyes, we do not always like what we see in the administration and the way they act.

"But I expect I will know a lot more of how the paths are interacting when I return."

Quthing — Monday, June 18, 1877

Hope relaxes in the office that he has set up in his new house as the late afternoon sun shines through the small window, lighting up the dust with its rays. He puffs at his pipe.

"I am really pleased you are here to help me as a clerk and interpreter. I think I will give you the title of Justice of the Peace."

Maitin smiles. The position is a senior one for a man aged 30.

"Griffith also has given me permission to appoint you agent of the post office. Of course, the number of letters passing through here is small, but the work will pick up in time. For this, you will be paid 6 pounds a year, with an allowance of 3 pounds a year, making a total of 9 pounds."

Maitin smiles again.

"I understand that you have been thrust into office quickly," Hope continues. "But now that you have been here a couple of weeks, I thought it appropriate that we review the duties of this office and discuss the way in which I plan to run it."

"I will be happy to do that, Mr. Hope," Maitin replies.

"I think we know why we are here," Hope continues. "We are preparing the native minds to understand and receive good government. Along with that goes respect for the law, for truth and for justice. Soon they will realize the benefits of good government and that will free them from the torpor of barbarism.

"Above all, it is important that we maintain peace and good order.

"And the native people understand that. Only their chiefs want to retain their hold on power to perpetuate their barbaric ways. In that regard, I think the Baphuthi people, under Moorosi, are far behind the other Basotho clans in civilization or industry. Also, the people are abject slaves to superstition. They listen to witch doctors who throw bones and say all kinds of mumbo jumbo.

"Nevertheless, things are getting off to a good start. I have received permission from Griffith to appoint more policemen. In addition to Sighata and the other three working for us, Griffith has approved the appointment of a corporal and the transfer of two privates from Mohale's Hoek and two privates from Mafeteng, as well as additional policemen, making a total of nine.

"So we will have a fairly strong police force, we have initiated a survey, we are mapping the territory, we will soon institute a census to ensure that all pay the hut tax — and now we have had our first court hearing.

"I have also requested £60 from Griffith to build a lock-up, where we can hold up to 10 prisoners," Hope adds.

"Griffith suggested I establish our magisterial compound at Alwyn's Kop, a mile or so this side of the Telle River," Hope continues. "But I preferred this spot. This place is closer to where the people live. The wagon road provides us with a good passage to the border of the Cape Colony. It means we can bring all we need by ox wagon.

"The stream here provides a steady supply of water. The ground is fertile. We can grow vegetables, graze our horses and have cattle here. When she joins me, my wife Mimmie can even have a flower garden here if she wants one."

Hope pauses and Maitin seizes the opportunity to talk.

"I think Griffith thought the site he suggested could be better protected. Here we are surrounded by hills on three sides and could be subject to surprise attacks."

"Yes, he would say that. But there have been no attacks on our magistrates here in Basutoland since the Cape Colony took over the running of the country six years ago."

Hope can afford to discount Griffith's authority. Or, for that matter, anyone's authority. Communications across Basutoland are slow. Mail posted from Quthing and carried on horseback will take two or three days, depending on the state of the rivers and weather conditions, to reach Griffith in Maseru, some 100 miles away by road. From there, the post takes five days to reach the seat of government in Cape Town. Telegraph lines have reached Aliwal North in the Cape Colony, to the south, but have yet to reach Basutoland. Because he is unable to consult anyone above him on decisions that have to be taken urgently, in most cases Hope will tell the authorities only what he has done, not what he intends to do.

Maseru — The same day

The resident colonial magistrate overseeing all of Basutoland, Charles Duncan Griffith, 47, comes from a long line of men who served in the British police and armed forces. His great-grandfather John Griffith was high sheriff of Penpompren in Wales. His grandfather was a captain in the Royal Marines. And his father, Charles Griffith, was a first lieutenant of the Royal Marines before he settled in South Africa in a Welsh party that arrived in Port Elizabeth in 1820. There, his father served as barracks master at Grahamstown.

Charles Duncan Griffith was born 10 years after his father arrived in South

Charles Griffith

Africa and was introduced to military life at an early age. At 14 he was assisting his father in the barracks and getting to know the soldiers who moved in and out.

At 18, Griffith joined the just-established Frontier Armed and Mounted Police where he was stationed at Queenstown in the Cape Colony. He soon demonstrated his leadership ability, becoming a captain during a frontier war in which he narrowly escaped death by starvation and fever, even as he was avoiding spear and gun attacks from the Ngqika people. At 20, he was displaying coolness and professionalism.

After serving as a lieutenant in the Cape Colony's frontier wars against the indigenous peoples in 1851 and 1852, Griffith made his first visit to Basutoland in 1855 on a mission for the then governor of the Cape, Sir George Grey, to the Basotho leader Moshoeshoe. Grey praised Griffith for the energy and efficiency he showed.

At the age of 28, Griffith left the military and served in magisterial posts in the eastern Cape where he displayed a commitment to open-minded justice, following the letter of the law and displaying fairness, persuasion and tact.

Six years ago he was appointed Resident Agent in Basutoland in place of James Henry Bowker who set up the first magistrate's office in Maseru under British rule. Griffith has imposed colonial rule gradually, trying to become a friend rather than a ruler. So much so, that he has on occasion been called "father" by the people.

Initial reports lead Griffith to fear that the man he sent to oversee the Baphuthi might be too strict. But, ever the bureaucrat, he is more concerned right now about the way Hope has presented his request for reimbursement for his wife and mother-in-law's move from Burghersdorp to Aliwal North in the Cape Colony.

"Sir," he writes to Hope. "With reference to your letter of the 9th instant submitting an account for £28-10-0, I have the honour to return the account to you and to state that I cannot comply with your request with regard to recommending the account for approval, for the very obvious reasons that it is not made out in compliance with Government notices No. 370 of 1856, No. 853 of 1858, No. 460 of 1858, and No. 323 of 1859, Pages 58 & 59 of Book of Circulars & Government Notices — I wish to draw your attention particularly to Government Notice No. 323 of 1859.

"I have, etc., etc.

"Col. Charles D. Griffith, Govrs Agent."

He will not tolerate anything but precise adherence to the rules.

Quthing — Thursday, June 21, 1877

It is 9 o'clock in the morning on which Raisa is due to appear in court. MaLebenya, ready to give evidence, sits outside in the weak winter sunshine. A small gathering of Baphuthi have gathered to observe the trial, the first of its sort on Baphuthi soil.

As Hope waits in his office for Raisa to arrive, the mail arrives from Maseru. Among the few letters is one from Griffith.

Hope stares in disbelief at Griffith's explanation as to why it has been returned. Is it not clear to Griffith that he was asking for £28-10-0 as a transportation allowance for his wife and mother-in-law who could not stay with him because of the dangers of his post? What difference does it make whether he wrote it using exactly the right forms? How does Griffith know which are the right notices to be followed anyway? Does he sit there reading the regulations all day?

Hope re-reads the letter, then angrily seizes it at each side, ready to tear it into little pieces. But reason takes over; he has no chance of receiving the allowance if he destroys Griffith's letter outlining what he should do. He sighs and takes up his pen, looking up the regulations to ensure his request is correctly submitted.

Hope is not surprised when Raisa fails to arrive by 11 a.m. After all, two of Raisa's sons visited him last night to tell him their father planned not to attend his trial today. Hope warned them consequences would follow such a refusal.

He calls to Sighata and two constables. "Go and arrest him," he tells them.

An hour later Hope hears talking outside the courtroom.

"We met him on the way," Sighata says, pointing to Raisa, who is slowly dismounting from his horse. "He says he was on his way here."

Hope asks Maitin to convene the court. Moorosi's son Lemena, who is eager to watch the white man's justice at work, and others gather once more to watch.

Hope composes himself with the dignity that should be accorded a magistrate and says he will start with the contempt-of-court charge. Raisa, he explains, did not obey the summons to appear last Thursday — a week ago. That action showed disrespect for the court.

"It is clear that you did not intend to appear in court today either," Hope says sternly. "I had to send policemen to arrest you. Have you anything to say in your defence?"

Raisa listens to the translation from Maitin, but remains silent.

"I said, Have you anything to say in your defence?"

"I have nothing to say."

"Do you admit that you failed to obey the summons, that you failed to appear in court when you were summonsed to do so?"

Raisa listens intently to Hope's questions as Maitin translates them. They have nothing to do with MaLebenya and the cornfield. They appear strange questions.

"The magistrate knows I did not appear," he says to Maitin.

"Don't you be cheeky to me," Hope responds when he hears the translation. "Did you appear or did you not appear?"

Raisa drops his head and stares at the ground. "I did not appear, boss."

"You are to call me: your honour."

"Yes, your honour."

"Very well." Hope fixes his eyes rigidly on Raisa. "I am fining you 5 pounds for contempt of court. You are to remain in a hut here until the fine is paid."

Raisa, not quite sure what he is supposed to do next, remains where he is. It is as well that he does so. The next step, Hope explains, is to hear the charges of destroying a cornfield and taking custody of two minor children.

After being sworn in, MaLebenya tells how Raisa destroyed her cornfield and her uncle Mapeshoane describes how Raisa came to his hut and took MaLebenya's young children from him, saying he would take care of them.

"Well," says Hope after the evidence is complete, "is what they have said correct? Is that what happened?"

Raisa, afraid of being called cheeky and of saying "no" to this angry man, looks down. "It is," he says.

"Have you anything to say in your defence?"

Raisa continues to look down at the floor. He remains silent.

"Well, then I find you guilty of unlawful destruction of property and the abduction of two minor children," responds Hope. "You have admitted what you did and what you did was wrong."

The next question catches Raisa off guard.

"And are you sorry it happened?" Hope asks.

At first, Raisa is unsure how to respond. He is not inclined to challenge this white man who appears to have so much power.

"Are you sorry it happened?" Hope repeats; the irritation in his voice is clear.

Better agree to this question, too. "Yes," Raisa replies.

"I am pleased to hear you apologise. This woman whose cornfield you destroyed is the wife of your dead brother. She is a relative and still you did this to her. I will not tolerate such action from you again. Do you understand?"

"Yes," Raisa responds.

"You have apologised, but you need to be punished for what you have done."

He orders that Raisa should compensate MaLebenya with three bags of corn and that he should pay the 5 pounds fine for contempt of court. A murmur runs through the crowd; they are surprised at the severity of the sentences. Five pounds is a lot of money and three bags of corn is a lot of food, both representing a substantial portion of any man's wealth.

After a collection of money from villagers, Raisa hands five pounds to Hope.

"Good. You are free to go and there is no need to keep you in custody," Hope says. "You must bring me the three bags of corn within the next week. I will pass them on to MaLebenya. That way I will know you have paid her."

Hope's eyes light up. Already, his influence is being felt. At first Raisa was clearly rebellious. Now he is willing to apologise and obey the law in the future. Hope has achieved an important victory for the rule of law. Griffith cannot fail to commend him for his judicial achievements — even if he fails to complete the right forms.

Raisa turns and leaves the courtroom. Accompanied by members of his family and friends, he sets off on his way back to his village.

He reviews the trial in his mind. He did the right thing, but the magistrate told him it was wrong. And punished him for it. He is bitter at such an injustice.

He must tell the king what has happened. He will know what to do to correct this unfair action by a unfeeling man whom they should never have allowed to set foot on their land.

3

Quthing — Friday, June 22, 1877

Hope has just sent off his amended request to be reimbursed for £28 and 10 shillings when, shortly after lunchtime, he sees a group of Baphuthi heading toward his compound. He wonders why they are here. When he sentenced Raisa yesterday, the headman paid his fine and was contrite and submissive, and he seemed prepared to pay the three bags of corn as compensation to MaLebenya in the next week, so it could not relate to that, could it?

At first, there are only a few. But the Baphuthi keep coming and soon Hope estimates they are 500 strong. Many of the men are armed, either with spears or with guns.

He is concerned because they are carrying weapons, even though their demeanour appears peaceful and their mood, while sombre, does not appear threatening.

Yet some of the men at the back of the crowd, unseen by Hope, are far from sombre. They are in a party mood. One wears a goat's beard around his face, mocking Hope's long grey whiskers. When the others see it, they point and laugh so loudly that they double over. Another pulls his blanket up to his neck and smooths it in an imitation of the magistrate's "uniform." He stands rigid and looks stern. Pointing at one of his fellow Baphuthi, he says, "You must be whipped." This, too, evokes laughter.

The armed men give way to allow Moorosi, riding on his white horse, to move through the crowd toward Hope. Moorosi is accompanied by his sons Letuka and Lehana and his leading advisers. Raisa rides nearby.

Moorosi stops as he reaches Hope, standing outside his house.

"I and my people have come here to greet you as my magistrate," he says. "I told them, Come all of you, my children, that I may introduce him to you. I wish you to hear for yourselves everything that he says to me."

Hope is suspicious of Moorosi's motives, given the chief's reputation for a rebellious attitude and the events of the last few weeks that culminated in yesterday's trial of Raisa. But he accepts the king's words at face value and calls on his policemen to bring two chairs, one for him and one for Moorosi. He invites Moorosi to sit. Moorosi walks slowly and eases himself into the chair. The old chief is starting to show his age, Hope notes, although he clearly remains fit. Many in the crowd draw closer and sit on the grass in a group around the men. Others talk among themselves and watch from a distance.

Moorosi and Hope ask after each other's health, discuss the weather and the state of the crops and share an occasional laugh. If Moorosi has come to confront the magistrate he shows no such intention, which makes Hope wonder why he is here. Is it mere coincidence that it follows yesterday's trial?

After a while, Moorosi says he will ride to the mission station at Masitise where he will sleep for the night. He suggests they should meet again tomorrow.

Hope agrees. No sense rushing the meeting.

He will find out more about Moorosi's intentions tomorrow.

Quthing — Saturday, June 23, 1877

The next morning, Hope awakens to the steady hum of speaking among a large gathering. Outside his house is a crowd larger than the one yesterday numbering as many as 600. Today every man is armed. They carry guns or spears; some carry many spears in bags slung across their shoulders.

Questions swirl in his mind. If Moorosi's motive is only to continue yesterday's rather superficial meeting why are the men armed?

If Moorosi is indeed seeking confrontation and these men attack him and Maitin, they would have no chance of escape. His small police force would be no match for this crowd.

Reflecting on the somewhat celebratory mood of the people, he thinks, "Perhaps they are holding a ball and the opening celebration today will be to slit my throat."

But Hope is hardly faint of heart. And, in a broader sense, he is not alone. He is confident that behind him stands not only the colonial government, but ultimately the British government and Queen Victoria herself.

He walks outside.

"What do they say?" he asks Maitin, who has been talking to the crowd.

"They say they are waiting for Moorosi to arrive," his assistant replies. "He told them to be here again today. And to bring more people with them. They say that is all that they know."

Before long, Moorosi arrives, riding on his white horse. A group of men who, Hope assumes, are his family and leading advisers, accompany him.

Moorosi rides up the slight incline that leads to Hope's house. He dismounts, greets Hope and Maitin, asking them to gather with him for a *pitso*, a traditional gathering at which important matters are discussed.

Talking is better than fighting, Hope thinks.

A constable provides chairs for him, Maitin and Moorosi. Maitin sits to the side, ready to translate.

Thoughts of a plot against him still coursing through his mind, Hope decides he should take the initiative. He tells Moorosi he has one stipulation before they start talking.

"What is that, magistrate?"

Hope rises and turns to face the onlookers, preferring to address them directly than to cede his authority to Moorosi. Asking Maitin to translate, he says, "I am glad that you have come to see me. I send you my greetings. But you must first put away your weapons — your guns and your spears. If you do not do that, I will not talk with you at all."

Moorosi's face tightens. Hope already is doing what he did with Raisa: bypassing him as the leader of the Baphuthi people. Hope is taking it on himself to give instructions to his people in front of him, demanding that the Baphuthi men weaken themselves.

Stunned, he remains silent.

Hope adds, "Go on then, put away your weapons. With weapons, there will be no talk. Without weapons, there will be talk."

The people are hesitant. They look to Moorosi for guidance. Carrying their weapons is a tradition — and they see no good reason to set them aside now.

Moorosi, carrying a rifle, also is reluctant to give up his weapon. He turns to his sons. They gather and talk.

Hope waits expectantly. He senses that he has disrupted their plan and counts it a gain.

Moorosi discusses with his sons whether he should upbraid Hope for addressing their people directly rather than through him. They conclude it is better to remain friendly because they have important matters to discuss.

Weapons are a tougher issue. But, after a lengthy debate and with reluctance, Moorosi and his advisers decide to concede this issue for the duration of the *pitso*. Moorosi steps forward, turns to his people and gives the order to disarm. Led by Moorosi, the men place their arms in a pile.

Hope is relieved. The tension lessens. He has taken control.

Moorosi launches into the first item to be discussed at the *pitso*: Hope has exceeded his bounds by sentencing Raisa. Griffith had reassured him he would remain king and would continue to implement the Baphuthi laws and customs. Now Hope is overriding that agreement by interfering.

Moorosi therefore wants to clarify what laws Hope plans to implement and how much they impinge on Baphuthi law. This will be his first move in a lengthy *pitso* on the subject of authority.

"I have brought all my people to hear the laws read so that they may know them," Moorosi says.

Hope, encouraged by Moorosi's apparent intent that his people obey the law, asks Maitin to read the regulations set out in "Courts of Law." He explains that amendments have been made recently and will be read to the people when they are available. For now, they will hear the existing version.

Moorosi listens intently as Maitin reads the laws:

• Each of Basutoland's four districts will have a magistrate. The magistrates will hold trials. Serious offenses are to be tried by three magistrates presided over by the senior magistrate. Death sentences must be confirmed by the governor. The scale of punishments and fines is laid down; females are not to be sentenced to a whipping. The magistrates are given criminal as well as civil jurisdiction.

• Marriage by force is unlawful. Church marriages have the same validity as traditional Basotho marriages. A man who marries in Christian or civil union cannot take another wife. The marriage is to be registered and a fee of 2 shillings and sixpence paid. The amount of the dowry is also to be registered. In the event of a parent dying, the survivor has custody of the children until the boys are 18 and the girls 16. Widows can remarry, but the children of the first marriage are to remain in the custody of a person selected, if possible, from among the relatives. Questions of inheritance or guardianship shall be decided by Basotho custom.

Moorosi and Raisa exchange glances, but say nothing.

• The right to allot land is vested in the governor. The chief in each district will have to provide the governor's agent with a list of the people to whom land has been given. A tax of 10 shillings a year is payable on June 1 for each hut except that a polygamist has to pay 10 shillings for each wife's hut as well as his own and an unmarried man who has a hut of his own is taxed 10 shillings.

• The governor's agent is empowered to issue trading and hawking licenses valid for up to a year and may refuse to grant or renew a license at his discretion. The sale of spirituous liquor is prohibited. Firearms and ammunition may be sold only with the sanction of a magistrate.

Maitin stops reading. "Those are the courts of law," he says.

Moorosi turns to the crowd. "You have heard the law," he says. "Those who have not yet paid their hut taxes for this year should pay up as soon as they can. You also heard again today, as you heard when Mr. Hope was installed as a magistrate, that they want you to obey the laws of the colonial authorities. But I am your king and you are responsible to me for following our laws and customs."

Moorosi turns back to Hope, sits down, and continues talking.

"I have a matter to raise with you," Moorosi tells him. "I hear my children crying because they say you have fined them as much as five pounds because they had not attended your court. In addition, in our country we do not fine people for damage to cornfields. What you have done is wrong and is against the laws of our people.

"I am very unhappy with you because you did not ask my consent for all that you did. You cannot do anything to my people without first consulting me. I am their king."

Before Hope can respond, Moorosi directs his attention once again to the crowd. "Who told you, my people, that you should bring your complaints to this man? It is only today that I am introducing him. You have not met him before. Why do you go to a man whom you have never met? Today, I am showing you the man who has been given me by the government, to help me. He has brought his own laws with him. You have heard them.

"But we still have our laws. I am your king. He is not your king.

"How is it that some of you go around me, that you go to the magistrate, the man you have never met until today, instead of to me?"

Moorosi turns to Hope.

"You did not ask my permission for what you did to Raisa," he says. "The agreement that I made with Mr. Griffith was that you would work here under me and be responsible to me. You did wrong to order Raisa to appear before your court. You should have come to me first."

Hope remains silent. What had started out as a conversation has become a confrontation. He knows that he needs to be firm, to assert his authority, but, while he is considering his best course of action, he will let Moorosi speak fully first and then respond.

Moorosi stands, turning again to the people gathered around him.

"Are you my people or are you the government people?" he asks. "If you are government people, you are fools."

Still addressing the crowd, he turns and points to Hope. "Do you obey him?"

He swings back, points to himself and faces the crowd.

"Or do you obey me?"

The crowd responds immediately. "We obey you," they shout in near-unison.

This support for Moorosi puts the magistrate over the edge. Hope stands, glaring at Moorosi. "How dare you?" he splutters, enraged at Moorosi's attitude toward a representative of the white government.

"How dare you?" he says again to Moorosi. "How dare you challenge my authority?" His face reddens with fury. "How dare you indulge in this display of insubordination?"

Now it is Hope's turn to address the crowd.

"Your chief agreed to be under the government," he says. "I do not need his permission to do anything here. I am not subordinate to him. He is subordinate to me. Every man and woman may appeal to me and bring complaints to me before complying with the judgments of the chief and headmen. You must not expect me to send cases to the chief. The chief must send cases to me."

Moorosi is quiet. He watches his people, trying to gauge their reactions to Hope's outburst. They, too, are quiet. They appear taken aback by Hope's angry disrespect of their king.

Hope pauses, even more angry that he is eliciting no response from Moorosi or from the people.

"This meeting is over."

Motioning to Maitin and his constables to follow him, he walks into his house, taking his chair with him.

The people in the crowd talk animatedly. Hope has turned his back on their king and on them, which is not only rude but also threatening. They are unimpressed with the white man who claims to bring justice and a superior way of life. This is not justice, this is an attack on their tradition, their culture and their king.

Sitting in his office, Hope's fury turns to concern. He fears that his direct challenge to Moorosi might invite a violent response from the people gathered around his house.

He tries to attend to his work, but his mind is outside. He hears the people talking and wonders what they are saying. He knows their pile of weapons is right there.

Maitin suggests Hope should sit down with Moorosi to talk further.

"If I go out there now and say I want to talk with him, it will be a sign of weakness. It will look as though I am recognizing him, giving him authority he does not have. He needs to accept that I am in charge here now and he is not."

Hope rises from his chair, running his hand through his thinning hair.

The only solution right now, he decides, is to wait for Moorosi to leave.

Almost three hours have passed. The crowd continues to mill around outside the magisterial offices. Hope and Maitin attempt to work, but regularly glance through the window. It is past midday; surely the people will return home soon.

A messenger from Moorosi walks to the door. Maitin speaks with him and then turns to Hope. "Moorosi wants to talk with you."

"He is having second thoughts," Hope tells Maitin. "He has thought it over and learned his lesson. I will talk with him because he has approached me and I am not lowering myself by going to him."

But this time, the conversation will take place on Hope's turf, in his house, away from the crowd and their weapons.

"Tell him he can come inside here and talk with me."

With Maitin acting as interpreter, Moorosi tells Hope he is disappointed that he left the meeting. The object of a *pitso*, he explains, is to discuss matters. A *pitso* can work only if people are allowed to talk without interruption, to make their wishes known in a straightforward way, and to answer one another until they have nothing more to say. They must talk and talk and talk.

Hope shakes his head in disagreement.

"Let me sum up what happened," he says. "You came here today with other subjects of Her Majesty the Queen to greet me as the chief government officer in this district. Although I had not summoned a *pitso*, I was pleased to see you and consented to your request to conduct such a meeting. But immediately after we read the regulations about the courts of law — at your request, I might add — you began to behave in an unseemly manner.

"When your people, in answer to a question from you, declared their intention of obeying you rather than me, I could not, consistent with my duty as a government officer, remain in the *pitso* any longer.

"Do you think I could sit still and listen to you insulting the government and, by implication, the queen?

"Also, I cannot accept your statement that before they make representations to me in my court they must ask your permission."

Moorosi repeats his assertion that he, and not Hope, is the ultimate authority in the area.

"When I met with Mr. Austen and Mr. Griffith and you were there, did they not say that in all cases you, the magistrate, would be subordinate to me?" he asks.

"You misunderstood what they said," Hope replies. "Or else the interpreter translated the words incorrectly. You agreed to be placed under British protection. I represent the queen and the authority of the Cape Colony. You need to respect me and to accept my judgment.

"The government is first and the chief second."

"To my people, I, their king, am first," responds Moorosi. "I cannot accept your judgment on our matters. You cannot judge any cases until you have consulted me. If you do not do that, you will be killing me. You will be destroying my authority over my people."

Hope smiles to himself. That is what he has every intention of doing.

"You went too far in judging Raisa," Moorosi continues. "Your authority as magistrate here is not valid. You cannot act until I have authorized you to do so. You must restore Raisa's fine."

Hope is tired of the discussion.

"I can see that you are refusing to listen to any of my arguments or to heed them," he says. "I am being patient with you, but I cannot continue arguing back and forth. Tomorrow is Sunday and I will not be at work. Let us meet again on Monday."

Moorosi agrees. He leaves the office.

Hope, who had been concentrating on the conversation with Moorosi, suddenly becomes aware that the people are singing outside. To him, it sounds like a war dance.

He looks through the window and sees that the people have picked up their weapons from the pile in which they had placed them after he had instructed them to put them down. Holding their spears and guns aloft in their right hands, they dance and chant in unison, repeating the same phrases over and over.

Wondering what they are singing, Hope's apprehension turns once again to fear as he realizes the strength of the force potentially arraigned against him. But he cannot believe that Moorosi will use their conversation to rouse up his followers against him. After all, the debate will continue on Monday.

His thoughts are interrupted by the sound of a shot. Within seconds, it is followed by another shot. Then another. The dancing turns into pandemonium as the people scatter.

Hope and Maitin shudder, unsure how to react.

Minutes later, chief constable Abraham Sighata enters the room.

"A man has been shot dead," he says.

Aliwal North — The same day

Mimmie Hope sits alongside her mother on the porch. Although their house lies along a main road in the first colonial town settled in the Eastern Cape, it is quiet. It also provides her a degree of security. Should she need help, her neighbours will come running.

She recalls the time five years ago when she was living with her brother, Emile Rolland, then an assistant magistrate in Mafeteng.

There she met Hamilton Hope, the man who was to be her husband. Hammy, as she calls him, was a clerk. She was impressed with his manliness, his strong moral convictions and his desire to protect and love her.

She and her widowed mother lived for a while with her husband in Mafeteng, but, when he was transferred to the wilds of Quthing, Hammy suggested that they move to her old home town of Burghersdorp.

A month ago he sent them money to move to Aliwal North. He would build a house in Quthing, he had said, in which they would live once he had settled into his new post. So far, however, he has not mentioned moving in any of his letters.

Mimmie's brother Emile now works for Griffith in Maseru. It is somewhat ironic, she thinks, that her husband and her brother should be linked in this way, both working for the same government 100 miles apart.

Aliwal North house, dating from the late 19th Century.

Mimmie grew up on her father's mission station in what is now the Orange Free State. She remembers the Boers attacking them because they befriended the Basotho and because the Boers believed that the mission station was on land that they wanted as part of their territory.

She recalls the sense of foreboding she felt before the attack and for reasons she cannot explain she feels it again. She has at times suffered under her husband's violent temper and is wary of his strong-armed approach.

She turns to her mother. "I wonder what Hammy is doing now," she says.

"I am concerned about him, mother. I am afraid that he will lay down the law too strongly and that the chief Moorosi, who is said to be wild and rebellious, will fight back."

"I am sure he can look after himself," Elizabeth Rolland replies. "Your father and I found the Basotho people not warlike at all until they were attacked by the Boers."

"That's what I worry about. I am afraid they will feel they are being attacked. I hope Hammy knows what to do.

"Please pray for him, mother."

Quthing — The same day

The dense mass of almost 600 Baphuthi surge forward to see the shot man lying on the ground. Their dancing forgotten, they shout, push and argue as they scramble for a look at the body. Guns and spears wave in the air. Now and then further shots are fired into the air, contributing to the chaos and creating frenzy.

Hope walks slowly and tentatively out of his house.

His first task is to make certain that the shooting was not aimed at him or his staff. When he sees the concentration around the man on the ground, and sees his constables in place, he relaxes somewhat. Had the incident been devised to draw him out and attack him, or his policemen, surely they would have done so by now.

Hope knows murder is highly unusual among the Baphuthi people. They sometimes have gone to war, and sometimes they kill a person accused of witchcraft. But Hope has heard no reports of Baphuthi people murdering one another. Suicide, too, is virtually unknown.

Unwilling to become directly involved — he is the magistrate, not the police — he instructs unarmed policemen, headed by Sighata, to investigate. He watches as they make their way through the crowd. Soon they disappear into the human mass, which continues to be uncontrolled and unruly.

When the policemen do not return, he fears the crowd might have mobbed them. He decides that he had better take charge after all. He had claimed control over law and order in Quthing in his confrontation with Moorosi. Now he had better demonstrate it. He will go and see for himself.

Casting aside the danger, Hope plunges into the seething mass of people. A frightened Maitin follows him. The crowd parts for the two white men.

At the centre of the turmoil is Moorosi. He is arguing furiously with Sighata, who has arrested the apparent shooter.

"Do not lay your hands on him," Moorosi says. "Let him go. I am here. I am in charge and I will see that he is put on trial. I assume all you want is your reward."

"I am not looking for a reward; I am only doing my work," Sighata responds, looking fearfully at the men around him holding spears above his head.

Moorosi pulls the accused man away from the constable and turns to Hope. "Here, sir, is the man who killed the one lying on the ground," he says.

"Why did he do it?" asks Hope.

"You question him yourself," Moorosi says, pushing the man toward Hope. This will be a test of how the white man handles the situation.

Hope and Maitin briefly examine the man lying on the ground. He is indeed dead, killed by a shot to the right side which appears to have penetrated his heart.

"Come with me to the courtroom," Hope says to the man identified by the crowd as the one who fired the shot.

Hope turns toward his house, Maitin with him. A knot of men follow.

Before he enters the courtroom, Hope delivers another lecture. With Maitin translating, he turns to face the crowd, which falls silent.

"You see what has happened," Hope says. "This is why I told you not to bring guns and spears to a meeting. Now this has happened. I want all of you to put down your weapons again. Then I will proceed with the hearing."

The men ponder the request. They cannot ask Moorosi, who, still questioning witnesses, is unaware of what Hope has said. They opt to obey the magistrate and place their weapons in a pile once again.

In his house, Hope has the prisoner brought before him. Onlookers crowd outside the window. Moorosi now has returned and stands among them, near the front.

The man, Kabi, says the gun misfired three times. He tried to fire it a fourth time, but had forgotten that the ramrod, used to load the musket, was inside it. When he tried to cock the gun, it was too strong for him and went off. The man was killed when the ramrod was fired from the gun.

"I do not know why you needed to try to fire your gun," Hope says. "But I find it impossible to decide whether this killing took place by accident or not."

Hope is pleased that Moorosi appears to have deferred to him to judge the case. It seems that Moorosi is unaccustomed to dealing with incidents like this, presumably because they are so rare and so serious. Now, believing he needs to press home his advantage, he invites Moorosi, accompanied by his son Letuka and his senior advisers, to continue the conversation that was interrupted by the shooting incident. The men sit together in the house.

Moorosi asks Hope why he left the *pitso* so abruptly. "You turned your back on us, which is a sign of disrespect among our people," he says.

"Do not accuse me of disrespect," Hope replies. "You were the one who was disrespectful. I was responding to your actions. You chose to act in an unseemly manner. The people, prompted by you, made a public display of their support for you as opposed to me, representing the government.

"You need to understand, Chief Moorosi, that I am in charge here now. I am the authority. I am the person your people need to obey, not you. You do not have the authority to give me permission to do anything," Hope says firmly. "I am the one who gives or withholds permission. You must accept that, Moorosi."

The men continue to talk. Neither will concede any ground, and each is determined to persuade the other.

As the sun sets, they agree to talk again on Monday.

Hope leaves the meeting fearful that Moorosi might have to be forcefully brought in line. To do that, Hope feels he needs a stronger police force to back him up. He writes a report to Griffith outlining what happened, including Moorosi's insistence on final authority, and asks for Griffith's instructions.

"I will maintain the stand I have taken, but as I expect open resistance to be offered to the constables should they be ordered to arrest any person, as Moorosi was at no pains to hide the fact that such would be the case, I beg you to take into consideration the incalculable advantage of crushing any such resistance at once, and to strengthen my hands by augmenting my police force."

Quthing — Monday, June 25, 1877

Light rain is falling this Monday afternoon as Moorosi, followed by about 100 Baphuthi, arrives at Hope's house to continue Saturday's discussions. Unwilling fully to concede to Hope's instruction that they do not carry weapons, the men are armed with their traditional spears, but none carries a gun.

Hope, for now, is satisfied with the compromise. He feels less threatened by spears, which — although they can effectively be hurled as far as 150 yards — are most effective only in close-up fighting.

Hope and Moorosi sit outside. Hope, making sure Moorosi is seated on a chair, says he would like to speak first. Moorosi agrees.

"First, I want to make clear that the language that you used at our last meeting was disloyal to the government," Hope says, speaking loudly so all can hear. "I am warning you, and that includes all the chiefs and all the common people, that, if it is repeated, I will not allow such disrespect to pass unnoticed. You will then be liable to be treated as rebels. We do not like rebels and we treat rebels in the way that they deserve."

He then tries to add a sweetener.

"But you do have some authority. You will continue to help me collect the hut tax," he says, "and continue to receive a stipend from the government for doing so. I will generously increase that from 20 pounds a year to 50 pounds. You should be satisfied with that."

Moorosi suggests it should be closer to 100 pounds.

The light rain has now become heavy and a cold wind adds to the worsening conditions. So the men continue their conversation indoors where the space allows only Maitin, acting as translator, and Moorosi's son Letuka, acting as an adviser to Moorosi, to be present. Without the crowd present, the discussion becomes more intimate.

"I would like to tell you of another issue with which I am dealing," Moorosi says. "I am angry that the people in a village near here — Lebetsa's village — are selling *joala*. For nearly a year now I have been telling the people to stop doing so."

Joala is a potent alcoholic drink brewed locally from sorghum. Unlike *leting*, which is only slightly alcoholic, *joala* is said to keep on fermenting in the stomach. Hope has seen the effects of over-imbibing on the drink, which causes severe headaches, bloodshot eyes, indigestion and renders the drinker ill for several days.

Some Baphuthi mix *joala* with brandy brought from the Cape Colony, making the effects even worse. Hope believes Moorosi, who, like all good chiefs, takes pains to stay sober, does not want his people to drink *joala*. But Moorosi is not concerned about the effect of the *joala* on his people; if they want to drink it, they can do so. He is upset because the liquor is being sold in the European way, rather than given as a gift, in the Baphuthi way.

Moorosi believes that asking strangers to pay for food and drink is contrary to a basic custom in which he and his people believe. This custom is reflected in the Biblical injunction to the ancient Hebrews to show love to strangers as recorded in the book of Leviticus — "the stranger that dwelleth with you shall be unto you as one born among you, and thou shalt love him as thyself." Moorosi is against foreign greed-inspired concepts undercutting traditional Baphuthi hospitality and so is raising the issue with Hope.

Yet Hope has no understanding or appreciation for this cultural custom and cannot identify with it. His immediate reaction therefore is to conclude that Moorosi is concerned about the harm, not of being uncaring to a stranger, but of strangers' imbibing a strong drink.

"I will not allow such a thing in my district," says Moorosi.

"Nor will I allow it," Hope replies.

Moorosi continues, "I know it will spread to other things, too, and will not stop at *joala*. Soon it will spread to bread and they will not only be selling *joala*, but will be asking sixpence from visitors to give them bread.

"The result will be that, if people visit from a distance, they will go thirsty and hungry because they will not have the money to buy the *joala* and the bread. This is not our way. We show hospitality to visitors. We share what we have with them."

Hope nods, failing to grasp the real intent of Moorosi's complaint, but satisfied that they are agreeing on a ban on the sale of a potent alcoholic drink.

"You are quite right," he says. "It should not be allowed. Give me the details and the names of those involved and I will inquire into the matter and take the appropriate action." The suggestion reopens the rift between the men once more.

Moorosi steps back, lines of anger crossing his face. With communication complicated by the language barrier, he is unable to understand why Hope is seeking to implement Baphuthi custom. He senses a trap.

"No," he says. "I have held a hearing. I have ordered the people to pay a fine. They will not do this again. I am merely telling you about this so you will know that I am seeing that my people do the right thing."

"To whom will they pay the fine?" asks Hope.

"To me, of course."

"Here is another example, Moorosi. You have no jurisdiction in this matter. It is my responsibility. I will fine them and they will pay a fine to me."

"I will never submit to you in this regard," Moorosi retorts. "I will judge the cases. I will not surrender my independence to you."

Moorosi presses his case with another example to indicate that the land belongs to all the Baphuthi people; no one person can own any of it, but, as the king, he can allot land on which the people can build huts, plants crops or graze cattle. When he allots a man a piece of ground to plant crops, the man pays him a goat for the privilege. "The goats are given to me," he explains. "I am the ruler. I decide how people can use our land."

"I must warn you that your language is rebellious," Hope says as calmly as his emotions permit. His tapping foot reveals his frustration. "I decide who can occupy the land and whether they should pay for the right to own it and to use it. The British law is applicable here."

Moorosi, detecting Hope's anger, remains unbowed. He repeats his contention that he will not yield to Hope. These matters might seem small, but they are symbolic of the wide cultural differences that divide them.

"Very well, Moorosi," he says, looking down at the seated chief and straight into his eyes. "I have been patient with you. I have taken a great deal from you. Now you are openly defying the government.

"I want to warn you, before it is too late, that if you openly resist me as magistrate, you will regret it. And the responsibility for doing so will be yours."

He waves his hand toward the door, indicating Moorosi should leave.

Moorosi rises. Hope has indicated he will not listen to any response, so, as he walks out, Moorosi turns to his son Letuka. "In spite of what the magistrate says, I will fine those who sell *joala* because they should give, not sell, drink to strangers . And I will keep the goats in payment for the use of the land."

Outside, all but the most devoted of Moorosi's followers — no longer part of the discussion — have left, driven away by the continuously falling rain.

Moorosi replays the confrontation in his mind. He will reassert his authority — and show respect to the magistrate as his subordinate at the same time — by assigning land to the colonial policemen on which to plant their crops. After all he is in charge of the land. It is his to assign.

He sends his chief messenger and son-in-law, Mafetudi, who has waited patiently in the rain, to tell Hope to meet him the next morning so that he may show him the ground that he will allot for the constables to plant their crops.

Mafetudi returns with the message that Hope refuses to meet him.

"In spite of his attitude, I will assign his policemen a good piece of land. That is our custom. I will show him two things at once — that I am in control of the land and that I am showing goodwill to him, a stranger on our land.

"But now it is raining too hard. Let us return tomorrow to complete this task."

⚜

Hope writes to Griffith: "I trust that you will see the urgent necessity of at once stamping out any attempt at open resistance, which resistance seems only too likely to be offered. I cannot allow matters to remain in status quo, nor yet let them drift until further and more serious complications arise. Hence I have the honour most earnestly to request that you will lose no time in giving me definite instructions as to how you wish me to act in the event of me being openly and forcibly resisted.

"You may depend upon my not precipitating matters, but at the same time I shall go steadily on, as I told Moorosi. I will do my duty, and let those who resist me by force take the consequences."

Quthing — Tuesday, June 26, 1877

Moorosi, accompanied by his senior sons and advisers, arrives at Hope's house around 2 p.m. He would like to show Hope the garden land he would like to assign to the policemen, he says.

Hope invites the group inside. Here, surrounded by the trappings of authority, he feels less vulnerable.

He insists that the chief and his retinue remain six feet from him at the one side of the room. He faces them with his two constables and the police corporal and asks Maitin to interpret. This is to be no casual discussion about land.

"Tell me again why you are here," he says.

Moorosi repeats the invitation sent earlier by his messengers. "I would like to show you the parcel of land I have set aside for your policemen so that they can plant their crops there."

Hope has no time to wait for Griffith's advice and assistance. He must deal with Moorosi now. Impatient and determined, he stares into Moorosi's eyes.

"Your offer is an attempt to show that you have some sort of control over me, isn't it? You want to prove that you have control over the land. You expect that, by accepting your offer, I will concede your authority over the land and submit to you.

"Well, let me tell you, Chief Moorosi, you cannot tell me what the policemen who work for the government can and cannot do. You cannot tell them where to plant their crops. You cannot tell me what I can and cannot do. I am in charge here. I have the authority.

"Yet you have the temerity to challenge me. You are seeking a confrontation with me — and let me tell you if you want one, you will get one.

"So, I must ask you again, chief. Will you submit to my authority? If you will, I will shake your hand as a faithful British subject. If not, I will regard you as a rebel. And I will treat you accordingly. I am sure you know what happens to rebels."

The atmosphere in the room is tense. The men are more or less evenly divided in numbers, with five on Hope's side and six on that of Moorosi. They stare across the room at each other, fearful of the consequences of the direct threat Hope is making to Moorosi. Although Moorosi remains outwardly calm, he is taken aback at Hope's more confrontational attitude. He remains silent.

Hope continues to stare at Moorosi.

"Well?" he asks. "What do you have to say?"

Moorosi looks across at his sons Letuka, Lehana and Lefata. Their faces are stern and resolute, but Letuka in particular shows signs of fear. He says this is not a good time to fight and urges Moorosi to back down. They are on Hope's turf. Lefata agrees with Letuka, but Lehana favours continued confrontation.

The Baphuthi king turns back to face Hope. He knows he is on dangerous ground, but the issue of who is in control over the Baphuthi people, their land and their lore, is vital. The tribe's moral code, its very way of life, is vested in him.

He cannot concede.

"I am unhappy with what you said yesterday," he tells Hope. "You threatened me and you said you would go against me. What do you say today?"

"I say the same today. And I will say the same tomorrow. You must understand, Chief Moorosi, that I have the power to force you to do as I say. I am not alone here. Mr. Maitin, here, and my policemen, over there, are only part of the power that I bring with me. I bring the whole authority and force of the government with me. If you do not listen and accept my authority, I will force it on you. The fines and the whippings I have administered in my career as a magistrate are only a small representation of what I can do when people will not listen.

"You agreed to be subject to the British government. I represent the Cape Colony, which represents the British government. You are therefore subject to me. That is the way it is."

Moorosi is silent. Hope seems bent on confrontation, not on discussion. This is not the way a debate is supposed to work.

He starts to take a step forward, to challenge Hope physically and directly. Then he thinks better of it and moves back.

"Well, what do you say, Moorosi?" Hope asks.

The Baphuthi leader is silent.

"Do you agree with me?" Hope asks Moorosi.

Moorosi bows his head, turning his eyes away from the magistrate.

Hope repeats his assertion. "You agreed to be a British subject," he says. "As a British subject, you must obey the British government. I am the representative here of the British government. You must therefore obey me. By failing to obey me you and your advisers are the aggressors. You are challenging my authority. By doing so you are forcing me to use the power I have to punish you.

"And, make no mistake about it, I will punish not only you but your councillors, too." Turning to face Moorosi's sons, he says, "You are the ones who are forcing my hand. I am not the aggressor. You are the aggressors. The law says you must obey me. By failing to obey the law, you are fighting against me. You are advising your father to fight against me. Why do you do that? If you cooperate there will be no reason for me to use any sort of force."

The men say nothing, but their eyes and gestures express their feelings. Letuka and Lefata say Moorosi should back off; Lehana says he should stand his ground.

Hope turns once again to look into Moorosi's eyes.

"I have to ask you, therefore: Are you willing to cooperate or do you want to force my hand with all the consequences that will bring? "

He raises his voice. "Do you agree with me, Moorosi?"

Hope's demeanour is authoritative, demanding, threatening, intimidating.

For the first time with Hope, Moorosi feels real fear. He has heard that, in his previous posting, Hope has gone so far as to order even chiefs to be whipped. Hope has made it clear that serious offenders will be sent to Cape Town where, cast into an alien culture, they will be put to work on building a new breakwater. Better to die than to be sent there.

Moorosi sees not only Hope the man, but Hope the government with an army behind him.

He feels cornered, like a snake under a rock.

"Your sons, particularly Lehana, are instigating you to work against me," Hope adds. "I trust you, chief, and I know you are willing to cooperate."

Moorosi looks at his sons. Lehana remains adamant; the others are quiet.

Fear takes over.

"I agree," he says, quietly. Realizing what he has done, he quickly adds, "Although I am dissatisfied." The message is clear. Hope is forcing him to yield in words, but not in spirit.

"Aha." Hope is brimming with the pride of accomplishment. "And so you give in to me on these issues?"

"I give in," Moorosi says reluctantly. "But I give in grudgingly."

Moorosi is disillusioned. He thought he had an agreement with the colonial government. Now Hope is bent on destroying him. He cannot believe he is actually yielding to this unyielding man.

Hope, delighted by Moorosi's concession, moves forward and takes Moorosi's hand. He shakes it vigorously.

"Remember what I said?" he asks. "I said if you agreed to do your duty as a loyal subject of the queen we would shake hands and give three cheers to the queen. So let's go outside and do just that."

As Moorosi and his contingent leave the room and as the people still gathered outside watch, Hope excitedly shouts, "Hip, hip, hooray. Hip, hip, hooray. Hip, hip hooray. May God save the queen." Moorosi and his sons simply watch in silence.

Hope suddenly bursts into singing. "God save our gracious Queen, Long live our noble Queen, God save the Queen: Send her victorious, Happy and glorious, Long to reign over us: God save the Queen."

The onlookers are bemused. These white people are strange. Their dance of celebration and their war chants are neither inspiring nor rhythmical.

"Now let us go and look at the garden," Hope says, a satisfied look on his face and his mood changed from belligerence to friendliness. "Let me see whether I agree that it is a suitable place for my policemen to grow their crops."

Moorosi walks alongside Hope, leaving with superficial peace between the men. But in Moorosi's heart there is no peace. His words were spoken in fear, not from the heart.

He has no intention of conceding to Hope.

4

Quthing — Tuesday, June 26, 1877

Hope is proud of himself. Today he broke the back of Moorosi's rebellious attitude. He was strong and resolute. That approach is the only way to deal with these people and in particular the sly, villainous Moorosi.

Before the day is over, he describes his victory in a report to Griffith. His supervisor must know how diligently he has worked and what he achieved today not just for the Cape Colony but for the British government.

"I do not wish to exaggerate the seriousness of this affair," he writes to Griffith. "But, at the same time, judging from the bearing of all his tribe, from Moorosi's own words, and from information which I have received from his messenger Mafetudi, I believe that we have reason to be specially thankful that no false step on the part of Government brought matters to a crisis, until I had succeeded in putting Moorosi into a false position, when I was able to show his councillors that they were the aggressors, and would be punished accordingly if I was unable to uphold the dignity of the Government without using force.

"Trusting that my management of this matter may meet with your approval."

Hope, proud of his achievement, is anxious that his action in this matter reach Griffith as soon as possible and that he receive instructions on any further moves he should make. But Griffith has not responded to his earlier letters and he wonders whether he is reading them; perhaps they are not written following the correct format as outlined in a hundred set of regulations.

He turns to his clerk and translator.

"Take these reports to Maseru. I would like you personally to report to Griffith on what has happened. Griffith must know of the victory I achieved today."

"I will leave in the morning," Maitin replies.

Maseru, Basutoland — Wednesday, July 4, 1877

When Maitin arrives in Maseru and tells him Hope is concerned that he has received no reply to his earlier letters, Griffith is apologetic. "I was in Bloemfontein when the first letter arrived," he says. "I read it only this morning."

Griffith reads the latest letter that Maitin has brought with him and listens to Maitin's description of the *pitso*. It confirms his fears that Hope is trying to take charge too quickly and drastically.

"I have attended many *pitsos* and I know the way they work," he tells Maitin. "Mr. Hope should have welcomed the opportunity to have heard Moorosi's views so that he would have known how the chief was thinking and could have acted more appropriately. Instead, Mr. Hope brought about a confrontation with Moorosi.

"I am worried, too, that Mr. Hope appears to be relying on being backed by armed forces. But war with the Xhosa tribes is brewing on the Cape Colony's eastern frontier and the troops are needed there. It will not be possible to send troops to Quthing.

"In any event, physical force is not an alternative. Mr. Hope must temper his firmness with diplomacy and understanding to reduce the tension with Moorosi."

Griffith chose Hope for the magistrate's position as he saw Hope as a firm, somewhat stubborn man who, in the way a good military leader would act, would stand his ground. But now he is afraid that those attributes have proven dangerous; the situation needs tact and diplomacy, neither of which is Hope's strong suit.

Griffith writes to Hope in an attempt to persuade him to be less autocratic. He praises Hope's "patience and firmness." But he adds: "It will, however, be very necessary for you to be most careful and judicious in carrying out the judgments and orders of your court, to see that they are not carried out by your policemen, etc., with too high a hand. Every possible care must be taken to prevent any of Moorosi's supporters being forced into open resistance or bringing on a crisis, as I am not in a position to say that you will receive any physical support if such an unfortunate result should happen.

"In any case in which resistance is shown to the execution of any orders or judgments of your court, it will be necessary for you before proceeding to extremities to make a full report on the subject to me so that I may be able to get instructions from the government before matters are brought to a climax."

Turning down Hope's request for more policemen, he writes, "The idea of crushing any resistance at once by physical force would require a very large body of men, which it is out of the question to suppose the Government would approve."

He directs Hope to "substitute diplomacy and moral persuasion for physical force or high-handed proceedings."

Griffith's years of experience have taught him that political advancement often is a two-sided effort. He not only must tone down Hope's intransigence, but also must seek cooperation from Moorosi whom he suspects conceded to Hope only under great coercion and will remain resistant to his rule.

He will approach the king in two ways. He will send a messenger to "tell Chief Moorosi that the course he is pursuing will inevitably bring trouble upon himself and upon his people." Secondly, on Monday he will send two of his most trusted messengers — Inspector George Moshesh and Sub-Inspector Sofonia Moshesh — to Letsie's headquarters near Maseru. They will ask him to send a messenger to Moorosi explaining that he should allow the Baphuthi people to lodge complaints with Hope and be satisfied to allow Hope to judge them.

He hopes that the messengers both from Letsie and from him will have the effect of changing Moorosi's attitude toward Hope.

Griffith also signs approval for the spending of £60 on a lock-up at the magisterial compound, for which he has received approval from Cape Town.

"Before you go, I need to write one more letter for you to take with you," Griffith tells Maitin. He hands it to him.

"With reference to your letter of the 25th ultimo relative to a transport account for £28-10-0 returned to you under cover of my letter of the 18th ultimo, I beg to inform you that Colonial Office circular of the 8th of August, 1853, page 57 of Book of Circulars, to which you refer me, rather tends to prove the unreasonableness of your charges than alters my opinion with regard to them.

"Again, let me draw your attention to Government Notice No. 323 of 1859, page 59 of Book of Circulars, in which you will find it distinctly stated 'that the allowance is granted, not upon the principle of defraying the officers' actual expenses, but simply by way of aiding him,' etc. etc."

He signs the letter, then adds a postscript:

"P.S. I may further point out to you that it is absurd in the face of it to expect the government to pay the expenses of the conveyance of your family to Aliwal North, just as well might you have sent them to Cape Town and then expect the Government to pay for their transport. — C.D.G."

He seals the letter and hands it to Maitin.

Even in the case of money, Griffith mutters to himself, Hope acts without thinking. He spends the money to move his family, realizes how expensive it is, and then expects the government to refund it to him.

He is not impressed.

Letsie's village, Basutoland — Thursday, July 12, 1877

When Griffith sends a message asking him to tell Moorosi to allow Hope to dispense justice in Quthing, Letsie faces a dilemma.

Having learned the virtues of peace from his father Moshoeshoe, the king of all the Basotho enjoys friendly relationships with the administrators of the Cape Colony as well as Moorosi. But now he is being asked to take the colonial side against Moorosi.

He is not one to stir up trouble with anyone. Compromise works just fine for him. He wants his people to retain the protection of the British and, by extension, now the Cape Colony. But he fears that Hope is imposing Cape rule too harshly on Moorosi.

Approaching 70, Letsie seldom leaves his village and his *khotla*, or meeting place. Overweight and unwieldy, he walks slowly because of his weight and the gout that afflicts his feet. Yet, even though he seldom mixes with his people, he wields great personal influence over them. Many are his relatives as he has 50 wives and has sired numerous children.

He realizes that from the time it took over the administration of Basutoland five years ago, the Cape Colony has been steadily undermining the power of the chiefs. The disinterest of the British is giving way to a more aggressive policy by the Cape Colony, which is now making itself felt more acutely among the Baphuthi.

But is this the time to resist the Cape rule? After all, Letsie admires Griffith. The "white chief" is a kind, understanding man. But, at the same time, Letsie wonders how long Griffith will be able to resist the government's steady implementation of its laws in place of the Basotho customs.

He wishes the situation would stay the same so there would be no confrontation. So Letsie decides to do as Griffith requests, but his tone will be soft.

He sends a messenger to Moorosi suggesting he attempt to seek cooperation rather than confrontation with Hope.

Quthing — The same day

Hope explains to the workmen the kind of building he wants for the lock-up. He has bought the materials and the building should be completed quickly. The courtroom and offices will follow; the jail must be built first.

He uses a spade to outline the dimensions of the building, 18 feet long and 8 feet wide. The walls should be 8 feet high and have an iron roof.

This jail will help him considerably. Should Raisa fail to pay the three bags of corn representing his compensation to MaLebenya, for example, this would be the place to put him. But he needs more to maintain law and order. He sends a request to Griffith for six carbines — a shorter version of the popular Snider-Enfield rifles — "and accoutrements" for the use of the police stationed at Quthing.

Quthing — Monday, July 16, 1877

Moorosi listens to the arguments from the messengers sent by Letsie and Griffith that he cooperate with Hope and be obedient to the person placed here by the British queen for, according to Griffith, his "protection and edification."

He tells the messengers to wait. He will counter the requests by demonstrating that he remains in charge. He will do so by conducting his own trial of Raisa.

After listening to their stories, he instructs Raisa to pay a fine for overstepping the boundary between persuasion and punishment. But, Moorosi tells Raisa, he is not to pay the fine to him and certainly not to the magistrate, but to MaLebenya. In that way, he will compensate her.

Raisa reluctantly accepts Moorosi's ruling. He offers MaLebenya two goats and one pound, eight shillings.

"That is not enough for the damage he did to my cornfield," the widow responds. "He caused me a lot of suffering. He took away everything I had."

Raisa increases the offer to a two-year-old ox and £1. MaLebenya accepts.

With the £5 he paid earlier to Hope for the contempt of court charge, Moorosi reckons Raisa has paid the equivalent of £10 altogether. It is a goodly sum.

MaLebenya leaves the meeting and makes her way to the magistrate's house. She will tell him that she has received sufficient compensation for Raisa's actions against her and that Hope no longer has to seek out Raisa and force him to pay. It's over.

As Raisa and MaLebenya leave, Moorosi calls the deputation that has been awaiting his reply for Letsie. "Tell him Raisa has already paid the fine," he says. "There is nothing more for the magistrate to do. Tell Letsie and tell Griffith that the matter is over. I have sorted it out."

Quthing — August 24, 1877

Hope rules the fatal shooting among the crowd outside his magistracy a month ago was an accident for which no one should be tried. He also decides to close the case against Raisa. MaLebenya has told him she is satisfied with the amount ultimately paid by Raisa and he will accept that because she was the complainant.

He is convinced that had it not been for his action Moorosi would not have intervened and Raisa would not have paid any damages. So he feels vindicated.

But that gain is diluted by Hope's increasing frustration at the administration's reaction to his confrontation with Moorosi. Although he is proud that he forced Moorosi to back down on several issues, he perceives that Griffith is still unhappy with his work, implicitly blaming him for Moorosi's rebellious attitude.

He is still smarting from Griffith's instruction of a few weeks back that "in any case in which resistance is shown to the execution of any orders or judgments of your court, it will be necessary for you before proceeding to extremities to make a full report on the subject to me so that I may be able to get instructions from the government before matters are brought to a climax."

He has pondered that phrase for a long time. What does "before proceeding to extremities" mean? Does it imply his earlier actions were extreme? Does it mean he should ask Griffith what to do in all court cases and then do only what Griffith says?

He succeeds in getting Moorosi to back down, and this is how he is rewarded?

He cheers up a little, however, when he receives a letter from Griffith in the afternoon post approving his request for a draft of £128 "for building a court room and offices at your seat of magistracy."

Maseru — Thursday, September 13, 1877

Telegraph office, Aliwal North [contemporary sketch by Arthur Pattisson]

The message turns Griffith's world on its end.

Dated Tuesday, September 11, it was telegraphed by the Under-Colonial Secretary in Cape Town, acting on orders from the Cape Colony's British Governor Sir Bartle Frere, who has been involving himself more and more in the running of the colony, to the closest telegraph office, in Aliwal North, and sent by express mail to Maseru.

It reads:

"Bowker is ill. Would it inconvenience you much to proceed to King William's Town to relieve him without delay, and, if so, what arrangements do you suggest for the discharge of your duties in Basutoland? Reply by telegram."

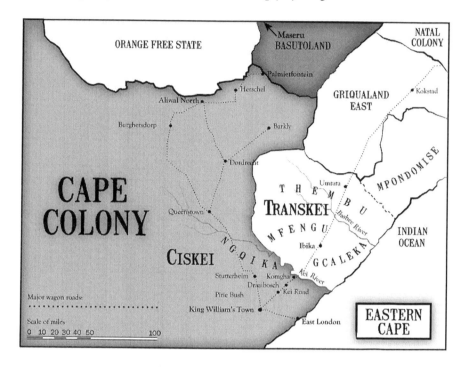

Griffith is aware that James Henry Bowker — the man who occupied his post as governor's agent in Basutoland from 1868 to 1870 — had returned to police and military duty several years ago and had been leading the Frontier Armed Mounted Police on the Eastern Cape frontier to the south of Basutoland.

Now apparently, at 55, he is getting too old for military service and his health is failing. Indeed Griffith had heard that Bowker was suffering from rheumatism, and had been complaining about shortness of breath and feeling tired.

Griffith thought his days in active military service were over, but now he finds himself called into action to take a major role in what looks like becoming the ninth frontier war between the colonists and the black indigenous people who live to the south of Basutoland. He is not eager to take up the post, but as a loyal civil servant he needs to drop everything and go.

He sits quietly for a while, considering the implications. What will happen to his wife and 11 children, the youngest of whom, Owen, turned a year old on Wednesday? What will be the reaction of the Basotho people? How will Hope handle Moorosi while he is away?

Two more telegrams that arrive in the next few hours tell him the prime minister of the Cape Colony, John Molteno, wants him to be in King William's Town four or five days after he receives the order. Griffith informs his assistant — Hope's brother-in-law, the missionary-turned-government-official Emile Rolland — that he will be filling in for him while he is away.

"When are you leaving?" Rolland asks.

"Molteno wants me to get down to King William's Town in four or five days."

"That means you will be leaving immediately as it takes five days to get there."

"I need a day to get ready. I will leave early on Saturday morning."

"This is really short notice. How long will you be gone?" Rolland asks.

"I am not sure. I assume it will depend on how long the hostilities last," Griffith says. "I am afraid I am going to be dumping everything in your lap, my dear Mr. Rolland. The most serious situation right now, of course, is what has been happening in Quthing. I am aware he is your brother-in-law, but I think you need to keep a close watch on Mr. Hamilton Hope. He is inclined to act high-handedly and I am concerned that the situation between him and Chief Moorosi could flare up.

"The main aspect to watch is that Mr. Hope should avoid using force to get Moorosi to cooperate with him. He should talk with him, reason with him and point out the futility of countering him before he tries to force him.

"I am afraid that Mr. Hope has a short fuse and so I have advised him to consult with me before he takes any further significant action against Moorosi or his sub-chiefs. Now, of course, while I am away, the duty to restrain Mr. Hope where necessary will fall on you."

Griffith intends to leave his wife and children in Maseru at least for a few weeks. "I am not sure at this stage what arrangements will be made for them to join me in King William's Town, where I assume I will be based," he says. "Please see that they are well cared for while I am away, Mr. Rolland."

Griffith replies to Frere's telegram, agreeing to accept the position and suggesting to the authorities that Rolland take his place while he is away.

Letsie's Village — Friday, September 21, 1877

The news that Griffith has been called to serve on the colony's eastern frontier has so shocked Letsie that he has become seriously ill, causing violent pain and fever to course through his body for several days. He had come to trust Griffith's calm, friendly and understanding approach, seeing him as a brother who was as interested in his welfare and those of his people as much as any white official ever could be.

Now he feels as though a rock has given way under his feet and he does not know where to turn. Without Griffith, he is left to deal with a government he distrusts, with people who do not understand him or care for his welfare. How will he and his people manage without their confidante and advocate?

Unaware that Griffith is already in the Eastern Cape, he believes he must protest this move with as big a demonstration of political power as he can summon to ensure that Griffith remains at his post. He calls 31 of his sons, counsellors and senior chiefs to his village to draw up a petition to the government in Cape Town.

After much discussion, the men draw up their message, which they will send to the governor of the Cape Colony, Sir Bartle Frere:

"The Petition of the undersigned humbly sheweth:

"That your petitioners have heard with great grief that it is the intention of your Excellency's Government to remove from his position at the head of affairs in Basutoland our present Governor's Agent, Charles D. Griffith, Esq.;

"That your Petitioners have been struck with dismay at this news, and not only they, but everyone else in Basutoland, from the old man with hoary head to the woman and the child.

"That your Petitioners, together with all the inhabitants of Basutoland, have enjoyed extraordinary benefits through the able and just manner in which the Governor's Agent has governed the country — saving it from invasion and war, overruling disputes, reconciling hostile factions, and establishing in the hearts of all confidence and security. Your Petitioners have, with all the people in Basutoland, felt that with such a man at the head of affairs they could rest in confidence.

"He has endeared himself to everyone, and we look upon him as the greatest and best gift Her Most Gracious Majesty has bestowed upon this land, and we contemplate with grief and consternation the prospect of that gift being taken away. Your Petitioners are unrepresented in Parliament, and have no other means of making their prayers and wishes known, but by such humble Petition as the present."

Paris — Sunday, September 30, 1877

Frederic Ellenberger is concerned about the reports from South Africa. He has heard from missionary colleagues of the trouble between Moorosi and the new magistrate Hamilton Hope.

He has read in the newspapers of trouble on the eastern frontier of the Cape Colony, and he fears that should war break out it might have ripple effects on the people in Basutoland, who face a similar colonial presence.

"We need to return to Masitise," he says to Emma. "I want to be there to help my people, to advise them and to protect them."

"I, too, feel we should return," Emma replies. "I want to continue my teaching and I want to help you with your work. But I am worried that you are not physically ready to return. You look wan. You are thin."

"Do not be concerned at how I look, my dear Emma," Frederic replies. "My strength has returned; I am sure of that. But before we leave, I feel we must do one more trip around the cities of Europe, particularly in France and Switzerland. We must tell the people of the great need among the Basotho and Baphuthi people, of the work we are doing at Masitise.

"We should not return before we have gathered enough funds to see us through the months and years ahead which could be turbulent if the stories I hear are correct."

Emma agrees. "When do you feel we should return to Masitise?" she asks.

"Early next year," Frederic replies. "Let us pray that conditions do not deteriorate further by then."

King William's Town — Friday, October 5, 1877

Cape Governor Frere, who has travelled to King William's Town to be closer to the hostilities between the settlers and the indigenous people, is holding regular meetings with the colony's Native Affairs Minister Charles Brownlee and de facto war minister John Xavier Merriman.

At the start of today's meeting, Frere tells them that Griffith has been appointed a colonel and commander of the troops on the eastern side of the Kei River, where they are preparing for an all-out attack on the Gcaleka people. The attack, which is ostensibly being launched out of fear that the Gcaleka will attack the settlers, is likely to become the ninth war to be waged on the frontier.

Sir Bartle Frere

"Talking of Griffith, here is the letter I have drawn up as your response to Letsie's petition asking that Griffith return to Basutoland," Brownlee says. It is addressed to "Chief Letsie and other children of Moshesh."

"Greeting. His Excellency the Governor directs me to say that he has with the highest satisfaction read your Petition addressed to him in regard to the removal of your late chief, the Governor's Agent. It is most gratifying to the Governor to find that after a period of six years residence among you, Mr. Griffith regrets his leaving you, and that you regret his leaving.

"When Mr. Griffith first came among you, you did not know him, but you have learnt to know, respect and love him."

"Love him? Love him?" Frere interjects. "We are talking about an administrator here."

Charles Brownlee

"I understand that, sir. But Mr. Griffith has endeared himself to these people. That much is clear from their petition."

"Very well. Keep that in, if you must. But add the words 'and obey him' after 'respect and love him.' We need some balance."

"So it would read, ...'you have learnt to know, respect and love him, and to obey him.' Is that right?"

"Let's say, 'and above all to obey him.' That puts it above the concept of love."

"It will then read, 'You have learnt to know, respect and love him, and above all to obey him.' Is that how you would like it to read?"

"Yes."

Brownlee notes the amendment. He continues reading the response that he has drawn up.

"In removing Mr. Griffith from your midst the Government honours him, and at the same time honours you. He has accomplished great things among you."

Frere says he thinks "great things" is a little vague. "Talk about the actual things he has done."

Brownlee suggests adding, "he has established the rule of law" and "he has initiated measures for your improvement."

Frere nods vigorously. "Then add, 'You have not looked to Mr. Griffith as much as you have looked to his measures.' I want to make it clear they respect Griffith because he is a firm administrator who has implemented British rule, not because he is nice.

"You can also add, 'and now the Government requires that he do elsewhere what he has done for you' after that. In other words, Griffith has been a forceful administrator in implementing the law in Basutoland and now we want him to be a forceful administrator in leading the police against Sarhili and the Gcaleka."

"What else have you written?" Frere asks.

Brownlee reads, "But of this you may rest assured that, in appointing a successor to Mr. Griffith, the Government will appoint a man who will follow in the course Mr. Griffith has so ably marked out, and one you so highly approve of."

"That's good," Frere comments. "Pray continue."

"The Governor, like yourselves, regrets that the necessity should have arisen for the removal of Mr. Griffith from Basutoland." Because Frere is interested in the wants of "all Her Most Gracious Majesty's people," the letter concludes, "it is his intention to visit Basutoland as soon as circumstances admit, and then he will have an opportunity of hearing fully what you wish to say, and to give you his views and advice."

Frere leans across and looks at Brownlee's notes.

"Is that it?"

"Yes."

"Good. You have presented my views well in the second part of the letter. I would make only one change. Instead of 'the wants of all her Most Gracious Majesty's people,' I would like you to write 'the wants of all her Most Gracious Majesty's children.' We need to make it clear that the relationship here between the government and the Basotho people is closer to that of father and child than adult to adult."

Brownlee takes up his pen and makes the change.

"I will see that this letter is sent tomorrow," he says.

Quthing — The same day

News of the fighting on the eastern frontier reaches Moorosi by word of mouth. Although the Gcaleka are Xhosa and so speak a different language and have different customs, the Baphuthi king feels an affinity with them. He assisted them with food during a great famine 20 years ago and 12 years ago the Gcaleka assisted the

Baphuthi in resisting attacks from the Boers.

Moorosi knows that the Gcaleka want to run their own affairs, as he does. They resent the intrusion of the white government and laws, as he does. They are prepared to resist the colonial government, as he is. Now that defiance is turning to war.

He is disturbed to learn that Griffith is the man leading the attack against the Gcaleka. His mind goes back to the meeting at his mountain fortress five months ago when Griffith introduced Hope to him. Suddenly it all springs into context. Moorosi had the impression then that Griffith was promising him a large degree of autonomy, but now it is clear Griffith misled him. Hope — who worked for Griffith — is doing all he can to take away his autonomy.

"If Griffith will fight against the Gcaleka because they want to retain their autonomy, surely he also will fight against me if I seek to retain mine," he reasons. And if Hope was appointed by Griffith and worked for him until recently, it follows that Hope is following Griffith's lead.

What, then, should he do to resist this intrusion?

Moorosi asks his advisers — doctors and rain makers — what his next moves should be with regard to Hope. He, too, is a diviner and he has his ideas. Now he is interested in knowing theirs.

The men, who throw their divining bones like dice, are used to identifying evil spirits, diagnosing illnesses and searching for lost stock. Often the bones will say whether a wife has cheated on her husband. The bones will say whether a person is bewitched and what sacrifice is necessary to exorcise the evil spirit. Should a chief contemplate a raid, the bones will say what ointments will make his followers invulnerable. They will indicate the direction in which to hunt or search for lost stock.

Now Moorosi wants to hear what the bones say about a white man; about Hope. It's an unusual request, but not beyond their powers.

The doctors throw their bones. Crouched beside them, they examine the way the bones have fallen and read them in the way that British people read tea leaves.

"The bones show this man Hope is trouble," they say. "He has come like a lion into our territory, ready to spring when the time is right. He will make small moves as he creeps up on our people. But one day he will pounce, just as the whites are pouncing on the Gcaleka.

"The crops are not good this year. Since Hope arrived, the rain has become less. Before he came, the crops were good.

"Our ancestors, who speak to us through these bones, are troubled by what they see."

Never afraid to profit from his practice, one of the doctors adds, "But he can be stopped. We can ward off his evil powers. You will need to protect yourself from him with medicine, which I can make if you will pay me a goat for each portion."

"Do so. I will pay you," says Moorosi.

The bones confirm what Moorosi suspected. They serve to prompt him into action. But he believes, too, in caution. As the great Basotho leader Moshoeshoe did, he should try to assert his authority through a combination of diplomacy and threats. He should be friendly at times, but assertive at others. If he can put those principles into action, he might be able to prevent an outright attack on his people.

Reluctant to move unilaterally, he will wait for an incident to occur. It needs to be the right incident and he needs to be ready to move when it happens. By the end of the day he has devised his plan of action.

Ibika, Transkei — Monday, October 8, 1877

Griffith has had trouble switching back into the role of military commander. In this position, he needs to plan and lead attacks against the enemy, to send his men to kill. These decisions are disturbing to him. Over the years as magistrate he has come to see war as a last resort, preferring to cultivate compromise; to choose diplomacy above death.

But his task now is not to make decisions. His task is to carry out the instructions of the government.

Sir Arthur Cunynghame

Chief Sarhili

"You are to break up the Gcaleka army," Sir Arthur Cunynghame, commander of the British and colonial forces on the eastern frontier, told him. "Destroy the kraals so the fighting men cannot rally again, and capture the people's cattle so they can be forced into submission. Allow those who wish to surrender to do so."

Griffith has had an initial success. Up to a thousand Gcaleka were killed in a skirmish at Ibika. Yet the war has only begun. The Gcaleka Chief Sarhili still controls most of his territory.

Although a lack of sufficient ammunition and food continue to prevent him from making an all-out advance into Gcaleka territory at this stage, Griffith determines the next step is to swing from defence to offence and attack Sarhili's Great Place. He will inflict as heavy a blow as possible on the leader, taking his capital. That objective can be realized with the supplies he has at present.

As evening approaches, Griffith orders the men to start tomorrow at first light and march in two formations to the Great Place, about an hour's ride away, and seize it.

"You will meet resistance on the way, I am sure of that, and that will slow you down so it might take you several hours to reach your goal. The enemy is well armed and can fight effectively at close range, as you know. But you are better armed and more skilled in warfare.

"I am relying on you to represent the Cape Colony, Britain and the Queen in this assault on the enemy. God save the queen!"

The men raise their guns and cheer, repeating in unison, "God save the queen!"

The Ninth Frontier War is about to be launched — officially.

Gcaleka territory, Eastern Cape — Tuesday, October 9, 1877

After a day of attacks on the Gcaleka, Griffith addresses the men at Ibika.

"The operation was a great success and I want to thank you all for the part you played in it," he says. "According to our initial count, 80 Gcaleka were killed.

"Our casualties, two killed and a seven wounded, have been small in comparison," Griffith continues. The effect on the enemy morale is great. Their defeat showed them they cannot stand against us, even in their own country, or their own stronghold. We captured a vast quantity of loot.

"Unfortunately we did not have the ammunition and the rations to continue to pursue them. We will give you instructions on the next mission soon."

Quthing — Thursday, October 11, 1877

Hope is settling into his new offices that have just been completed. After receiving permission and money from Griffith a few weeks ago before the resident magistrate left for the eastern frontier, he has constructed a courtroom 27 feet by 14 feet and two side rooms, each 10 feet square. The rooms are sparsely furnished and the walls are rugged. But the structures represent the colonial presence. They also allow Hope and Maitin to conduct their business and store their records away from their houses, which, together with the lock-up and the new offices, form the magisterial compound.

Today Maitin enters Hope's office to tell him of information he has gleaned from the local people.

"I have heard reports that tell of a group of shepherds who, apparently without any flocks of their own to tend, stole goats from a nearby kraal at night, slaughtered them and ate them.

"Another case of stock theft," Hope replies. "It's the most serious crime around here.

"We should send Sighata to arrest the people who have stolen the goats so that they can be tried. They must learn that even when food is scarce, stealing is against the law. After a good whipping, they will have second thoughts about doing it again.

"And it will give us a further opportunity to put our courtroom to use and to establish ourselves as the authority around here."

Quthing — Monday, October 15, 1877

The message from the chief constable is not what Hope wanted to hear.

"I went with two of my policemen to arrest the young shepherd boys who stole the goats," Sighata tells Hope.

"When we got there, Moorosi was there. He refused to allow us to arrest the boys."

"What did he say?"

"He said he is the chief and he had already tried the boys for stealing the goats."

Hope is furious. Once again, Moorosi is interfering in the judicial process. "He has already tried them?"

"Yes, sir."

"Did he say what he had done with them?"

"Yes, sir. He said he had fined their parents six times the value of the stolen goats. They had already paid him the fine. He said the matter was over and there was no need to arrest the boys."

Hope calls to Maitin in the adjoining office.

"Can you believe this man's guile? I thought he had learned his lesson last time I confronted him and forced him to back down. I thought he had accepted that I am the authority here."

"It does appear he is intent on rebelling against your rule here," Maitin ventures.

"Appear?" Hope blusters. "He *is* rebelling against my rule. "We cannot allow this to continue, Mr. Maitin. We have to stop him from doing this and explain to him in no uncertain terms that he is not the law here. I am."

Hope calls Sighata.

"I want you to go to the place where the goats were stolen. I want you to arrest the people responsible.

"I do not care whether Chief Moorosi says he has already tried and sentenced them. We need to disregard that action as illegal and irrelevant. They are to be tried in a proper court of law."

Sighata asks what he should do if Moorosi refuses to let him arrest the people, as he did before.

"You are to confront the chief and tell him that the magistrate has sent you and he must be subservient to my orders. Remind him of what happened before and how he was forced to back down. Does he want that to happen again?"

Nervous about confronting Moorosi, Sighata reluctantly agrees to return to the village.

Ibika — Monday, October 22, 1877

For four days, the combined forces of the Frontier Armed and Mounted Police, pro-government Mfengu and volunteers have been scouring the Gcaleka people's land.

The Gcaleka have offered little resistance. The soldiers report that the Gcaleka, who have broken up into small groups, are moving eastward.

As he prepares to continue, Griffith receives a visit from the Eastern Frontier commander Cunynghame who asks Griffith for his assessment of the campaign.

"We are driving the whole Gcaleka people before us," he tells Cunynghame.

"Where are they going?"

"I believe they are leaving Gcalekaland and dispersing among other tribes. I also suspect that Sigcawu — Sarhili's son and a cunning strategist — might be planning a surprise attack.

"My scouts have questioned people in the surrounding areas, but no one professes to know where Sarhili and his forces are hiding.

"But we are ready for such an attack.

"Gcalekaland will soon be vacated."

To Cunynghame the victory seems too easy.

He tells Griffith that his forces should destroy the property the Gcaleka left behind. Their huts must be burned and their food supplies decimated. 329Doing so will ensure that the people cannot return to their land and survive.

Quthing — Wednesday October 24, 1877

Early summer rain is falling lightly outside as Hope speaks to Maitin.

"I have received an instruction from Mr. Rolland to travel to Maseru to attend the annual Basotho *pitso* on Thursday next week," Hope tells him. "He also has asked me to speak.

"After that, I will be involved in discussions with Mr. Rolland and my fellow magistrates before I travel to Aliwal North to spend a couple of weeks with my wife and mother-in-law.

"My plans are to return in about five weeks, toward the end of November, depending on how much rain falls and the condition of the roads.

"While I am gone you, my dear Mr. Maitin, will be in charge here."

Maitin looks perturbed. Five weeks is a

long time.

"What about the boys who stole the goats? Do you want me to pursue that matter while you are away?"

"I think that can wait until my return. Sighata failed in his second attempt to arrest them, but we did prosecute two cases of stock theft in the past three weeks.

"Our policemen are to continue to spread the message around the villages that all cases of criminal wrongdoing must be brought here and not to Moorosi or any of his subordinates.

All cases, no matter how small, must be brought before me. Should any incidents be reported to you while I am away, I would like you to record them and to set a date for the trials after November 26th."

Maitin remains concerned. "I have heard rumours that Moorosi is planning to reassert his authority among the Baphuthi," he tells Hope.

Some, he says, even go so far as to say that, should Hope fail to acknowledge Moorosi's authority, Moorosi plans to expel Hope from the district by force.

"One informant told me that Moorosi has seen what has happened to Sarhili and the Gcaleka people and he fears that the same thing is going to happen here," Maitin says. "If Griffith can attack the people there, take over their land and give it to the whites, he thinks you are planning to do the same thing here and he wants to prevent that happening."

"Stuff and nonsense," Hope says. "He would not dare to challenge me with any sort of force. I think what you are hearing is rumour and nothing more." In any event, his mind is on the Maseru *pitso* and his trip to his wife and mother-in-law.

But Maitin is worried. "What am I to do should Moorosi take some sort of action while you are away? Is there any way I can consult with you?"

"Yes, by messenger, but there will be a week's delay," says Hope. "Fear not, Mr. Maitin; I am sure you can handle anything that should occur."

5

King William's Town — Thursday, October 25, 1877

The decision seems logical to the colonial Secretary for Native Affairs, Charles Brownlee: Give Bowker — former commandant of the Frontier Armed and Mounted Police — Griffith's post as senior magistrate in Basutoland. After all, Bowker set up the office in Maseru 12 years ago before handing over to Griffith six years ago. His service was widely praised. Now Bowker's rheumatism has rendered him unfit to lead a police force, but it does not prevent him from serving in his former office position in Maseru.

It's a simple switch of roles. Griffith replaced Bowker; now Bowker replaces Griffith.

Brownlee notifies Bowker of his appointment and suggests he take up his new office as soon as possible. He also notifies Rolland he should return once more to the role of assistant to the senior magistrate as soon as Bowker arrives.

Maseru — Thursday, November 1, 1877

Today is the day for the Maseru *pitso*, or annual meeting, at which the Basotho chiefs gather with the magistrates to discuss events in the country and to tell them what is on their hearts. It is an opportunity, too, for the magistrates to bring the chiefs up to date on any changes in the administration or any new regulations that are to be put into effect. It serves as an effective two-way communications channel.

Rolland had hoped Bowker would have arrived in time to lead the meeting, making it a fine introduction to his second tenure as senior resident magistrate. But Bowker is suffering from such a severe bout of rheumatism that he has been detained at his home in Pietermaritzburg, in Natal colony. So Rolland is going ahead with the meeting as planned.

Once all the chiefs and headmen have taken their places outside the magistracy, many on horseback, Rolland greets them. Sitting alongside him outside the magisterial office, are magistrates from the five districts, including Hope from Quthing, and several missionaries who have travelled from Morija, 25 miles south of Maseru.

Rolland attributes the Basotho turnout, which is smaller than he had hoped it would be, to Griffith's absence. Rolland reminds the Basotho that this meeting is their chance to speak their minds.

He starts by outlining recent events. "With regard to what the government has done here during the past year, I may tell you that a new district has been made over the Orange River. There was no one at hand there to collect revenue, issue passes and settle complaints, and the people were put to great inconvenience when the river was full. The Government, therefore, found it necessary to give Moorosi's people over there a magistrate and Mr. Hope has been appointed."

Rolland outlines the new laws, an updated version produced in March by a government commission that first met in December 1872. Many chiefs and people were called to give evidence to the commission and spoke freely about the changes that should be made, Rolland says. Now, after four years of deliberation, the laws have been published.

"This is the way the government works," Rolland tells the gathered Basotho. "It consults the views and feelings of the people, and then enacts laws that seem the best. The amended laws are not very different from the old, as you will see. I have had a number of copies printed in Sesotho for your information, and I will now ask George Moshesh to read them to you."

After Moshesh reads the laws, several chiefs comment that, although the commission might have listened to what the Basotho people said, they did not necessarily follow their suggestions. And the people who sat on the commission were all whites who thought like white people. Rolland does not respond.

Rolland leans down and picks up a packet. "I am now placed in a difficult position," he says. "I have a certain packet which I am ordered to deliver publicly and the man to whom it belongs is not here. The packet is this beautifully embossed letter from Sir Henry Barkly (governor of the Cape Colony before Sir Bartle Frere was appointed) to Letsie and the other sons of Moshoeshoe. Where is Letsie?"

A few among the crowd respond, "He is not here." Someone says, "He is sick."

"If he is sick," Rolland continues, "where is his eldest son, Lerothodi?"

No one responds. He is not here either.

This is not the first time Letsie has failed to attend a *pitso* and it annoys Rolland. He adds, "The queen grants you this annual opportunity of speaking to her, and Letsie is always sick, so is Molapo. I cannot help thinking that this is an excuse, and, I tell you, frankly, I am dissatisfied.

"This absence of the principal chiefs is a bad thing. It is not bad for the government, but bad for the chiefs, and for you all. It shows that they do not care any longer what becomes of the people, nor anything about their welfare."

Chief Masupha [*Illustrated London News*]

The crowd murmurs. Rolland hands the engraved letter to Masupha, a son of Moshoeshoe, as the highest ranking chief there, asking him to deliver it to his eldest brother, Letsie.

He introduces Hamilton Hope, the new magistrate of Quthing district.

"The difficulties of a magistrate are great," Hope tells the attendees, "but if every man helps his magistrate to see that the law is kept, those difficulties will be easily overcome. If you obey the laws you will prosper and eventually become a great nation. A country cannot progress without law and order. Let every man assist his magistrate. I greet you all, and I am glad to see so many present."

Rolland asks whether the chiefs have any comments.

"I know you are dissatisfied that Chief Letsie and other chiefs are not present," George Moshesh says. "The reason is that they are old and they are infirm. Besides, they know that the government will manage everything all right."

Not all agree. As the *pitso* continues, several delegates hint at another reason for the chiefs' absence: The chiefs were not consulted about the new laws.

"I have already told you that they were consulted," Rolland says. "Again last year you were told at this *pitso* that the new laws would soon be established, but none of the chiefs took the trouble to inquire. Was this from indifference, or was it because you fully trusted the government? I think the latter. You all know full well that the government never has, and never will, treat you ill."

Transkei — Tuesday, November 6, 1877

Sir Arthur Thurlow Cunynghame, commander of the British and colonial forces on the eastern frontier, reviews the campaign against the Gcaleka with Griffith and his senior officers.

Their conclusion: Over the course of 18 days, the men have made a clean sweep of the Gcaleka territory, burning down vacated kraals and seizing the people's corn and cattle. The Gcaleka no longer have huts in which to live and would have little

Burning of Sarhili's kraal [*Illustrated London News*, November, 1877]

to eat should they return. An operation originally intended to defeat the Gcaleka turned into a scorched earth campaign.

Although he has reservations about the long-term effects of this action, in an official despatch to the governor, Sir Bartle Frere, Cunynghame commends Griffith for carrying out his orders "with correctness and judgment."

"Commandant Griffith has been unremitting in his endeavours to carry out to the best advantage his military operations, in which he has been very successful," he writes. "The whole of the country known as Gcalekaland has been entirely freed of the enemy, much cattle has been taken, and the enemy routed from their strongest position. Circumstances lead to the indication that the termination of this war is not far distant."

Quthing — Thursday, November 15, 1877

Moorosi believes his plan to push quietly against Hope is working. His refusal to allow the men to be arrested by Hope's policemen was effective. As a result, the magistrate — who has taken no further action on the matter — yielded to him on the issue of the stolen goats, recognizing his authority to punish the offenders.

He must push this advantage further and discuss matters with Hope in another *pitso*. Perhaps this time, given his victory over the stolen goats, he will advance his cause more effectively and persuade the magistrate that he remains in charge of his own people.

Transkei — Friday, November 16, 1877

Griffith's men are exhausted. After seemingly endless days of marching in the rain and mud, they have covered almost every square mile of the deserted territory, burning huts, seizing cattle and gathering stores of food, but have come into contact with only a few Gcaleka. The horses, too, are tired. The provisions are almost gone and the rugged terrain and wet weather make it difficult for the supply wagons to reach the men with food and ammunition because virtually no roads exist in most of the area.

Some of the men are sick with fever and dysentery. All need a rest. The pro-government Mfengu and Thembu fighting with them are anxious to return home.

Griffith orders most of the troops to return to Ibika, but sends a team to guard the Bashee River near the sea to prevent the return of the Gcaleka to their land. He thanks the settler volunteers for their services and allows them to go home.

The news spreads throughout the colony. The war is over, the Gcaleka cease to exist as a community. Their land has been taken. Their chief and leaders have fled.

Merriman, the de-facto war minister, is beaming. He had feared, he confesses, that the fighting would have been much worse. "We can now move toward setting apart about 500 farms of 300 acres each for occupation by Europeans," he tells Governor Frere. "Clearly, they will select the most fertile areas. The less fertile areas will be given to the Mfengu, who assisted us in our campaign against the Gcaleka. What is then left will be open to occupation by those Gcaleka who, we believe, will return, surrender, give up their arms and agree to live under colonial rule."

In the barracks in King William's Town, Griffith sits alone, on the edge of his bed. He sees again in his mind's eye the shooting, the shouting and the shelling as his men chase the panicked Gcaleka.

He sees the vivid orange and red of the huts on fire. He sees the troops pillage food from the deserted kraals and capture the disoriented cattle. He sees the fury in their eyes, reflecting those streaks of cruelty and hatred every soldier needs to perform his task efficiently.

Griffith had been determined to lead the operation with his head and not his heart. He would serve his country as he had been trained — as a good soldier, following orders. But, unable to ignore the murmurs of his heart entirely, he had tempered his instructions with compassion. He had opted to do so with the least loss of life possible. He had instructed his men to force the enemy to flee. Rather let them depart their land than depart this earth.

At least, Griffith consoles himself, the loss of life was not as great as it could have been. He and his men might have driven people from their land and destroyed their means of survival, but they had not killed people unnecessarily and, he is convinced, had avoided needless cruelty and suffering.

The thoughts tumble through his head, vying with one another for primacy.

But enough of this. He had implemented justice fairly and with compassion. He will struggle to be content that he served both his country and his conscience.

Quthing — Monday, November 19, 1877

Maitin feared something like this might occur in Hope's absence. For more than an hour, groups of armed Baphuthi have been gathering at the Quthing magistracy tethering their horses and talking loudly to one another. Their numbers have been steadily increasing for some hours; now hundreds are here.

Maitin's mind jumps back to the occasion five months ago when a large gathering of armed Baphuthi, led by Moorosi, confronted Hope. He recalls how threatened he felt when the men asserted that Moorosi was their leader and they would obey him and not Hope.

How should he respond now?

Maitin approaches a man who is leading one of the groups.

"Why are you here?"

"King Moorosi told us to come because a *pitso* is being held here today," the man responds. "He told us to bring our weapons."

"I know of no *pitso*," Maitin replies. "Did he say what the *pitso* would be about?"

"No."

Maitin is debating whether he should tell the crowd to leave as no *pitso* is to be held, when a man makes his way to the front. Maitin recognizes him as Moorosi's messenger, Mafetudi.

"King Moorosi is coming to pay a friendly visit to Mr. Hope," Mafetudi says. "He wants to talk about things that friends discuss with one another. Last time they met they did not have a chance to talk as friends. Now he wants to do so."

"Mr. Hope is not at home. He has gone for some days. I suggest you tell Chief Moorosi that he should postpone his visit. I will pass the message on to Mr. Hope when he returns."

As the messenger leaves to convey the message to Moorosi, Maitin retreats into the relative safety of the office where he discusses the situation with the policemen. They are as puzzled as he is.

"Look at them," says sergeant Isaak Masin.

"They are walking around and talking as though it is a party. I don't think they know why they are here, either. Their king told them to come here and so they are here. That is all."

"At least they look relaxed," replies Maitin. "They do not seem bent on any sort of confrontation."

Later, the messenger returns. "King Moorosi says to thank you for the information. When Mr. Hope comes back, we will ask him to set a day for a *pitso*."

The messenger shouts to the crowd to leave. Maitin heaves a sigh of relief.

Quthing — Thursday, November 22, 1877

Hope disembarks from the new Cape cart that he bought with government money in Aliwal North while visiting his wife and mother-in-law. He has been on the road for three days and away from the Quthing magistracy for a month.

He wastes little time conferring with Maitin, who describes the arrival of armed men four days ago. Hope is convinced Moorosi does not want a *pitso*. He wants a confrontation.

"I have been giving this matter some thought while I have been away," he tells Maitin. "I listened to what the Basotho said at the Maseru *pitso* and discussed their attitudes with the other magistrates. I'm convinced Moorosi is more rebellious than any of them. He is rash and fearless. He is clearly defying the government.

"I have done what I believe is right to counter the chief. I do not know what else I can be expected to do. During our private discussions in Maseru, Rolland kept quoting Griffith's letter to me in which he warned me not to precipitate any crisis. He said, too, that he would be unable to back me up with force should matters get out of hand. He said that by being 'calm, firm and reasoning' I will be more effective than if I use force.

"Calm, firm and reasoning.

"I'll try to be calm. I think I have shown I can be firm and, well, I have reasoned with him over and over again.

"This time I will set out my message to Moorosi in writing so that the authorities can see what I have said to him. Then they will be unable to second-guess me."

The letter, in scrawling handwriting, will be passed on to Maitin to translate.

"Yesterday I returned to my office and was informed by Mr. Maitin of your message sent to me by Mafetudi," he writes to Moorosi. "I was much pleased with the words you sent me by him. I will also be very glad to see you; for, as you say, when we last met we had so many affairs which we were forced to talk over in order that we might understand each other, that we had no time for friendly discussion.

"Mr. Maitin advised you to postpone your visit because I was absent, and I was very glad to hear this, as I should have missed seeing you, my friend, had you come when you first intended."

He reads over what he has written. He smiles as he reads the words "my friend." Surely those are "calm and reasonable" words.

He lays down one stipulation; one with which he is sure the authorities in Maseru and King William's Town will agree. "I trust that you will not bring trouble on yourself and your children by omitting to tell all your friends to leave their arms at home when they come to this or any other friendly meeting."

He has no intention of facing the same armed threat he faced before.

After Maitin has translated the letter, Hope hands it to the chief constable, Abraham Sighata. He tells him to read it to Moorosi and to wait to see whether he has a reply.

Hope also suggests Sighata remind Moorosi of the events in the eastern Cape — verbally of course — and to bear in mind what has happened to his friend Sarhili.

Quthing — Friday, November 23, 1877

As Moorosi listens to the letter from Hope, read to him by Chief Constable Sighata, he is pleased that Hope is ready to see him again and to discuss the issues causing trouble between them. He is also anxious to hear from Hope about the *pitso* in Maseru. He likes that Hope calls him friend.

But he baulks at one stipulation: That he and his people leave their weapons at home. "I will not leave my guns at home when I go to a *pitso* to speak with a chief," he tells Sighata. "Tell the magistrate I cannot leave my weapons. It is our custom to take our weapons with us wherever we go. Even when I move among my people I take my spears.

"Explain to him that when a Baphuthi is initiated into the privileges of manhood, the elders place a weapon into his hands. The weapon is a sign of manhood. With his weapon he is to defend his chief, his country and himself.

"We say, 'Hold on to your arms.'

"Tell the magistrate that when a bull goes out to pasture, he does not take off his horns and leave them in the kraal. They are part of him. He uses them to defend himself. He gores his assailant if he is attacked.

"The horns are part of the bull and our weapons are part of us, too.

"Even when I visited Moshoeshoe I would take my weapons with me. Even when I go from one hut to sleep in another I go carrying my quiver of spears to the place where I sleep.

"Abraham Sighata, explain my view to the magistrate for me. Tell him I would be weak if I were unarmed. I would be walking around naked.

"Even when I go to pay my hut tax, I go with these arms to the magistrate's office. The weapons do not prevent me from paying tax. I pay it anyway. No one tries to stop me from paying the tax because I have a weapon with me.

"If the magistrate replies that I must leave my weapons behind, he is telling me he refuses to see me. What matters is where your heart is. These weapons cannot hurt anyone unless your heart is crooked. I will visit the magistrate with a happy heart, not a crooked heart. That is what is important.

"Tell the chief that I will attend this *pitso* with a glad heart. The arms mean nothing. They are only the appendages of manhood. True manhood is in the heart.

"Please convey my very best greetings to Mr. Hope and also to Mr. Maitin."

As he mounts his horse, Sighata promises to convey Moorosi's sentiments, but he already knows what the answer on the weapons will be.

Quthing — Saturday, November 24, 1877

Hope remains convinced that Moorosi has an ulterior motive in bringing the weapons with him to the *pitso*.

"All that contention about arms being a part of him and his people is utter nonsense," he tells Maitin. "He wants to back up with force his assertions about being the ultimate authority here. He knows he can stand up to me more effectively with a crowd of armed followers behind him."

Hope's first reaction is to tell Moorosi he must leave his weapons at home or else the *pitso* is off. But he realizes, too, that, as Rolland emphasized in Maseru, he needs to keep communication open.

After some thought, he decides to start with the positive and move to the negative. He will first set a date for the meeting: Monday December 3, a little more than a week away.

He will follow with the negative: Whatever Moorosi might say, no one — neither him, his staff nor Moorosi and his people — should be armed.

In the meantime he will send copies of his correspondence with Moorosi to Rolland in Maseru. Let Rolland tell him what he has done wrongly. In that way, at least Rolland will not be able to criticize him afterward.

"It is all very well for them to sit in their offices in Maseru and King William's Town, or wherever they happen to be, and warn me not to act with a high hand," he says. "But what would they do if they were here? How would they act if they were faced with an aggressive and defiant chief, backed by hundreds of warlike armed savages, who is determined to subvert my authority? And to chase me out of the country if necessary? Or to kill me if that will achieve his aim?

"And the man who told me not to be so high-handed, whom we now should correctly call *Colonel* Griffith, has himself been leading troops against Sarhili. Why is he acting correctly when he makes war, yet I am *not* acting correctly when I ask for a few score troops to back me up against a rebellious chief?

"I will do my work here to the best of my ability. I will bring justice and civilization to these savages and I will do it effectively — whatever it takes. When they see what I have achieved, they will thank me for my work.

"One thing is for sure. I will not tolerate arguing once more with Moorosi with a force of armed warriors arraigned against me without some sort of armed force backing me up.

"Either it is unarmed against unarmed, or armed against armed. In equal numbers. Otherwise, I do not meet with him at all."

Hope also decides to cover himself more fully by sending a telegram via Aliwal North to Brownlee, the Secretary for Native Affairs, who is in King William's Town.

"Moorosi is to be here on 3rd December to repeat his old argument. Has warned the whole tribe to assemble armed. District a good deal unsettled at this, and at exaggerated reports of what he is going to do. I sent a message to warn him not to bring guns or spears; he sent civil reply, but says he insists upon the guns. I think he does not believe the news I have given him about Sarhili's collapse. This being a direct defiance, please send me instructions at once, meanwhile I will act as before. Have reported to Rolland, who will send letters by post."

Now, Hope decides, he will await the replies from Rolland and from Brownlee. Their responses will determine the approach he will need to take on December 3.

Quthing — Tuesday, November 27, 1877

Hope has not heard back from Rolland or Brownlee, but time is getting short. The *pitso* he arranged with Moorosi is less than a week away and he is convinced he needs to have a visible armed force in place when he meets Moorosi so the chief will know that he can back up his words with force if necessary.

He will request West Fynn, who is in charge of the troops at Kraai River 50 miles to the south, to send as strong a patrol as he can spare — say 40 or 50 men — to the

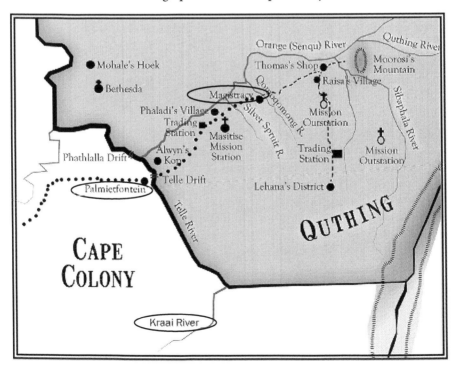

border of Moorosi's territory, at Palmietfontein, less than a day's ride from here.

"I will tell him that I need the troops to be there no later than Sunday, December 2nd. That will put them in place a day before the *pitso* with Moorosi. The news that they are there will reach Moorosi and he will be reminded that the government is watching his actions and is prepared to restrain him with force if necessary.

"I will ask Fynn's men to remain at Palmietfontein and not enter Quthing without instructions from me. You see, if the men come here to meet Moorosi's force a collision will inevitably take place. But when Moorosi hears that the men are in position at Palmietfontein, ready to attack, he undoubtedly will abandon the idea of the so-called *pitso*, which I suspect is a way to confront me with an armed force once more. He will postpone it to a later date. At that time we also may have an even stronger force to back us up."

Hope writes a letter to Fynn, and orders Maitin that it be sent "by special express post if necessary." Only six days remain before the *pitso* and he needs to have the troops in place by then.

Maseru — Wednesday, November 28, 1877

It is more than a month since Acting Resident Magistrate Emile Rolland was told Bowker would take over the office and Bowker still has not arrived.

Realizing he cannot put pressing matters indefinitely on hold while waiting for Bowker, Rolland decides he needs to step in and try to calm the troubles engulfing the Quthing magistracy.

After reading the letters and statements from Hope that arrived in this morning's post and studying carefully Hope's report of the events immediately following his return from the *pitso* in Maseru, Rolland accepts that Moorosi will not easily back down on his demand that his people be armed at the *pitso*. Nor will Hope back down on his demand that the men come unarmed.

It appears to be a recipe for conflict that, sparked by an incident, could easily get out of hand.

Rolland would like to travel to Quthing himself to try to calm the situation. But such a journey will take a few days in preparation and travel time and he cannot risk being out of the office for that long should Bowker arrive. He needs to do something now. The *pitso* is less than a week away.

Firstly, he will order that the *pitso* planned for December 3 be postponed, providing breathing room. Secondly, he will send a message to Letsie, asking for his help. Then he will write a letter to Moorosi, which he will enclose with the letter to Hope, instructing Hope to see that Moorosi receives it.

He must work quickly. A new daily police express service will ensure that his letter arrives in Quthing by noon the following day, but he must complete his letter today so that he can get it in the Thursday morning express post, which will reach Quthing on Friday, three days before the *pitso* planned for Monday. Doing so will provide Hope just enough time to send the letter to Moorosi before Monday.

Rolland's approach to Moorosi will be colonial and British. Even though his father was French, Rolland was born in South Africa to a mother of British descent and grew up with English as his home language. Even though Rolland spent only four years in Britain, he is as British as any born and bred British national.

In line with that approach, he regards Moorosi as a disobedient child, as one who needs to show respect to the authorities and to obey them because it is the right and only thing to do. To Rolland the British, and now the colonial authorities, have brought light into darkness for people who were mere savages. The British system is civilized and just. Its basis in Christian principles underpins it with moral authority. There can be no question the British system of government is superior to anything anywhere else in the world.

British rule is in the best interests of the Basotho people themselves, Rolland believes. Left to their own devices, they will wallow in heathenism.

Unlike Hope, who grew up in a home with a military and administrative background, Rolland was reared in a missionary home. His approach, therefore, is rooted in persuasion and conviction and an appeal to a higher standard. To Rolland, the Baphuthi people will accept the colonial system because they will be persuaded that it is just and in their best interests, although he believes, too, that government officials should bring about such persuasion by speaking quietly, but firmly, making clear that they are in charge and not tolerating any attitude other than complete obedience and profound respect. Like children, the natives will be persuaded by the higher reasoning, will obey and will be subservient.

In his letter to Moorosi, therefore, Rolland believes he needs to show firmly that the government holds the power and that Moorosi needs not just to obey, but to obey happily; not merely to be content with British rule but to show how admirable it truly is.

He writes a letter to Moorosi in English, which he will then translate for onward delivery to the chief. Hope will be sent both versions, the English original for him to read and the other for him to send to Moorosi.

"Your words have greatly amazed me," Rolland writes to Moorosi. "I am sure that the Queen's government will also be greatly astonished to learn in what way Moorosi speaks to his magistrate."

Moorosi's duty, he continues, is to go to Hope unarmed, no matter what his custom might be. By not obeying Hope's instruction to leave his arms at home, he has shown no respect for the magistrate, let alone the queen's government.

"You say there is no harm in carrying arms if a man's heart is right, and that arms are only dangerous when the heart is crooked. Yes, but when you come with armed bands how will the magistrate see into your heart to ascertain if you come with white hearts or with hearts of another colour? Supposing that the governor came to you with many armed warriors, what would you think of it? Would you not conclude that he had come to fight you?

"In the old time you used to go armed to chief's meetings, because, very often, warlike expeditions were ordered and planned at these meetings. Now, under the Queen's government, all that is over; there are no longer any warlike expeditions to which the people may be summoned by the chief.

"But all that is beside the question.

"The great thing is that it is not you, Moorosi, who must dictate your customs to the Queen's government; it is the Queen's government which must teach you its custom, and that is that people do not attend a *pitso* armed.

"We are not like God who can see into men's hearts whilst they are afar off; we are only men, and when we see armed men coming to us, we suppose they want war. Although your words may deny it, your actions call out in a loud voice.

"No, Moorosi, your duty is to obey and humble yourself. If you go about with bands of armed men after you have received an order to the contrary, it will be impossible for the government to recognize you as a subject.

"A bull that carries its horns with it in order to gore its assailant (to use your own words) is very like an enemy."

He tells Moorosi the *pitso* is off. It is not Moorosi's place to take the initiative and dictate to the government that a meeting shall take place.

"I entreat you to recognize that you have done wrong and to remain peacefully at home," he writes. "If you have any cause for dissatisfaction bring your complaint to your magistrate or to me. The government does not wish to prevent any man from speaking his mind or bringing forward his complaint. What will not be permitted is the use of threats."

The correct way to discuss a matter is to sit down in council and discuss it, Rolland adds.

"That is the way men behave. To flaunt your weapons is not manliness, it is only the bragging of a bully."

Rolland concludes: "My words to you are the advice of a true friend."

In his letter to Hope, Rolland once again urges restraint.

"I am of the opinion that the greatest caution and prudence should be exercised in this matter," he tells Hope, "and that there is everything to gain from delay, whilst on the other hand no advantage can possibly accrue from a *pitso* held at the suggestion of this unruly chief and which will give him the opportunity of being insolent to his magistrate and of contrasting his large physical resources, in the shape of a body of armed men, with the (to the native eye) defenceless and weak position of the magistrate.

"The chief Moorosi is evidently trying to make use of these armed demonstrations in order to convince his people of his power and supremacy, being unaffected by the presence of the magistrate, and to a tribe of ignorant barbarians no argument could be more conclusive, especially if the demonstration be accompanied by a defiant bearing."

Rolland adds, "It is quite impossible for me to give you any specific instructions. If, for example, Moorosi should, in spite of my letter, come down with his armed followers, you would have a good reason for declining to attend the *pitso*, by alleging the order contained in the letter.

"In any case, your wisest policy will be to keep quiet, avoid trials of strength, gain time, and allow the moral influence of the government to gain ground insensibly as it has in the more advanced districts.

"Should Moorosi visit you, unless there are special reasons to make it advisable, I should counsel that you receive him in your office, or at your residence, and that you should avoid giving him any opportunity of making a display before his people of his power and eloquence, a display which must necessarily be at your expense as long as he remain in his present sentiments.

"You will continue to exercise that friendliness and forbearance which you have already shown under trying circumstances, and to bear in mind that your highest and most lasting triumphs will be those which are the most gradually and noiselessly obtained, and that profound tranquillity is the most successful result of good government.

"In all other matters you must use your own judgment and discretion, in which I have every confidence."

He hopes this coordinated action will calm matters in Quthing.

Maseru — Friday, November 30, 1877

As he reads the copy of Hope's letter to West Fynn that reaches him today, Rolland crashes his fist on the desk. What does Hope think he is doing? It is bad enough that Moorosi intends calling up an armed band to confront Hope at the magistracy. Hope now counters by summoning troops to the border.

The 40 or 50 men on the border would be no match for the thousand or so warriors Moorosi would be able to summon. They would not serve as a threat, nor would they force Moorosi into docile submission.

They would serve only as a provocation.

The Baphuthi people know of the war against Sarhili to the south; now they would see the build-up as the first moves in a war against them.

Surely, Rolland mutters to himself, Hope should have listened when Griffith warned him before that no forces could be sent. Could Hope not read? Did he not understand Griffith? Could it possibly have been any clearer than it was?

Above anything else, Hope had been told to leave the responsibility of taking drastic action with his superior, the resident magistracy in Maseru. Yet here he is taking it upon himself to send his request directly to Fynn.

Although Hope is his brother-in-law, Rolland feels he must tell him he has dangerously overstepped the mark. He fears that his actions will upset Mimmie, his sister and Hope's wife, who eventually will hear of them. But another part of him suspects Mimmie will understand the reason for his words. In any case, he must say what needs to be said.

"Your action in calling for troops to go to Palmietfontein," he writes, "meets with my most serious disapproval. As a counter-demonstration to anything Moorosi may do, it is most inadequate and is only calculated to irritate and provoke that chief without overawing him. Moreover, the arrival of an armed force under such circumstances might produce a scene on both sides of the Telle River, amongst a population so given to spreading false and exaggerated rumours.

"If Moorosi supposes you have been instrumental in it, your moral influence with him will be greatly undermined. Under these circumstances, I should feel obliged if you would inform Mr. Fynn that it will no longer be necessary for him to send the patrol as requested by you.

"I trust that the disturbance caused by Moorosi's armed demonstration, which is the only cause I can see for the present uneasiness, will, by this time, have passed away. We are not at present in a position to meet force with force, nor is it desirable; and our only wise policy is to keep quiet as much as possible to avoid giving the chiefs opportunities of displaying their physical superiority."

Letsie's village near Maseru

In the afternoon, a concerned Rolland visits Letsie at his village and asks him to send a confidential messenger to Moorosi, telling him to submit to the orders of the government and warning him against making any armed demonstration.

Letsie is not inclined to foment confrontation.

He smiles, nods and agrees with Rolland to send a messenger to Moorosi. Doing so will keep Letsie on the good side of the colonial government and will remind Moorosi that he believes he should act with tact and not provoke the colonial powers.

But he knows, too, that Moorosi will not necessarily heed his advice and that trouble could ensue.

Quthing — Saturday, December 1, 1877

Rolland's letter, which arrived in the post at noon, leaves Hope steaming. Rolland's instructions do not anger him as much as the way the letter is written.

He goes over it once again, re-reading the reprimand on his decision to request Fynn to move troops to Palmietfontein.

The reprimand is so blunt that he begins to fear that his position as magistrate might be in jeopardy.

But Hope decides to fight back. He must reassert the necessity of his action. He must explain that, with the *pitso* due on Monday, he needed to act soon and could not wait for instructions by post on what to do.

Hope drafts a letter saying that Rolland does not understand the threat he is facing from Moorosi, and fails to understand that he needs an armed force, not to provoke Moorosi, but simply to back him up. "It would serve as a display, not a threat," he writes.

Having second thoughts, he deletes the word "display" and writes "protection."

He adds a paragraph arguing that he still needs an armed force to back him up. Convinced the chief is bent on attacking him and ousting him from Quthing, Hope fears that Moorosi could arrive at any time with hundreds of armed men and confront him.

He reads the letter over once more, deleting sections and substituting others. He takes up a fresh sheet of paper and writes out the letter again.

As he does, fear reasserts itself and pushes fury into second place.

He decides he had better do as he is told. He crumbles the second letter and throws it on the floor.

He begins with the required acknowledgment: "I have the honour to acknowledge the receipt of your letter of the 28th ultimo, enclosing letter for Moorosi." He says he has sent the letter with his chief constable to the Baphuthi leader.

With that out of the way, he once again tackles a response to the letter of reprimand. Like a good soldier, he must stand his ground. But, like the good whist player that he is, he must recognize when the cards go against him.

If only there were a way, he thinks, he could go back in time and erase his request to Fynn. Yet there is a way he can partially do that.

"I have also just received yours of 30th ultimo," he continues, "and have the honour to state that I had already seen my mistake, and sent to countermand Mr. Fynn, telling him not to come."

The letter is uncharacteristically short for someone who even writes long telegrams. So be it. It is a lie and lies are better short.

He signs the letter and readies it for the next post.

Now he needs to ask Fynn not to move his troops after all. And to mark the instruction with yesterday's date.

⚜

Dating the letter a day earlier does not help it arrive earlier. Fynn, unaware that the instruction has been reversed, already has moved almost 50 men to the border.

News of their arrival soon reaches Moorosi on the word-of-mouth pipeline that stretches across the kingdom.

Why, the chief asks himself, are they there? Is it a coincidence that the *pitso* was postponed and the troops gathered on the border at the same time? Do the colonists want to fight rather than talk?

Moorosi wants to comply with Letsie's request that he act with tact. But that attempt at dialogue has been answered with an armed threat. Even as the colonial authorities are telling him that he should not arm his men, they are arming theirs. Is it because they want to attack him without facing any resistance?

It all makes sense. They think they can score as easy a success over him as Griffith did over Sarhili.

They deceive themselves.

He calls his messenger, Mafetudi.

"Go to the people who live between the magistrate's office and the Telle River. Inform them they are no longer to come to the *pitso*. Tell them they should move closer to the border and watch with guns and horses at the ready. They will see that there are armed police across the border.

"Should the police cross the Telle, they are to defend themselves and attack them. But they are not to cross the river if the colonial men stay on the other side. They are to attack only if the troops cross the river into our territory."

6

King William's Town — Tuesday, December 4, 1877

Scouts report to William Raymond, deputizing for West Fynn — who is occupied at Palmietfontein on the Basutoland border — that large parties of Gcaleka are gathering in all parts of the territory from which they were forcibly driven a little more than a month ago.

Raymond, in turn, reports to Griffith who realizes what he should have expected all along — that those Gcaleka who had eluded his forces had been lying low, both within their territory and across the Bashee River, and they have returned to reclaim it.

Griffith, in turn, reports to Cape Colony Governor Frere what has happened and asks for reinforcements to build up the military forces once more.

The war against the Gcaleka — the Ninth Frontier War — has not ended.

Before the day is over, moves are under way to collect an active and larger force, including the drafting of soldiers from as far away as Cape Town, to stop the Gcaleka from returning to reclaim land taken from them at the outbreak of the Ninth Frontier War.

Quthing — Wednesday, December 5, 1877

Fynn is puzzled by the change of orders from Hope, whose latest letter asking him to withdraw his troops has reached him in Palmietfontein. But, as an obedient soldier, he does as he is told.

As Fynn's troops dismantle their tents and leave Palmietfontein, Moorosi's armed and mounted men across the Telle River watch with fascination.

For Moorosi, the withdrawal is a victory. Clearly, once he placed his men near the border, the colonial soldiers were out-matched. Had he not moved his men into position, the colonial forces might have marched right up to the magistrate's office and perhaps beyond, with the aim of backing Hope's assertion that he is in control in Moorosi's territory and possibly even challenging him head-on.

The sudden withdrawal gives Moorosi confidence that taking on Hope with force will have the desired effect of causing him to back away from asserting his authority.

Once all the colonial troops have left, Moorosi tells his men on the border they can return to their homes.

He will call on them once more should it become necessary. For now, the recent events have shown that their mere presence has the effect of frightening off the colonial troops.

Maseru — The same day

Acting Resident Magistrate Emile Rolland regards it as a good sign that he has received no express letters from Hamilton Hope in the last two days. The cancellation of the *pitso*, his letter to Moorosi, the withdrawal of the troops from the border, and his admonition to Hope to avoid the appearance of seeking armed confrontation all seem to have had an effect. As far as he can tell from a distance, calm has settled over the area.

Rolland reports to Secretary for Native Affairs Brownlee that Hope committed "an error of judgment" in acquiescing to Moorosi's holding a *pitso* at the magistracy and thus giving that unruly chief an opportunity for a trial of strength and that he had "erred again" by summoning the police to the border, "a step which might have occasioned a general scare."

"As far as I can ascertain everything has quietened down," he adds.

Quthing — Monday, December 24, 1877

Two challenges face the Baphuthi people as the summer heat bears down on the mountainous territory.

One concerns the conflict between their chief and the magistrate.

The other is an increasingly worsening drought. The rains have been few and far between. Small and less hardy corn, sorghum and millet plants, planted just a few months ago, are withering under the relentless sun. The vegetables, too, are not as vigorous as they should be by this time of year. Unless plentiful rains fall soon, many plants will die.

Meanwhile, the supplies from the last harvest, which were not as plentiful as in previous years, are dwindling. Many Baphuthi are supplementing their stored grain with roots and berries.

Livestock remain plentiful and areas of green grass on which they can feed remain. But the Baphuthi do not want to slaughter too many cattle to supplement their food supply. Cattle are their wealth and their sources of milk and future herds.

The situation is worsened by the arrival of those Baphuthi who have worked for years on the diamond fields in Kimberley. In returning to their families and friends, they place additional strain on the grain supplies.

Many blame Hope for the ailing crops. He has been ardent in attempting to challenge their king, collect hut tax and throw offenders in jail. But he has done little to help them with food.

To many it appears — in spite of what he says — that Hope is bent more on hurting than on helping them.

But they appreciate the help given by Thomas and other traders who have been assisting the Baphuthi by selling them grain from other parts of the country, even though their prices are high.

For their part, the Baphuthi Christians are waiting for the Ellenbergers to return. Frederic Ellenberger is a wise man, a kind man and has done many things to help the Baphuthi people. Emma Ellenberger teaches them many things that help them.

They believe the situation will improve when the Ellenbergers return.

In the meantime, they will gather tomorrow, Christmas Day, at the church built by Ellenberger to celebrate the birth of Jesus and to ask him to help them, too.

Maseru — Monday December 31, 1877

Rolland is reflecting on the events of 1877 as he prepares to write his annual report for the Minister of Native Affairs in Cape Town. As he reads through the reports from the six magistrates in Basutoland, he concludes that progress has been made during the year.

The main event he decides, was the transfer of Griffith from the post he filled so long and ably. Rolland ponders why the move upset the Basotho people so much. He concludes the reason is that the Basotho people are accustomed to personal rather than amorphous government rule. They look to a chief, and Griffith was their respected white chief alongside their Basotho chief, Letsie.

The Basotho never have identified with a political system, a set of laws or a dogma, he reasons. They have identified themselves with a person who embodies those elements: the king, or paramount chief, and the sub-chiefs who lead them. A chief would not be expected to establish new laws, or introduce a new system. He would be expected to act in terms of the unchanging mores and customs that have existed for generations.

So it was that when the British and later the Cape Colony began to implement their governmental system the Basotho people put their trust in the man introducing it. Here was a new chief, whom they expected to work alongside their old chiefs, to respect them and their traditions, to help them and protect them from their enemies.

Griffith excelled at that, Rolland believes. He understood the Basotho character, imposed justice impartially and handled emergencies with tact. He displayed a kind disposition toward the people. He succeeded in never setting himself up as an opponent of the Basotho chiefs, rather working alongside them.

In doing so, he won the hearts and the confidence of the Basotho chiefs and people alike.

When he went to fight against the Xhosa-speaking Gcaleka, the Basotho did not identify with the people he was fighting against. They believed they were superior to the Xhosa and that Griffith recognized this. Griffith was their father, not the father of the Gcaleka.

Rolland suspects that such feelings are not shared by Moorosi and the Baphuthi. Not only have they had fewer direct dealings with Griffith, but they see Griffith's representative, Hope, as an enemy of their chief, a man setting out to impose his traditions and customs on them rather than working with them.

In addition, the Baphuthi are more likely than the other Basotho clans to identify with the Gcaleka. Their ties of history and geography with the Xhosa-speaking people are stronger and they see Griffith's attack on the people to the south as something that could be directed at them.

Rolland accepts that he has been an inadequate replacement for Griffith. He has tried, but failed to win the people's confidence in the way Griffith did. He can sense this lack every time they ask him when Griffith will return. He hopes Bowker will be a good replacement as, by all accounts, he, too, won the hearts and minds of the

Basotho when he first served in the post.

This "paternal" attribute accorded to Griffith seems to run counter to Frere's belief expressed in a recent letter that it is possible to turn the attention of the Basotho away from "men" to "measures," Rolland reasons.

The nature of the Basotho is to react to men, not measures.

In Quthing, too, Rolland muses, the people have looked to the man more than the measures. Even though the laws and system of administration are the same, Hope has not been a Griffith-like person to the Baphuthi.

Same measures, different man.

The one was loved, the other was disliked.

Rolland is grateful that Quthing is quiet for now. He hopes Moorosi has accepted Hope, and that Hope has found his feet.

But he fears that the man — not necessarily the measures — has been found wanting and that will continue to be a problem.

Quthing — Friday, January 18, 1878

In checking out his 1877 tax receipts and the recent preliminary census he has undertaken since his arrival, Hope notices that five widows in Lehana's district did not pay their hut taxes.

He discusses the situation with Maitin, back from his week's leave of absence. The government needs to gather taxes from everyone, he says. The money is used to run the administration in Basutoland and taxes cannot be allowed to go unpaid. It is the law and it must be obeyed.

"In Baphuthi custom, when a widow is beyond child-bearing age, and has not remarried, her son is responsible for seeing to her welfare," Maitin explains. "Therefore, I would assume that the widows' sons would be seen as being responsible for paying the taxes."

"Very well," Hope responds, "let us tell them that the widows' sons should pay the taxes."

He dispatches his senior police officer, Sighata, to tell the men that if they do not pay the taxes for their mothers, they will be summonsed and face punishment.

Quthing — Tuesday, January 29, 1878

The headman Maikela and four other Baphuthi stand silently in Hope's courtroom as they listen to the charges against them.

Through a translator, Hope tells them their widowed mothers failed to pay their hut tax. "Because you are responsible for them, I hold you responsible for the failure to pay the tax," he says.

The men show no outward reaction.

"Do you admit that your mothers are active and have gardens that they cultivate?"

"Yes," the men say.

"They have separate fields, which they are well able to attend to?"

"Yes."

"Good. When I find a woman is really too old or infirm to support herself, I give her a certificate of exemption. But in this case, these women have their own separate gardens, which they are able to cultivate. Is that not so?"

"Yes."

"Why then have you not gathered the hut tax from them or paid the tax for them?"

As the headman, Maikela, answers on their behalf. He has learned that it is important to answer Hope and not agree with him out of politeness.

"These taxes are a burden on us," he says. "The widows must not pay the taxes. You say we are responsible for them. But we do not have the money to pay their taxes and also our own taxes.

"Mr. Austen, the magistrate in Mohale's Hoek, when he sent his men to collect the hut tax from this area, he said these widows do not have to pay the tax."

"Mr. Austen exempted them?" Hope asks.

The men agree.

Hope is taken aback. They are unlikely to have made up such an explanation. For a brief moment, he considers telling them if that is the case then they are free to go. But he cannot back down now. And who is to say Austen — a man who, in Cape Colony terms is a Coloured man — is right? Although he has more experience, Austen does not have the education that he does and Hope has little respect for him. And the law is clear. Everyone who is capable of working in their fields must pay hut tax, even if someone pays it on their behalf.

"So what you are saying is that because Mr. Austen exempted you, I must exempt you too?"

"Yes."

"Do I look like Mr. Austen?" he asks the men.

"No, you do not look the same," Maikela says. "But you and the other magistrates all live in the same kind of houses. Two horses do not look alike, but they eat the same grass in the same field and they carry the same people on their backs."

Hope accepts that Maikela's contention, couched in the symbolism favoured by the Baphuthi, is reasonable. In their eyes, Austen is equal to Hope. But Hope is unwilling to concede the point completely. He would show himself as weak and lacking in judgment should he suddenly change his mind and throw out the case. Instead, he will toss the issue back at the accused men.

"Very well," he says. "I will need proof that you are not lying to me. I will give you 14 days to go to Mr. Austen and get from him a certificate of exemption."

The men, after listening to the translation, ask what a "certificate of exemption" is. After an explanation from Maitin, they say that they understand.

"If I receive no proof of exemption, you will need to pay me a total of five pounds for the widows' hut taxes."

Hope declares the hearing over.

The men leave the courtroom and gather outside.

"I do not understand why Hope says we must show him we are not lying," Maikela tells the others. "We are telling the truth, why does he not believe us? He says we must go to Mohale's Hoek. But the river is full and difficult to cross. Why does this magistrate not know what the other magistrate did?"

"Why cannot he ask the Mohale's Hoek magistrate what he did?" asks one of the men. "He wants us to talk to that man, Austen. Why must we do it? Why does he not do it?"

Their opposition to Hope's ruling goes further. Their mothers are part of their family. The gardens that their mothers cultivate are the family fields, granted by Lehana, a senior son of Moorosi, for which the family is responsible. Their widowed mothers occupy the same position as children in Baphuthi custom — and just as their children do not pay hut tax, so, too, must their widowed mothers not pay it.

Hope says they, as their sons, must pay the tax for them. He is not right. No one must pay hut tax for them. The family already is paying hut tax, so why should anyone pay it again?

"In the same way that Hope punished Raisa for doing the right thing, so now Hope is punishing us for upholding what is right," Maikela says. "Raisa upheld his family responsibility; we, too, want to uphold our family responsibility. Our responsibility is to see that our widowed mothers do not pay the tax. We want to look after our family members and protect them. He wants us to act like the white people who do not help their family members. Hah!" He shakes his head in disgust.

The men know what will happen if they fail to obey Hope's instruction. He will act as he has in the past, sending a policeman with a summons. If they resist, the policeman will arrest them and Hope will punish them.

But Hope is not their chief. He does not understand them and shows no concerns for their way of life. Lehana is their headman. Moorosi is their king. They know, as all Baphuthi do, what is right and what is wrong and they keep to those ways. Hope wants to impose false laws on them, laws that want to take away the love and support they have for their mothers.

Moorosi understands. Lehana understands. Even Austen understands. But Hope does not want to understand and is always looking for ways to punish them.

They climb on their horses, return to their village and report back to Lehana to seek his counsel on what they should do.

Quthing — Friday, February 1, 1878

Lehana has travelled two days to ask Hope to explain the hut-tax charges.

Hope sighs, muttering to himself about the inability of these people to understand anything.

He goes over the case, explaining that the widowed mothers must pay the hut tax but, if Austen has given exemption, the men must show him proof of such exemption.

Lehana listens intently.

"What if the men do not agree that their widowed mothers have to pay the hut tax?" he asks. "The mothers are members of their family. They are not separate families. The mothers do not have rights of their own. Their rights are the rights of their sons.

"And the sons do not have the money to pay the hut tax for themselves as well as for their widowed mothers."

Hope, feeling under pressure, but determined to stand by his decision, replies that his ruling was that they need to pay the tax.

"I do not care whether you agree or disagree with my decision," he tells Lehana. "That is irrelevant. The law is clear, even if it makes the sons feel bad and regardless of whether they have the money. If the mothers cannot pay it and the sons do not have it, they will have to find it."

When Lehana remonstrates further, Hope holds up his hand, indicating he should stop. "I cannot argue with you any further, Lehana. If they do not bring proof of exemption from Mr. Austen, I will fine them. But if they still disagree with my verdict, they are free to appeal my ruling."

"To whom do they appeal?" Lehana asks.

"They can appeal to the resident magistrate in Maseru."

Lehana shakes his head and looks down. The men cannot cross the river to get to Austen in Mohale's Hoek right now, let alone Maseru.

It is apparent Hope does not understand and does not want to understand. Concluding that further discussion is futile, Lehana leaves for his village.

As Hope sits alone in his office, feelings of frustration well up within him. He might have erred on the hut-tax issue, but he cannot reverse his decision; that would not only embarrass him in front of the Baphuthi people, but also lessen his effectiveness as an administrator and judge. But at the same time he fears he will be condemned for his action. Already, he can see the letters from Rolland telling him he is wrong. In diplomatic language, of course. He will be blamed for disagreeing with Austen — of all people. It will be another black mark against him.

It feels to Hope as though he is being thwarted in everything he does. He should not be so "high-handed." He should not have arranged a *pitso* with Moorosi. He should not have called on Fynn to move his men to the border. He should not ask for more armed policemen. And now he is sure he will be told he should not have charged the men.

What does the government want from him? Do they want him to control Moorosi, or do they want him simply to cooperate with the Baphuthi leader and allow him to take control?

"How can I complete the task that they have assigned me if I am criticized for every move I make? How can I serve my country when they stand in my way?"

Perhaps, he reasons, he can get rid of his frustration by working for a different authority, one in which the rules are much clearer. He writes to Rolland, placing himself at the disposal of the government for military service. At least there his services will be appreciated.

Transkei — Thursday February 7, 1878

Within minutes the battle is over.

An attempt by the Gcaleka — assisted by another Xhosa clan, the Ngqika led by their chief Sandile — to take back their land has failed. The 5,000-strong combined attack on white forces at Kentani in the heart of what once was Gcaleka territory is beaten back by superior fire power and the Gcaleka flee, leaving behind 400 dead.

The Gcaleka chief, 62-old Sarhili, is a broken man. This battle was decisive. It was more intense than anything his people faced when they fled Griffith's advancing troops a few months ago. Today his men gave their all and failed. His chieftainship itself has been found wanting.

"We must return across the Bashee River into the land of the Bomvana," he tells his men. "It will be a long time before we are able to fight these settlers again. Their fire power is too strong. We must hide where they cannot find us."

Ngqika Chief Sandile says his people, too, will find refuge where the colonists will not find them. "We will return to our territory across the Kei River. There we will hide in the rugged country along the lower river. There we will discuss how we can defeat the settlers. But, for now, we must accept that the future does not look good for us. These people who say they are superior to us have today shown us that, when it comes to the use of guns in war, perhaps they are."

⁂

News of the victory reaches Griffith at the military barracks in King William's Town. He has mixed feelings. As a commander of the joint forces, he takes pride in the accomplishment. But he is disappointed that the victory had to come at the cost of so many Gcaleka and Ngqika lives.

Nevertheless, he reasons, the lesson is that armies like the Gcaleka and Ngqika can be defeated by standing up to them with superior fire power and mowing them down. He sighs. If that is how it has to be, then so be it.

Quthing — Monday, February 11, 1878

When messengers from the south bring him news of the defeat of the Gcaleka and the Ngqika, Moorosi ponders its meaning.

He reaches several conclusions.

One is that any thought of ousting the white government from their territory by armed force should be set aside until they can obtain more guns. Although the two Xhosa chiefs had thousands of people under their command, and they did have firearms, they were largely using spears to attack guns.

His second conclusion is that the colonial forces had an advantage by fighting from a hill, looking down on their attackers. Moorosi had found for himself in earlier battles that those on higher ground have an advantage. From now on, he will ensure he always defends himself from higher ground.

A third conclusion is that he must fight with his mind.

A lion usually does not run straight at an antelope, warning it and giving it a chance to escape. The lion stalks his prey, slowly and carefully. He watches until the time to spring is right.

Sarhili acted too soon, without thinking through his strategy. Moorosi notes that he, too, must be careful not to act too soon.

Battle at Kentani [*Recent British Battles on Land and Sea, 1897*]

SARHILI'S ATTACK

24TH REGT

Fight at
KENTANI
Feb. 7th 1878

SANDILE'S ATTACK

Adapted from a map in *My Command in South Africa* by General Sir Arthur Thurlow Cunynghame.

The messengers have told Moorosi how, at Kentani, a small group of white police went out first and tricked Sarhili and Sandile into believing the white forces were small. They told him how Sarhili thought the government force was only about 100 strong when in fact it totalled about 600. They told Moorosi, too, how the rest of the colonial soldiers, hidden on the hill, jumped up into sight when the forces commanded by Sarhili and Sandile came into range.

It was a clever trick. He vows to use such tricks. He must avoid confronting the government soldiers directly. He must have his warriors draw them into a trap, make the government people think his forces are small so that they will not summon big forces to attack them. Then the Baphuthi will come out from hiding and overpower them. The white government people will be frightened away and will be hesitant to attack the Baphuthi people again.

It will also help if the government thinks Moorosi is not involved and that only a small group of Baphuthi people are in rebellion.

He will do to the white authorities what the white soldiers did to Sarhili and Sandile. He calls Lehana to his fortress to outline the role he must play in his strategy.

Quthing — Thursday, February 14, 1878

Sixteen days have passed since Hope instructed Maikela and the four other accused men to obtain proof from Austen of their hut-tax exemption. Hope has heard nothing. He told them to return in 14 days; he has given them two additional days. No one can accuse him of being unfair, of being "high-handed."

Clearly, the men are purposefully ignoring him. He is afraid, too, that Rolland will not back him up.

He feels threatened on both sides.

Adding to Hope's frustrations is his receipt of a copy of a letter Rolland sent to the Secretary of Native Affairs in King William's Town. The letter is in response to Hope's request to be transferred to a military post.

"Although I do not doubt that Mr. Hope might do good service," the acting senior magistrate writes, "I cannot see my way clear to recommending his proposal unless the Government should see fit, in accepting it, to replace Mr. Hope at Quthing by some other officer experienced in the native service."

In other words: "No."

He has no choice right now but to continue to pursue the men accused of not paying the hut tax for their widowed mothers.

Quthing — Saturday, February 16, 1878

Isaak Masin, the sergeant, knocks on the door of Hope's office.

"What is it?"

"I have something to report, Mr. Hope. For the past week Moorosi's son Lehana has gathered all his men, armed with guns and spears. They are assembled in the mountains behind his village. They have orders that if you send your constables to arrest Maikela or anyone else for not paying their widowed mothers' hut taxes they are to shoot the constables.

"I am told, too, that Lehana has told his father, Moorosi, about the situation."

"Very well. Thank you for informing me. You have done well."

The men's resistance has elevated the hut-tax dispute to a new level and makes Hope temporarily forget his frustration with Rolland. He will refuse to allow these men to defy him. He will not tolerate their disobedience. He will show them he cannot be intimated by a display of force.

Hope writes out a summons. He calls chief constable Abraham Sighata.

"I want you to go to Maikela and serve this writ on him," he says. "Take four men with you. There are four others who must be served the writ, so I am sending five of you, one of you for each of them. Tell them they must pay the hut taxes for their mothers, or face the consequences. You must all be unarmed. I do not want Moorosi or any of his people to accuse me of breaking the rules that I set up for him."

He warns Sighata the men might resist, might be backed by an armed force and that Lehana is likely to help them. But should he encounter resistance, he should not create a disturbance. It is sufficient to serve the summons and return.

⁕

When Sighata and the four constables arrive on horseback at his village, Maikela is nowhere to be seen. But the rocky outcrop behind the huts is lined with 70 to 80 men, all armed. The men see them arrive, but show no reaction.

"Let's go to Lehana's village," Sighata tells his constables. "I am sure we will find Maikela there."

They do.

"We have come from the magistrate to demand that you pay the five pounds you owe in hut tax for your mothers," Sighata tells Maikela.

"You must ask Lehana about that," Maikela replies. "He is my headman and he has told us not to pay the money."

"Where is he?" asks Sighata.

"I don't know. He is hiding somewhere."

Sighata turns to the constables accompanying him. "Let's go back to Maikela's village and see whether we can obtain the tax there," he says.

As they ride to Maikela's village, a group of men, all armed with spears, follows them, all also on horseback.

At Maikela's village, the government representatives see the armed men are still on the rocky outcrop. Sighata notes that the cattle are still in the kraal and have not been released to graze in the fields for the day.

"Come," he says to the men with him. "We will take two cows. That will take the place of the hut tax they owe."

To the Baphuthi watching them, the policemen's action is tantamount to theft. As Sighata and the assistant ready their ropes to seize the cows, the armed men who were gathered behind the rocks above, run down the slope, waving their sticks and spears above their heads. "Stop," they shout. "Leave those cattle alone!"

Sighata throws a noose over the cow's head and pulls it tight. He is determined not to be intimidated, believing that the men would not dare to attack him and his police cohorts. But, as the armed men running toward him show no signs of slowing down and continue to yell insults, Sighata has second thoughts.

He releases the cattle as the armed men reach the kraal. The men stop. Maikela tells them to lower their weapons, which they do. Sighata, imitating Hope, addresses Maikela and the men gathered around him.

"You are making it bad for yourselves. If you had let me take the cattle, that would have been payment for the hut tax and the matter would be over. Now you are liable to be punished even more.

"I will report this to Mr. Hope."

The armed men watch quietly as Sighata and the four constables ride away.

On hearing of the events, Hope decides that Lehana must be included in the people charged over the hut-tax issue because he is inciting Maikela and the others not to pay the taxes.

Hope is convinced, too, that Moorosi also is behind the stand-off on the issue.

"I have another duty for you," he tells Sighata. "I want you to go to Moorosi and tell him I need his help. Ask him to let me know where Lehana is so I can summons him, as the chief of those who owe the hut tax, and obtain the hut tax and the fines that these people owe from him."

As Sighata sets off, Hope writes to Rolland in Maseru. This time he wants to ensure his actions meet with Rolland's consent. After summarizing the events, he writes, "I think you will agree with me that I should summons Lehana on a charge of instigating the people in his ward to resist the authority of the magistrate. I do not, however, expect that Lehana will attend upon a summons of this kind; and I also doubt if Moorosi will be able, truthfully, to deny having advised Lehana to this course. I shall have a reply from Moorosi tomorrow, which I will send to you. Moorosi has been very quiet for some time, and I imagine this is merely a pretext to cause some excitement without which he apparently thinks he cannot exist."

Quthing — Monday, February 18, 1878

Sighata tells Hope that he has spoken with Moorosi, who denies all knowledge of Lehana's conduct, expresses his greatest regret for what happened and asks Hope to be merciful to his erring children. The message sounds false to Hope. He is convinced Moorosi knew of the events surrounding the widow's hut tax. For him to deny all knowledge of it does not ring true. Hope perceives Moorosi is avoiding direct confrontation, leaving Lehana and Maikela to lead the defiance against him.

Hope's suspicions are confirmed when a policeman reports to him. "I am told that Maikela and the four other men tried twice to come here and pay you, but Lehana threatened to kill them if they did," the policeman says. "To make sure he does not pay the tax, Lehana has kept Maikela a prisoner in his hut. All the men from the surrounding villages, their wives and families have fled to the mountains with their cattle."

Hope issues a criminal summons against Lehana and Maikela, as well as the 30 who threatened Sighata and the constables to appear before him on Thursday.

When he reports the latest events to Rolland, Hope is sure that the acting chief magistrate will turn to Letsie for help to resolve the issue. But he is convinced, too, that Letsie and Moorosi are working together behind his, and Rolland's, back.

"I would respectfully suggest that an appeal to Letsie in this matter will most probably only result in another deputation being sent to Moorosi as in December last and end in a more cleverly planned scheme being hatched between those two chiefs to be developed upon in the next favourable opportunity."

Quthing — Wednesday, February 20, 1878

Hope's policemen have rounded up 16 of the 30 Baphuthi who threatened Sighata and his constables. The accused men, appearing before Hope in his courtroom, plead guilty to a charge of interfering with the administration of justice. Hope fines them two head of cattle each.

In some ways it is a hollow victory. Although the men surrendered when confronted, Hope is aware they did little more than follow Lehana's orders in threatening the policemen. His real quarrel is with Lehana who is continuing to subvert his authority. But his policemen report that Lehana and the rest of his cohorts have left their village and are in the mountains, presumably hiding in one of the many caves along the Qomoqomong or any of the other rivers in the area.

Sending his constables to try to track them down will be an exercise in frustration. How then to get Lehana?

The only way is through Moorosi, Hope concludes. The chief almost certainly knows where his son is and is probably spurring him on. He sends a message through Moorosi's messenger, Mafetudi, asking Moorosi to see that his son Lehana appears before him in court.

The hut-tax confrontation is escalating from an incident over a relatively small amount of money into another stand-off between Hope and Moorosi.

Quthing — Thursday, February 21, 1878

Frederic Ellenberger walks past the first house he built when he arrived at Masitise 11 years ago. It looks as good as when he built it.

He climbs the twisting stone stairs up the hill through the trees. As he reaches the top step, the cave house comes into sight. He sighs with relief and satisfaction when he sees it. It, too, is still there, just as he left it. The row of 60 aloes lining the open space in front of the house on the edge of the steep drop to the cattle enclosure below are still there. He is home. He has returned to work among the people he loves.

Satisfied after a brief walk-through that the house is in good order and the books and papers he left behind are all there, he walks back to the wagon in which he brought Emma, their family and belongings to the mission station.

Soon the news gets around. The Ellenbergers have returned. People emerge, seemingly from nowhere, flocking around Frederic and Emma. They alternately laugh with joy, sing, and try to tell the couple all that has happened since they left. They carry the missionaries' supplies up to the cave house. They reassure them the mission work was well conducted by local evangelists, but, they are quick to add, they are pleased to see their spiritual leaders back. And they try to tell them everything all at once.

The Ellenbergers listen patiently, tired after their journey over the rugged African roads, but anxious to hear the news.

Frederic Ellenberger's senior pastors tell him of the new government presence that has moved into the area. The magisterial compound and police camp, his people tell him, lies a little more than two miles away where a magistrate named Hamilton

Hope is imposing direct government rule on the Baphuthi people. They tell him, too, of the trouble that has arisen between Moorosi and the magistrate.

The missionary listens intently. When he moved to Masitise, colonial magistrate Austen, still based in Mohale's Hoek, had little influence in the area beyond collecting hut tax. Austen did little to impose colonial law on the people directly. Now a magistrate, police post, court and jail two miles away present a whole new dispensation. One of his most trusted evangelists, Philemon Seboka, tells him the tensions between Hope and Moorosi have become thwart with danger.

"At one stage, we thought there might be a violent conflict when King Moorosi and hundreds of armed men gathered at the magisterial compound," he tells Ellenberger. "We heard them singing war songs and we were afraid."

Tensions lessened a few months ago, but now are growing again, Seboka says. "This time the magistrate is angry because some of the widows are not paying their hut tax." He tells Ellenberger how the sons defended their mothers, Lehana defended the sons, and they are now hiding in caves. "The magistrate wants to find them and punish them, but he has been unable to do so."

Ellenberger, not one to waste time, decides he must do what he can to reduce tensions as soon as possible. He will visit Hope tomorrow.

Quthing — Friday, February 22, 1878

After spending the morning in further discussions with his Baphuthi staff, Ellenberger rides on horseback to Hope's offices. After the men swap stories of their backgrounds and the reasons they are there, Ellenberger gets to the point. Although French is his primary language, his English is good. "I have heard of disputes between you and Moorosi, whom I know quite well, and I wondered whether I could help perhaps to reconcile some differences that you and he might have," Ellenberger says. "In the past, he visited me from time to time and kept me in touch with what was going on. I have not yet been to see him as I arrived only yesterday morning. I thought I would speak with you first."

Hope senses another threat. He has had enough criticism from Griffith and Rolland for his actions. Now this man comes here to tell him what to do. What does a holier-than-thou missionary know about government? Because Ellenberger is friendly with Moorosi he will take Moorosi's side against him. After all, the missionaries are known for siding with the native people against the government.

"Will you be instigating the chief to challenge my authority?"

Ellenberger is taken aback.

"Not at all," he says, trying to remain calm. "Sometimes confrontations come from misunderstanding. Because I think I understand Moorosi and his people, their traditions and their beliefs, I might be able to help you to understand him better and work with him more effectively."

"I understand him perfectly well," Hope responds. "He is cunning, crafty and rebellious. Now he has turned to lying as well. He refuses to accept that I am in charge here now and he shows a reluctance to accord me the respect that I and my office deserve. The only way to deal with him is to show him in no uncertain terms where the authority lies around here.

"Reasoning does not work with these people. They respond only to power and, where necessary, the use of force to back that power. I am not afraid to confront him and to show him the error of his ways. No longer can he carry on as though he is the only authority around here."

Ellenberger listens quietly, takes a deep breath, and responds.

"I believe it is important to understand that King Moorosi has ruled his people here for many decades," Ellenberger says. "He carries on a long line of rule that extends into history. Until you arrived here, he was, for all practical purposes, subject to no other authority except when it came to collecting hut taxes — and that itself was only a recent introduction. Now that you have arrived and are asserting your authority it will disturb him. He sees his power challenged and potentially usurped."

"I'm surprised at your attitude, reverend," Hope responds. "You are spreading Christianity among these people; we are bringing them a Christian government."

"We do preach Christianity," Ellenberger responds. But we don't believe in forcing people to become Christians. We try to persuade them that their sins will be forgiven and they will live happier and more fulfilled lives if they are Christians."

Hope is quick to respond. "But these people practice polygamy, witchcraft and barbarism. We must impose laws that enable them to live as Christian people and as civilized people. The British laws are Christian. The laws of these people are heathen."

"Their customs are not necessarily heathen," Ellenberger responds. "Some of their values are similar to ours and those of the Israelites thousands of years ago. They might not all know of the ten commandments, but they respect and honour many of them. They are not wild savages. These people are orderly and law-abiding within their code of conduct. I am sure you have found that crimes of violence are rare."

Hope is quiet. True, he has had to deal with few such offences. But he is suspicious of the track that Ellenberger is following.

"A natural love of order and respect for authority are part of the Baphuthi character," Ellenberger continues.

"That is why you probably have found they are reluctant to criticise you or to argue against you. It doesn't mean they agree with you. It is that they respect you and are being polite to you."

"I find little respect from Moorosi," Hope responds. "He argues with me continuously. He does not always say yes."

"I cannot speak for him and I am not here to defend him and all that he does," responds Ellenberger. "But he and the Baphuthi people accept that they need British protection from their enemies and so are willing to accept your presence here as a representative of the British."

"You are right," Hope says. "Moorosi found it an admirable set-up. If Letsie attempted at any time to tyrannize him, he could appeal to the white government. As long as he paid as much hut tax as he and his people could conveniently spare, he went on his way, deciding civil and criminal cases as he chose, always taking care that the fees of court amounted to a comfortable sum for himself."

"That might be true," Ellenberger says. "I am not suggesting that Moorosi is without fault. But I would suspect that he and his people believe the Cape Colony's motive is to annex this territory so they can secure the bounty of this fertile land for the monetary benefit of the Cape Colony."

Hope rises from his chair and steps back, physically and symbolically distancing himself from Ellenberger. "And that is what you are going to be telling them? That is the way in which you will incite them to action against us?"

Ellenberger remains calm. "Please understand, Mr. Hope. I am telling you what these people believe, not what I tell them to believe. There is a difference. I am suggesting how I believe they feel based on what I have heard from them since first moving here 11 years ago.

"We need to understand other people's points of view. But we need to go further. We need to understand why they hold that point of view. That is key."

Hope is defiant. "I suggest you turn from supporting these people and their heathen beliefs and uncivilized way of life to helping to show them that they are wasting the government's time and resources by trying to rebel against our authority. We will impose civilized government on these savages whatever it takes to do so."

Ellenberger, realizing it is of little value to continue, promises to return to talk again. He mounts his horse and rides home.

Ellenberger's next move will be to talk with Moorosi. He will inquire into the tax issue and see whether he can convince the men to meet somewhere in the middle. Although he fears that persuading Hope to take a less belligerent attitude will be a tough hill to climb, he will try nevertheless. He owes it to his people.

7

Quthing — Saturday, February 23, 1878

This is Hope's first summer in Quthing and today, with the temperature climbing, he is finding that by mid-afternoon his small stone walled office has become a baking oven. His official English heavy clothing adds its own complement of heat, causing perspiration to run down his body. His face is red and his breathing laboured.

Outside, the Baphuthi are sitting in the shade of the occasional trees, dressed in only the barest of clothes. For him to do the same would be to act like a savage. He is above them and must sit in his office, wear his official clothes and sweat. Only tomorrow, Sunday, might he be able to find some respite from the heat in his house, which, with its thicker walls, is a little cooler than this office.

The heat also affects his thinking. He feels anger boiling within him, ready to be taken out on the nearest victim. Today his temper, usually short, has no length; it is poised to spring.

He is angry at Lehana for evading capture. He is angry at Moorosi for sheltering him. He is angry because he has been unable to control them, the reason he was sent here in the first place. He is angry at his supervisors who reprimand him for everything he does.

Yesterday he had a lecture from the missionary, just returned from France with his other-worldly, anti-European attitude. Does Ellenberger really think these black savages have any decency in them? Any redeeming features at all? Even Ellenberger, as a minister of the Gospel, is against him, failing to realize the good work he is doing for Christianity. He is angry at him, too.

He is angry at everyone. Look at how he has been thwarted every inch of the way. Moorosi intervened and finalized the Raisa case. Moorosi settled the issue of the stolen goats. Austen's ruling on the widows' tax was deemed more acceptable than his. The planned *pitso* with Moorosi, which he thought was a good idea, was cancelled. He was forced to reverse his action in calling up troops to the border.

He pours himself a glass of brandy and water, hoping it will provide a measure of relief. He has worked all day and, although it is only mid-afternoon, the time for his end-of-the-day drink is soon approaching; all he is doing is taking it a little earlier — and with a little less water.

As he takes a gulp of the brandy and water, Hope glances down at the recent correspondence from Rolland, neatly copied over into a one-and-a-half-inch lined book. He takes more gulps and tops up the glass with more brandy as he reads them through again. The letters remind him of how angry he felt when he received them.

The alcohol fuels his fury. Griffith, Rolland, Austen. They are all to blame. They have failed him.

But no one is more to blame than his brother-in-law Rolland. He never helps him, never praises him, only hinders him. How can he be expected to apply the law when Rolland tries to block his every move?

Rolland turned down his requests for more ammunition, for more policemen and for help from the Cape Colony. When he went around Rolland and ordered back-up forces to be sent to Palmietfontein, he was countermanded. You need no help. Battle on your own. Fight Moorosi with one hand tied behind your back. Go on, see what you can do. And we'll stand here and mock you.

Rolland might be Mimmie's brother, but Hope has had enough of his superior attitude. He had hoped Rolland would be better than Griffith. And, for a while, he was. But now he has proven to be even worse.

Do these people have any idea how wily this rebellious old chief is? Do they really think they would have handled him any better?

"When does Rolland ever say, 'Thank you?' When does he ever say, 'Well done?' They say that to Austen all the time, but never to me. And he's a coloured man!"

He gulps the rest of the brandy in the glass, takes up his quill, dips it in the ink well and writes. He will tell Rolland exactly what he thinks of him and his government superiors.

When he has completed the letter, he places it for delivery by the next post.

As the afternoon drags on and his rage intensifies with the rising heat, Hope adds more brandy to his glass, slugs it down and picks up another piece of blank paper. The first letter was not forceful enough, hinting rather than telling. He will send another, stronger letter to Rolland.

Quthing — Monday, February 25, 1878

When he receives Hope's message relayed through Mafetudi, Moorosi smiles with satisfaction. Hope has failed to find Lehana. Now he wants his help to do so. He is recognizing his authority.

"Tell the magistrate that I thank him and praise him," he tells Mafetudi.

Moorosi has no intention of helping the magistrate to achieve his aim of finding his son Lehana and punishing him. Nevertheless, at this stage, he will give Hope the impression that he is helping him.

He will use his messenger, Mafetudi, as an unwitting part of the plot to deceive Hope. "You are to go to the village and tell Lehana that I want him to accompany me to the magistrate's office," he tells Mafetudi. "After you give the message to Lehana, take my message of thanks to Hope. I am flattered that he is recognizing my authority and seeking my help."

⚜

The sun is setting as Mafetudi returns to Moorosi, saying he could not find Lehana in his village. He decided it best to return to Moorosi for further instructions before proceeding to Hope's office. Moorosi nods. That is as he expected. He knows Lehana has left his village and is hiding in a cave. But it will enable Mafetudi to tell the magistrate truthfully that Moorosi instructed him to find Lehana and he could not find him.

Now Moorosi will go further in seemingly meeting the magistrate's request for cooperation. He will do the same as he did with Raisa and MaLebenya, when the magistrate eventually conceded his right to judge the matter, and with the issue over the stolen goats, when Hope abandoned the matter after Moorosi acted on the case.

Moorosi turns and goes into his hut. After a short while he emerges with a rag, folded and tied at the corners, which he hands to Mafetudi.

"Give this to the magistrate."

Quthing — Wednesday, February 27, 1878

Mafetudi arrives on horseback, conveys Moorosi's message of thanks to Hope and tells him that Moorosi had sent him to tell Lehana to accompany him to the magistrate.

"I am pleased to hear that the chief is ready to cooperate with me in imposing the law," replies Hope. The message lifts his sagging spirits and helps him recover somewhat from his bout of weekend anger. "Did you do as he said? Did you give Lehana the message? When will Lehana and the chief be here?"

Mafetudi takes each question at a time.

"I arrived at Lehana's village yesterday, gathered the people together and asked them where Lehana was," Mafetudi reports. "I told them I had been sent by King Moorosi to take him to the magistrate. They all said they had no idea where he was."

As Mafetudi is speaking, Hope notices he is holding a piece of rag.

"What do you have there?"

"This is King Moorosi's appeal to you on behalf of Lehana," he says.

Hope opens the rag. It contains nine pounds and five shillings — two pounds more than the total owed him for payment of the hut tax and the fines for non-payment.

He looks up at Mafetudi.

"What does this mean?" he asks.

"This is King Moorosi's offering to you," he says. "He has weighed up the situation and decided that Lehana should have collected hut taxes from the widows. The taxes have now been paid and, because you represent the government that imposes the taxes, the taxes must be paid to you.

"King Moorosi also has imposed a fine on Lehana. In a spirit of friendliness, he wants you to accept the fine as well as the taxes that should have been paid."

"This is not the right way to do this," Hope tells Mafetudi. "Lehana must come here, he must stand in front of me, I must try him and he must admit his wrong. Lehana must pay the penalty himself. I cannot have Chief Moorosi deciding the issue and then paying the taxes and the fines himself to shield Lehana and to prevent him from appearing in my court.

"He is playing with me."

He thrusts the rag back into Mafetudi's hands. "Take the money. Tell him that I do not want it. He has played with me long enough."

Mafetudi is taken aback. He holds out the rag and its contents once more toward

Hope. "He wants you to have it," he tells him. "He wants to pay the penalty for Lehana and the five men."

Hope folds his arms so that Mafetudi cannot put the rag in his hands once more. "I have told you, Mafetudi, I will not accept it."

Hope's caustic tone causes Mafetudi to move backward. He does not want to upset the magistrate and be faced with charges of insubordination himself.

"Yes, magistrate," he says and walks out the door.

"I know what Moorosi is doing," Hope tells Maitin. "He is acting as the authority here. He is trying to defeat me. Again. He is trying to show me that he is able to collect the tax because the Baphuthi people look to him as their chief. He is saying they will obey him, but not me.

"If I accept this money I will, in effect, be telling Moorosi that he is in charge and that I should approach him when I want the law obeyed. He seems to think that if he offers me enough money the whole matter will go away and he will be victorious once more."

Hope's face reddens as his weekend display of anger rises to the surface once more. "No. No. No.

"I want to see Lehana punished and humiliated for inciting his followers to disobey me. I want to see him brought to trial. I want him to be responsible to me, not to his father. I want the people to see that I am the authority here, not Moorosi."

Hope calls Sighata.

"Go to Lehana's people," he tells him. "Tell them I will not receive their hut tax and their fines if they are paid through Moorosi. I want them to pay the fines and the taxes to me because I am the authority, not their chief Moorosi.

"And tell them I will refuse to grant them passes to leave this area until this matter is settled."

Maseru — The same day

The rancorous letters from Hope take Rolland by surprise. He understands Hope's frustrations. He knows the work is difficult. And he knows Hope can lose his temper.

But for Hope to take out his frustrations on him is unacceptable. He leaves the letters on his desk for several hours, returns to them and re-reads them. They are damning in their accusations of him and others in the government. They are acts of insubordination. Hope should lose his position for writing letters like these.

The Hamilton Hope he knows is an intense hard working, intelligent person, serious and determined. Clearly his emotions have blurred his senses, causing him to exaggerate perceived wrongs. Rolland is unsure why Hope wrote what he did and suspects that Hope was acting irrationally when he wrote the letters.

For the sake of his sister, he will give his brother-in-law another chance.

"I have the honour to acknowledge the receipt of two letters from you dated 23 instant," he writes. "As I cannot but think that you will regret what you have probably unadvisedly written both with regard to direct expressions as well as to covert and implied sentiments, I shall defer any reply until you have had an opportunity of withdrawing or amending these letters."

He sets the offending letters aside, readying them to be discarded. Better that no one else ever sees them.

King William's Town — Monday, March 4, 1878

The new colonial Native Affairs Secretary, William Ayliff, has been in his post for only a few days, but is bringing himself up to speed on issues concerning the native affairs administration he now heads.

As he reads through the reports on the situation in Basutoland, the events in Quthing stand out.

To him it seems clear that Hope has created problems that might not have existed had he handled affairs better.

He shares his views with Rolland in a letter.

"Judging from the report of Mr. Hope, I infer that the whole affair originated in the fact of certain widows now being asked for hut tax who had been exempted by Mr. Austen," he says. "If such is the

William Ayliff

case, and Mr. Austen with his large experience in the management of the Basotho saw fit to do so, it is a subject of regret that Mr. Hope should not have followed out Mr. Austen's view, whatever his own may have been; and it seems from the tone of the report that Mr. Hope has allowed temper more than prudence to guide him in the matter.

"Mr. Hope's refusal to accept even a portion of the hut tax when tendered was perhaps not the wisest thing he could have done, the fact of any portion being tendered being an acknowledgment of liability for the whole, and might well have been taken as a part of the debt.

"It seems hardly fair to those of Lehana's people who have been willing and anxious to have the matter settled by offering to pay the debt with the fine, that receipts for hut tax or passes should be refused them.

"The government gladly accepts your idea that force may not be needed," Ayliff writes, concluding the letter to Rolland by saying that Hope should know that calling in troops "could only be resorted to as a resource when every other effort had failed."

Basutoland, — Tuesday, March 12, 1878

Heavy rains have swollen rivers and rendered the road across the mountains from Pietermaritzburg in Natal Colony harder to negotiate than usual. But James Bowker, now 56, is finally on his way to his appointment as new resident magistrate at Maseru.

He realizes he should have been in his office in January, two-and-a-half months ago, or even earlier. But his rheumatism had played up again and he had waited for the severe summer rains to ease off. That strategy did not work out, however. The rains have come late this year, slowing his progress even further.

The driver assures Bowker that once they have crossed this river they will not have long to travel. Although the roads will be muddy, they should be in Maseru tomorrow.

As his cart and the wagon carrying his goods wait at a river crossing that is deeper than usual, Bowker talks with another traveller also waiting for the river to abate before crossing. Bowker is a big man. Taller than 6 feet and heavyset, he towers over many of his contemporaries, giving him an advantage in negotiations.

James Bowker

Unmarried, he is the youngest of 11 children born to Miles Bowker, a settler who arrived at Port Elizabeth in 1820, and his wife Ann. He became active in military service, fighting in three wars on the eastern Cape frontier. An accomplished negotiator, he helped settle several boundary disputes.

Bowker tempered physical adventure with a streak of compassion, gaining a reputation for combining military prowess with humanity, enabling him effectively to broker disputes between antagonistic groups of farmers and their black workers.

As the two men sit down and talk, Bowker tells his new-found fellow traveller that he will once again be the most senior colonial official in Basutoland, the position he occupied for three years from 1868 to 1871.

"Did you find you had to be firm with the Basotho people?" the traveller asks. "How did you force them to obey the colonial laws?"

"I found little resistance among the Basotho to colonial rule," Bowker replies. "At first, they were ready to accept almost anything for protection against the Boers. But as time progressed, dissatisfaction arose now and then.

"I must say that sometimes I felt I had more resistance from the missionaries," he says. "I often criticized them for opposing annexation of native territories. I believe that the natives are better governed by whites, but the missionaries always seem to take the side of the blacks against the whites, although I learned later they were often expressing the views of the Basotho, who dislike confrontation."

Bowker cannot resist saying that he spends a lot of his time observing and catching butterflies and has gathered one of the best collections in South Africa.

But, he adds, he will have little time for butterflies in his new post. "I have been told that pressing issues await my attention."

Quthing — Monday, March 18, 1878

The cave in which Lehana is holed up with his followers is protected by stone walls, behind which armed men stand guard. Because the cave is situated above a wide valley, the guards can see every approach to it. They know when a person is nearing long before the person is aware of the cave or them.

Late this morning the guards call out that someone is approaching. As the person nears, they inform Lehana that it is a man from their village.

"He is a friend. Let him approach; I will talk with him," Lehana replies.

"I have not told anyone where you are hiding," Philemon informs Lehana. "But I went to the service at the missionary Ellenberger's church yesterday. He spoke with me afterwards and asked me whether I could get a message to you. He wants to talk with you and asks that you meet him on the path to the mission station. He will not tell the government people that you are meeting with him."

Lehana, who learned to trust Ellenberger when he was at Masitise before his visit to Europe, agrees. He follows Philemon down the hillside and along a path to the mission station.

He meets up with Ellenberger along the way and the two sit down on nearby rocks to talk. Ellenberger lays out his argument that resistance will provoke violence and bloodshed.

"I suggest you go to the magistracy and talk to Hope," Ellenberger says. "That is worth more to you than facing the possibility of armed forces attacking you and your followers."

Lehana is resolute.

"Hope never listens to the Baphuthi," he says. "He does not even let you explain how you feel or what your view is. When you answer him, he threatens to throw you in jail or be whipped for not showing respect to him. I would rather be killed by the government forces than that I should be whipped like a dog or sent to Cape Town to work on the breakwater. If I go there I will never be able to return home."

"Would you be willing to go to Mr. Hope's office if you could be given the assurance that you would not be whipped or sent to Cape Town?" Ellenberger asks.

"If I could talk to him, if he would listen to me and if he would promise not to whip me or send me to Cape Town, I would be willing to see him. But he will not do that."

"We will see whether that is possible," says Ellenberger.

He thanks Lehana and leaves, pleased that he has hold of a potential compromise. Now he needs to find someone on the government side to assure him Lehana will not be harshly sentenced. But who? Ellenberger's previous visit to Hope was not encouraging. He needs to go over his head. He has heard that Bowker, whom he knows from the magistrate's previous service in Maseru, has taken up the office again and is planning a trip to Quthing. Bowker has a reputation as a good negotiator and a man of compassion. Ellenberger will send him a letter of welcome in the hope he might be able to talk to him about Lehana and the hut-tax issue.

Maseru — The same day

It is less than a week since he arrived in Maseru, but Bowker already is focusing on the growing confrontation between Hope and Lehana. After reading the reports from Hope and the responses from Rolland, he discusses the situation with Rolland.

From the discussion, several aspects become clear to him.

One is that he needs to help to settle the matter peacefully. For one thing, he has only 70 untrained Basotho policemen he can send to Quthing. For another, the ammunition stored at Maseru is ineffective; a quick examination shows that half of the few thousand cartridges would not fire if used. In addition, he has no money in his budget to pay for colonial armed forces and, in any event, the forces are all needed in the Transkei.

A potential non-violent solution would be to withdraw the charges against Lehana, particularly as they do not seem to be well based, but doing so, Bowker decides, would depict the colonial rule as ineffective. The law must be seen to be enforced.

Bowker is convinced that to achieve resolution he needs to go around Hope. The magistrate has precipitated the trouble he is now being called upon to resolve and Hope appears unlikely to be able to broker some sort of settlement of the standoff. He would not even accept the money from Moorosi. The government records reflect a man who is abrupt and stubborn and whose temper has a short fuse.

Bowker decides to call on his old friend — paramount chief Letsie.

Letsie's Village — Tuesday, March 19, 1878

In visiting Letsie at his headquarters near the Morija mission station, 35 miles south of Maseru, Bowker is not treating him as a subordinate by summoning him to his office, but is meeting him on his ground. The symbolism, he is convinced, will not be lost on the paramount chief.

He asks "my true friend" to send his most trusted messenger to persuade Moorosi to help in bringing Lehana to book and to bring the matter to a peaceful resolution.

"I will be glad if upon my arrival there, I find that you have accomplished and peacefully arranged the matter in accordance with the orders you have received so that when I see Moorosi I may find all old and crooked things done away with and be enabled to commence afresh without any grievance."

Letsie nods vigorously. He says he is pleased to see Bowker back in his old position and will do all he can to help resolve the conflict.

Maseru — Monday, March 25, 1878

Just as Bowker made a special trip to Letsie, so today the paramount chief, in an unusual foray outside his village, has made the journey north to see Bowker, responding to Bowker's gesture with one of his own. Walking slowly, the chief, who recently turned 70, moves to a chair in Bowker's office and slumps into it.

"I sent my messenger to talk with Moorosi, as you requested when we met on Tuesday last week," he says. "He returned to say that Moorosi says his son Lehana will not go to see Hope. Moorosi says he does not accept that Hope is the ruler of the Baphuthi people and he does not accept the magistrate's authority to punish Lehana."

The response is not entirely unexpected. But Bowker has learned that diplomacy takes time, skill and perseverance. These moves are only round one in the battle of wills and the balancing of alternatives. The carrot has not worked. His next move will be to try the stick; experience has taught him the threat of force can be an effective diplomatic tool.

Bowker has no forces on which he can draw, but Letsie does. Faced with a threat from Letsie's men, Bowker believes, Moorosi will yield.

But how to persuade Letsie to commit his forces on behalf of the government?

"We cannot allow Lehana to continue to confront the government," he tells the paramount chief. "Not only does it mean he is not respecting our authority, it sets a bad example for others. We cannot tolerate such disobedience or disrespect."

Letsie finds the words hard. He sees the relationship between the white authorities and the Basotho chiefs as shared power, in which the white people's laws apply in some cases and the black people's laws apply in others. But he simply nods and lets Bowker continue talking.

"If Lehana continues to refuse to do as he is told, and Moorosi continues to back him in that refusal, I want to draw you a picture of what can happen to the Baphuthi and the others who live in Moorosi's territory."

Letsie listens intently.

"Let us say that Lehana persists in refusing to go to Hope's court to stand trial and to pay the fine and face the prospect of jail. Let us say that Hope calls for military help from the government to force Lehana to attend the court hearing.

"Let's say, too, that Moorosi backs Lehana in his fight against the government, meaning that all of the Baphuthi people are drawn into the fight. Then let's say that the government forces win. The next step would be for the colonial government to take over the Baphuthi territory and to divide it up and give it to white farmers. That land would be lost to the Baphuthi nation and also to the Basotho people. It would be occupied by white people.

"You have seen this happen in the south where the land that Sarhili's people once occupied has been annexed and is now being given over to white farmers."

"What do you want me to do?" Letsie asks.

"I want you to help me with your men so that we can capture Lehana and his followers, punish them for what they have done and put this matter to rest. By using your forces you will make it unnecessary for white forces to enter the territory."

Letsie realizes that he is trapped between two tough alternatives.

On the one hand, he can cooperate with Bowker. The result will be a higher standing with the colonial government. It also will mean a removal of any threat that Moorosi would be attacked by the colonial forces and his territory taken over by the settlers.

On the other hand, if he refuses Bowker's request he will be seen as a rebel who, in effect, sided with Moorosi. When the whites take over Moorosi's territory, they will turn on him next.

Letsie looks down. As he thinks through the alternatives, he wonders if he has any choice at all.

After a while, Letsie looks up once more.

"Tell me what I should do."

Bowker smiles with relief.

"I would like you to assemble some of your best warriors," he says. "Only then will Moorosi take you seriously. Only then will he understand that the consequences of disobedience are greater than simply words.

"Remember, chief, that a lot is riding on this. We need to settle this matter and to settle it quickly."

Letsie pauses one more time. Reluctantly, he looks into Bowker's eyes and asks, "How many men do you need?"

"I think if you asked your son Lerothodi to assemble between 600 and 700 men on the border of Moorosi's territory that would be a good start," Bowker says.

Although Letsie has not appointed an heir, it is clear that his eldest son, 41-year-old Lerothodi, the leader of Basotho who live in Kornet Spruit, adjoining Baphuthi territory, will be paramount chief when Letsie dies. Lerothodi, whose name means "drop of dew" and who has 10 wives, is — in contrast with his overweight and sedentary father — a man of energy and activity even though he, too, is on the plump side. He is highly intelligent, has a quick temper and is proud and ambitious. He remains obedient to his father, knowing he must do so if he is to inherit the kingdom. Like his father, therefore, he remains outwardly loyal to the colonial administration, although he sometimes questions its motives. He lives near Mafeteng where 5,000 people recognize him as their chief. Although a number of his subjects have become Christians, Lerothodi dislikes Christianity, but he does not oppose it openly.

Lerothodi [sketch by Arthur Pattisson]

Letsie replies, "I will instruct Lerothodi to send his men to help you."

"I think you're doing a wise thing," Bowker replies. "Have Lerothodi's forces gather in Mohale's Hoek. I'll meet them there and tell them what to do next."

Mohale's Hoek — Sunday, March 31, 1878

Bowker sees another ray of hope for reconciliation in the Lehana affair when he receives a letter from Ellenberger, who sees the possibility of compromise should Hope promise he would only fine Lehana and not whip him or send him to prison.

Bowker writes back to Ellenberger, reassuring him that such punishment will not be inflicted. He asks Ellenberger to pass on the assurance to Lehana.

Yet, on deeper reflection, Bowker wonders whether his assurance is worth anything at this stage. The situation has gone beyond the issue of the hut tax, of exemptions to widows, and even of a fear of being flogged. It has turned into a clash of wills that has been waiting for a spark to light it. Feelings have hardened; neither side will easily make concessions. The dispute now is no longer between Hope and Lehana. It is between the colonial government and Moorosi.

So much has the dispute over the widows' hut tax escalated that rumours are spreading that war between Moorosi and the colonial government is imminent. Bowker realizes that the rumours might feed on themselves and worsen the situation.

To enable diplomacy to succeed he will march Lerothodi's forces to the border of Quthing to confront Moorosi.

This action might be a step closer to war, but it might also be the only way to assure peace.

Phathlalla Drift is on the left of the hill, and Telle Drift on the right, on the border between Basutoland and the Cape Colony in this contemporary sketch by Arthur Pattisson.

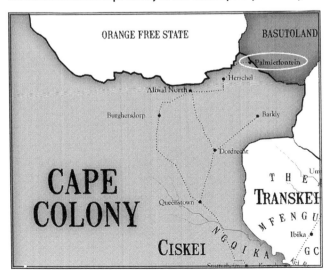

Bowker selects Palmietfontein, just south of the Phathlalla and Telle drifts that cross the Telle River between the Cape Colony and Basutoland, as an ideal location for his camp. A seven-pounder cannon placed there and aimed into Basutoland, for example, would be as effective as a regiment. Not only that. Bowker believes Palmietfontein is key to the entire Cape Colony's north-eastern border area.

He often has said that the town and police camp, with roads leading in every direction, is one of the most advantageous military positions in South Africa. A wagon road runs west to Natal colony, another east into the Orange Free State and a third into Basutoland.

But he faces another obstacle. Palmietfontein is outside Basutoland and so is out of his jurisdiction. He cannot simply set up camp there. So Bowker writes to Secretary of Native Affairs Ayliff in King William's Town, requesting authority to operate in the district of Herschel, in which Palmietfontein falls.

Bowker also is unsure how motivated Lerothodi's people will be to fight against the Baphuthi. The two groups are similar in culture and Lerothodi is married to one of Moorosi's daughters. How determined would they be in a fight to the death?

So, in the midst of these preparations, Bowker decides to give negotiation another chance. He sends a message to Moorosi, offering to meet with him in a *pitso*.

Quthing — Tuesday, April 2, 1878

In recent days Ellenberger has met twice with Moorosi at his mission station in an attempt to persuade him to hand over Lehana for trial. Doing so, Ellenberger assures him, will avoid a violent confrontation, in which Moorosi would come off second best.

"I realize that you want to retain your independence as a chief and that you are not willing that the colonial government rule your people," Ellenberger tells Moorosi. "But I think you must realize that, if you do not try to negotiate a solution with the colonial government, you stand to lose everything.

"Is this dispute over the hut tax worth risking a war — a war that you might lose? Particularly if there is a middle way out, a way that does not involve violence on either side?"

"But I refuse to give in to him and let my son be flogged or be sent to Cape Town or to jail in Aliwal North," Moorosi replies.

"That will not happen," Ellenberger says. "Colonel Bowker has told me that will not happen."

He looks into Moorosi's eyes. "Sometimes," he continues, "we have to meet in the middle. If two people are stubborn and refuse to concede anything, they can destroy each other with their stubbornness. They fight so hard and they hurt one another so much they both lose. But if each concedes a little, well then each wins a little, too. If you are willing to yield a little by handing over Lehana, Colonel Bowker will be willing to yield on the punishment, too. I am sure of that.

"Remember, too, that Colonel Bowker is a bigger man than the magistrate. I believe you can trust his word."

"I do not trust the white people," Moorosi replies. "If I yield too much to them, they will take over my country and my people." He pauses and thinks for a while before responding: "But your words are wise. I will think about what you say."

Ellenberger, realizing that is all he can hope for, returns to Masitise, praying for peace and hoping he has helped avert an outbreak that could lead to war.

Mohale's Hoek — Thursday, April 4, 1878

Ellenberger's efforts at negotiations are bearing fruit. Moorosi has agreed to hand over his son Lehana to the government for trial — on condition that Hope is not the magistrate and that no floggings will be administered. Bowker has assured him he will conduct the proceedings himself, that they will not be held in Hope's courtroom and that flogging will not be a form of punishment. The trial will be held in place of the *pitso* he had proposed. Everything is falling into place.

But Bowker is not taking any chances. Ayliff has given him permission to move his forces — largely Basotho provided by Lerothodi — to Palmietfontein and to operate from there. Bowker has also requested from Aliwal North a wagon load of cartridges. It will be of little use confronting Moorosi without ammunition. If the compromise carrot fails, he might have to threaten with the more potent stick.

An obstacle remains, however. Moorosi tells Bowker he will not attend the trial unarmed.

Bowker, working in Austen's office in Mohale's Hoek before moving to Palmietfontein, needs to resolve this remaining issue.

He asks King Letsie's son Lerothodi, who has brought his forces here, to join him and Austen for a discussion. Austen is an important attendee because he was the magistrate who had authority for Quthing before Hope's arrival, and was the one who waived the fines on the widows.

Hope is in Quthing and was not invited to join this discussion.

"First of all, I think the trial must go ahead," Bowker says. "We cannot afford to show that we are not in charge here. Hope has charged Maikela and Lehana with instigating people not to pay their hut taxes and we must stand by it. We cannot allow our courts to be treated contemptuously or their precepts disregarded. Whether the ruling is considered fair or unfair, it must be obeyed.

"Failure to do so undermines our whole system of government. Having said that, let's see whether we can resolve this issue peacefully."

Bowker outlines the agreement he has received by messenger from Moorosi to hand over Lehana for trial.

"What do you think?" he asks. "Do you think he will honour it?"

"I am convinced he will honour it," Lerothodi replies. "But I also am convinced that he would rather declare war on the government than meet you without his people being armed.

"Please, Mr. Bowker, you must agree that he come armed. I am fearful that if you do not agree he will not come and then we will face big trouble.

"Please. It is the only way of saving the country from a war. You have never objected to armed meetings with the chiefs before. I know that for myself as I have been at meetings at which we have been armed and you have been there. Please, Colonel Bowker. You must listen to what I say."

Bowker turns to Austen, "Your opinion?"

"I agree with Chief Lerothodi on both points," says Austen. "Chief Moorosi will not back down from any agreement he might make with you. But I, too, am convinced he will not meet with you unarmed."

"So you, too, believe that I should allow him to attend the meeting armed?"

Austen hesitates for a moment and glances across at Lerothodi who is fighting back tears of concern for his people and the consequences that war could bring and whose eyes plead with him to agree.

He turns back to Bowker. "If you want to pursue every avenue short of war, I think you should do so," says Austen. "After all, you yourself will be backed by an armed force, won't you?"

Bowker nods. He looks at each of the men, weighing his decision. He is nervous that if such a meeting gets out of hand, he will have an armed conflict on his hands, but he realizes that refusing Moorosi's request (and Lerothodi's passionate plea) could destroy any chances for a peaceful resolution. And, Lerothodi is right. His practice always has been to allow arms at meetings.

Lerothodi looks across at him anxiously. His face becomes contorted in fear as he watches Bowker weigh up his decision. "Please, Mr. Bowker. Please."

Bowker raises his hand, indicating that Lerothodi should cease his pleas.

"I am a soldier as well as an administrator," Bowker says. "My people will be armed. I can see no reason, therefore, that Moorosi should not come armed."

Lerothodi is so relieved at Bowker's decision that he offers to send one of his messengers to take the news to the Baphuthi leader.

"Thank you, chief," Bowker replies. "I would like you to do that. But let's make this the final message to him. We need to move forward and hold this trial. Please tell him I must have an answer before Saturday on whether he will bring Lehana to trial. If his answer is yes, we will meet on the following Friday, April 12."

Bowker is confident that the ammunition will have arrived by then.

Lerothodi agrees. As he leaves, Bowker turns to Austen.

"This meeting of two armed forces will either prevent war or start it," he says. "I sincerely hope it will be the former."

8

Palmietfontein — Saturday April 6, 1878

Moorosi sends a message saying he is ready to meet and hand over Lehana for trial within a week at the Telle River crossing where the Cape Colony meets Quthing. As his Palmietfontein quarters, Bowker has selected an abandoned mud hut from where he can see Moorosi's territory across the Telle River. In one of the rooms he sets up a bedroom and office for himself. The other room will accommodate six white officers from the Basutoland administration who are accompanying him.

Palmietfontein camp [contemporary sketch by Arthur Pattisson]

Another hut serves as a mess hall where a cook prepares meals for the colonial officers and the Basotho National Police.

Lerothodi's men have two major complaints.

One is the lack of food. For two days now many have had little to eat.

The other complaint is the apparent senselessness of their call-up.

They have been instructed by their headmen to be there, but they feel the fight is not theirs. They know, too, of Moorosi's reputation as a mighty warrior and they fear many lives could be lost should fighting erupt.

Comments one, "If Moorosi broke the white law, why does the government not send the white soldiers against him? Why should we leave our wives and our fields to fight other people's quarrels?" Another agrees. "It is the white people who have caused this. Let them fight their own battles."

As the dissent spreads, some quietly make their way back to their homes.

Others, however, are satisfied to follow their chief, Lerothodi. If he says they

Inside Palmietfontein camp [contemporary sketch by Arthur Pattisson]

should prepare themselves to fight, they will do so. Even a lack of food, their absence from their families and the unpleasant living conditions will not deter them.

This afternoon Lerothodi arrives. He moves among the men, encouraging them to stay on. By helping the whites now, he says, they will be helping their own people. By joining in with the white government, they will show them that they are honourable, trustworthy people and so the government will treat them well.

"It is better to stay on the government side in this dispute," he says. "By doing that, they will treat us well and will not fight against us as they are fighting against Moorosi."

To many, the argument makes sense.

"But we have no food," complains one man. "How can we fight without food?"

"And we are not being paid, as the white soldiers are," says another.

Lerothodi promises he will talk to Bowker about those issues. In the meantime, he says, they should stay and be ready to fight.

Quthing — Monday April 8, 1878

Maitin offers to leave Quthing for Palmietfontein to represent Hope, who — fearful of more criticism should he leave — is determined to stay at his post. "You need to go," he tells Maitin. "You will be safer there. But my duty is to stay here and maintain the government presence."

In spite of his frustration with his administrators, Hope remains determined to do what he believes is the right thing to do, no matter what anyone says, even though his feeling of insecurity has been increasing daily.

For the last two days, each evening, around dusk, Baphuthi men have been gathering around his house, dancing and singing war songs. Others stand on the hillsides, yelling loudly.

Maitin, translating the threats to Hope, say they tell of what they will do to Hope. Few details of how they would tear him apart are omitted.

Hope tries to ignore them. Although he now has 30 policemen, he knows they will be of little help against a serious attack. But he will remain in the compound.

Palmietfontein — Saturday, April 13, 1878

Reports reach Bowker early in the morning that Moorosi is on his way to the Telle River crossing. Accompanying him is a body of armed men. The day Bowker feared might never arrive has arrived. And now that it has arrived he fears what its arrival could bring.

At least, the ammunition is here and during the morning the officers place their 50-strong police force in position to guard it.

Moorosi's men assemble opposite the Telle Drift. They travelled most of yesterday, slept in the vicinity overnight and now look across the rapidly flowing river, which is shallow here as it passes over a series of sandbars, toward the military outpost on the opposite river bank. Some dismount and talk animatedly; others sit quietly on their horses.

For Moorosi, this place at the junction of the Orange and Telle rivers, where his kingdom meets the northernmost boundary of the Cape Colony, is heavy with memories, both good and bad.

Here, 30 years ago, he built a fortress on the nearby flat-topped mountain the Baphuthi call Tulumoneng and the whites call Table Hill. He abandoned the fortress when war broke out between the Basotho and the Boers, believing he and his people would be safer farther into his territory.

It was near here that nine years ago that he met with Sir Philip Wodehouse, who persuaded him, in the interests of peace, to give up his land on the west of the Orange River, to be placed under British protection, and to allow Quthing to fall under the jurisdiction of the resident magistrate in Maseru.

This junction of rivers is a natural place for the meeting of opposing forces, whether they be hostile black nations, the Boers or the colonial government. Here they have confronted one another before — and will do so again today.

Slowly, as the rising sun warms the earth, government officials, the Basotho police-men and the troops under Lerothodi take their places on the Cape Colony side of the river and stare across at Moorosi's men. Apprehension mixes with excitement at the confrontation ahead.

Bowker knows that crossing into Moorosi's territory with even a small armed force would be an act of war. Hoping his protocol will be correct, Bowker crosses the ford with only a couple of men and invites Moorosi to join them on the colonial side.

Moorosi accepts, signals to his followers, whom Bowker estimates at 700, to follow him across the ford. The riders, well-built men armed with rifles and spears, are ready to do battle should their chief call upon them. Many are eager to demonstrate their hatred of colonial government rule.

By 10 a.m. more than 1,600 men — the vast majority black — have gathered in two groups outside the camp's mess hut. To the south are the colonial government's men, to the north, the Baphuthi men. Their presence has changed the essence of the event. Had Bowker been the sole representative for the colonial government and had Moorosi arrived only with Lehana and Maikela the meeting would be confined and there would be less chance of a wider confrontation. Now, anything is possible.

As they reach the designated place for the trial, Moorosi, his sons, grandsons and headmen take up their positions, with Moorosi standing in front. Near him stands a sullen-looking Lehana, angry at being forced by his father to be there, and a wide-eyed Maikela.

Behind Moorosi, his sons, grandsons and headmen, totalling about 80, stand in two ranks, one behind the other. All are holding rifles.

Behind them sit or crouch a dense mass of Baphuthi warriors, alongside their horses. All are armed, some with spears, others with rifles and some with both.

Seated facing them with their backs against the mess hall are five colonial authorities. In the centre is Bowker, dressed in his red-coat-and-black-trouser military uniform, and next to him Austen, the magistrate at Mohale's Hoek, dressed in his magisterial garb. Dr. Henry Taylor — surgeon to the Basutoland Police Force and stationed in Thlotse Heights, to the north of Maseru, who is serving as the medical officer in charge — sits on the other side of Bowker. Alongside him is Hope, who arrived in Palmietfontein yesterday. Having been summoned by Bowker, he had no choice but to abandon his magistracy. "You are to speak only should I ask you to speak," Bowker has told him. Maitin, sitting next to Austen, completes the official retinue.

About 70 members of the colonial-appointed Basotho National Police are gathered on both sides of the officials. They clutch their rifles. Off to either side are Lerothodi's men, armed with spears and rifles, numbering 500. Another 200 policemen brought by Austen from Mohale's Hoek are close by.

Slowly Moorosi's men and those of Lerothodi edge forward until they form two big semi-circles with Bowker, the magistrates and officers, and Moorosi, Lehana and Maikela and his retinue in the middle. The right wing of Lerothodi's force almost touches the left wing of Moorosi's force.

Bowker sizes up the situation. In his police and army days, he was present at many confrontational meetings and discussions, and faced incidents that called for careful strategy, some to discuss peace terms after a war. Now he draws on that background. Although it is unlike any other he has experienced, this meeting contains similar elements, including a volatile mix of emotions.

As he sees it, any attempt by Moorosi's men to fire would be met with a quick response from the well-armed policemen gathered on either side of him, among them a few sharpshooters, as well as the senior officials themselves, all of whom are armed. Yet Moorosi would hesitate to give the order to fire first unless he and his family could escape within seconds after firing, an almost impossible feat. Should Moorosi flee to his rear, he would be blocked from a hasty retreat by his own men.

Clearly, Bowker reasons, Moorosi is aware of this. Not unlike Bowker's own support force, his warriors are there for insurance and to demonstrate his power. They are not there to stage an attack. Nevertheless, he is prepared for a confrontation should one occur.

Yet the potential for violence lies even beyond the power of the leaders. Any stray shot, fired perhaps as a result of a misunderstanding, would ignite latent mistrust like a match cast into a field of dry grass.

Bowker pushes those thoughts aside, confident that a resolution to the conflict is well worth the risk he is taking by allowing arms at the meeting.

He is aware, too, that some in the colonial government will condemn him for dealing directly with the chiefs — Letsie, Lerothodi and now Moorosi — virtually as equals and not as subordinates. He will face that criticism later. Here, Bowker's experience convinces him that dealing with chiefs as equals is the only way to resolve this clash of wills. At the same time, he knows he must not back off the government's assertion that Lehana has done wrong.

So much, Bowker realizes, depends on how he handles the situation.

Lerothodi's men are restless. As they look across at the Baphuthi opposite them, they, too, are nervous that shooting might result and that they might be asked to kill men whom they regard almost as brothers. But they remain at the ready because obeying their chief is more important to them than any other consideration.

Moorosi — dressed for the occasion in a silk hat and a black cloak draped over his shoulders — looks around and behind him, satisfied that all his people are there. He looks across at Bowker. The crowd lapses into silence and only the buzzing of insects hangs in the warm air. The king steps forward and, after shaking hands with Bowker, sits on an overturned ammunition box, placed there for that purpose.

"Your instruction to me was to bring Lehana and Maikela here," Moorosi says quietly, looking at Bowker. The men who are gathered behind him peer forward, hoping to hear better.

"I have brought them here."

Moorosi swings his right arm outward toward the men.

"Here they are."

With that, the men lined up immediately behind Moorosi lower their bodies until each is kneeling on one leg. Their rifles rest on their thighs. The silence is broken only by the clicking sound of the men, acting on instructions given them earlier, cocking their rifles, ready to be raised to their shoulders and fired within seconds.

Bowker stares at 80 rifles pointed in his direction. Tension ripples through his body. He is one wrong word away from a riot. Never has he felt more responsibility for life and death than now.

"There is Lehana," Moorosi repeats. "With him is Maikela. Take them to face trial before you."

Bowker fears that, in spite of Moorosi's invitation, if he takes hold of the men and leads them to the centre, such a move could be interpreted as taking them into custody and therefore a call to arms. The men with the cocked rifles are sending a message: Don't touch him or we'll shoot. Taking them now would be too dangerous.

Yet Moorosi is saying: I'm telling you to take them. He is throwing down a challenge to Bowker, taunting him to move first.

"Here they are," Moorosi repeats aloud. "Take them."

Bowker knows he must take action against Lehana. Yet he must also show respect to Moorosi. He must not be seen to be undermining Moorosi's power over his people. Already, Moorosi has made a major concession in making Lehana available to face trial.

He must find a middle way, one that enables both sides to save face. The compromise bartered by Ellenberger is such a middle way and should avoid violence. But he must be careful how he approaches it. The peaceful outcome might be available; achieving it might be more difficult. Bowker decides to lessen the chance of losing the compromise by using an intermediary.

He turns to Lerothodi.

"Bring the prisoners to me," he says.

Lerothodi walks up to Lehana and Maikela and leads them forward so that they stand between Moorosi and Bowker. Lehana and Maikela hand over their weapons to Lerothodi who lays them down alongside Bowker.

The time has come for action. Bowker knows he cannot vacillate. He must act and he must act now. He rises and steps forward until he is about two yards from Moorosi.

"Chief Moorosi, I am glad to see that you have listened to the word of the government," he says. "I am pleased you have brought Lehana and Maikela here today."

Without allowing time for Moorosi to respond, Bowker turns to Hope.

"I ask that the charges be read."

Hope stands up and reads out the charges — the one part of the trial in which Bowker has agreed that the magistrate can participate. The charge against Lehana is that he instigated the people in his ward to resist the magistrate. The charge against Maikela is that he instigated people in his village not to pay hut tax.

"How do you plead?" asks Bowker.

As they hear the translation, both men reply almost simultaneously.

"Guilty."

Bowker sighs with relief. One obstacle out of the way. He responds almost immediately. "They have pleaded guilty to these charges. And I therefore find that they are guilty. The next step is to punish them for what they have done."

The men holding the rifles grasp them more firmly.

Bowker addresses Moorosi, as though he were the only person at the trial. "First of all, let me assure you that I shall not put them in prison," he tells him. "I will not send them to Cape Town, nor will I have them flogged."

Moorosi smiles in relief. The tension noticeably lessens. He had hoped that would be the case. Ellenberger had said it would be likely. But to hear it confirmed by Bowker is reassuring.

"I do that out of consideration for you, his father," he tells Moorosi.

"But Lehana and Maikela have committed an offence for instigating people not to pay their taxes and for failing to appear in court when called upon to do so. They admit to that offence and they must be punished for what they have done," Bowker adds. The tension rises once more.

As the men with the rifles stiffen again, Bowker realizes he must press ahead and deal with the sentencing as quickly as possible.

He draws Moorosi into the discussion and, to avoid any misunderstanding, repeats himself. "Are we agreed that Lehana and Maikela have committed that offence?"

Moorosi says he agrees. Lehana and Maikela watch in silence.

Bowker continues. "I must now punish them for what they have done."

Silence. Now for the fine itself. Will it prove to be too harsh?

"I believe that a suitable punishment for this offense will be 25 pounds for Maikela and 100 pounds for Lehana. Those amounts are equivalent to a total of 24 head of cattle. Hand the money or the cattle to me today and the matter will be over. Do that and you, Lehana and your people, can go home in peace."

The penalty is far higher than the original payment offered by Moorosi. But it is not physical. The reaction is immediate. The men kneeling behind Moorosi lower their rifles and stand. Cries of "*pula, pula*" ring out from Moorosi's followers. Bowker is delighted. He is aware that "*pula*" means rain and is an expression signifying joy.

"Before you go, I want to thank you all for coming here today," Bowker says, raising his voice as talking breaks out among the assembled crowd. "I want to thank everyone for the fairness that they showed today, which enabled us to resolve this issue in a way that is acceptable to both sides. I am satisfied that now we can return to the peace that prevailed before this event arose."

Satisfied there is little harm that Hope can do now, and that many are no longer listening, Bowker asks the magistrate to say a few words. Hope echoes Bowker's comments and is followed by Austen, who says he is thankful everything turned out well.

With the speeches over, the hundreds of potential warriors gathered in the background break up in a disorganized mass. People, it seems, are everywhere. But they are relaxed. They are pleased. A great danger has been averted.

As the Baphuthi cross over the Telle River drift, 24 head of cattle are herded in the other direction.

Intense relief rushes through Bowker's body. He will relax and accept his achievement. But he is aware, too, that, although he might have solved the present confrontation, the underlying tensions have not disappeared.

As the crowds thin out, a tall bearded man with compassionate eyes moves toward Bowker and Moorosi. "May I speak to you both?" he asks.

Masitise — The same day

Ellenberger sits at the table in the cave house with Moorosi and Bowker, exchanging pleasantries as they eat the evening meal his wife and the servants have prepared.

"Thank you for inviting us here today," says Bowker, still dressed in full military regalia. "I appreciated the letters you sent me indicating that the charged men feared being flogged or sent to work on the breakwater in Cape Town and this was a major problem. You helped a lot in enabling us to understand how Lehana was thinking and how we might respond."

"I am pleased by the outcome," Ellenberger responds. "I thought you and the chief might like to sit quietly and talk for a while before you return to your headquarters."

"I am always pleased to visit you here in the cave house," Moorosi says quietly, directing his remarks to Ellenberger, rather than Bowker. Ellenberger translates for Bowker's benefit as Moorosi continues. "I recall that you opened your house nine years ago, in 1869, for a meeting at which Colonel Bowker and I met with Sir Philip Wodehouse, who was then governor-general of the Cape Colony."

Sir Philip Wodehouse

"To me that was a special visit," Ellenberger adds. "Not only did I have the pleasure of you two great men visiting with me, but never had I had anyone of such a high government position as Sir Philip in my house. After all, as governor-general, he was Queen Victoria's representative in the Cape Colony. A man of power and, I must add, a man of compassion and diplomacy. You will recall that he brought about peace to this part of the world by drawing up the boundaries of Basutoland and giving British protection to the Basotho people within those boundaries so that they would no longer be attacked by the Boers.

"Although the British then became their rulers and Wodehouse did introduce a ban on liquor sales, a hut tax and a few regulations — which were acceptable to most people — he largely allowed the Basotho people to continue running their affairs.

"It is true that some criticize him because his boundaries caused the Basotho people to lose a significant portion of their original land, which he gave to the Free State. But I am afraid that trying to regain that land would have meant a great war and might have resulted in tragedy for the Basotho people. He understood that compromise is almost always the price we pay for peace. We have to lose something to gain something greater."

"Indeed," Bowker says. "The meeting in this room was to define the boundaries to the Baphuthi people." He turns to Moorosi. "Chief, you had already agreed to fall under the government as the other chiefs had done. You might recall that Sir Philip came to explain where the boundaries were to make them clear to us all."

"That is so," says Moorosi. "It was here on this bench that the governor sat when he talked with us." Moorosi refers to a 10-foot three-seater bench, that Ellenberger sculptured from rock, set against the inner side of the living room, on which he is sitting.

"I see the governor's name is on the side," Bowker says.

Wodehouse bench in Ellenberger's cave house. Below: Name etched on side of bench.

Ellenberger explains that, after the Wodehouse visit, he carved out an area on the side of the bench and etched in capital letters the name "PHILIP WODEHOUSE," which he painted white to stand out against the dark red background. "That's how special his visit was to me," he says. "I named the seat after him. Whenever I look at it, it reminds me of a great man of peace.

"But not everyone understood his achievements. The British government reprimanded him. Some of the Basotho people were upset that they lost some of their land. It was as though he could not fully satisfy either side. But I am afraid that often happens. When we achieve peace through compromise, not everyone appreciates it. They fear they have lost something. They think they have not just to win, but to win completely, destroying other people in the process, or else they are weak. But in thinking that way they fool themselves and are the poorer for it. When you destroy other people you destroy a part of yourself, too. You lose your moral integrity.

"Peace achieved through compromise demonstrates your values of concern and respect for others. It demonstrates love, the greatest of human values, not hate, the basest of all values.

"Peace is worth making sacrifices to achieve. Those who encourage peace are the real heroes. And I believe as Christians we should be always looking for a peaceful solution to our problems. After all, Our Lord said, 'Blessed are the peacemakers, for they shall inherit the earth.' Those who encourage war and urge victory at all costs, but do not search for a peaceful solution — well, eventually they are the losers, not the winners.

"War seldom achieves anything of lasting value for anyone — for the winners as much as for the losers.

"It might achieve short-term gains for the winners, but the underlying conflict will re-emerge over time.

"The reason is that war does not change people's minds; it only makes the losers bitter and even more convinced they are right. They will explain why they lost — the other side was so much stronger, for example — but they will not change their views.

"The cost of war, in lives and money, therefore, is not worth it.

"And war destroys our finest values. It makes us lesser human beings, turning us into cruel killers rather than compassionate lovers of our fellow humans."

He pauses and looks at Bowker and then at Moorosi.

"And that is why I am so happy today that you both prevented an outbreak that could have led to war. You ensured a peaceful outcome. Through compromise. It is a wonderful thing."

The room falls silent for a moment.

"But I fear I am preaching too much," Ellenberger continues.

"As I was saying, the British government criticized Wodehouse. In his defence, after serving six years as governor, he wrote to the British Secretary of State, who had reprimanded him, pointing out that not a shot had been fired in war by a British soldier during his government, and that he had never applied to her Majesty's Government or to the British parliament for the smallest sum for the purposes of war.

"Yes, he was a man of peace.

"And I would invite both of you to sit on that seat — the Wodehouse bench — today because that seat is a seat of peace and I am anxious to do all I can to reduce tensions, to reconcile differences between the Baphuthi and the government, and to establish a platform for an enduring peace."

Bowker, taking a seat on the bench alongside Moorosi, says he appreciates what the missionary is saying.

"I served under Sir Philip and I can identify with everything you say about the man," he adds.

"It is a pity he did not serve even more than the eight years he did."

Moorosi says he is willing to compromise in the future, even as he did today. Rather than insist that Lehana go unpunished, he was willing to accept a lesser punishment in the interests of peace.

"What you did was good," Ellenberger responds. "I think we can all agree that it is better to talk things out rather than resort to force. You are worthy, my friends, to sit on the Wodehouse bench."

"For my part, let me say that this discussion has helped me focus my thoughts," Bowker replies.

"But now you must excuse me.

"I must return to Maseru where I have an important action to take, one that has been advanced by this discussion. And one that I think might help restore calm to this area."

Quthing — Wednesday, April 24, 1878

Hope is furious. Bowker, with approval from the new Secretary for Native Affairs, William Ayliff, has ordered him to vacate his office in Quthing as his duties there will end at the end of next month. He will be moved to a post at Qumbu in the Transkei where he will begin serving at the beginning of June, giving him a month to make the move. Austen, of all people, will replace him.

Steaming with fury, he throws the letter on his desk, kicks the wall and paces the floor with heavy steps.

Clearly Rolland has persuaded Bowker that he should go. Why did Rolland refuse to let him take up a military position? Instead, he was to stay and follow instructions. Instructions that would not work. They set him up for failure. Now they have declared him a failure.

"Come here, Mr. Maitin," he calls.

"I have been told my services are no longer required here," he says, his hands shaking as he holds the letter.

"I will be sorry to see you go," replies Maitin — to whom the decision does not come as a surprise.

Hope ignores Maitin and continues talking.

"I am proud that the Baphuthi are afraid of me because it means I am doing my job.

"Yes, I am firm.

"Yes, I am strong-willed.

"Yes, I am courageous.

"Are not those the very qualities required of someone in my position? The very fact that this office is still standing is testimony to my resoluteness. Even though they denied me armed back-up, I held firm.

"But now they are moving me because they are dissatisfied with what I have done here. Colonel Bowker does not care for me. I know that from the way he treated me at Palmietfontein.

"I will write to Ayliff and protest my removal.

"I will call for an official government inquiry.

"In this way, everything will come to light. It will show what I did and why I did it, and it will clear my name. I will not meekly back down and accept this slap in the face."

Maseru — Thursday, April 25, 1878

When Bowker receives a copy of Hope's protest and his request for an inquiry, he shakes his head. He writes to Ayliff to cut it short.

An inquiry, he says, "would show the natives that there was disunion amongst us which might lead to further troubles," he writes.

He tells Ayliff he is convinced the magistrate's arbitrary and injudicious actions were a major cause of the deepening trouble between the government and Moorosi.

None of the other magistrates in Basutoland is having similar trouble, he writes. "I need hardly comment upon the tone of Mr. Hope's letter, which speaks for itself."

Aliwal North — Saturday, April 27, 1878

Bowker and Ellenberger might be pleased with the peaceful outcome at Palmietfontein three weeks ago, but the white settlers in the Cape Colony, who view Bowker as an appeaser, are not. Their criticisms are harsh and reflect a fundamental policy difference between the settler community and Bowker.

Most settlers believe in total submission of the indigenous blacks. They seek control, not compromise. Attack, not arbitration. Subjugation, not settlement. That is why they were critical of Griffith when he failed to destroy the Gcaleka rather than chase them off their land. Now similar reasoning lies behind their attack on Bowker.

Their opinions are reflected in an editorial published today in the Aliwal North newspaper, *Northern Post*.

"The first thing that struck us as being strange was that Moorosi should have been allowed to meet Mr. Bowker accompanied by an armed retinue of several hundred men," the editorial says. "This we consider was a blunder of a very serious kind and one that ought not to be allowed to pass over without comment.

"The circumstances were simple: A son of Moorosi defied his magistrate (Mr. Hope). For weeks, Moorosi openly supported his son and Mr. Hope's life was for several days placed in serious jeopardy, his house being menaced by threatening agents of Moorosi's people...

"Moorosi required he should be allowed to meet Mr. Bowker with an armed demonstration and he was allowed to do so."

The newspaper quotes from a letter it received from "a gentleman who was on the spot."

"It was a very critical matter," the letter read, "and the least false step might have caused a general rising of the Basotho. Their sympathies were all with Moorosi, whom they believed to be in the right.

"It is my firm belief that, had we acted differently than what we did, and attempted to take Lehana away, he would have been rescued and we would have been left in the lurch by Letsie's people. They would have run away and not fired a shot on Moorosi's people, and the chances are that everyone of us would have been killed."

The *Northern Post* continues: "How was the difficulty met? It was not met at all. It was evaded. Mr. Bowker fined Lehana — a rebel who had been in arms for weeks — 24 head of cattle! The colony is saddled with expenditure of some £10,000 and this district is left to suffer the losses it sustained through his and Moorosi's conduct without any reparation whatever. This is the surprising result and is most unsatisfactory."

The crucial issue, the newspaper adds, is "the evil of allowing or recognizing native chiefs in any way. They should be done away with in Basutoland as well as here — not in a spirit of maliciousness but as a matter of high policy. The British government in South Africa cannot permit such petty chieflings as Moorosi to threaten to disturb the peace and any overt act of a pretence to exercise the functions of a chief ought to be made punishable."

Such views find an echo in the approach of Cape Colony Governor Sir Bartle Frere who believes the reason for Moorosi's conduct is not as much the disputes with Hope, which to him are minor, but the spirit of opposition to colonial rule that has spread from the Eastern Cape into Basutoland. He remains convinced Moorosi's defiance is part of a plan hatched by the black chiefs across South Africa to unite against the settlers and to drive them into the sea.

The government must not think of shrinking from war because of its costs or because people are tired of fighting, Frere says in a speech. "You must not cease to fit the front with the men required to keep up the strength until all opposition is effectively put down." His mission remains to unite and strengthen the white-ruled colonies in a confederation, but for now the Cape Colony must destroy the opposition on its own.

King William's Town — Monday April 29, 1878

On a visit here, the newly elected Prime Minister, Gordon Sprigg, has an urgent task to complete before he returns to Cape Town. He walks across the wide street to the barracks to talk to Commandant-General Griffith.

"Have you been reading the reports about the meeting between Bowker and Moorosi?" he asks.

"I have and I must say I find it inconceivable that Bowker allowed Moorosi to attend the meeting fully armed," Griffith replies. "I would not have allowed it."

"Indeed. It seems that the situation was such that war was on the verge of breaking out," says Sprigg. "I can't say I appreciate what Bowker is doing there. Not only does he arrive some three months later than his date of appointment, but when he arrives there he plunges himself into the affairs relating to Moorosi and comes up with a solution that is nothing short of an appeasement and an embarrassment to the government."

Sir Gordon Sprigg

"I am reluctant to criticize Bowker," Griffith says. "But I would have tackled the issue differently. I would have built on Moorosi's good relationship with Letsie to achieve a settlement of the issue that did not cause the government to lose face."

"That is the reason I have come to speak with you," Sprigg says. "I would like you to return to Basutoland and take over the office you vacated last year."

Griffith is taken aback.

"Well, I am not sure that..."

"The salary will be £1,200 a year. You will take over the house that Bowker built. I am sure we can arrange to hire or purchase it from him."

Leaving Griffith dazed at the sudden turn of events, Sprigg walks to the temporary office that Ayliff is occupying in a nearby building.

"I have spoken with Commandant-General Griffith and he is willing to proceed to Basutoland as soon as we require his services there," he tells Ayliff. "I think we require him to be there as soon as possible. I leave it to you to inform Colonel Bowker that his services will no longer be required. You might want to allow him to resign rather than face dismissal."

Maseru — Monday May 13, 1878

Bowker asks Rolland to see him in his office.

"I know I have been here for only three months, but my rheumatic problem is recurring and it is time for me to move on," he tells Rolland. "I am racked with pain and short of breath, which makes me extremely tired, and I am unable to perform my duties in the way that they should be performed."

"But, Colonel Bowker, you have been so effective in this position," Rolland responds. "The way you handled the Maikela affair was outstanding. I thought at any stage that the situation could spill over into violence. And who knows what might have happened had that occurred?"

"Thank you, Mr. Rolland. But I have no choice in the matter. My breathing is becoming constricted, the pain is increasing, and the doctor says I must rest. I am confident that this phase will pass, as others have, but it is imperative that I stop working for at least a few months."

"When will you be leaving?" he asks.

"I am leaving for Leribe today."

"You are leaving Maseru immediately?"

"Yes, I am afraid this attack has come upon me quite suddenly. And I know from previous experience that it will tend to linger for some months.

"In Leribe I will be able to rest and there I will await instructions from the secretary for native affairs, whom I have already told of my intention to leave. I understand they will instruct Colonel Griffith to return to resume his previous office. Apparently he is occupied right now on the eastern frontier, but I am told he should be able to return in about a month.

"In the meantime, I am sure you will be able to continue performing the same duties that you performed before I arrived."

Rolland has developed a respect for Bowker and his compassionate and diplomatic approach.

"I would be pleased," he says, "if before you go, colonel, perhaps you could give me some insight into how you view the ongoing situation here and how you would have handled it had you stayed in office."

Bowker is happy to oblige. "The disarmament act — the so-called Peace Preservation Act — being cooked up in the Cape Parliament is worrying," Bowker replies. "Its intention is to take arms away from every black person while keeping them in the hands of the whites. Word has spread here quickly and the local Basotho have spoken to me about it. Letsie was here just yesterday. We discussed it then. I believe he might be forthcoming with a petition against it."

"But will the law be applied to Basutoland?" asks Rolland.

Bowker takes a deep breath and pauses.

"As far as I understand the situation, yes, it will be," he responds, breathing heavily. "Because Basutoland is administered by the Cape Colony I assume it will be applicable here. But that is not to say it will be implemented here."

"I agree that it could cause trouble," Rolland responds.

Bowker's breathing becomes easier as he continues. "As you know, I enlisted the help of Lerothodi in confronting Moorosi. I think the presence of 500 of Lerothodi's men at Palmietfontein was extremely helpful in persuading Moorosi to yield. I believe that we can effectively pit one group against the other and, in that way, keep the peace here in Basutoland. And, at the same time, we can gradually increase our control here — with the emphasis, I might add, on gradual."

Rolland understands. "And disarmament will not be helpful in keeping the peace, no matter how gradually we move."

"It certainly will not, Mr. Rolland. And that is what Letsie told me. He asked how effective Lerothodi's people would have been in helping me against Moorosi if they were not allowed to possess arms."

"What did you tell him?"

"I told him that disarmament will not be applied here as long as he is being called upon to fight the Queen's enemies," Bowker says.

"You told him their arms will not be taken away?"

"I told him I *thought* they would not be taken away. Obviously I cannot give any promises. It is up to the government. But I think the authorities would be foolish to implement the law here."

"Have you told the government of your views?"

"Not yet," Bowker responds. "The measure has not been passed. But if they do ask I will tell them I am dead against disarming friendly tribes. I believe that if you put that law into operation in Basutoland you would at once have 20,000 men against you. I have no doubt about that. The feelings here are bitter about this new measure."

Rolland is surprised at the strength of Bowker's conviction. He notes, too, that Bowker seems to be breathing normally as he becomes more vigorous in his argument against the disarmament law.

"What about Moorosi?" Rolland asks.

"I believe that the passage of the act in itself, even before any action is taken, will be a cause of great dissatisfaction in Moorosi's territory and also in Basutoland generally. Already, merely a discussion of it is causing trouble."

"Some say Letsie is moving in Moorosi's direction," Rolland says.

"I don't believe that," responds Bowker. The only problem is the matter of disarmament. I think if the government tries to impose disarmament here, you would have trouble. But from no other cause."

"So your belief is that the only ill will here is the threatened disarmament?"

"Entirely. Nothing else. I think the Basotho are a wonderful people. They are willing to pay their hut taxes, although they do complain that the money goes to building roads and conducting wars in the colony and is not used in Basutoland.

"Also, they work hard in their fields, feed themselves quite effectively and give less trouble than any other nation I know of. But I think disarmament would affect the loyalty of all the people. It could even bring on a general war.

"If you ask me, the application of disarmament to Basutoland would be insanity. The only way you could apply it would be with six regiments. And then the people would retire into the mountains. There are many fortresses, as you know, similar to the one Moorosi has in the mountains in Quthing."

"So you think that to forcibly disarm them would be a greater evil than to allow them to possess their arms?"

"Decidedly. It is moral castration. If it is applied across the whole country it will unite every black face in South Africa against us. The impact would be as strong here in Basutoland as anywhere else, and with Moorosi the strongest of all. I had thought that, with Mr. Hope out of the way, we could have peace with Moorosi. But, if this law is implemented in Basutoland, we will have trouble.

"The authorities seem to think they know best. They will dismiss me — and my views — as irrelevant. So be it."

Cape Town — Wednesday May 15, 1878

Introducing the second reading in Parliament of the Peace Preservation Bill, which most commentators call the "disarmament measure," the attorney general, Thomas Upington, removes any pretence that the measure will be fair to all races. "In no ordinary instance would licenses to own firearms be refused to white people," he says. "Native persons might also come to apply for licenses, but the magistrates would have the strictest instructions not to grant such licenses, except under special circumstances."

Upington explains that the law is based extensively on the Irish Arms Act, which obliged gun owners to license their firearms.

The second reading of the bill is approved. It will now go into committee where adjustments will be made before it is sent to a third reading for approval.

Quthing — Thursday May 23, 1878

Austen is satisfied that his work in the Quthing magistracy is off to a successful start. Rebels from East Griqualand have been tracked down and sent off to Kokstad.

The victory, however, does not impress Hope, who — even though he was placed on a month's leave of absence by Bowker two weeks ago — remains in the office, continuing to wrap up his affairs before leaving for Qumbu in the Transkei.

"You received more help in that one mission than I ever received in the entire time I was here," he complains. "They never gave me that sort of help in tracking down rebels, even though I requested it."

"I am sure they would have given it to you, too," Austen replies. "These rebels were from outside the Quthing area and so we needed help from outside."

"Hmph."

The men do not exchange words often. Austen wishes with each passing day that Hope would leave. But Hope is trying to put his paperwork in at least some sort of order. He reluctantly admits how slack he was in organizing the office, but reminds himself that he was busy on other duties.

King William's Town — Saturday June 8, 1878

An attempted rebellion by the Ngqika people in the Ciskei has collapsed, but to prevent an uprising occurring again Colonel Samuel P. Jarvis, stationed in King William's Town, has been appointed the first commandant-general of a newly created Defence Department, which organizes the military forces into a single organization. Jarvis oversees the new Cape Mounted Riflemen, reorganized as a military unit from the Frontier Armed and Mounted Police, which will be disbanded.

The authorities hope that the new unit and the disarmament measure will combine to ensure peace in the Eastern Cape and surrounding areas, including Basutoland, should they be needed there.

Quthing — Tuesday June 11, 1878

Ready to leave, Hope looks out on the valley, brown from the dry winter.

He will miss the area. He will, believe it or not, miss the people, too. Although the position was a lonely one, it was challenging. If only the government had supported him more, he would have been able to achieve much more.

He is sorry Mimmie could not have spent time with him here.

He loads his wagon and harnesses the oxen.

He must not look back. What he has done, he has done. What has happened has happened.

Now he must look forward to a new post, new people and, inevitably perhaps, new problems. But he is determined to face them with the same fortitude and resilience with which he faced the problems that Moorosi presented.

Cape Town — Friday, August 2, 1878

After debating the Bill "for the better Preservation of Peace within the Colony" the legislature is ready today to vote on it.

The Bill provides for licences for those who own firearms and imposes a fine of £500, more than a year's earnings for many, and imprisonment and seven years' hard labour for those who possess unlicensed firearms.

Following suggestions from members of the opposition in the committee debate, no racial groups are mentioned in the legislation. But members know whites will be given licences and blacks will not. Disarm the natives and they will be unable to fight any prolonged war.

The law will, as its name implies, preserve the peace within the colony — peace meaning the inability of the black people to defend themselves against the white authorities.

After a brief debate, members — anxious to return home after a long session — approve the Bill. In a few days Frere will approve it and the disarmament measure will become law.

Quthing — Monday, September 16, 1878

Reports have reached Austen that five months ago, when King Moorosi and Bowker were meeting with the Rev. Ellenberger at Masitise, three of Lehana's followers rode into the Cape Colony where they stole horses, sheep and goats.

Before they could return, the men were arrested in the colony for stock theft, were tried and were sent to jail in Aliwal North, the reports suggest. But they escaped from the jail and have now returned to Quthing where they have stolen sheep and goats from local villagers.

Austen accepts the reports as reliable.

"We need to take action immediately," Austen tells Maitin. "But I do not think we should send out our policemen to arrest them. The area in which they are hiding has a labyrinth of caves and it will not be easy for a small group of policemen to track them down and capture them."

"How do we bring them to justice then?" Maitin asks.

"I think this case is one in which we need to involve Moorosi," he tells Maitin. "After all, Moorosi does not condone stock theft and they deliberately acted while they knew Moorosi was occupied at Masitise. So they were trying to deceive Moorosi, too.

"By enlisting the help of Moorosi in capturing these people I will not only achieve my aim of arresting the stock thieves, I will also keep Moorosi content that he is involved in the running of the territory."

He summons chief constable Abraham Sighata.

"I want you to go to Chief Moorosi," he says. "Tell him that I request him to bring about the capture of these thieves for trial in my courtroom. Tell him I know that he does not want the property of innocent people to be injured.

"He has a week to carry out my instructions. If I find he is acting promptly and taking steps toward bringing these thieves to face trial, I will extend that week, but if not then I will take the matter into my own hands."

9

Quthing — Friday, September 20, 1878

Moorosi, sitting outside his hut on the top of his mountain fortress to the north of the magistracy, scans the sky, as he does each morning, for an indication of the weather headed his way. Off to the west, fluffy grey clouds move slowly toward his redoubt. They hold a hint of rain, but one that does not seem likely to be realised.

For weeks now they have waited for the spring rain, but still it does not come.

In the valleys, the brownness of the long grass, heightened by the contrast with the green shrubs that draw sustenance from the water in the creeks, is unusual for September. By now rain should have transformed it into a sea of light green. Instead the singed grass looks morose and sullen as it slumps over from a lack of energy.

Even worse, the crops are suffering, too. The lower leaves on the tiny struggling corn plants are brown and many are not growing strongly. It has been more than a year, perhaps even two years now, that the rain has been insufficient for their crops. Last year, they succeeded in harvesting some of them, but this year it looks worse.

They have stored food, but last year's smaller crops have rendered the supplies less plentiful and, if the drought persists, they will not be able adequately to replenish them at harvest time. Already, some of the Baphuthi people are on meagre rations.

For Moorosi, the scene before him is a reflection of the ravages of colonial rule.

"They sent a magistrate here who said he would show us how to live better lives, who told us we did not know what we were doing," Moorosi tells a group of people who have joined him for their regular meeting. "Is this dryness not a sign of the failure of the white people to improve our lives?

"The white government says their way is better.

"But, I ask you, is it really better? Is it really better when they want to put us in jail and flog us for doing things that they think are wrong but we know are right? Or for doing things they think are right but we know are wrong?

"Is it really better when they make it clear that they want to take away our land and turn it into farms for the white settlers as they have done in the south? Is it really better when they tell us we must follow their customs and not our own? Are they happier than we are? Are their families stronger than ours?

"Is it really better when the result is a tearing apart of our people, a fighting between the new ways and the old ways?"

"No, king, it is not," says Lemena, a son of a lesser wife, and one of his listeners.

"Now I hear from messengers from the chiefs at Thaba Bosigo that the white men want to take away our weapons from us," Moorosi continues. "They want to make it so that we cannot fight back against colonial rule. We must not allow that to happen. We must fight to keep our weapons.

"They are destroying our ways. They are not helping us with our crops now the rains have stopped. Now they want to destroy our ability to defend ourselves."

"Do you think the new magistrate is better than the old one?" asks Lemena.

"I am not sure whether he will be better," the chief replies. "We will have to see. He did say that the widows need not pay the hut tax. So perhaps he will be better. Perhaps he will be more like Bowker than like Hope.

"But I am afraid of what the white government to the south wants to do. I am afraid that they want to take our land from us, as they did with Sarhili and others who have resisted them.

"When they have taken away our land they will put up fences and white men's houses as they are doing on the Gcaleka land. The land will no longer belong to our people, it will belong to individual white people. One man will own the same amount of land that can provide food for 50 of our people. He will raise many more crops than can feed him and he will sell them for money. We will be left with nothing. They will destroy our crops and plant their own. We will have to work for them for nothing and we will have to follow their laws. Our people will be broken.

"I am old and I will have to suffer for only a short time if that happens. But many of you are young. What hope is there for you if the white government comes and takes away everything you have? What help is it to you if you are protected from your enemies but are not protected from the people who say they are your protectors?"

As Moorosi looks down at the ground, Lemena slowly rises and walks toward the highest point on the flat-topped mountain. He looks down again at the scene below, casting his eyes north and south. He wonders how it will be if the valleys were to be filled with white farms, with the Baphuthi people working on them, forced to do the white farmer's bidding every day of the year, while the white farmer sits back and becomes fat and lazy.

Lemena knows from his travels to Kimberley that that is what happens when the white man takes over the land. He has seen children being taken and forced to work like slaves for white farmers.

The images tumble through his mind. He does not like what they portend.

Lemena swings around and walks back to Moorosi.

"We must stop them," he says. "We must resist the colonial authorities and their rule. We are better without them."

Lemena is interrupted when a messenger from Austen appears on the path.

"I have a message from the magistrate," he says.

As the messenger outlines Austen's request to apprehend the men responsible for stock theft, Moorosi ponders his position.

He asks the messenger to walk away, out of earshot, and he turns to Lemena.

"What is your advice on this matter?" he asks.

"I do not think we should help the magistrate at all."

Moorosi shakes his head.

"We must be wise. If we let him have the stock thieves he talks about, he will be quiet and not go after my son Lehana and all the others living in the caves. They will be free to continue their plans to help us resist the government. We must be willing to compromise. We must give up a little to gain a lot. That is what the missionary told me. Perhaps we must give up these men to gain more."

He does not wait for Lemena to comment, but calls to the messenger.

"Tell the magistrate he must leave it to me," he says. "I will take the action that is needed."

Quthing — Saturday, September 21, 1878

Austen is pleased to hear that Moorosi will help apprehend the stock thieves, but in the last few days he has concluded the stock theft is a symptom of a deeper problem.

He outlines his conclusions to Maitin.

"I have pieced together reports from informants on the stock thefts committed while Lehana and his men were holed up in caves. From them, I have built a picture of a group of Baphuthi who are more rebellious than Moorosi himself. They number about 30 men, led by Lehana, three of whom are the prisoners who escaped from the jail at Aliwal North, who are living in caves in the mountains on meat from stock stolen from the villagers and are said to be plotting to eject us, representatives of the colonial government, from Quthing.

"Their original plans were to entice government troops to cross the Telle and confront them in a battle. They were confident they could win and send the troops fleeing back across the border, at which time they would oust the magistrate and his staff from the territory. Their plans were thwarted, however, when Moorosi agreed to hand over Lehana for sentencing by Bowker.

"But I fear their sentiment remains intact. They might not have exactly the same plans now, but I believe they are determined to resist the colonial presence here in every way they can.

"Any incident, no matter how trivial, that involves an intrusion of colonial rule provides them with an excuse to rebel.

"I am convinced the young tyrant Lehana is trying to mislead his father. The old chief Moorosi has seen the danger that could arise in an all-out battle and is anxious to avoid that. Lehana wants to fight; Moorosi is afraid of an all-out battle.

"The immediate task facing me now is to see that the two men accused of stealing sheep and goats from villagers are brought to justice. After that I can take steps to act against those who stole stock across the border and thereby get at the heart of the rebellious group."

Quthing — Wednesday, September 25, 1878

Austen is pleased when Dethlama and Thaba, prompted by Moorosi, answer the summons and report for trial on stock theft.

When tried by Austen, the men confess their guilt.

He sentences each to six months' imprisonment with hard labour and they are placed in the lock-up built by Hope.

But Austen's task is not yet done. The testimony at the trial confirmed his belief that the men did not act alone. He is convinced Lehana was behind the stock thefts

and the two men who appeared before him for trial are, in effect, sacrificial lambs. Austen needs to apprehend and convict Lehana to remove the person most responsible for the turmoil among the Baphuthi people. With Lehana out of the way, he believes, Moorosi will be more conciliatory.

This is Austen's big chance to consolidate the colonial presence and maintain peace.

Having gained Moorosi's cooperation in the case against Dethlama and Thaba, he will enlist his support once more. He sends a message to Moorosi, telling him that he needs to ensure that his son Lehana and a grandson, Thladi, also appear before him on a charge of stock theft.

Maseru — Friday October 11, 1878

As Griffith prepares to occupy his Maseru office once more, Rolland attends a gathering of 27 Basotho chiefs who present him with a statement that they would like him to translate and deliver. It is addressed to Griffith and reads:

"Our hearts are filled with a wonderful gladness at hearing of your arrival in Basutoland and we ask you to receive herewith our greetings with which we welcome your coming into this territory.

"This day we are in truth satisfied that the Queen does indeed love the Basotho people, since she has once more yielded you back to us, you whom we know to be greatly regarded by the colony!

"May the Lord bless you, Sir, you and your family; and grant you many years in this land and may the Basotho nation learn through you to honour and love the law.

"God save the Queen!

"God save the 'Darling of the Warriors!'

"We salute you our honoured Chief, may God pour upon you endless blessings. We are your subjects and children."

Maseru — Wednesday, October 16, 1878

Today Griffith, after spending a week organizing his office, addresses a challenge from his own government which he fears will render his second term of office in Maseru radically different from the first.

Awaiting him is a letter from the Prime Minister, Gordon Sprigg, written from King William's Town.

"The disarmament, as you are probably aware, is proceeding very successfully from the sea right up to (the area known as) Wodehouse," Sprigg writes. "I want you now to commence with the Basotho. Assemble the leading men and acquaint them with the native policy of the present government, which I believe you thoroughly understand to be a government ruling over a barbarous people in the proper sense of the word.

"Tell them that they are not to be allowed to arm themselves and everybody else, but that our superior intelligence is to be beneficially exercised on their behalf, that they are to be held in hand and guided and trained with the view of raising them out of barbarism into civilization.

"Tell them that the proof of manhood is not the possession of a gun, but the capacity to observe and maintain order and to assist in advancing the moral and material prosperity of the community. The guns after delivery will be valued and each man will receive compensation — and an assurance that the government recognizes its duty to protect the people from oppression and will perform that duty.

"If you report to me that the people are willing to submit to the orders of the government in this respect then a day or days can be appointed for the delivery of the arms, spears, etc...

"If you find any unwillingness on the part of the Basotho you will oblige me by informing them that the government are resolute in the matter and are determined to carry it out, but I prefer doing it with the consent of the people.

"I suppose you may experience some difficulty with Moorosi, but you will know how to deal with him. If he is obstinate and you require a force to overcome him it shall be supplied. After the bulk of the natives in the several frontier districts is disarmed the Peace Preservation Act will be proclaimed making it illegal to carry a gun without a license and when that is done I shall feel somewhat more easy than I do at present."

Griffith does not like what he reads. He is an obedient soldier and administrator and will do what his government says. But he is fearful of the reaction of the Basotho and in particular Moorosi.

He finds a way to stall Sprigg by resorting to the letter of the law, a favourite tactic. He writes back:

"Your note of the 5th October in re disarming the Basotho has just reached me and of course your orders will be obeyed whatever they are. I wish, however, to point out to you that by Act No. 12 of 1871 — The Basutoland Annexation Act: Section II — it is provided that no act passed by the colonial parliament shall extend or be deemed to extend to this territory unless such act shall be extended thereto in express words contained therein or in some other Act of Parliament or unless the operation thereof shall be extended to such territory by the Governor by a proclamation.

"Under these circumstances the disarming act does not at present apply to this territory and cannot legally be put in force here."

Realizing that the government will surely have its way and extend the measure to Basutoland anyway, Griffith tells Sprigg that he has not the slightest doubt that Moorosi will refuse to give up his arms and will resist any attempt to take them. And, he adds, he will present the issue to a *pitso* to be held in two weeks.

Maseru — Thursday, October 24, 1878

Thousands have gathered for Griffith's *pitso*, the first since his return. Four resident magistrates from the area around Maseru are here, as are several missionaries belonging to the French Protestant Missionary Society and the recently arrived Roman Catholic Mission. Traders and several white investors in the country also are here. Once again, Letsie, the paramount chief, is absent, but the next in rank, Chief Masupha, is there. Also among those who are absent is Moorosi, although there are those among the crowd who will report to him everything that is said.

Griffith begins with warm greetings and apologizes for having left the previous year without having said goodbye.

He reports that "after several months' fighting the Gcaleka have been driven out of their country and all their cattle taken, hundreds of the people killed, also many of the chiefs killed or taken prisoner, and their chief Sarhili is now hiding himself away like a wolf. The Ngqika have shared the same fate, only in a worse degree; their old Chief Sandile and many other chiefs have been killed."

After describing the destruction and suffering, he adds: "From all I have told you I hope you will learn a lesson and see what the result of rebellion is. The Gcaleka and Ngqika were living in much the same way as you are. No one bothered them or interfered with them and yet they were not satisfied. The chiefs listened to bad advisers, and thus brought themselves and their people to destruction. And thus will it ever be with people who rebel against the just and mild rule of the Queen.

"During the time that I was away from this country, I heard of the unsettled state of the Baphuthi and the proceedings of Moorosi and his son Lehana, which news astonished me very much, as when I left the country I thought all the chiefs and people in the country were loyal subjects of the Queen, but when I heard that Moorosi and the Baphuthi came to meet Mr. Bowker at Phathlalla Drift all armed with guns and spears, as if they were going to meet an enemy, my astonishment knew no bounds and to this day I cannot understand what Moorosi and the Baphuthi meant by such conduct."

Having laid the groundwork, Griffith moves to the major issue: disarmament.

Griffith explains that the government will call on the people to disarm. His listeners understand that, in this context, "people" means black people and that it means them. The mood of the crowd perceptibly changes.

"This policy has been adopted by the government because it wishes the country to be at peace," Griffith continues. "The government says the people have no use for guns as there is no game in the country to shoot, that if they are allowed to keep their guns they will only fight with each other. The government will protect everyone.

"I mention these matters to you today because you Basotho will also be called upon to give up your arms and I hope you will all do so willingly; and you will suffer no loss by doing so, as it is the intention of the government to pay you the value of your guns."

The Basotho have little to say on the issue of disarmament, largely because they have just heard about it. They need time to consider it and want first to discuss it with family and friends. But those who do respond to Griffith's announcement on disarmament reluctantly accept it. After all, it comes from their white "father" whom they so greatly respect. Says government-supporter Sofonia Moshesh, "Though we may be called upon to make a painful sacrifice like Abraham, we can do it. We will find it bitter; but what the government sees fit to do must be right." He fails to add that Abraham was later relieved from having to perform his sacrifice.

Still, the concession comes more from a desire to be polite and avoid confrontation rather than agreement. They were taken by surprise and need to think it through. Clearly, however, the disarmament issue is likely to be the one to ignite anti-government feelings in the months ahead, particularly among the Baphuthi, who will soon hear about it.

Quthing — Friday, November 1, 1878

Moorosi climbs the winding stone staircase to the Masitise cave house and asks Emma Ellenberger whether her husband is there. She tells him he is in the new church he is building. Moorosi finds him there.

"I have heard that Mr. Griffith held a *pitso* and he said there that the government is to force our people to give up their arms," he tells Ellenberger. "No longer will we be able to own rifles, let alone carry them. Even spears will be forbidden.

"The white authorities and their allies, the police, will be armed. I and my people will be left like bulls without horns. When the government wishes to impose its will on us it will be able to do so with force and we will not have the ability to fight back."

Ellenberger reassures Moorosi that, according to his information, the law has not yet been imposed in Basutoland, even though it has been passed by the Parliament in Cape Town.

"But Mr. Griffith says that it will be imposed on us."

Ellenberger speaks quietly, reassuringly. "My missionary colleagues and I are opposed to this measure," he says. "We are sending a message to the government in Cape Town that we think they should not impose this law on the people of Basutoland.

"So do not take any action now that you might regret later. Do not try to fight the authorities on this. We are doing what we can to stop them. We cannot stop the law, but we can ask them not to impose it on this country."

Moorosi sits for a while and thinks.

"What you say is good," he replies. "You can talk to the white people for us because you know what we think. They will listen to you even though they do not listen to us. I hope that now you can help us with this bad law. It will destroy us as a people, it will take away all my power as a chief and it will mean we will have to obey the white people's laws whether they are just or not."

Ellenberger holds up his hand.

"You must not seek to fight against the white authorities with your weapons," he says. "As you know, I am a man of peace. I do not want to see anyone fighting. I believe that God is unhappy when he sees anyone fighting. You should be patient and let us, the missionaries, talk to the government about this. Give us time to see whether we can stop them from imposing the law on you and your people.

"In the meantime, I suggest that you do not take your weapons when you meet with the magistrate. Doing so will only make them fear you and will give them reason to want to take away your arms."

In his heart, Moorosi fears an attempt to disarm his people is inevitable. He has had many dealings with the white authorities and he knows that the government does not suggest one thing and do another; it does what it says it will do. And it does not always listen to the missionaries.

"I want to talk to you about another matter," Ellenberger says. "I have heard that the magistrate wants you to tell Lehana and Thladi that they must appear in the magistrate's court to face trial and I would like to suggest that you tell the men that they must appear in court."

"But they are afraid of what the magistrate will do to them," says Moorosi.

"This magistrate is not like the other one," Ellenberger replies. "He does not order men to be whipped in the way the other magistrate did. Only the other day I heard that Mr. Austen had asked permission from Mr. Griffith to withdraw a sentence of lashes that Mr. Hope had imposed on a man.

"So you need to tell them they must not be afraid, but must act as good citizens and appear before the court. God wants us to obey the authorities that he has put there for our good.

"If Lehana did not commit the offense of stock stealing, the magistrate will find him not guilty. If he finds him guilty he must face the consequences because stock stealing is not right."

"But I do not know where the men are," Moorosi says.

"King, I know that you can find out where they are," Ellenberger says. "If you do not do so and you do not send them to trial then the magistrate is going to call in other people to help him find them and we will have a battle on our hands. That is another reason you should tell them to appear in court.

"We do not want to have a war over a matter that is not big enough to warrant one."

Moorosi accepts Ellenberger's advice and decides he will tell Lehana and Thladi to appear before Austen in court. But they will not be the only ones in court. He will attend the session himself and help the magistrate make his decision.

Quthing — Tuesday, November 12, 1878

Persuaded by Moorosi to appear in court, Lehana and Thladi are here, ready to face trial.

Word of the trial has spread. The small courtroom is filled with about 30 spectators, the maximum that can be accommodated without causing some to faint for lack of air. A few — including Lemena who arrived early to ensure he could get a seat — occupy the few benches and the rest stand.

Moorosi sits in the front row, alongside Lehana and Thladi, ready to come to their defence.

Some 70 more spectators stand outside, jostling one another for a view. Those closest to the door say they will report to those outside.

Austen is pleased to note that none of the crowd is armed. They are quiet and calm.

Maitin, serving as the clerk of the court, stands.

"I call the case of the Queen versus Lehana and Thladi," he says.

"What is the charge?" asks Austen.

"The accused are charged with the crime of being accessories before and after the act of theft and with receiving stolen property," Maitin intones.

The crowd is silent as Maitin translates the charge, explaining that it means that the men might not have committed the thefts themselves, but that they caused others to commit them, which is an equally offensive act, and that they took possession of the goods that had been stolen.

"How do you plead?" asks Austen.

The men protest that they are innocent.

The first witness takes the stand and the testimony begins.

Now, Austen thinks, is my chance to put the troublemaker Lehana away for good, in a place where he will no longer be able to stir up trouble among the Baphuthi people. He believes he owes that to the cause of law and order and the future of colonial rule in the territory.

Quthing — Friday, November 15, 1878

Cattle grazing under the watchful eye of a herder.

For three days, witnesses have testified that they heard that Lehana, his son Thladi and others crossed the border twice to steal cattle in the Cape Colony — firstly when Lehana was awaiting trial in the Maikela affair and secondly after he was fined by Bowker at the meeting at Palmietfontein. The cattle provided food for the thieves and their 20 followers holed up in a cave in Quthing, the witnesses said.

Some said they saw Lehana riding toward the border and later heard that he had returned with stolen cattle.

Some suggested that the animals were a replacement for those they had paid to the government as a fine in the trial held by Bowker.

Lehana and Thladi, encouraged by Moorosi to argue in their defence, insisted they are innocent of the charges laid against them. They told Austen no direct evidence had been produced to show that they had either stolen the cattle or ordered the thefts. None of the witnesses had heard the men specifically instruct anyone to steal cattle, nor did they see them stealing cattle.

The question before Austen now is: Although no direct evidence has been presented that Lehana stole cattle and Thladi assisted him, is it a reasonable assumption that they must have done so or, at the least, took no steps to stop it?

As sole judge and jury, Austen finds himself influenced by two factors, neither directly related to the theft charges. He is convinced Lehana was not hiding in the cave simply to escape capture from the contempt charges levelled against him by Hope. Austen believes the rumours he has heard — that Lehana's plan was to taunt colonial forces into invading Baphuthi territory, giving him the justification for hitting back and thereby starting a rebellion against colonial rule.

The other factor is Austen's belief that Bowker imposed too lenient a sentence on Lehana at Palmietfontein. Because he was not imprisoned, Lehana could return to his cave and continue to foster his incipient rebellion against the colonial government and steal cattle. Now, Austen believes, is his chance to impose the sentence Bowker should have imposed.

Finding Lehana guilty would, therefore, serve a dual purpose. Not only would justice be done in the stock-stealing case, but imprisonment would remove Lehana and Thladi, and their influence, from the Quthing district. Without their influence, Austen is convinced, the Baphuthi people would be more cooperative and respectful of the government. No longer would Moorosi be subject to persuasion by his wild, aggressive and rebellious son.

Austen clears his throat.

"Does anyone want to say anything more?" he asks. The court room is silent.

"Very well, I will deliver my verdict."

Austen summarizes the case, outlining the charges and the evidence presented to him. The crowd of onlookers listens in silence. He reaches the end of his summation and he instructs the accused men to stand.

"Lehana, I find you guilty of the crimes as outlined in the charge sheet. I am convinced that you committed the stock theft, you encouraged others to assist you in stealing the cattle, sheep and goats and that you took the animals to your hideout in the caves along the Orange River.

"Thladi, I find you guilty of receiving stolen property. There is not enough evidence to find that you actually stole stock, but I am convinced that you lived off that stock when you knew it had been stolen."

A few members of the crowd gasp, but for the most part they are quiet. The verdict was not entirely unexpected. Their main concern is the punishment.

Austen continues.

"Lehana, you were the leader of this group that hid in the cave," he says. "Because you are a headman and because you are able to influence more people — and because I am convinced you took a leading role in the thefts — I am going to give you a harsher sentence than the one I will impose on Thladi.

"I want to point out that I cannot tolerate such action as you have both taken. The law condemns stock theft as a serious offense and this court will not take it lightly.

"Lehana, I sentence you to four years' imprisonment with hard labour.

"Thladi, I sentence you to two years' imprisonment with hard labour.

"The police will take you to the jail near this courtroom where you will start to serve your sentence immediately. Later you will be taken to another jail in the Cape Colony.

"The court is dismissed."

A cry of shock rises from the crowd. To fine a man is one thing, but to put him in prison, to remove him from his family and his people is another. Under Baphuthi laws, Lehana likely would have been told to return the stolen cattle and would have been fined an amount equal to the stock he had stolen. Imprisonment as a punishment for such a crime is a white people's concept. In addition, he would have to perform hard labour, which consists of working on the roads.

But, even if imprisonment is accepted as a form of punishment, why was he not given six months imprisonment as the other convicted stock thieves were? That was the worst case that Moorosi had imagined. The reason for relief when Bowker sentenced Lehana at Palmietfontein was that the magistrate did not impose a harsh jail sentence on him. With this sentence, there is no relief. The king is devastated.

Lehana is shocked. He stands still, looking down. His heart drops. Above all, he cherishes his freedom, his ability to go where he wishes, to enjoy his family and to sit for hours, eating and talking with those close to him. Take those freedoms away and he is nothing. Without being close to his family, he might as well cease to exist.

Thladi, too, is downcast. Like Lehana, he stands motionless.

They are bitter and angry. Why did they listen to Moorosi and agree to the trial? He said he would protect them — and now look at what has happened.

The policemen place the men in the jail, give them prisoners' shirts and blankets, and secure the door with a lock. The prisoners reluctantly put on the shirts and throw the blankets on the ground.

Already in the small jail are Dethlama and Thaba, sentenced by Austen to six months in September, and two other men sentenced recently to a short jail term.

"Did the magistrate also send you to jail?" asks Dethlama.

"For four years." Lehana spits out the words angrily as he and Thladi look around them. The stone walls are about eight feet high and the building is covered with an iron roof. The mud floor is smooth from the trampling of others who have preceded them in the jail. The realization sinks in that their freedom has been taken from them. The years of the sentence — particularly in contrast with that of Dethlama and Thaba who have a little more than three months left to serve, seem like forever.

As a rat scurries away through a hole under the wall, the men wish they could follow it. They wonder how long they will be kept in this ill-smelling, dark confinement before being sent to work on the breakwater in Cape Town, an even worse punishment.

In the court room, Moorosi, still numb from the severity of the sentence, slowly rises from the bench on which he had been sitting. These sentences are wrong. Lehana is being punished not for stock theft, but for defiance. He is being put away because he is seen as a threat to them. He should have realised Austen would do this.

Not only will his love for his son and grandson not allow him to rest in peace while they are being held in the government's prison, but he will also lose the counsel and support of the one who has become his favourite son and so to whom the kingship of the Baphuthi people will surely pass when he dies. In the later years of Moorosi's life four years seems an eternity. He might be dead when they are released. If the men are taken out of Basutoland, he may never see his son and grandson again.

He will devise a plan to fight back. He will not confront the authorities now lest they take that as an excuse to act against him. Of what use will he be to his people if he, too, is put in jail? He will prepare quietly.

Of one thing he is sure. He will do all he can to prevent the authorities taking his son and grandson out of Quthing to the Cape Colony.

❧

Moorosi rides to Masitise, where he sees Ellenberger outside. "How are you doing today, chief Moorosi?"

"I am not doing well," Moorosi replies as he dismounts. "I am deeply saddened by the action taken by this magistrate. You advised me to tell Lehana to appear in court. You said Mr. Austen would be fair as Mr. Bowker was fair. Now he has sentenced my son Lehana to four years in jail. He will be sent away to Cape Town. This sentence, it is too harsh. It breaks my heart to see my son and grandson treated in this way."

"I can understand your feelings," Ellenberger responds, shocked at the severity of the sentence.

"I should not have listened to you," Moorosi continues. "I did what you said I should do.

"You speak of the Wodehouse bench, the bench of peace. This is not the way to achieve peace.

"This magistrate is not sitting on that bench.

"I am the one who has made all the sacrifice. The magistrate has done nothing."

Ellenberger nods. He had thought the sentence would be along the lines of that imposed by Bowker. Now Austen's action will render his efforts at peacemaking much harder and will erode Moorosi's trust in him.

Yet he must try to retain Moorosi's confidence.

"I admire you for playing your part in helping to ensure peace," he says. "You have acted in a good and noble way. What you have done will help to achieve peace, to ensure that the government will not wage war on you.

"Remember, as I said, we each have to give up something to achieve compromise and thereby peace. You have given up something big. You have taken a big step to ensure peace."

Moorosi looks down at the ground. Ellenberger is a man of God, a man who speaks wisdom. But he finds this wisdom difficult to accept. He looks back up at Ellenberger. His eyes tell of his feelings of betrayal and despair more eloquently than words can do.

"Do not despair yet, King Moorosi," Ellenberger continues. "Perhaps Mr. Austen will change his mind. Or perhaps the authorities in Maseru will reduce the sentence."

The king raises his head and looks into Ellenberger's eyes. He sees compassion in them. He knows it is not Ellenberger who has sentenced his son. He can see that Ellenberger is saddened by what has happened. But he feels betrayed.

"I cannot accept this action," he says.

"Don't do anything rash," Ellenberger replies.

"Let me see what I can do."

⁂

Ellenberger rides to the magistracy where he urges Austen to reverse his judgment and impose a less severe sentence on the men.

"I helped you by encouraging Moorosi to bring his son for trial," he says. "He trusted me and did what I asked him to do. Now he feels betrayed because of the severity of your sentence.

"These men fear jail, and fear being sent to jail and hard labour in East London or Cape Town more than anything.

"You will recall that was the issue when Mr. Bowker held the hearing at the Telle River. When he imposed only a fine and not jail on the men they were happy and shouted with joy at the relief they felt because the men would not be sent to work on the breakwater in Cape Town.

"Perhaps you can do the same thing this time. There is still time to call them back and tell them you have changed your mind and you want to impose a less strict sentence."

Austen sighs. "You do not understand, Rev. Ellenberger," he says. "Not only can I not change a sentence once it is imposed, but also these men are not just stock thieves. They are rebels. They want to overthrow our government and chase us out of the country."

"If they do want to rebel, it is because you are imposing severe sentences on them. To achieve peace, we have to compromise, Mr. Austen. Moorosi gave up his son to you for sentencing. I am asking you also to give up something to secure peace."

Austen displays a flash of anger. "The rebelliousness came first; the severe sentences followed," he says. "The latter is a result of the former, not the other way around."

"That may or may not be so, but, for the sake of peace, I am pleading with you to meet compromise with compromise and lessen the sentence," Ellenberger says.

"Impose a fine — a severe one if necessary. But lift the jail sentence, or reduce it to a few months in jail here.

"We have been living in peace here for many years. There were no problems when you were governing Quthing from across the river in Mohale's Hoek. I would hate to see that peace shattered and all the work you have done here destroyed by this act.

"I plead with you to follow the same action as Mr. Bowker. He prevented violence breaking out by imposing a sentence on Lehana that did not involve going to jail."

"No, Rev. Ellenberger. You are looking at it in the wrong way.

"If Mr. Bowker had put Lehana in jail, he would not have been able to continue his rebellious ways.

"We cannot afford to make the same mistake that Mr. Bowker did. If anything, perhaps my sentence was not strong enough."

Maseru — Wednesday, November 20, 1878

When Griffith receives notice of the verdicts in today's express post, he supports the harsh sentence imposed by Austen, but realizes that keeping the convicted men in the insecure jail in Quthing can be no more than a temporary measure. They must be sent first to Aliwal North and then on to a convict station in East London or Cape Town.

Because he does not have the authority to order the Aliwal North magistrate to hold the prisoners, he will go to the top and ask the Secretary of Native Affairs Ayliff to approve the men being held in a colonial jail.

Maseru — Monday, December 23, 1878

Today, six weeks after Lehana and Thladi were confined to the small jail in Quthing, Griffith finally has the authority to move the prisoners to Aliwal North, from where they will be transferred to East London and then to Cape Town. Griffith's request has gone through a lengthy and slow bureaucratic process, through Ayliff in Cape Town and even through the British colonial secretary, Michael Hicks-Beach, in London.

Griffith sends the relevant permission form to Austen in Quthing, asking him to send it to Aliwal North, which should take a few days.

Aware that the men's removal from Quthing to Aliwal North might be Moorosi's chance to prevent the sentence from being carried out and to get his son back, Griffith also requests an armed escort be sent to accompany the men to Aliwal North.

He insists, too, that the plans be kept secret so that Moorosi will not know when the men are being moved. Even the members of the escort should be told only at the last minute of the exact timing of their mission so there is no chance of the details leaking out.

Griffith is confident that the plans for the men's removal will succeed and that once Lehana is out of Quthing the spirit of rebellion among the Baphuthi will wane.

Now, two days before Christmas Day, everything seems to be in place to achieve that goal before the end of the year.

10

Aliwal North — Wednesday, January 1, 1879

We leave for Quthing tomorrow at dawn, Sgt. James Thorne tells four policemen who are to help him to escort Lehana and Thladi to the jail in Aliwal North. "Although we haven't received the formal papers, we have been informed by telegram the papers are on their way. We are aware there is some urgency to the removal of the prisoners and so we will saddle our horses at first light tomorrow. If the weather holds, we should be at the Quthing magistracy by the end of the day."

Quthing — The same day

The New Year's Day festivities have been going on for some hours in Quthing. Indeed, it has been a time of rest and relaxation at the magisterial compound for a week. Last Wednesday was Christmas Day and the following day was Boxing Day, also a holiday. By the time Friday and the weekend rolled around, it seemed a good idea to take a few days off until the next holiday — today, New Year's Day.

The holiday festivities are confined largely to the colonial authorities. It is a British concept, after all, and today is just another day to most of the Baphuthi people.

But, as colonial government employees, the native policemen can take part in the festivities — and do so with some eagerness. Their position entitles them to Cape brandy, banned for sale in Basutoland, and it flows freely among them today.

Now, as the sky darkens, the men are suffering the after-effects. The weather is not helping. A strong wind, carrying with it light rain, is sweeping down from the ridges around the magisterial compound, making outside duty unpleasant.

A sleepy and not entirely sober Second Class Private Mohomo is standing prison guard with Jeroboam, who shares the same rank and now shares the same impaired ability. After taking an evening meal to the prisoners, the two men sit a few yards from the entrance to the jail.

Two men on horseback pass the jail. Mohomo recognizes one as Mponya, a grandson of Moorosi, who stops his horse, dismounts and walks toward the jail where he exchanges a few words with the prisoners.

"Tell that man he has no right to come here," says Jeroboam, reluctant to do so himself. Mohomo slowly rises and walks in a zigzag line toward Mponya. He passes on the instruction.

"Why are you stopping me from seeing the prisoners?" asks Mponya.

"If you want to see the prisoners, ask the magistrate," Mohomo replies, pointing to Austen's house. "You see the magistrate's house? Go to him. Don't ask me."

Mponya pursues his argument for a while, but receives the same slurred answer. Finally, he rides off with his colleague.

Jeroboam and Mohomo check the jail door is secure with a padlock and that a

141

bar is in place across the door, the usual nightly routine. They return to their huts. They will sleep well tonight.

Quthing — Thursday January 2, 1879

His head pounding in spite of his long deep sleep, Jeroboam walks to the jail to start his day's duties. As usual, he is to take the prisoners to work in the gardens where they will be closely guarded.

But the sight that greets him indicates that today's activities will not be usual. The jail door is closed, but the bar across it to prevent it being opened from the inside is hanging down. The padlock is missing and the door is dented about quarter of an inch deep. The damage appears to have been made with the same blunt piece of iron used to smash the padlock.

The jail is empty.

Jeroboam runs to the policemen's huts. "The jail has been broken open and the prisoners have gone," he tells sergeant Isaak Masin.

A dazed Masin, also suffering from the New Year's festivities, runs outside.

"They have gone? They cannot have gone."

He looks across at the jail house.

They have gone.

"Why didn't you stop them?"

Jeroboam is quick to defend himself. "They broke out during the night. I was asleep." Determined not to be the scapegoat, he quickly adds, "And so were you."

The men walk slowly to Austen's house, as if delay by even a few minutes will make it easier to tell him what has happened.

Pietermaritzburg — The same day

Ever since he left Basutoland almost eight months ago, Bowker has wanted to speak with Cape Colony governor Sir Bartle Frere about the situation in Basutoland. He believes Frere has little more than a cursory knowledge of what the Basotho and Baphuthi people think and feel and does not realize the effect that the disarmament act will have on them.

Since being branded an "appeaser," Bowker has shared his thoughts only with close friends. Now, he decides, is the time to make himself heard — and who better to tell than Sir Bartle Frere?

"The Basotho looked upon themselves as a nation taken into British protection," he writes in a letter to the governor, "but never by any act of theirs assented to incorporation with or subjection to the Colony of the Cape of Good Hope, to which they seem to have been handed over in the most arbitrary fashion.

"The Basotho are quite clever enough to take unfavourable note of the fact that by such transference they became, without getting any 'quid pro quo' in the shape of representation, a province of a mere dependency."

Up to that point, Bowker notes, they had managed with the aid of Her Majesty's Commissioner, to rule and restrain themselves through their grand councils. The money collected in the hut tax was used in Basutoland.

"Under the Cape Parliament, however, they were threatened with taxation without representation; in fact, their surplus revenues were actually taken away from them without their consent and paid into the colonial exchequer."

Bowker advises Frere to take note of the strength in arms, horses and men in Basutoland.

"I must warn you, Sir Bartle, that if you do not allow them to keep their arms a Basotho war against the whites must arise, when colonists would have to face a people united against them."

Quthing — The same day

Mponya rides astride Moorosi's favourite white horse, lent to him for the occasion. Behind him are Lehana, Thladi, Dethlama, Thaba and two other released prisoners as well as the men who helped Mponya break open the jail.

They have stayed away from the regular routes to avoid detection, moving instead up and down steep hills. Now it is mid-morning; they have travelled five miles and are tired from little sleep.

They make their way to a cave that, Mponya says, will be their hideout for a few days. It is hidden in a deep valley and they are confident that the government people will not be able to find them here.

"I knew you wanted to free us," says Lehana, "but for a while I thought you might not make it in time. We overheard the guards talking about men arriving soon to take us to Aliwal North and then to Cape Town to work on the breakwater."

"We knew the time was getting close," replies Mponya. "We started planning around the time of the Christmas celebrations because we knew then that the magistrate and the policemen would be distracted. Then Jantji Xaka, a Thembu, told us he had heard that white policemen would come to this office from Aliwal North on New Year's night and remove you.

"We knew we had to act soon, but we needed to find out whether King Moorosi was supporting us. Three days ago we received a message that we were to go ahead with the plans to break open the jail and release the prisoners. He sent us a key to use in the padlock.

"Some of the people who wanted to release you were afraid because the police sleep nearby and they said the policemen would shoot us. But we went anyway."

"That's when you came the first time and the policeman told you to leave."

"Yes. We also heard voices in the magistrate's office. So we told you we would return."

"You did. And I told you not to be slow about it. 'Come quietly and do it at once,' I said."

"And did we not do as you asked?" asks Mponya, his face breaking into a smile.

"You did. But you took longer than I thought."

The men laugh.

"We did. But we waited until it was quiet in the office; no candles were burning and the wind was blowing strongly enough to cover any noise.

"We tried to open the padlock with the key, but it did not work. That is why Nepa broke the padlock with a piece of iron."

Lehana turns his thoughts to the future.

"Now, tell me, what is this I hear? They are going to take away our weapons?"

"Yes, Lehana, it is true," Mponya continues. "The government says they will take away our weapons — from us and from everyone in Basutoland. Not only our rifles, but also our spears.

"All the people are talking about it. The Maseru magistrate, Griffith, held a *pitso* and told everyone there that there is a new law to take away the arms from all the black people in South Africa — and we will be among them.

"When they do that, the people say, war will break out. They are talking about it in Letsie's territory and in other parts of the country. Even King Moorosi said that after we have released you we must hide the children because there might be fighting. Another reason he wanted you released before they could send you away was so that you would be able to fight with us when the government tries to take away our weapons.

"Do you really think that war will break out?" asks Thladi.

"Yes," Mponya replies. "They will come to take away our weapons. We will not want to give them up. War will break out."

"Have you found out when the government will do this?" Lehana asks.

"A messenger has been sent to King Letsie as he is in contact with the top chiefs of the white government. We have not heard back from him yet."

"They already are waging war on us by putting me in jail for four years," says Lehana. "They are slowly herding us like cattle into a kraal. We have to be ready to fight. But we must also be careful not to be caught and be put into jail again."

"I have made plans for us to stay here in the cave for a few days," says Mponya. "Later, we will move to King Moorosi's Mountain. You will be safe there. King Moorosi has told me that he and his men are ready to fight off any attempt the government might make to recapture you."

⚜

"How could this have happened?" Austen asks when Masin tells him of the breakout. "Nothing like this has ever happened in Basutoland. No prisoners have ever escaped. Were your policemen not guarding the jail? Why were they not on special guard?"

Masin and Jeroboam say they received no instructions to post a sentry at night.

"But was that not an obvious thing to do?" Austen asks.

Even as he puts the question to the men, he suffers a twinge of conscience. Because the prisoners had shown no signs of wanting to escape, Austen had given no instructions to guard them at night.

But the men, too, feel guilty and are quick to change the focus of the discussion. "This is the work of King Moorosi," Masin says. "It would not have happened if he had not been behind it."

Austen believes that is an excuse. The policemen were negligent, but it is of little use remonstrating with them now. He needs their help to get back the most important prisoners he has ever held.

He needs to act before it is too late.

"I want you, Isaak, to go to Chief Moorosi. Tell him this is a very serious offense. It will make a very bad impression on the mind of the government against him and his people, especially as it comes after the time when Lehana fostered rebellion while hiding in his cave.

"Tell him I expect him to use his utmost attempts to find and capture the men and to send them back to me and I can put him in jail."

Masin says he will leave within the hour for Moorosi's Mountain.

In addition, Austen will launch his own search. He turns to Jeroboam.

"I want you to take Mohomo with you. You must take the same message as Isaak is taking to Chief Moorosi to the people who live in Lehana's village and the area that he oversees. I want you to go to the villages along the Silver Spruit River and the Qomoqomong River. I want you to talk to the people and find out where the escaped prisoners are hiding so we can then recapture them."

Austen retreats to his office. Suddenly, Quthing looks a lot different than it did just a few days ago when he penned his annual report. The calm of which he was so proud has gone. The leading rebel he thought he had removed from the area is back with his people, with an even stronger reason to rebel than before. Moorosi, who clearly was not happy with the sentence imposed on his son, will be even less cooperative now.

Austen fears the chances of his policemen finding Lehana and Thladi are slim. The mountains, hills and crags offer a thousand hiding places. Unless they are lucky and find someone who will talk, it will take weeks to scour the mountains and during that time the fugitives — whose spies will keep them informed — will move continually, making the search almost impossible.

"Why did this have to happen?" he shouts, banging his fist on the table. "How could the policemen have been so careless?"

Hearing the noise, Maitin enters the room.

"I am convinced Moorosi was behind this act," Austen says. "He is no longer working with us, my dear Mr. Maitin; he is working against us. We are back where we were two months ago," he continues, sitting at his desk once more and jabbing his finger toward Maitin. "Only matters are now worse. We have not just a rebel on the loose, but a man who is out to get me for the sentence that I imposed on him. He will stir up not just his own family, but his father, the chief himself, against me.

"I am going to have to ask for more protection."

Austen pounds his fist on the desk one more time.

"Why, oh why, did this have to happen?"

Maitin returns to his office. Austen sits at his desk for what seems like an hour. He is unable to concentrate on his routine duties. If only the prison break could have been avoided. If only...

Darkness is approaching when there is a knock at the door.

"Come in."

The door is opened and a head pokes around it.

"Sergeant Thorne reporting, sir. We have come from Aliwal North to pick up the prisoners and escort them to the safety of our jail."

Quthing — Saturday, January 4, 1879

Sergeant Isaak Masin returns from his visit to Moorosi in the mid-morning.

"I delivered your message," he tells Austen.

Over the last two days, Austen's mood has turned from anger to anxiety. He fears not just for his safety in Quthing, but also for his position as a government servant. After all, even the British government in London was involved in deciding where the prisoners should be sent. Lehana and Thladi are now known far beyond the confines of Quthing, Basutoland and even South Africa. It seems to Austen that he is operating under the eyes of the world. And he does not relish the position in which the escape has placed him.

"What did the chief say?" he asks Masin.

"He did not seem surprised when I told him what had happened. He said the magistrate locked them up and he should know where they are. He said he is not responsible for them. But he said nevertheless he would send two messengers to try to find them. The messengers would go to the villages that lie along the Quthing River on the road over the mountains that leads to Matatiele in the east."

"That might sound good, but, Isaak, I think we cannot rely on Moorosi to find these men for us," he replies. "He is likely sending the messengers in the wrong direction."

Masin nods. "I agree with you," he says. "He did not seem eager to find them."

Austen draws up a warrant for the arrest of Lehana and the other prisoners and asks Maitin to make several copies. He believes Moorosi was trying to mislead him in saying that the men might have sought refuge over the mountains, but he sends a copy of the warrant to M.W. Liefeldt, the magistrate in Matatiele, just in case.

Austen decides it is time to tackle a duty he had hoped to postpone, but knows he cannot. He writes to Griffith, telling him he believes Moorosi was behind the break, having heard that the policemen were about to arrive to move the prisoners to Cape Town.

He says he hopes to be successful in finding the men, "especially if you would sanction a reward to informers."

Austen includes statements from the policemen involved, folds the letter and places it in the box for the post that leaves tonight. He is under no illusions about how Griffith will take the news.

Maseru — Monday, January 6, 1879

Griffith is furious. Waving the letter from Austen in his hand, he strides into Rolland's office.

"Mr. Austen has allowed the prisoners to go," he tells him.

"He has released them?" Rolland gasps with disbelief.

"No, they have escaped."

Griffith tosses Austen's letter on Rolland's desk.

"And one of those prisoners is Lehana?"

"Yes."

"Did he not realize how important a prisoner he was?" Rolland responds, ignoring the letter.

"Apparently not," Griffith responds. "At least not from the way he acted. It is clear from his report that proper precautions were not taken. He does not say so specifically, but I am convinced a proper guard and sentries were not placed over the lock-up at night. Had they been, the prisoners would not have escaped."

Rolland realizes the seriousness of the situation. Lehana was known to be plotting rebellion against the government. He was the ringleader. With him out of the way the tension would have been lessened. Now he is on the loose once more, likely more rebellious than before.

Griffith continues.

"The guards were there when the prisoners were having their supper, but, after locking them up, the policemen did not return again until the next morning, when they found the lock-up empty. That much is clear from statements by the policeman and constable involved.

"Somebody has been very careless here."

"And you think Mr. Austen is to be blamed?" Rolland asks.

"Of course. Clearly. When last I heard, he was in charge over there. He is the person who should have given the policemen orders to guard the lock-up at night.

"Perhaps he gave them orders and the policemen did not follow his orders," Rolland ventures.

"Well, then, he should have seen that those orders were obeyed. But he does not say he gave them orders or that anybody disobeyed anything. Surely if that were the case he would have protected himself by explaining it in his report.

"No, there are no excuses for him. He is to blame."

Griffith picks up the letter once more. His eyes glance down again at the contents, which he already has read several times.

"And then he goes on to suggest that Moorosi is responsible for the break-out."

"Is he not?"

"I do not know, Mr. Rolland. But before he tries to hold Moorosi responsible he must be in a position to prove that Moorosi has aided in the escape or that he harboured them after the escape. He and his policeman Isaak are trying to throw the blame on Moorosi in order to avoid their own responsibility in not having taken proper precautions to keep the prisoners in safe custody. Before we act against Moorosi, make demands on him or hold him responsible for finding the prisoners, we need to know for sure that he organized this affair. If we do not know that, we are acting unjustly."

"Do you think he should have refrained from telling the chief about the breakout?"

"No. It is fine that Mr. Austen reported the break-out to Moorosi. I think the chief needs to know that it happened — assuming he did not already know. But I do not think Mr. Austen should go beyond that. I think it would be much better for him to work out the matter with his own police constables.

"I will inform him that he needs to take his own steps to find these men and show Moorosi that the Government is independent of him. Working through Moorosi is a mistake. It is important that we do not ask chiefs to do our work for us. Doing so only makes them believe they are still in full control of their own people, that their word still counts and that they are responsible for law and order in this country. It also gives the impression that we are weak and incapable of administering justice ourselves.

"We need to show Moorosi that the government is quite independent of him."

"Will you tell Mr. Austen of your concerns?"

"I certainly will. But I will wait a few days while I make inquiries among the people here. I would be pleased if you would help me do so. The chiefs around here are in contact with Moorosi and we might be able to glean information from them.

"But, unless I hear something that changes my mind, I will let Austen know how I feel about what has happened and his neglect in allowing it to happen. I am going to call on him for a full report as to what steps he took to secure the safe custody of these prisoners. I also plan to inform the Secretary for Native Affairs and to express to him my concern about Mr. Austen's actions.

"First, Mr. Hope causes trouble among the Baphuthi with his high-handed, tactless and undiplomatic attitude. Now Mr. Austen, who seemed to be getting to grips with the situation, aggravates those problems with negligence.

"If we are not careful, we will be facing an extremely serious situation in Quthing. For now, we must find Lehana and the other prisoners — particularly Lehana. At all costs."

11

Transkei — The same day

Hamilton Hope has produced his first annual report as magistrate at Qumbu in the Transkei. It reflects a pattern that characterized his dealings with Moorosi.

Hope says that Mhlonthlo, paramount chief of the Mpondomise, of whom he has had charge since July 1, 1878, "is a brave and warlike man and far more outspoken and straightforward than most other native chiefs; and as a natural consequence he is somewhat impatient of control.

"I believe that before I came here he had not infrequently offered a good deal of opposition to government authority; and when I was installed as magistrate of the district he expressed great dissatisfaction at my appointment.

"But I am glad to be able to say that, after one or two feeble attempts at opposing me at first, he accepted the position I allotted to him as in all things subordinate to me, and he has since then rendered me cheerful, and I may say prompt obedience in all matters."

In spite of Hope's rosy outlook, however, signs of resistance are growing to his demand that the chief be subservient to him in all matters, his frequent use of the whip, and his cracking down on the payment of arrears hut tax.

"I have many obstacles to overcome," Hope confesses. "But I do not despair."

Pietermaritzburg — Saturday, January 11, 1879

Unaware of the turn of events in Quthing, Frere is in Natal colony, where he has been since August, planning the downfall of the Zulu king Cetshwayo. He has organized wagons of supplies for the troops and given instructions on how the battle will be waged. The Zulu king has been warned, but refuses to concede.

So today British troops, accompanied by several hundred pro-government natives, are invading Zululand to force Cetshwayo to agree with Frere's demands.

Quthing — Friday, January 17, 1879

The messengers sent across the mountains to Matatiele report back this morning that the magistrate Liefeldt has not seen the escaped prisoners, but will do all he can to find them. He has sent detectives to inquire in the area and will report back on what they tell him. He also has sent a copy of the warrant for the prisoners' arrest to the chief magistrate's office in Kokstad.

"Thank you," says Austen. "At least Liefeldt is trying to help."

Chief constable Masin enters the office.

"I have some good news," he says.

"If it is, it will be the first I have heard in the three weeks since the breakout."

"One of the escaped prisoners has been apprehended," Masin says. "His name is

Magerman."

"But he was not one of the rebels," Austen says. "He was in the jail awaiting trial on charges of theft."

"Yes, but he can give us a clearer picture of how the break-out took place and who was responsible for it. We also have apprehended one of the accomplices in the jailbreak, a man named Mapara."

Austen recognizes that, although the men are not involved in the rebellion, they are important witnesses and they also can implicate Moorosi as the one who planned and gave instructions for the rescue of the prisoners.

Austen instructs Masin: "I want you to put them in the jail and place additional guards at the door to ensure that Moorosi does not help them break out again to prevent them giving evidence against him."

He adds, "I have just heard from Mr. Griffith that he has approved my request to increase my police force to a total of 18 men, including a sergeant, a corporal, three first-class, three second-class and 10 third-class privates. He also has agreed to send me two additional pairs of leg irons."

"Another piece of good news," Masin says.

"I suppose it is," Austen says. "Finally, they listen. It takes something like this before they realize that we need additional policemen and equipment. He also has approved my request that, as a last resort, I can send prisoners to Palmietfontein where the officer commanding there, Captain James Surmon, will place them under guard. But, he has emphasized, this action should be taken only as a last resort."

Natal colony — Wednesday, January 22, 1879

The rout is complete.

In a furious battle at Isandhlwana, a rampaging force of 20,000 swift and mobile Zulu warriors take the slow and cumbersome British, led by Lord Chelmsford, completely by surprise. They outwit, overwhelm and kill 900 white and 500 black soldiers — members of the Natal Native Contingent — leaving only a few of the troops alive.

C.L. Norris-Newman, the first newspaper correspondent to reach the scene, writes, "The corpses of our poor soldiers, whites and natives, lay thick upon the ground in clusters, together with the dead and mutilated horses, oxen and mules, shot and stabbed in every position and manner; and the whole intermingled with the fragments of our Commissariat wagons, broken and wrecked, and rifled of their contents, such as flour, sugar, tea, biscuits, mealies, oats, etc., the debris being scattered about and wasted as in pure wantonness on the ground."

After rampaging over the British forces at Isandhlwana, the Zulus continue on to Rorke's Drift where a small group of soldiers battles for hours to hold the group of houses that constitute a British base. Led by Lieutenants Chard and Bromhead — who are lauded as heroes for their bravery — the group holds out until sunset, when the Zulus retreat.

But, in spite of Chard and Bromhead's stand, the story of the day is that the

Zulus imposed a stunning and humiliating defeat on the British, who boast the most modern weaponry and the strongest army in the world.

Quthing — Monday, January 27, 1879

The news of the British defeat at Isandhlwana five days ago has spread to Basutoland. It is stark: a black indigenous army defeated the white colonial power. The casualties, the sources say, were the heaviest to white soldiers in any battle in South Africa and the greatest defeat suffered by the British army anywhere in the world.

The news is encouraging to the Baphuthi leaders. Up to now the white-won battles to the south have led the Baphuthi people to believe that black Africans cannot win. Moorosi's response has been that his people's independence is so important that it is better to die at the hands of the whites than to succumb. The Zulu victory has reshaped this debate. It demonstrates, as Moorosi had suspected all along, that a black army can win.

As a result, Moorosi feels more emboldened to stand up to Austen and more convinced that Lehana is right that war is the only answer. Indeed, the Zulu victory gives him a feeling approaching invincibility.

"He has completely lost his head," Mafetudi, Moorosi's chief messenger, tells Lemena. "He says the Basotho will join us in our fight against the government and we will be even more victorious than the Zulu people. He is convinced that this time Letsie's son Lerothodi will be fighting on our side — against the whites."

⁂

For the colonial authorities, the loss at Isandhlwana is a cause of consternation, alarm and dismay. They have relied on a show of force to back up their authority. They have used colonial victories in the south, such as that against Sarhili, to drive home their point that they have powerful forces to bolster their rule.

Suddenly, their power is less impressive.

During the morning, Arthur Barkly, who took over Austen's post at Mohale's Hoek, arrives unexpectedly at Austen's residence.

"The news from Isandhlwana is disturbing," he says. "I knew most of the officers of the regiment well. Now they have been killed by Cetshwayo and his *impis*.

"But it goes beyond that," he adds. "I am afraid this catastrophe is the beginning of great trouble for us. Already the Basotho people have been angered by the disarmament proposal and have been showing greater and greater resistance to colonial rule. And I hear that the Zulu people are sending messages trying to stir up the Basotho to join them against the government."

Barkly's assessment comes as a surprise to Austen.

"Our people here are quiet," he replies. "The people are not showing strong support for the would-be rebels."

"I am surprised to hear you say that," responds Barkly. "Our people around Mohale's Hoek are becoming more and more sullen every day. As they do, we are becoming more and more nervous. We feel the time is becoming perilous and I am not sure what each day might bring forth."

Austen and Barkly discuss Lehana's conviction and the jailbreak. As they do, Barkly becomes concerned that Austen is not taking matters seriously and does not realize the degree of discontent prevailing in his district — discontent that has spread to Mohale's Hoek. After a while he concludes that the discussion is going nowhere. His hope of formulating a cohesive plan of action with Austen has faded.

"I cannot linger," he says. "My wife is expecting a child in a week or so, but it could arrive early and I need to be there."

"I am anxious for her safety should rebellion of some sort spill over into our district."

Soon Barkly is on his horse back to Mohale's Hoek. Surely, he thinks, Austen must understand that his conviction of Lehana, his excessive sentence and the subsequent jail break — all of which are known in Mohale's Hoek and in much of Basutoland — have prompted strong feelings against him. By denying that and suggesting everything is peaceful he is living in a dream world.

Barkly leaves more worried about events in Quthing than when he arrived.

Quthing — Wednesday, January 29, 1879

Barkly's comments have made Austen wonder whether he has failed to notice rising tensions in other areas of Quthing.

So today he takes two steps. He asks Griffith to send him more arms and ammunition. And he sets off on a trip into the interior with two of his policemen to see if Barkly's information about widespread discontent is grounded.

Passing through a village, Austen talks with the people who live there, trying to gauge their feelings. He finds them reluctant to talk with him. He can assess little and realizes anew that the Baphuthi are good at hiding their feelings and often will say only what they think an inquirer wants to hear, partly out of politeness and partly out of a fear of saying something that will upset the questioner.

As he leaves the village, he and the policemen ride along a narrow mountain path. Here, he comes across a man who says his name is Japhta who lives in Lehana's village. He tells Austen he has been shown boxes of ammunition in his village and has been told that they have been sent there by Moorosi.

"The men of my village sleep with their guns at their side," Japhta says. "And they take their arms with them when they go into the fields. Some of the people in my village have taken their cattle to hide in a kloof near the source of the Sibaphala River, high in the mountains."

"Have you heard where Lehana is hiding?" asks Austen.

"They do not tell me," Japhta replies. "But they say the government will not get him again. This is not the work of ordinary men; this is the work of King Moorosi."

As he returns Austen realizes that, although those who live near the government offices appear quiet, the people farther away seem to be preparing for a confrontation.

Maseru — Wednesday, February 5, 1879

More than a month has passed since the jail breakout and tensions are rising not just in Quthing, but throughout Basutoland. Griffith realizes it is now more important than ever that Lehana and his fellow escapees be brought to book before matters get out of control.

He summarizes the situation: If Moorosi is innocent of orchestrating the jailbreak, he nevertheless is unlikely to persuade his favourite son Lehana to hand himself in, as he did before the trial. If Moorosi is guilty of assisting Lehana, however, the Baphuthi chief definitely will protect Lehana and prevent him from being captured.

Whichever way you look at it, Moorosi is the key and he must be confronted.

Griffith ponders his strategy. He must enlist Letsie's help. Without realizing it, he echoes the argument Bowker used to enlist Letsie's support when Lehana's first trial was held in Palmietfontein.

He will begin by warning Letsie of the consequences of using colonial forces to capture Lehana and pacify Moorosi.

The government will throw all it has at Moorosi to force him to hand over Lehana, he will say, and it is inevitable that Moorosi will lose. The Zulu leader Cetshwayo might have won, but Moorosi has fewer men and will suffer the same fate as the Xhosa chief Sarhili.

Once white forces take Moorosi — he will tell Letsie — they will take his land in the same way they took Sarhili's land. From there, they will look toward other parts of Basutoland to annex as well. The argument will be that the Baphuthi and Basotho are rebels and the only way to treat rebels is to take over complete control of their territory and annex their land.

So Letsie's first task should be to persuade Moorosi to hand over Lehana and the other fugitives to the authorities. Suggestions that his territory should be annexed to the Cape Colony will be defeated; Griffith would personally see to that.

Griffith has another argument to use to persuade Letsie, one that Bowker did not have. Griffith will tell the chief that, should he use his arms on behalf of the white government, the government will have every reason to exclude his people from the disarmament law. If Letsie can use his arms to defend the Queen, why would the Queen want to take his arms away?

Griffith knows he is on shaky ground by making such promises; if the Cape government should decide to impose the disarmament law on the Basotho, he will be powerless to stop it. But he is confident, too, that he will be able to wield some influence over the decision should Letsie use his arms to assist the government.

Also, he will tell Letsie, the Basotho will be able to keep many of the cattle taken from Moorosi should they join forces with the whites in bringing him to book.

Greed, the chance to avoid disarmament, and Letsie's desire to avoid confrontation with the colonial government, Griffith hopes, will outweigh any sympathy that Letsie might have with Moorosi.

He hopes desperately that Letsie will buy it.

London — Tuesday, February 11, 1879

Details of the defeat of the British forces in Zululand are reaching London, where Colonial Secretary Sir Michael Hicks-Beach believes that it puts the confederation policy in jeopardy.

Defeat, especially at the hands of savages, is unacceptable. And the greatest defeat ever inflicted on a British force is intolerable. It must be reversed. Cetshwayo must be crushed.

Hicks-Beach decides to send reinforcements to South Africa.

Quthing — Thursday, February 13, 1879

For some days now, Quthing sergeant Isaak Masin has been watching a man named Pindu who has been sitting under a tree or talking to people around the magistracy. Masin talked briefly with Pindu a few days ago. The man said he had fled the turmoil in the north to seek a safer area in which to stay.

But Masin is suspicious and today confronts Pindu once more.

"You, Pindu, you are a rebel," Masin says. You are listening to other people speaking, you are watching what we are doing. I know you, Pindu. I know you are a rebel."

"Alright, then, Isaak, let's have a test," Pindu replies.

"If I tell you where some of the rebels are hiding and you find they are hiding there, will you then believe me that I am not a rebel? Would I tell you, a policeman, if I, too, am a rebel?"

"That makes sense, Pindu. You show us where the rebels are hiding and we will no longer call you a rebel and we will not lock you up. Wait here and I will call Mr. Austen, the magistrate."

Inside his office, Austen is reading a letter from Griffith. It reminds him of Nero who was said to have fiddled while Rome burned.

"With reference to my 'circular memorandum' of the 7th of November 1878, setting forth a uniform system for conducting correspondence in this territory, I have the honour to draw your attention to the third paragraph thereof and to explain that when your communications extend beyond the first page of a sheet of foolscap such sheet must remain intact. Should your communication be short and written on the first page, or in other words, on one side of a half sheet, then, in such case only, must the corresponding half sheet be torn off."

Typical of Griffith, Austen grunts. He instructs how pages should be torn while the world explodes around him.

"I am sorry to interrupt you, sir," Masin says.

"Yes, what is it?"

Masin recounts his talk with Pindu. Austen resists the temptation to respond, "Did he say that on a half sheet of paper, or did the message go on to a second page? And where did you tear off the page?" But he resists the temptation.

"I will talk with him." The men walk out of the office; Pindu is waiting.

"So, Pindu, you will lead us to a rebel hideout?" Austen asks.

"Yes. I will take you to where Nepha and Sieponi are hiding. They helped Lehana to break out of the jail. They are rebels. I am not a rebel. I am here because I want to be safe."

As Masin did, Austen fears Pindu might be laying a trap for them. Yet he is willing to take the chance because he desperately needs to vindicate himself. And arresting these men could lead them to Lehana.

He devises a plan to protect himself should the offer be a ruse. "Here's what I suggest, Pindu," Austen says. "You will go ahead of us, lead us to the place where the rebels are hiding and talk to them. While you are talking, we will arrive and arrest them."

Pindu agrees. Austen says he will meet Pindu at the magistracy on Saturday.

Quthing — Saturday, February 15, 1879

Austen leads the group of policemen, on horseback, toward the village, a little distance behind Pindu, who is walking on ahead. With Austen is an informant named Mapara who is willing to identify the men who broke open the jail.

Austen carries a rifle. Rather than relying on the policemen, who botched the last attempt to find the prisoners in a cave, he is taking the lead himself.

The group approaches a stream with thick bushes into which Pindu has walked. This is the place Pindu said the rebels were hiding. Austen signals his men to walk slowly and hunch down.

"There they are," Masin whispers. He points ahead. Two men are standing on the path, talking. One is Pindu.

As they get closer, they hear the men arguing. Mapara, the informant, identifies the other man as Nepha, one of the men who broke open the jail. They creep closer until the men are in earshot.

"You are going to tell the magistrate where we are," Nepha says to Pindu.

"No, Nepha, I will not do that. I will not tell him where you are."

"Why then are you here?" he asks. "Why have you come to talk to me about nothing? You are a traitor."

Nepha pushes Pindu backward. Pindu slips on the stony path and falls into bushes at the side of the path. "I will show you what people like you deserve," Nepha shouts at Pindu. "I will show you what it means to be a traitor to your people."

He pounces on Pindu, hitting him in the shoulders and chest.

Austen walks quickly to the fighting men. He raises his rifle.

"Nepha, you are under arrest for releasing Lehana from jail," he says.

Nepha stands upright. "You did betray us," he shouts at Pindu. "You deserve to die." He spits on the ground.

"Stop that immediately," Austen says. "You will come with me."

The policemen surround Nepha, seize him and bind his hands. Pindu realizes that if he does not reveal the whereabouts of Sieponi, who is close enough to hear what is being said, that Sieponi will track him down and possibly kill him.

"Sieponi is in the bushes over there," he says, pointing.

Austen raises his rifle and fires several shots into the bushes.

"Do not shoot anymore," a voice shouts. "We will come out."

Three men emerge from the bush. Another flees upstream. Austen orders two policemen to pursue him.

"I am here to arrest you," Austen says, pointing his rifle toward them. He turns to their informant. "Mapara, is this one of the men who broke open the jail?"

"Yes," Mapara says reluctantly as Sieponi glares at him.

The policemen tie the men's hands and escort them up the hill to where the horses are waiting. Austen and the policemen ride slowly alongside the men, who are forced to walk back to the magistracy.

As they make their way on a trail along the side of a mountain, the two policemen who pursued the fifth man join them, saying that the man got away. They identified him as Ditlame, a son of Moorosi. They also saw blood spots on the ground, indicating that Ditlame had been injured.

Austen is annoyed that once again his policemen have allowed a man to escape. But he is satisfied that he has caught the ringleaders of the breakout group. And he is confident they will help him track down the prisoners, including Lehana.

Quthing — Monday, February 17, 1879

Austen's first tasks today are to obtain confessions from the men arrested on Saturday and then to try them. He orders them to stand in front of his desk and two of the policemen who accompanied him to act as witnesses.

Nepha says Moorosi himself instigated the breakout. He says he worked under instructions from Moorosi's son Somathube who was riding his father's white horse and who said he was following his father's orders.

"Somathube said his father would never consent to the disarmament of the people," he adds.

In his confession, Sieponi says he also acted under instructions from Somathube who said Moorosi wanted Lehana to be rescued because the white people would take him away to the colony.

Austen sentences Nepha to three months and Sieponi to six months imprisonment, each with hard labour. But he still has not come any closer to finding out where Lehana is hiding.

Quthing — Wednesday, February 19, 1879

Moorosi's mountain is today the scene of an urgent discussion among the Baphuthi king and senior family members. Other family members and advisers sit in a large circle facing the men.

Every man is armed with a gun or spear.

"You might have heard that the white soldiers have been sent to Palmietfontein," Moorosi tells the assembly. "I ask you, my people, the people whom I love, is this not a sign that our country is to be invaded and they are to seize us? Why would they assemble there if they do not intend to use those men to attack us?

"Has the government not said we will be punished? Have they not said they will capture us if we resist their orders?"

The listeners are quiet.

"Now, this magistrate, Austen, has fired on my son Ditlame. Fortunately, his wounds were not too bad. But Austen tried to kill him and he also shot and killed two other of our people when all they were doing was standing in the bushes with the others. Why?

"Chief Letsie is talking with us about Lehana and the other escaped prisoners. Why is Austen acting like this and shooting us when we are talking to Letsie about these matters? Is Letsie nobody that he should be passed by in this way? Why do they not wait to hear what we have decided?

"When I attended a church service at Masitise on Sunday, the missionary Ellenberger had a long talk with me. He told me I should hand over Lehana to the government people. He said that if I do not do so, they will come after me and that Letsie and other chiefs will also send their people after me. He says that Lehana is one man and one life, but if I resist the government in this matter I will put the lives of all my people at risk.

"He said it is better to concede one thing than it is to be hard-hearted and to invite a war.

"I thought carefully about what he said because Ellenberger is a good man and I know that he wants the best for me and my people. That is why I asked him to be my missionary. He is a man of peace who is always looking to prevent trouble.

"But I said I did not want to do that as the last time I did so Austen wanted to send Lehana to a jail in Cape Town for four years. At the time, the missionary told me that he would talk with the government and tell them to take away the jail sentence on Lehana, but that did not happen.

"Now he again wants me to hand over Lehana because he says it will bring peace. I thought about it again. But it is difficult for me to take that step because this time I know they will punish him more severely because he has broken out of the jail. I know they will send him away and we will not see him again. I will prevent them doing so because he is my son and because he will take over as king when I go.

"Now I thought I would like to talk to the magistrate about the sentence, but I could not because I am afraid he will arrest me for hiding Lehana.

"I was not sure what to do because I also want peace.

"But now the decision has been made for me. I can no longer talk to the government people or hand over Lehana. When Austen fired on our people he showed he does not want peace. He will attack us whatever we do."

Moorosi stands to give his words more impact. He shakes his fist in the air. He shouts so all can hear.

"My people, listen to what I say.

"Austen has started a war against us. He did not wait to hear what we would say. He showed he will shoot us if we do not do as he says.

"We cannot let that happen.

"The white government has assembled soldiers on the banks of the Telle River because they want to invade us in the way they invaded the land of Sarhili. They want to destroy us in the way they tried to destroy Cetshwayo.

"We cannot let that happen.

"They have said they will take away our weapons. They want to take our guns away because they know we will be unable to defend ourselves when they invade our land.

"We cannot let that happen.

"They will try to take me prisoner, too, to try me in their court, to sentence me, and send me to the breakwater in Cape Town.

"We cannot let that happen.

"If we let these things happen, they will take away our freedom. They will take away our land and give our land to white farmers and build European houses and European towns on our land. They will force our people to work for them on the farms and in their towns. They will break up our families. They will destroy our way of life — the way of life our ancestors taught us and that has served us well for generations and generations.

"They will make us their slaves. They will rob us of our happiness and make us miserable people.

"We have tried to be good to our visitors, as our custom demands. We have accepted the magistrates on our land because we know they can teach us new things, show us new ways, and protect us from our enemies. We have tried to work with them. But now they have shown they are not interested in working with us or among us or helping us. They are interested only in destroying us.

"We say to them now: This is enough.

"If you want war, you will get war.

"I would rather die fighting for my people, their land and their way of life than live under white people, forced to live according to their laws and to work for them for long hours and little money.

"So it is that we will go out and fight when they come to get us.

"If the people they send against us outnumber us and try to defeat us the way they defeated Sarhili, we will make our homes here on this mountain top where we can defend ourselves and where we can live for many months and even years. We are stronger than Sarhili. We have more ways to protect ourselves. I have fought many battles and I know we can chase away the whites so they will leave us to live on our own. They will run from us like dogs with their tails between their legs.

"I know some of you do not want to fight. You say you also do not want to send your sons and your brothers into battle only to die at the hands of the white man.

"But we can do nothing else. To surrender is to give up life. You will be like a lion that is put in an enclosure where it cannot run where it wishes, where it cannot live with its family, where it cannot hunt and where it depends on people to feed it. That lion will say to itself, 'I will rather die than live like this.' But once he is put in the enclosure he cannot choose to die; he is forced to live in such a way that life has lost all meaning. It is better for that lion that he dies when they try to put him in the enclosure than to live as a captive.

"So it will be with us and with our wives, with our sons, with our daughters, with our brothers, with our sisters, with our cousins and with our uncles if the white government takes away our weapons, takes away our land, forces us to live according to their laws and makes us work for their people. It is better for us to die than to live in their enclosure."

The men around him nod in agreement.

"We will fight," they say in unison. "Wherever King Moorosi leads us, we will fight. We do not want to be like a lion in an enclosure.

"Lead us on, King Moorosi. We will fight with you."

Moorosi smiles. He sits.

He is pleased at the support he receives.

"Now," he says, "we must discuss how we are going to fight. We must be prepared to attack them before they build up their strength and attack us."

Quthing — Friday, February 21, 1879

Reports of Moorosi's preparations for war during his mountaintop summit are reaching Austen. "This is grave news," Austen tells Maitin after the men leave. "All the stories point in the same direction and so there must be some truth in them. We cannot allow ourselves to be overrun. We have no means of defending ourselves against the hundreds and possibly thousands of men that Moorosi will bring with him when he attacks us here."

"We need to act before Moorosi does. We cannot afford to be taken by surprise." Still smarting under the criticism of his inaction on New Year's night, Austen is determined to take the initiative.

"First, I will send policemen out as scouts to let us know when Moorosi and his warriors start to head in our direction.

"Second, I will send an urgent note to the commanding officer at Palmietfontein telling him that Moorosi intends to attack here tonight and asking him to send every available man up here at once to defend this office tonight.

"If I send the request by special messenger it should reach Palmietfontein in a few hours, giving the officer time to gather his troops and be here by nightfall."

Conceding that Austen's idea is an appropriate one, Maitin nevertheless is afraid that Austen's actions might precipitate war rather than prevent it. "Should you not inform Griffith of your intentions and gain his permission?"

"How can I possibly do that?" Austen snaps back. "He is two days' ride away — and that by express post. Don't you understand, Mr. Maitin? Did you not listen as you translated and wrote down those words from the informants? The chief is planning to attack us here tonight. *Tonight.*"

"With all respect, Mr. Austen, sir, I understood the informants to say that Moorosi would attack at night, but not necessarily tonight."

"They might have not used the word 'tonight', but they said he intends to start the war immediately. To me, that can mean only one thing. 'Immediately' and 'at night' mean tonight."

Austen writes to the commanding officer in Palmietfontein: "I have just heard from a reliable source that the Chief Moorosi sent this morning to call up all the people who acknowledge him on the northeast side of the Orange River to catch their horses and come up to him; that he is tired of seeing the forces at Palmietfontein and is coming down to attack this place tonight and kill all the officers and sweep the country down to the Telle River and stop your forces there.

"Under these circumstances I have to request that you will be good enough to march every available man up here at once, in light marching order, to defend this office tonight.

"Have also to request that you will be good enough to send an express to Captain Hook, the resident magistrate of Herschel, to move up with all his available men to the Palmietfontein Camp to cooperate with us if necessary; and I think it would also be advisable that you should ask Captain Hook to send an express to Aliwal North and telegraph this intelligence to Government."

Bearing in mind Maitin's advice about consulting Griffith, Austen adds, "I am sending an express letter to the governor's agent with this information at once."

He makes two copies of the letter for his records, seals it, summons a messenger and tells him to deliver it immediately to Palmietfontein.

His next step is to write to Griffith. Enclosing the copy of his letter to the commanding officer and outlining his course of action, he adds, "I have no other course open to me, but to take the present precautionary steps," adding, "I will stay at my post to the last."

Quthing — Saturday, February 22, 1879

Austen sleeps fitfully, expecting to hear blood-curdling yells at any time. But the night is quiet. He rises before dawn and assesses the situation: The troops he requested did not arrive, but neither did any attack. He remains convinced, however, that an assault from Moorosi's warriors could come at any time.

"As you noted, the report said he would attack at night," he tells Maitin. "We have survived one night and should be grateful for that. I expect the troops from Palmietfontein to arrive today so that we will be ready tonight."

At his mountain fortress, Moorosi considers his strategy in his fight to retain his independence and how he should defend himself against the colonial troops should they be sent to arrest him and to take his arms away from him. Most important is the degree of support he will receive from the paramount chief, Letsie. But the Basotho king has been sending him mixed messages. A message from Letsie says "The government wants to disarm the Basotho, but Letsie will refuse to give up his arms." But in other messages, Letsie advises Moorosi to surrender Lehana and the men who broke open the jail. "If you refuse to hand over the men and want to fight against the British Government (which is the government given to me by my late father Moshoeshoe) you had better fight your own battle, wherever you like, but not in my country," one message said.

Letsie cannot have it both ways, Moorosi reckons. "Either we are to fight the government or we are not to fight the government. Either we cooperate or we don't. Either we hand over our guns or we don't."

Sketch of northwest end of Moorosi's mountain. The grotto is on the top of the mountain, on the right, and the Orange River is below [contemporary sketch by Arthur Pattisson].

Moorosi, sitting outside a grotto on the northern end of the mountain top, calls Lemena to sit alongside him.

"I hear two messages from Letsie so I cannot depend on him to help me," he says. "What do you think we should do, Lemena? You have lived on the diamond mines, learned how the whites live, and how they think. What do you think?"

As they talk, men move forward to listen. Soon a hundred or more — headmen, relatives, doctors and advisers — are sitting or squatting in a semicircle around them.

"I do not like war," Lemena says in a quiet tone. "We are not soldiers like the whites. No one will pay us for the months to be away from our fields, hidden behind rocks or watching the roads that lead to the white government's houses. War takes men like us away from home, it makes us hungry, tired and cold. Some will die. We will lose our cattle."

His listeners nod.

"The animals that fight, they are always miserable. The lion must skulk and hide in the daytime. He has no rest. In his old age he is thin; then he is weak and his end is unhappy. But the sheep rests. He is fat and people take care of him instead of fearing him. The quiet horse is well treated and loved, but the ill-tempered one is starved and beaten. So it is with people. If we have war we cannot improve ourselves. We will have no rest. We will become thin and weak.

Kimberley, 13 years after the discovery of diamonds in 1866. Many Baphuthi men worked on the diamond mines where they often bought rifles to take back home. [*Souvenir Album of the Orange Free State, 1954*]

"There can be nothing better than for a nation to be at peace."

The audience nods again. Some murmur their agreement.

For a while everyone is silent. Moorosi starts to speak. "What you say is —"

"But," Lemena interrupts, his mood turning from solemnity to shouting. "But I... But I...." He jumps up, tearing off the shirt he bought at the diamond mines. "But I do not believe that to be true now. This shirt is holding me back. Like the life I was told at the diamond mines in Kimberley that I would like, it is confining me. The shirt has been telling me what to say.

"No." He throws the shirt to the ground. "No, it is better to be free than enslaved. The whites' way of life is like slavery. Clothes are slavery. School is slavery. The church is slavery. These are the things that make people children all their lives when they would be men and women."

Lemena kicks the shirt away from the area in front of the hut.

"Must these things take our manhood from us? Are the whites going to come here to insult our king, Moorosi, to walk over our mountains, to trample over our graves, to steal our cattle, to take away our horses and must we, because of ploughs and clothes and box-shaped houses and books and things our fathers never knew, and comforts they never sought, sit still when we should spring up to defend our chief, his honour and our homes?

"The white man's houses are built only of brick. He is only a man in a house. Our home is the mountain. All the land is ours. We are above the white man.

"Let those who want King Moorosi and freedom join with me. Is not freedom worth more than a blanket from the white man's store, and the name of a Baphuthi warrior better than the name of a white soldier?"

Moorosi stands up alongside Lemena.

"You are right, Lemena," he says. "I do not care what Letsie thinks because I must protect myself, my son and my family. If I don't do so, I will be a dead man.

"Will you fight with me? Will you protect our people? Will you drive the whites out of our land when they attack us?"

The Baphuthi listeners stand up, raise their fists and cheer.

"We will fight with you our King. We are yours, our King Moorosi. We are yours."

As they are cheering, a messenger walks up to the hut. He says Ellenberger is asking Moorosi to meet with him. The missionary is concerned, the message says, that the state of affairs appears to be heating up and would like Moorosi to come to the cave house and sit on the Wodehouse bench.

"Tell the missionary I would like to talk with him, but I am busy right now."

Maseru — The same day

When Griffith receives a copy of Austen's request for soldiers from Palmietfontein to defend his office, his anger is once more aroused.

"Look what this idiot Austen has done now," he says, walking into Rolland's office and throwing the report on his desk. Rolland quickly reads it.

"You don't think it is a good idea to send troops to protect Austen?" asks Rolland.

"Of course it is not," splutters Griffith. "Austen is panicking. Imagine what Moorosi's reaction will be when he sees that our forces are crossing the Telle River and marching into his territory, ready to fight against him."

"Does Austen have the authority to give orders to those forces?" Rolland asks.

"He does not, and I can only hope that the officer commanding at Palmietfontein would have the good sense to decline his request. In any event, I do not believe the officer would act without authorization from a more senior source. But if he does, we could have an extremely serious situation on our hands."

"Austen believes he is facing a serious threat," Rolland responds. "He is trying to protect himself and our offices."

"I do not believe Moorosi would dream of attacking Mr. Austen unless he felt sure that he had the support of Letsie, which I am convinced he has not got.

"Moorosi is an obstinate old man and will very likely continue to refuse to give up his son and the others, but he will act strictly on the defensive. I have spoken about these things with George Moshesh and other trustworthy Basotho and they agree with me.

"Letsie tells me he has sent messengers to Moorosi pleading with him to hand over his son Lehana rather than face a confrontation that could end up badly for him. We should give an opportunity for that advice to have an effect. Moorosi respects Letsie and will be inclined to go along with what he advises him to do."

"Yes, I suppose that is a good idea," Rolland says. "But Mr. Austen is worried about his own safety should these reports prove true. I know you say they are false, but can you blame him if he seeks to protect himself should they prove to be true?"

Griffith paces up and down the room. Perhaps he has been hasty in dismissing Austen's concerns. But Austen cannot be allowed to call out troops. There must be another answer.

"Very well, you have a point," Griffith says. "Let us assume, even though I do not for one moment believe it, there is good reason for Austen to believe that it is unsafe for him and the other officers to remain at their post. Then the proper step would be to go to Palmietfontein, taking with them the government chest and the records of the office.

"Calling for armed support is madness. Even if half the men stationed at Palmietfontein were to be moved north to Quthing, they would be unable to defend the buildings anyway. Given its physical situation and the number of men Moorosi would be able to muster to sweep down on it from the surrounding hills, it would be impossible to defend it.

"Also, moving armed men into the magistracy is likely to precipitate matters with Moorosi. All doubts he might have had about intentions to attack him would be wiped away. It would also cause great confusion and excitement in the Quthing District as well as Basutoland generally.

"In addition, the small force at Palmietfontein would be divided in two, leaving both vulnerable to attack. No, if Austen feels he is in danger, then his course is to fall back on Palmietfontein. It is only ten miles from his office."

Griffith telegraphs the officer commanding at Palmietfontein, telling him not to accede to Austen's request for troops. He sends a letter to Austen telling him if he really feels in danger he should leave for Palmietfontein, but he should under no circumstances call up troops to his office.

Ibika, Transkei — The same day

Ox wagon travels across a rough road in the eastern Cape Colony.

The war fever in Baphuthi country is reverberating in the Cape Colony, where the authorities feel the need to strengthen the forces at Palmietfontein so they can be ready for any contingency.

Today, members of the Cape Mounted Riflemen who fought in the war against Sarhili and the Gcaleka start their journey after being ordered to take three ox-wagon loads of supplies and ammunition to the front at Palmietfontein.

Among them are three friends — Alex Granville, Peter Brown and Robert Scott — who have been stationed at Ibika for eight months. They often saw action together in the frontier war, where they developed their friendship, but have been conducting routine police activity in Ibika since they were stationed here.

"Something must be going on up there," Brown says. "I guess the natives are giving trouble, otherwise why would they need the troops and the ammunition? Well, I am ready to fight again. Let me at them."

Towed by 16 oxen each, the heavy wagons make their way slowly across the flat plain. The men know the going will be rougher as they encounter hills and rivers fed by the summer rains on the road ahead, but soon they will be in Palmietfontein, ready for action.

Quthing — The same day

It is early afternoon as Joseph Thomas closes his trading store near Raisa's village for the day, and mounts his horse on his way to spend the evening and Sunday at the home of Henry Buckland, manager of his store near Masitise. From there, he plans to travel into the Cape Colony where he needs to attend to business. He has placed his store in the hands of a Baphuthi assistant while he is away.

As he makes his way down the hill leaving his trading post, Thomas senses that something is different in Raisa's village.

At first, he is unsure what it is. Then he notices that horses are being kept near the kraals. Normally at this time of day they are in the fields where they can graze. The large group of horses in the village suggests they are being held ready for immediate use or for protection — the sort of measure taken only in emergencies.

Thomas rides down the path to Buckland's store, convinced that the rumours he has picked up of war readiness may be more than mere hearsay.

Buckland is waiting anxiously outside the store he runs near the Masitise mission station as Thomas rides up. "A Baphuthi man who lives nearby arrived here a short time ago and told me to remove all my stock from the country without delay," Buckland says. "I know him to be a reliable source of information."

"Why did he say you should do that?" Thomas asks.

"He said war could start at any moment."

"It is all starting to add up," Thomas says, keeping his voice low. "I have been hearing these rumours, too. And, as I left my shop near Raisa's village I noticed the horses were being kept in the kraals.

"I am going to tell Mr. Austen about this warning and find out what he knows. I must go down to the Cape Colony for a few days. But I will return as soon as I can. It looks as though we must be ready to leave at any time."

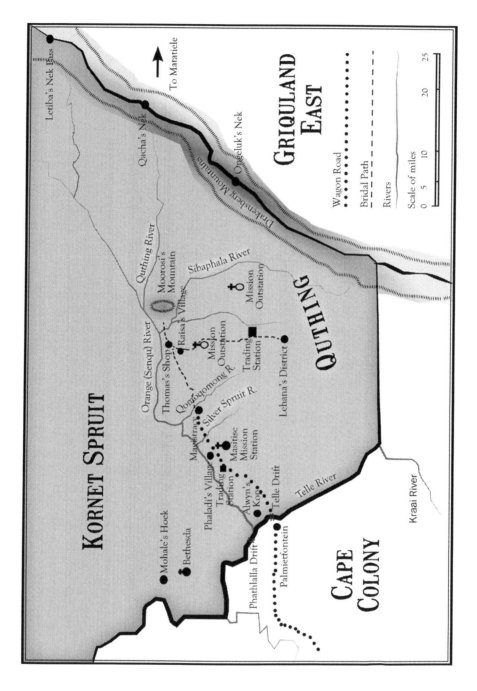

12

Quthing — Sunday, February 23, 1879

Usually, Austen is able to relax on a Sunday, but not today. Reports of an imminent attack continue to reach him.

He feels isolated and vulnerable, particularly as Captain Surmon, the commander in Palmietfontein, has refused his request for a platoon of soldiers. The only help he received was six volunteers from the Herschel district who had read reports in the Aliwal North newspaper of unrest in Quthing. They arrived yesterday, but would be of little help in a full-scale attack.

He rises early today after a sleepless and nervous night and sees Ellenberger and another white man passing the magistracy.

"Good morning, reverend," Austen calls out, walking up to speak to him. "Where are you headed?"

"My friend, Mr. Vernet, who is from Geneva, and I are on our way to Sunday church services at our outpost at Qomoqomong, south of Thomas's Shop. One of our church leaders, Philemon, is preaching this morning at Masitise."

"You seem calm in spite of the crisis."

"What crisis?"

"Moorosi is about to attack us."

"He is?"

"Yes, I have received numerous reports that he is about to sweep down on our magistracy, attack us and destroy our buildings and then make for the border where he intends to confront the forces at Palmietfontein."

Ellenberger is surprised. "I have heard rumours that Moorosi will protect himself against any invasion from the forces at Palmietfontein, but I have not heard of any attack and I have heard nothing along the lines of what you describe."

"I find your response surprising, reverend," Austen replies. "All my informants have told me that the forces are being gathered for an attack. They are armed. They are aggressive. And they are ready to fight."

"My people are going about their business as normal," Ellenberger replies. "I have invited King Moorosi to the opening of my new church, which is now complete. I am expecting to hear back from him this afternoon. Should I hear of anything untoward, I will let you know."

Austen thanks Ellenberger. He shakes his head in disbelief as he walks back to his office.

Before long, Baphuthi whom he regards as reliable arrive to tell him that Moorosi has sent a force of armed men to Raisa's village, a few hours' ride to the north. There they will gather more men and from there, Austen is told, Moorosi intends to attack the magistracy.

Austen is aware that Raisa has wanted revenge against the government ever since Hope fined him for destroying a widow's cornfield. He also recalls the time in Mohale's Hoek when he issued a hut-tax waiver to widows in Moorosi's district. Hope's refusal to accept the waiver created resentment in Raisa's village. It is not surprising, therefore, that his village should be among the first ready to rebel.

Austen's scouts also report that Moorosi has ordered that cattle be driven to his mountain top.

More preparations for war.

Maitin, too, is anxious, but cannot believe rumours that they are to be killed. He has never encountered any feelings of hostility directed at him personally by the Baphuthi people. But he accepts that if the magistracy is to be attacked he might be in the way.

"Are you sure these threats are serious?" he asks.

"I am. I think anyone would be delusional not to believe them. There have been too many reports and all are so similar. We are left with no choice but to leave here," Austen tells him. "I think we need to leave for Palmietfontein and consult with Captain Surmon and Captain Grant there."

Maitin agrees.

And so it is that the magistrate who professed two days ago that he would stay at his post to the last decides to abandon the magistracy.

"Once we reach Palmietfontein, I will apply to the commanding officer for a couple of wagons to remove all the government property and my furniture from here," Austen says. "I will return with the wagons, but I will need an armed escort. All I hope is that we can take them across the border in time."

He and Maitin pack a few personal belongings and strap them on pack donkeys. They saddle their horses. "We should be able to reach the border and safety at Palmietfontein by late afternoon," Austen says.

Austen instructs the policemen to follow them and drive their own cattle and those of the magistracy to the border.

As Austen and Maitin ride along the wagon road to the border, they spot scouts on the hillsides above them. Austen knows they will be reporting what they see to Moorosi.

Passing the mission station at Masitise, Austen suggests they ride up to the cave house to check that Emma Ellenberger is safe in the absence of her husband.

She tells Austen and Maitin that, along with her husband, she has not heard any reports that the Baphuthi are planning to attack.

"I am convinced Moorosi is determined to fight and I am expecting him to attack the magistracy tonight," Austen tells her. "My situation has become untenable. I believe I am acting prudently by leaving."

"You mean you are leaving us to the mercy of people bent on war?"

"I do not believe that Moorosi has any quarrel with you, your husband and the mission station," Austen says. "I believe his quarrel is with us. But you are welcome to join us and seek safety across the Telle."

"Thank you, but I am sure that, as you say, the king has no quarrel with us. We intend to stay here, Mr. Austen. No matter what happens we will trust in God to see to us and protect us. My husband quoted only yesterday the verse from Psalms, 'It is better to trust in the Lord than put our confidence in princes.' That is what we will do if there is trouble."

As Austen and Maitin prepare their horses before leaving, Ellenberger and his companion Vernet, arrive back from conducting a service at the outstation.

"I told you I was unconcerned, but, after talking with our people at the outstation, I am afraid there might be some reason for concern," Ellenberger says.

"I asked them pointed questions about their king's attitude and I now understand your concern a little better. I still do not think there is any reason to leave here, but I was able to confirm reports that Moorosi is regarded as being in open rebellion against the government. Whether that will translate to actual fighting, it is impossible to say, although I consider it unlikely, at least at this stage."

Austen asks Ellenberger to write a note outlining what he has heard about Moorosi's rebellious plans.

"I would like to pass it on to the authorities," he says.

Ellenberger agrees. "I will write what I have heard, but I still do not think there is reason to panic," he says.

Austen thanks him and takes the note. He will enclose it with a letter to Griffith telling him why he has fled the magistracy.

After they have ridden four or five miles farther down the road, Austen looks back and sees a party of mounted men in the distance following them. He had seen them earlier, but now they are much closer.

"We need to move faster, Mr. Maitin; they appear to be gaining on us."

They whip their horses and donkeys, shouting at them and encouraging the slow animals to pick up speed.

Austen and Maitin round a bend and the drift over the Telle River comes into view. They can gain speed now because the rest of the road is downhill.

The men who have been following them stop at a hilltop and watch them.

As they cross the drift into the Cape Colony, Austen breathes a sigh of relief. They are safe. At least, for now.

Austen tells Captain Surmon what has happened. He says he wants to return to the magistracy to retrieve the rest of his goods.

"I would like a wagon and an armed escort," he says.

"I am afraid I cannot do that, Mr. Austen."

"Why not?"

"I have no authority to cross the Telle," Surmon replies. "We are not permitted to operate outside the Cape Colony. Even though the colony has responsibility for Basutoland, this is still the border and unless I have specific orders from the Cape colonial government, I cannot enter Basutoland. That is why I had to turn down your request a few days ago to send a group of men."

Austen is too afraid to return on his own. He will wait in Palmietfontein.

⚜

The mounted men on the Quthing side note that the magistrate is talking with a man dressed in an army uniform. They head back to report to Moorosi.

Clearly the white men are preparing for an attack, they will tell him. The magistrate has left his offices and joined the troops and has been talking with the leaders of the government army.

It adds up to one message: An attack from across the border is imminent and their king must be ready to defend himself and his people.

Maseru — Monday, February 24, 1879

Griffith, unaware that Austen and his staff fled across the border yesterday, feels pleased with his progress in enlisting the support of Letsie. He is heartened when he receives a copy of a message Letsie has sent to Moorosi. Clearly Letsie is trying to be a peacemaker.

"Last year, I was unhappy with the white authorities," the message says. "I was dissatisfied with them because I thought Lehana had been wrongly treated. He was sentenced to a long term in prison only because he had run away. But now, it is clear that Lehana stole horses from white men in the Cape Colony."

Griffith smiles. Letsie clearly changed his mind when presented with the white authorities' view of the situation.

"The white man has taken nothing belonging to anybody," Letsie continues. "Why did Lehana capture white men's horses? Had those white men ever taken anything of Moorosi's?"

Good, Griffith thinks. He reads on.

"A great many of Moshoeshoe's sons have been imprisoned, but no one has broken open the jail to let them out. As far as I am concerned, they were justly punished. I have not yet experienced any injustice from the white men. I say to Moorosi: Are your children so very precious that they should be protected more than the children of Moshoeshoe?"

Letsie falls back on the Basotho claim that Quthing is part of their land.

"If you, Moorosi, lived in your own country, I would say nothing, but the territory that you occupy is my father's country.

"There was a time when you, Moorosi, defended my father, the great chief Moshoeshoe, while he was yet alive. Anyone who tried to attack Moshoeshoe would also be attacking you. In the same way, when you say you will fire on the white men, does it not mean that you will fire on me? I am at peace with the Queen. The inheritance from my father, Moshoeshoe, is to respect the white men because they are protecting us from our enemies.

"I believe that you should support me and, in supporting me, should support the white government."

Letsie adds in a note to Griffith: "I have sent this message with Molomo to Moorosi.

I have told him he must give the men who broke open the jail to me. If he is afraid to hand them over to Austen, let him bring them here and give them to me. I will take them to the court to be tried. If they are innocent, they will be returned to him. If they are guilty they will be put in prison."

Griffith is pleased with the message, but he is concerned that the time to reach Moorosi with Letsie's message of reconciliation is wasting away; the longer the message takes to reach Moorosi, the greater the chance that events will spiral out of control. Griffith is convinced it is time for him to step into the fray. He calls for three of his senior policemen.

"I want you to go to Moorosi as quickly as you can," he says. "You must tell him that I demand that he surrender Lehana and the other escaped prisoners," he tells them. "Also warn him of the danger he runs, to himself and his people, if he disobeys the order that I am sending him."

Griffith is hoping Letsie's message will have a stronger impact if it is backed up with his own. Together they will present Moorosi with the prospect of a conflict he cannot win.

War can still be prevented, Griffith believes. He is confident that the combined messages and threats will be sufficient to cause Moorosi to back down, hand over the prisoners and agree to cooperate.

But Griffith's confidence in a peaceful resolution of the conflict is shaken when he receives a telegram from Native Affairs Secretary Ayliff in which he says the urgency of Austen's telegram has prompted him to send Col. R.G. Southey and the 260 troops of the 2nd Yeomanry to join the troops at Palmietfontein. Additional ammunition and supplies are already on the way.

Griffith laughs mockingly when he reads the final sentence: "Hope this affair may be settled without the use of force."

He wants to shout so loudly that the secretary can hear him wherever he is, "Not if you support Austen in his panic. The more troops you send to Palmietfontein, the more likely war becomes."

Quthing — The same day

The news that Austen and his staff have fled the magistracy conveys a strong message to Moorosi. Talk, he believes, does not always reflect what is in a man's heart, but action does. The lion's roar might be a pretence; it is only when the lion starts running toward its prey that you know it means to attack.

"His flight means only one thing," Moorosi tells Lehana. "They are preparing for war. He is joining the white soldiers at Palmietfontein. From there they will attack us."

Lehana agrees. "When a snake defends its position under a rock, it does not wait in the darkness at the back of the rock for you to attack it," he says. "It comes to the front and it shows you its fangs. It shows you it is ready to fight to defend itself.

"So we must show the white government we are ready to defend ourselves when they come to attack us. "

"You are right, my son," says Moorosi. "Tell the men in the villages they must be ready tonight to confront the whites and to defend ourselves from their attack. They must have their weapons ready and be prepared to use them in the way that the snake shows its fangs. They must show the whites we are not afraid of them.

"We must also show our fangs to those Baphuthi who support the government. Tell our people to take their cattle. The Christians who follow Ellenberger will not support us; their cattle must be taken, too, so they will know we will not tolerate any support for the enemy.

"But also tell them not to attack the missionary. Respect him, for he does good work; he does not want to attack us and we must not attack him. It is the government that wants to attack us, to take our weapons and our land from us."

The men from the surrounding villages start to gather at the base of Moorosi's Mountain. Hundreds of Baphuthi warriors dance and chant in unison, raising their spears and their rifles, echoing the words of their lead singer Lemena. Before long, their war songs are reverberating across the valleys.

"Tonight, we will resist the invaders.

"We will drive away the government men.

"We will show them we will not be subjugated.

"We will resist their attempts to disarm us.

"We will defend our land, the land our ancestors gave us.

"Tonight we will fight to keep our freedom."

Lemena stands and faces the warriors as he sings a praise-poem to Moorosi, asking for God to bless him. The warriors wave their spears and dance in time with the rhythm of the song.

"The Protector of the son of Mokuoane,

Who darkens the sun and makes it as dusk,

Saying that the orphans should walk in the shade,

That those should live whose fathers have died.

Protect now the son of Mokuoane

As the guns point their mouths at each other

Protect the one who was born a warrior."

Lemena turns to face Moorosi:

"We're yours, son of Mokuoane,

"We're dogs, bulldogs of yours

"We'll strike with you at the nations."

The warriors raise their spears in a salute to Moorosi and shout their support, echoing the words of Lemena. "We're yours, son of Mokuoane. We're dogs, bulldogs of yours. We'll strike with you at the nations.

"We're yours, son of Mokuoane. We're dogs, bulldogs of yours. We'll strike with you at the nations."

As the intoxicating singing and dancing continues into the darkness of the night, the line between defence and attack becomes blurred. A display of defensive force-fulness transforms into a demonstration of determined fire power.

Some of the men start moving forward, eager to turn their ardour into action. As they move, others join them and the throng of advancing warriors grows in number.

Still singing and dancing, they leave the mountain. Some turn toward Lehana's village. Others take the trail to Thomas's shop.

"We're yours, son of Mokuoane. We're dogs, bulldogs of yours. We'll strike with you at the nations."

"We're yours, son of Mokuoane. We're dogs, bulldogs of yours. We'll strike with you at the nations."

Their singing grows dimmer as they head south from the mountain.

"We're yours, son of Mokuoane. We're dogs, bulldogs of yours. We'll strike..."

Maseru — Tuesday, February 25, 1879

When he sees Maitin riding toward the Maseru magisterial compound, Griffith wonders what can have happened in Quthing to warrant his traveling the long distance to him. Seeing a look of urgency on Maitin's face, he strides to the door to greet him.

"What brings you here?"

"I have a letter from Mr. Austen that I thought it important to deliver it to you myself. Mr. Austen agreed to my request to bring it to you. Once you have read it, I will be able to elaborate on its contents."

The main content is a copy of a telegram Austen sent from Palmietfontein to the Secretary for Native Affairs "for the information of government." Once again, Griffith notes, Austen has gone over his head.

The telegram, dated Sunday February 23, reads: "I have to inform you that I found it absolutely necessary to vacate my seat of magistracy this morning, having had reliable information that the Chief Moorosi had called a considerable armed force to come down to the village of a subordinate chief named Raisa, about two hours' ride from my office, with the intention of attacking me and all loyal people and driving the cattle toward his mountain, which he had strongly fortified."

Griffith's jaw tightens as he reads how Austen abandoned his post, leaving all his furniture and government records behind.

"But I thought...I thought he was going to stay at his post to the last," he responds in anger.

"Only yesterday I received a letter that he was doing all he could to suppress reports about a supposed attack by Moorosi. He said he was fully aware of the exaggeration used by his informants. And now he leaves."

"He did intend to stay," Maitin ventures. "But..."

Griffith gives him no time to continue.

"What could possibly have happened to make him change his mind like this? First he says he will stay at his post to the end. Then he asks for armed support. When that does not happen, he gives up and abandons his post."

"We received reports that an attack was imminent, colonel. We were told that Moorosi would attack last night."

"And did he?"

"Well, colonel, I do not know yet. I left from Palmietfontein yesterday. I slept overnight on the way and rose early today to reach here as soon as possible."

Griffith grunts. "Very well. Thank you. But let's get this straight. These reports of an attack originated as a result of three causes.

"One was the presence of the force at Palmietfontein. That made the Baphuthi chief and his people afraid. I had always said that would happen and advised against sending additional troops there, but, as you know, I was overridden by the authorities in Cape Town.

"A second factor was Moorosi's anticipation of an attack from us to take away his guns in terms of the new disarmament law, which, as you know, has not yet been applied here and, I hope, might never be.

"We should have been telling him that it is not yet law.

"A third cause of these reports was undoubtedly the sad Natal disaster which has emboldened the native people around the country who see us as vulnerable in a way that they never saw before."

Maitin agrees that these were all contributory causes, but adds that the reports of an imminent attack by Moorosi were persistent. It was these reports on which Austen acted.

"Some of them came from people we know and trust," he says.

"Yes, my dear Mr. Maitin, that might be so," Griffith continues. "I am not suggesting that the people who gave you the reports were not reliable. I am suggesting that the reports themselves were not reliable. Your informants were merely passing on information that they had heard from others. Who knows where the 'others' received their information?"

"That is a good point, colonel. But surely, if I may say so, sir, the persistence and similarity of reports must testify to their veracity."

"Perhaps. But I continue to hold the view that this information has not been proven to be reliable.

"I am surprised that he should have found it 'absolutely necessary' to vacate his seat of magistracy, upon information that could be highly questionable. Now he is leaving the loyal natives to take care of themselves — and that in itself could drive them into the ranks of the hostile ones.

"All the evidence shows that Moorosi's people were acting more on the defensive than being aggressive.

"Now it is up to me to try to rescue what we can from this situation and to prevent a war. I intend to send Mr. E.O. Davies, acting resident magistrate here and one of my most senior officials, to assume the duties of acting resident magistrate at Quthing.

"We need to waste no time in showing the Baphuthi we will continue to run the magistrate's office as we have been doing for nearly two years. I do not want to give the impression that we have abandoned our presence there.

"I will direct Mr. Austen at once to send the constables he took with him to Palmietfontein back to Quthing.

"I intend to write to Mr. Austen informing him that his actions are unacceptable and that, pending further instructions from the government on the subject, he is to take two months' leave of absence."

Hearing reports that trouble in Quthing is becoming more serious, and concerned about the safety of his three trading stations, Joseph Thomas has cut short his visit to the Cape Colony and returned to Quthing.

At the trading station near Masitise, Thomas seizes the reins of a couple of pack horses and ties them together. He will take them to his trading station near Raisa's village and pack his most valuable goods on them. He has heard enough to concern him, and he wants to save at least some of the goods that represent his livelihood should fighting break out.

He sets off, riding past the vacated magistracy and on to the bridle path along the steep slopes of the Orange River to his shop near Raisa's village.

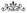

When Moorosi's lesser son and praise singer Lemena arrives at the Quthing magistracy no one is around. Austen and Maitin have gone and so have the policemen. Even the cattle and the horses are not there. He wonders where Austen and Maitin are. Why have they left? Have they taken some sort of break from work? The Europeans like to take holidays and go away. But when they do, they leave someone in charge. It never happens that no one is around.

The door of the courtroom is broken open. Lemena assumes someone was here earlier and broke it; surely Austen would not have left it like that. It is strange to see no policemen, no magistrate, no one in the jail. He wanders into the courtroom, picks up a criminal record book, looks through it, noting the names of people charged with crimes, found guilty and their sentences, and throws it down.

Surely, the explanation for their absence cannot be that they are afraid of Moorosi. The government is strong. Hope always said he was more powerful than Moorosi. Austen seemed to be more fearful than Hope, but surely he would not run away?

Perhaps they left the magistracy so they could prepare a big force across the border to invade Quthing. Why would they do that? Why would the force not join them at the magistracy and advance northward?

No explanation makes sense to him.

Lemena hears voices outside, one of which he recognizes as that of Matushela.

Five other men, including Moorosi's son Ratsuanyane, enter the courtroom. Lemena smiles. Casting aside the puzzle of the vacated magistracy, he is ready to turn the absence of the government officials into a party. "Let's hold a court hearing," he says. He sits behind the desk in the chair in which Hope and Austen have so often sat. He takes a record book, opens it and looks around. He had always wanted to be a magistrate.

"I call the case of the Queen versus Ratsuanyane," he says.

"Ratsuanyane is here. But where is the Queen?" asks Matushela. "Are you going to call her, too?"

"Yes, the Queen will come. She will be here any minute, wearing her crown and her long robes, but in the meantime we will go on with the case." Lemena says, laughing loudly.

Ratsuanyane takes up his position in the dock.

"You are accused of stealing cattle, telling lies and being a bad boy," Lemena says. "How do you plead?"

"I am not guilty," replies Ratsuanyane as more men join the group in the courtroom to watch the proceedings. Lemena dips an imaginary pen in an imaginary ink pot (the original seems to have gone) and pretends to write in the book.

"Let's have some witnesses," Lemena continues. "Who wants to say bad things about this man?"

Nk'a, one of the newly arrived men, walks up and enters the witness stand. Lemena leans forward and intones, "Do you swear to tell the truth, the whole truth and nothing but the truth?"

"I do," Nk'a says in a deep voice.

"You must put your hand on the Bible in the witness stand," Lemena shouts. "Why did you not do that when I first asked you to swear to tell the truth? Are you so stupid that you do not know what to do? You boys are all so stupid."

Nk'a quickly obeys.

"I am sorry my magistrate. I am sorry. I will do whatever you say, my magistrate."

The group in the courtroom, which has now grown to some 20 men, are enjoying the display.

"Tell the court, did you see the accused doing something wrong?"

"He always does something wrong," Nk'a says.

"When you speak to me you must say, your honour."

"I am sorry my magistrate. I am sorry. I will do whatever you say, my magistrate."

"I said: Your honour. You must say 'your honour.' I am so important you must call me that."

The assembled crowd laughs.

"He is a bad, bad boy, your honour."

More laughter.

"Please tell the court why he is a bad, bad boy," Lemena intones.

"Because he does not do what the white people tell him to do."

"He doesn't do what the white people tell him to do? Now I know why he is a bad, bad boy. That is a very, very bad thing to do."

More laughter. This is the most fun they have had in years.

Lemena calls for quiet.

He turns to Ratsuanyane. "I sentence you to be whipped twenty-four times with the cat-o'-nine-tails."

"If he is whipped once with the cat-o'-nine-tails, is that nine whippings all at once?" asks Matushela. "How many then is twenty-four whippings with nine cats? It is a lot."

"No, you are a stupid boy," Lemena replies. "It is one cat. But it has nine tails. It is not nine cats. Aw, you boys. I don't know what to do with you. You are so stupid."

As more laughter erupts, Lemena stands up from the desk and glares at the assembled men in a look reminiscent of Hope. "I am going to whip you all," he says. "I am so angry with you that I am losing my temper and I will punish you all."

His face wrinkled with mock anger, he seizes the desk with the books on it and throws it over.

Now the humour has made his onlookers realize how much they hate the system they are mocking. Suddenly, Ratsuanyane, reverting from laughter to seriousness, takes his spear and plunges it into the record books several times until they are in tatters. Others follow. Shredded books lie strewn across the floor and spears fly through the air as they are directed at any symbol of the government the men can find.

After destroying the desk and benches in the court room, the men run to Austen's house where they smash furniture and carry off clothing.

Still holding his spear, Ratsuanyane walks outside, raises his arms above his head and shakes them in victory.

"Now the government is dead," he shouts. "I must go and tell the king."

Thomas's trading station is on the right, his house on the left [contemporary photograph].

Approaching his trading station near Raisa's village, Thomas sees several Baphuthi gathered around the entrance. January, the assistant he had left in charge of the store, runs to meet him.

"I am sorry, Mr. Thomas," says January, son of a Khoisan mother and a Baphuthi father. "When I came to open the store this morning, I found it had been broken into last night. They took some things."

Thomas dismounts and enters the store. He can see that goods have been taken, although it has not been heavily looted.

"I must leave here and take as many of my goods with me as I can carry, January," he says. "It is not looking good. I will pack what I can on my horse and these two horses I have brought with me. I will return later to take the rest of my goods. I must close the store."

He grabs some of his most expensive blankets from the shelves, places them on the back of one of the horses, and secures them with a rope. He ties several shiny new pots to the rope.

As Thomas is attaching another set of blankets to a second horse, a number of armed men appear, almost, it seems, from nowhere. All are mounted.

"What is happening here?" asks Madekoni, as he dismounts. "King Moorosi says no goods are to be allowed to leave the country. But here the white man is getting ready to take the goods away."

Madekoni's men raise their rifles toward Thomas and January.

"Leave your goods here or we will shoot you," Madekoni says. "King Moorosi tells us the goods must stay."

For the first time as a trader here, Thomas feels real fear.

For the most part the Baphuthi people have been friendly, cooperative and grateful for his services. As they sold him their farm goods and bought saddles, blankets, pots and pans from him, they enjoyed talking with him; some swapped jokes with him; some even shared their personal stories with him. When January was in charge and Thomas was away, the store operated as normal and there was no attempt to disrupt trading.

Now it seems this group of warring men are furious at him for wanting to stop trading. He moves toward his horse.

"He is trying to take the goods away," Madekoni tells his men, their rifles still pointing at Thomas and January. "We must stop him doing so.

"Shoot him."

13

Quthing — The same day

Thomas stands still, frozen in place.

"I said: Shoot him," Madekoni repeats.

The men are reluctant to follow the order. For one thing, Thomas is standing still and not actually taking the goods, so shooting him does not seem justified. In addition, the men have a sense of respect and fear toward whites and they bear no personal animosity to Thomas.

As the seconds pass, Thomas, realizing that should he turn and run he almost certainly will be shot, stares at his would-be assassins. Their rifles loaded and cocked, the men remain poised to pull the triggers.

"What are you waiting for?" demands Madekoni. "Do you not know how to shoot? Let me show you what you need to do."

He cocks his rifle and raises it to his right eye. As he does, a group of men from Raisa's village, who have heard the loud talking and remonstrating and have come to find out what is happening, enter the room. It does not take them long to take in the scene. On one side stands Thomas, ashen-faced. Facing him a group of Baphuthi men are pointing their rifles at Thomas. Madekoni seems ready to shoot.

"Put down the weapons," one shouts. "Mr. Thomas is a good man. He is our friend."

Madekoni briefly lowers his rifle and turns to face the men. He is insistent. "None of the goods must go from here. The trader wants to take his goods. He must be stopped." He raises the rifle once more and aims it at Thomas.

The men continue to try to dissuade Madekoni from shooting. "If he wants to take his goods away for a while let him do so," the man says. "He will return them soon."

Madekoni shouts back, "Our orders are not to let him take the goods."

"Don't you see, he is not taking the goods. Take the rifle off your eye and you will see he is not taking the goods."

Madekoni lowers his rifle, turning to face his challenger and pointing to the horses loaded with goods. "Look at the pack horses over there. He has put his blankets and saddles on them. He wants to take the goods."

"Well, tell him not to do so. Why do you want to shoot him? Let him leave the goods. If you shoot him, bad things will happen."

As the men argue, January leans across to Thomas. "You must leave here as soon as you can," he whispers. "These men come from the area where King Moorosi lives. They are under orders from the chief. Ride only on your own horse from here. Do not take your goods or your pack horses with you. We will look after them."

Madekoni, conceding his challenger's argument has merit, moves closer toward Thomas, his rifle lowered, but still pointing toward the trader.

"Take those blankets and pots off the horses and put them back in the store," he says.

As Thomas starts to unpack one of the horses, Ratsuanyane arrives. He is on his way to tell Moorosi of the devastation at the magistracy and is attracted by the noise in the store. He goes to investigate. He is senior to Madekoni in the Baphuthi clan which immediately places him in command.

"What is going on here?" he asks.

"This man Thomas, he wants to take away his goods and King Moorosi told us he must not take them away. We are following the chief's orders."

Ignoring Thomas, Ratsuanyane turns to January. "You and Madekoni are to ask Raisa for someone to help you run the store," he says. "They must see that nothing is taken away. None of the goods must leave here."

Thomas is relieved at Ratsuanyane's approach. He knows that, in the absence of Moorosi, Ratsuanyane's word is effectively law to these men. Although Thomas is unhappy with him taking charge of his store, he prefers it to losing his life.

Leaving the pack horse half-laden, Thomas walks slowly to the side of the store to his horse. Now that Ratsuanyane effectively has taken possession of the store the men's attention has turned to the inventory and whether they can share in it. Their noisy talking and arguing attracts more people from the village.

Thomas gingerly mounts his horse and walks it away from the store, moving some distance before stopping to glance back. No one is following him. He digs his heels into the horse's side and heads south.

Thomas arrives at his trading station near Masitise where, with some helpers, he piles as many of his goods as he can on a wagon and rides off. He and his helpers have gone only about half a mile when armed men on horseback ride down a hill ahead of them, shouting to those who are riding with him to stop.

"You must ride on to the border," his assistants tell him. "They are more interested in the wagon and what it is carrying than in you."

Thomas gallops south, leaving his merchandise in Baphuthi hands.

Maseru — Wednesday February 26, 1879

It is the note from Ellenberger that reaches him today which, more than anything else, has given Griffith second thoughts on his reaction to Austen. Combined with two further statements from agitated Baphuthi sent him by Austen, Griffith realizes that the magistrate might indeed have had cause to flee to Palmietfontein. For the first time, he accepts that Moorosi is in open rebellion, and conflict could erupt at any time. He regrets his reaction to Austen's flight, but brushes that aside; attending to the situation at hand is more important right now.

Maseru — Thursday February 27, 1879

After spending the better part of a day assessing the new situation in Quthing, Griffith has gone from taking steps to prevent an uprising to planning to put down a rebellion. The way to do it, he concludes, is to assemble a large force with mountain guns at Palmietfontein, most of them Basotho forces under Lerothodi, and march them into Quthing. Invasion by such a force would have a sobering effect on Moorosi, who might be driven to surrender before the shedding of too much blood.

He cannot take this action himself without government authority. Southey is in charge of the troops at Palmietfontein, not him.

But he can take certain steps and he must take them immediately. He must withdraw Austen's two months of leave and ask him to stay on and help Southey in Palmietfontein. Austen can advise Southey on the nature of the terrain, where the roads are, and where the people live — all valuable information for an attack on Quthing.

He must change the directions he gave to Davies and Maitin, who by now should be with a party of Basotho, crossing the Orange River on their way to Quthing. He must tell them that, rather than try to take over the now-plundered magistracy, they should do all they can to give support and help to the loyal natives.

He must put together a combined force under Letsie, his son Lerothodi and other chiefs who, Griffith believes, would want to prove their loyalty to the Queen and demonstrate thereby that they should be allowed to keep their weapons.

Griffith will tell Letsie and other Basotho chiefs that, by his actions, Moorosi has thrown off the cloak under which he had been hiding and has openly rebelled against the government of the Queen.

Griffith decides he can go even further with his plan. He will pack supplies and set off tomorrow for Mafeteng, from where he will travel to Mohale's Hoek, about five miles north west of Palmietfontein.

On the way, he will gather fighters from Letsie and the other chiefs. Because he has no authority to act outside Basutoland, he will ask them to cross the Orange River into Quthing rather than go through Palmietfontein and thereby cross into Cape Colony territory. It will not be long before he will have a large fighting force of Basotho warriors eager to prove their mettle against Moorosi.

Quthing — The same day

Moorosi, accompanied by a commando of fighting men, leaves his mountain fortress and, riding his favourite white horse, follows the course of the Orange River, a few miles down the road to Thomas's Shop.

He is distressed to find it in disarray. Goods lie strewn across the floor. The few blankets that are left lie in ragged piles. Saddles, once carefully arranged on poles, lie haphazardly on the ground. Shelves, normally filled with pots and other items for sale, are bare.

"By whose order was this shop looted?" Moorosi asks Raisa as he surveys the scene.

"I do not know," Raisa replies. "I have been keeping guard since yesterday to make sure that no more items are taken. When I am not here, others help out to make sure nothing more is taken."

"I want you to make sure that all the goods that have been taken from here are found and returned," Moorosi says. "The trader Thomas did not hurt us. He did not take things from us without paying for them. He did not try to rule us. He was a guest in our land and we do not treat guests in this way. We have no argument with him. Our argument is with the government."

"I have heard that the people stopped a wagon on which Thomas had piled goods from his store near the mission station," Raisa says. "He wanted them to be taken across the border, but the people took the goods for themselves and then returned the wagon and the oxen to the missionary."

"I will have to talk with them, too, and get the goods back," Moorosi says before continuing south.

⚜

After a few hours, Moorosi, followed by hundreds of men, travels through the narrow valley of the Qomoqomong River, turns a bend in the path and comes across the scene of destruction at the magistracy.

Maitin's house, grain store and horses are untouched, reflecting his popularity with the people. But what were once Austen's office, his house and the courtroom are now little more than a pile of rubble.

Moorosi dismounts and walks into the ruins of Austen's house. The doors and windows have been smashed. Broken tables and chairs and torn mattresses give evidence of the force with which a group swept through and destroyed everything. The harmonium that he had once heard Austen play is damaged beyond repair.

In the garden alongside is a piano, its legs broken and many of its keys torn away by the force with which it was flung out of the house.

Books and drawings lie in confused heaps in the house and in the garden.

Moorosi walks to the courtroom, which he enters through a jagged hole where the door once stood. Inside, the overturned desk and benches are broken.

The windows are smashed. In adjoining rooms in which records were kept, torn books and government papers lie in heaps on the floor.

He walks slowly across to the prison, where the iron bars have been wrenched off and the door — repaired after the New Year's Day breakout — broken down.

Moorosi is disturbed by what he sees.

True, he derives a degree of satisfaction that the symbol of the government's attempt to take away his people's independence lies in tatters, its dignity crushed and its authority dented.

It was here he confronted Hope and later Austen, standing up to their attempts to rule his people and their land.

Here is where he experienced their so-called justice, where his son was sentenced to banishment to the Cape for a crime he believes he did not commit.

In some ways, it is good to see it all destroyed in this way.

But his satisfaction is tinged with apprehension.

His men wrought this destruction on the magistracy without his approval. He meant it as a possible plan for later, not an instruction for now. Yet, under the intoxication of the war dances and their anger, a band of his men, including two of his sons, moved on their own, convinced this was the action the chief wanted to defend their freedom.

The government does not know that and will assume he orchestrated it.

But there is nothing he can do about that now. The deed is done. It will provide the government with an excuse to attack him.

He and his people must prepare to fight.

⁂

Volunteer troops and police in Palmietfontein, now at 400 and strengthened by new arrivals daily, are told they should be ready at a moment's notice for an attack on the camp from Quthing and should make entrenchments for themselves. In addition to placing 40 men on guard to give advance notice of an assault from Moorosi's men, Southey issues an order that the men should keep their guns and ammunition close to their beds at night.

⁂

Moorosi sends a message to his people to meet at a cave near the mission station. With his body of fighting men gathered in the valley around him, he stands in front of the cave entrance.

"I want all the goods looted from Thomas's shops to be collected and returned to the trader," he says. "I am disappointed that you destroyed the magistracy. I understand why you acted as you did, but if you had asked me I would have told you not to attack it. But the deed is done. We can discuss that matter when it is peaceful again. Now we no longer have peace in this land."

Pointing to the hills to the south, he adds, "The government forces are across the Telle River, waiting to attack us. And they will attack us soon.

"Every Baphuthi man must fight; only in that way can we achieve victory.

"The war is upon us."

Cape Town — Monday, March 3, 1879

Secretary for Native Affairs Ayliff, ready to leave for the scene of the action in Basutoland, has been giving the rising turmoil in Moorosi's territory much thought. Earlier in the week, he heard of the plundering of the magistracy by telegram and today receives an express letter from Griffith telling of his plans to enlist Basotho against Moorosi. Ayliff has steadily pieced together a plan of action. But his plan relies more on government troops than on friendly Basotho.

Ayliff orders a strong force to be sent to support Southey at Palmietfontein and any pro-government Mfengu willing to fight with him be encouraged to do so, believing the people who live on the Eastern Cape frontier will be better fighters than the Basotho provided by Letsie.

In correspondence with Ayliff, Prime Minister Gordon Sprigg has urged him to appoint Griffith head of the combined troops. Sprigg points out that Griffith has proven himself a competent commander, in civil as well as military affairs. And, after all, he is the government's main administrator in Basutoland. It seems that he is intent on gathering the Basotho forces together to attack Moorosi and he would encourage him to continue to do that.

Telegram from Ayliff to Griffith

Yesterday Ayliff sent a telegram to Griffith by way of Aliwal North informing him he should take over from Southey as commander of the colonial forces, which includes the 2,000 men assembled by Lerothodi, as soon as he arrives in Palmietfontein.

As such, Griffith will continue to take orders relating to civil matters from Ayliff, but will report to the recently appointed commandant-general of the defence forces— Colonel Samuel P. Jarvis, stationed in King William's Town — on military matters.

He recalls the words of Sprigg in a recent meeting.

"I cannot emphasize enough the necessity to win this war, if that is what it turns out to be," he reportedly said. "We cannot afford another setback like that in Natal. The sooner this chief Moorosi is brought to justice, the better."

Maseru — Wednesday, March 5, 1879

The telegram from Ayliff authorizing Griffith to take over from Southey as commander of the invasion force has emboldened Griffith.

Only a week ago, he felt the situation was spiralling out of his control and he was trying to do all he could within Basutoland. Soon he will be fully in command on the ground in Palmietfontein, both as a military officer and as the chief representative of the Basutoland government, and in a position to implement his plan to impose justice on Moorosi who has rebelled violently against colonial rule.

Griffith outlines his plan to his senior officers. "In order to wage this war, for that is what it is now, I will assemble a large force to invade Moorosi's territory and to arrest him, his son Lehana and other offenders," he says.

"We will subdue the rebellion. We can expect Moorosi to fight back vigorously. He has already shown he has no intention of yielding without a fight and he can summon a strong force of warriors.

"I will be in command of all the forces, consisting of regular troops as well as volunteers from the surrounding districts, as well as the men supplied by Lerothodi and the other Basotho chiefs. They are good fighters, men who understand the terrain and who know the thinking of the people against whom they will fight.

"We will need a few days to prepare, to ensure we have the requisite number of guns and ammunition, but we will have to move soon."

Griffith adds that he will ask Maitin, for whom he developed considerable respect as the events unfolded in Quthing, to serve as his aide-de-camp and interpreter

Palmietfontein — Thursday, March 6, 1879

Robert Scott, on afternoon picket duty near the Telle River, notices them first. Several mounted and armed Baphuthi have crossed over the fast-moving river, and are riding on the Cape Colony side, toward the police horses tethered near the police station. Scott estimates their number at 20.

The Baphuthi have not seen the pickets, who are bunkered down behind an earth-

Robert Scott

works about 100 yards east of the police station. Scott turns to Alex Granville.

"What do you make of this?"

"We have been told that they could be planning to attack. But these people don't seem intent on any kind of attack. Surely they would be charging forward and firing if they were."

"But it looks as though they might be trying to round up our horses. We cannot allow them to do that."

Granville stands up, raises his rifle, shoots in the air, and shouts.

"Leave those horses alone or we'll shoot you."

The men turn their horses around, and head back across the river.

"That was easy," Granville says.

"Not so fast," Scott responds. "Look across the river. I believe they are planning to return."

On the other side of the river, the Baphuthi men shout toward the hills. More riders appear until they number about 150. This larger group crosses the river, yelling instructions and encouragement at one another. They seize two horses belonging to a trader named Jones whose house is close to the river and head back across the drift once more.

Granville jumps up again. "Return those horses!" he shouts. "They are not yours. Return those horses at once or I will shoot."

His demand is answered by a volley of fire. A shot grazes one of the pickets, who runs to the police station to alert Southey.

At the sound of the volley, hundreds more Baphuthi riders emerge from the hills, most mounted on horses, and some running alongside. They charge down the slope toward the water, yelling.

Alerted by the injured yeoman, Southey orders the alarm to be sounded and mounts his horse to see for himself close up what is happening.

The Baphuthi appear to be gathering for an attempt to capture more horses.

Leading them is a man on a white horse. The pickets assume he is Moorosi, whose presence makes matters much more serious than an attempt to seize a few horses.

Granville, who is most senior among the half-dozen men behind the earthworks, takes charge. He advises the others to fire should the Baphuthi come any closer.

"We shouldn't take any chances," he says.

"They are armed and they are on our territory and we have every right to shoot to kill. If they get past us and attack the police station, we will be in big trouble. We are on the front line here."

As a few warriors come within 20 yards of their position, Granville issues an order to respond.

He fires.

Scott follows, aiming into the midst of the gathered men. A Baphuthi man falls from his horse.

The riders turn toward the pickets and fire back. The pickets return the fire.

Chaos erupts among the Baphuthi who thought the closest troops were in the police station a mile away and were not anticipating a fire fight over the horses.

The reinforcements summoned by Southey arrive to find the Baphuthi and colonial forces firing furiously at one another.

As puffs of smoke cloud the air and the smell of gunpowder wafts across the bush, several Baphuthi run toward the colonial soldiers, holding their spears, ready to fling them.

Scott and Granville cut down a number of them. But several succeed in evading the fire and run toward the pickets. As they do, a Baphuthi warrior hurls his spear over the earthworks directly at Scott.

⚜

The 2,000 Basotho led by Lerothodi and armed with spears or rifles, have crossed the Telle River and are approaching Palmietfontein.

They are sombre, appearing unsure what is required of them. They have heard of rising tensions in Quthing. Now and then a rumour has rippled through their villages that war has started, but it soon proves to be false. Now they are told they are to fight against Moorosi and the Baphuthi people. If it is not war, what is it?

The men have been raised to believe that every man should be brave enough to be a warrior, to defend his family and his people. They have been trained to fight with their spears and many have learned how to fire the guns they have bought. They feel a sense of assurance in being ready to fight. But, although they have heard stories of war from their elders, most of these young men have known only peace in their lifetimes.

Now they are being called upon to show their prowess.

But they are confused about why they are being called upon to fight. For most of their lives they have been told that the white government is there to defend them from the Boers. They have heard how their fathers fought against the Boers, how they were driven from their land and faced losing all their land until the British soldiers came to their aid.

Now, however, they are not fighting the Boers. They hear that Moorosi and his people are upset with the government. The Baphuthi, they are told, want to fight against the colonial authorities because they do not like the way in which they rule them. Now Moorosi and the Baphuthi people, and not the Boers are the enemy.

They have heard, too, that the white government wants to take away their weapons from them. But now Lerothodi tells them that if they fight on the side of the government against Moorosi they will get to keep their weapons as a reward for fighting for the government. And they have been told that they will get to keep any cattle that they might capture in a fight against Moorosi.

So they have, most a little reluctantly, followed Lerothodi's instructions to gather here today to prepare for what could be a fight against a group of people with whom they really have no quarrel. Perhaps, they think, it will turn out as it did nearly a year ago when Bowker faced off with Moorosi. They will stand there, listen to the two sides argue, see them sort out their problems peacefully, and then go home.

Above all, however, they will do as they are told. Lerothodi is their leader and they will follow him. If he says they must fight, they will fight.

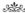

Scott jumps to the side. The spear glances his leg, drawing blood, but the wound is not deep.

The Baphuthi warrior continues advancing, presumably to follow with another spear — he carries several — and a hand-to-hand attack. Granville raises his rifle and fires. A few feet away, the warrior falls, fatally wounded.

Southey summons more men.

Soon members of the Cape Mounted Riflemen and the volunteer Queenstown yeomanry are tumbling out of their barracks. Halfway to the river, they kneel, load and fire on the rampaging Baphuthi whose numbers have now swollen to 450.

For more than an hour, the Baphuthi fight back with spears and rifles and the fighting becomes intense. Several Baphuthi fall from their horses. Others, on foot, collapse as the colonial soldiers' bullets find their targets. Some of the Baphuthi risk death to gather the bodies, put them on horses and take them back across the river as the firing continues around them.

The fighting is in full swing as Lerothodi arrives with his men.

Unexpectedly the man on the white horse gives instructions to retreat over the Telle River. The Baphuthi follow, abandoning most of the cattle and horses they had seized.

Southey, in command until Griffith arrives, is reluctant to cross into Basutoland. He orders the troops to hold their positions.

About 20 Baphuthi have been killed in the skirmish.

On the colonial side, a sergeant in the Basotho police has been shot in both legs and a trader named Kelly has suffered a superficial wound to the chest.

As a medical officer tends to Scott's wound, Southey walks across to thank Scott for his action.

"Did you see the way we made them run?" Scott says, wincing as the officer wipes away the blood and bandages his leg. "They sure were afraid of us."

Quthing — Friday, March 7, 1879

Riding on his white horse, the Baphuthi king is subdued as he makes his way back to his mountain fortress. His face reflects disillusionment.

When he led his warriors across the Telle River, he believed he would be joined by a large number of Basotho, who had promised him support. "I had thought that even Letsie's son Lerothodi would join me with thousands of warriors," he says. "Did you not yourself tell me that?"

"It was what we heard from Lerothodi's messenger," Lemena responds. "He said you were like family. If you were attacked by the whites, Lerothodi would feel he was being attacked, too, and would come to your aid. Then I heard that he was gathering his men at Mohale's Hoek and I assumed he was there to help you."

"I thought he would help me," Moorosi continues. "I wanted to attack the settlers first, before they could gather a larger force and, with Lerothodi's support, defeat them. There are only a few hundred across the border.

"But now I see Lerothodi is supporting them, not me." Moorosi sighs, looking at the ground, still shocked by the sight of his friend becoming his enemy.

"If Lerothodi will not support me, now I know that Letsie will not support me. It is not only that he will not support me; he will fight against me.

"How can that be? How could Letsie dishonour his own word? How could he turn on me and make me his enemy when two days before I was his friend? And how can I fight against my brothers?

"I want you to send a message to Lerothodi. I want you to tell him that he sent me promises of help, but now I have been completely deceived. But tell Lerothodi I will not yield. I will not let the government seek me out and try to kill me, even if it means I have to fight against him, too.

"Tell our people that they must go into the mountains and defend themselves and their cattle."

As he stands awash in disillusionment and abandonment Moorosi becomes certain of one thing. He will fight to the end against the colonial forces, even should Lerothodi fight alongside the whites. He cannot turn back now. He will defend himself and his people against all who try to oust them from their land, whoever they are.

14

Palmietfontein— Saturday March 15, 1879

Griffith, now on the ground in Palmietfontein, is anxious to move as soon as possible against Moorosi, even though Southey is still urging the colonial forces to wait until they receive instructions from Cape Town. His plan, he tells Southey, is to attack Moorosi from four sides, leaving him no escape except to surrender or to fall back on his mountain fortress where we will confront him head on.

"The first group will be led by Colonel Edward Brabant, who is now in Umtata, and will consist of 150 men. They are to enter Quthing from the southeast and will mop up any rebel forces on their way to Moorosi's Mountain.

"A second group, led by Captain Wood, will move in from the northeast, from Ongeluk's Nek. They will prevent the rebels from escaping across the Drakensberg mountains to the east.

"The third group will attack from the west. Seven hundred Basotho that I have assembled will go to the Kornet Spruit bank of the Orange River where they will take up posts at staggered positions northward along the river as far as the mountain above Raisa's village. Their task will be to prevent rebels from crossing the river to the west and to capture stock from any who try.

"Our men, the fourth group, will march tomorrow with the rest of the contingent across the Telle River, from where we will advance into Moorosi's territory on Monday.

"As we advance northward, to make sure we cover all the territory, a fifth group

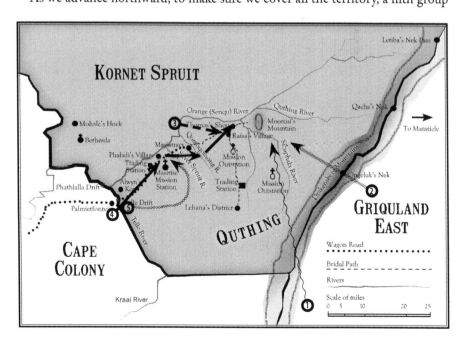

189

consisting of Captain Henry Davies, leading the Basutoland Police, and another group of the Basutoland Native Contingent, will march to the east, working their way around the hills toward the head of Silver Spruit River. From there, they will move back west to Phaladi's Village, occupied by the family and friends of Phaladi, a Christian Baphuthi who lives close to the mission station at Masitise and, I am told, has renounced his allegiance to Moorosi.

"We'll meet Davies at Phaladi's village. From there, we will patrol the surrounding territory, dispersing any rebellious groups we might find or inviting them to surrender. We will send a patrol to Lehana's cave in the valley of the Qomoqomong, oust the chief's rebellious son from his hiding and bring him to face justice.

"Should Moorosi find sanctuary on his mountain we will confront the chief there directly — after capturing the rebel groups in the rest of the country. There, we will surround him and force him to surrender."

Quthing — Monday, March 17, 1879

It is an impressive show of force. At nine o'clock this morning, under skies heavy with the threat of rain, Griffith, Southey and Colonel E.T. Minto, commander of the 104-strong 3rd Yeomanry, which arrived in Palmietfontein on Saturday, cross the Telle River, accompanied by 100 Cape Mounted Riflemen, 300 Cape Mounted Yeomanry, 100 Mfengu and 2,000 members of the Basutoland Native Contingent. Maitin, special aid to Griffith, accompanies them. Their destination: Phaladi's Village.

Granville, Scott and Brown are among a contingent of the Cape Mounted Riflemen instructed to remain at Palmietfontein. They are told they will be called upon once the troops advance to Moorosi's mountain; for now they should serve as a back-stop in case of trouble.

The troops under Griffith, Southey and Minto are surprised when they encounter no resistance on their 12-mile march in intermittent rain into Quthing, where they set up camp close to Phaladi's village.

Phaladi's people welcome the troops.

With the rain increasing, the men move quickly to pitch their tents. Some have to settle for sheltering under blankets.

As they work, Davies arrives with his group. "Our march appears to have been almost as uneventful as yours," he tells Griffith in the commander's tent, raising his voice against the patter of rain on the canvas. "But we did drive off a small party of Baphuthi shortly before we arrived here. We took one of the rebels prisoner."

"Good work, Davies," Griffith replies.

"Because it appears so quiet, I have instructed a large part of the Basutoland Native Contingent, who are on the other side of the Orange River under Letsie's son Lerothodi, to join us here, but I have just received word that they cannot cross the Orange River until the waters have abated a little."

With the tents erected, Griffith instructs the men to fortify the camp.

"We cannot afford to take any chances," he tells the men. "Moorosi might be planning a surprise attack. I need you to build earthworks to protect our camp."

The men reluctantly swash their way through the mud to start the arduous task of digging trenches and surrounding them with sandbags.

Southey and the senior magistrates accompanying him join Griffith through another heavy downpour to visit the missionary, Frederic Ellenberger, and his wife, Emma, in their cave house at Masitise.

Griffith reassures the missionary. "My men will provide aid and protection to you, your good wife and family, and to those Baphuthi living close to you who have not joined Moorosi in his revolt. Let me assure you of this: You have nothing to fear from the rebels. We will see to that."

Ellenberger thanks him, pointing out that he has postponed the formal opening of his new church — which he had spent nine months building and can seat 400 — until next month. Moorosi is to be a special guest and he hopes the tension will have abated by then and the king will be able to attend.

"Talking of tensions abating and seeing you are sitting on the Wodehouse bench," Ellenberger tells Griffith, "I would have liked to have heard you discussing a way of

Church built by Ellenberger

bringing about a peaceful resolution to this conflict."

"It is up to Moorosi to bring about peace," Griffith responds. "If he is prepared to hand over Lehana and the other escaped prisoners, and present himself for trial for his rebellious acts, we will take a big step toward resolving this issue peacefully. But as long as he resists our moves to capture Lehana and the others, and as long as he persists in attacking us, we have no choice but to go and get him."

"I'm told Moorosi didn't want his men to attack the magistracy," Ellenberger replies.

"Whether he wanted them to do so is immaterial," Griffith responds. "He must take responsibility for the actions of his people. In any event, I cannot believe that he did not encourage them to do so. After all, he crossed the Telle River with his people just a few days ago and stole some of our horses. That is an overt act that belies any pretence he might have of being the defender rather than the aggressor."

Quthing — Thursday, March 20, 1879

The rain returns to Phaladi's Village — and Griffith's camp — during the early hours. Apart from yesterday's brief respite, heavy rain has been falling for almost a week, not only breaking the drought but also saturating the ground to overflowing.

Rivulets form in areas that previously were little more than tracks through the bushes. Together, carrying mud and debris, the newly formed streams rush to the nearest creeks, which fill to overflowing and hasten toward the Orange and Telle rivers, turning them from meandering waters into brown torrents and causing them to overflow their banks.

Every road turns into a quagmire of mud, slowing the three 14-foot colonial supply wagons to a crawl as they slip and slide their way along the 14 miles to Phaladi's Village. For three days, the drivers and leaders of the wagons have exhorted the oxen to pull harder and move faster; their voices are hoarse; their arms are weary from repeatedly whipping the oxen's backs. Their task has been frustrating at best, impossible at worst. Not only do the oxen have to work harder to pull through the mud, but the water-drenched canvases that cover the wagons add to the weight of the load.

At times, where the road crossed creeks, the mud reached up to the axles, forcing

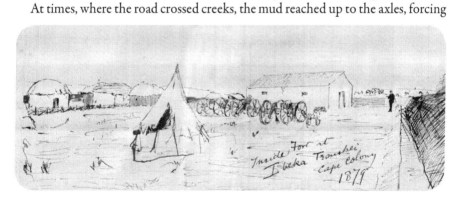

Cannon at Ibika, seen here, were sent to Quthing through Palmietfontein. [Arthur Pattisson]

the drivers to dig the wagons out before proceeding.

Today they reach Griffith's camp where Griffith tells them they need to return to Palmietfontein tomorrow for more supplies.

On the surrounding hills, unseen by Griffith, armed men are watching and sending reports to their king, who is now their commander in chief.

Barkly, Cape Colony — The same day

For three days, Colonel Edward Yewd Brabant has been on the road with his men from Umtata. They are, as requested by Griffith, bound for Baphuthi territory.

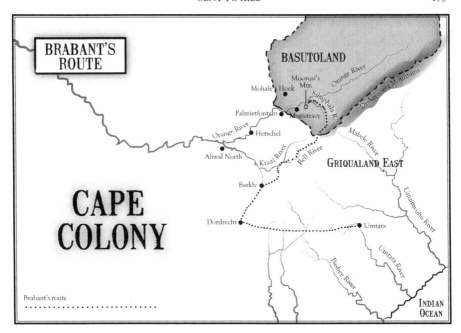

Brabant, who has a reputation for being a strong commander, fought with the Cape Mounted Riflemen in various native wars before being appointed leader of the First Cape Yeomanry.

Today, as he arrives in Barkly, a message reaches him from Griffith ordering him to send him two of the cannon he carries by way of Palmietfontein so they will reach him more quickly. Brabant directs a small group to take the big guns that way.

The rest of his force will advance up the valley of the Kraai and Bell rivers, across the Drakensberg mountains to Moorosi's Mountain, a way white troops have never taken. "Because of the recent heavy rains, we will have to cross several flooded rivers," the colonel tells his men. "That might be a problem. But our presence is urgently required as war has broken out with Moorosi.

Colonel Brabant

"We likely will encounter rebels along the way and once we reach the chief's mountain fortress with our supplies we will certainly be needed in the fighting to capture it.

"I am sure you will be up to it, no matter what conditions we may encounter.

"Once we leave here we will be out of postal or telegraphic contact with the main forces under Colonel Griffith, so we are to try to make as best time as we can and arrive at the mountain when he is expecting us."

But if the march of the last three days is any guide, Brabant fears the journey is not going to be straightforward. In traveling from Umtata to Dordrecht, they negotiated five flooded rivers. But, even though they made it in tolerably good time to Barkly, it has been raining steadily since they arrived. Fearing the journey ahead will be hazardous for their wagons, Brabant instructs his men to remain until the rains cease and the roads become passable.

Ahead of him, he has been told, is a ravine called Rebel's Kloof which is so difficult to negotiate that no timber has been brought down from the district on the other side of it for two years; it simply has been considered impossible to make the journey bearing the loads of timber. Brabant, too, has wagons and loads that need to be taken through the ravine, but he reckons he has soldiers who are able to see it done.

Quthing — Friday, March 21, 1879

Leading his men across the hills toward Raisa's village after successfully crossing the Orange River during a lull in the rain, Lerothodi was confident that the Baphuthi would yield when his forces arrived. But as they clash today, Moorosi's men, although outnumbered and out-gunned, fight back.

Soon what started out as a skirmish turns into a wider battle and the front line becomes a scene of chaos. Amid war cries, both sides fling spears and fire at one another.

At times it becomes difficult to tell one group from the other.

A runner brings Lerothodi the news that a bullet has struck his uncle Chief Lenkoane, a brother of the late chief Moshoeshoe. A horrified Lerothodi makes his way forward through the mass of dead and wounded men.

By the time he reaches Lenkoane, the advancing warriors, flush with success against the retreating Baphuthi, have moved on. The shouting from the advance warriors already is becoming quieter with distance as Lerothodi reaches down and examines his uncle. The bullet has pierced his heart.

Lerothodi carries his uncle's body back toward the village, tears streaming down his face. As he stumbles across the rock-strewn earth, still slippery from the rain, he recalls the days he and his brothers spent as children, swapping stories with their uncle in the kraal before they set out to herd their family's cattle.

Before he reaches the village, he lays down the body. He is angry at the men who have robbed him of one who was like an older brother to him. He looks up and sees another body being brought back from the front lines, followed by another.

Soon nine bodies lie in a row, a silent testimony to the horrible reality of this day.

The bodies convey a message as nothing else can: The lives of his family and friends are little more than a means to an end in the whites' strategic game.

The adventure of war that would yield them bounty has turned into the horror of conflict. By his efforts on this day, the white government has won, and he has lost.

As he looks again at his uncle's body, Lerothodi finds his emotions driven in a direction he never envisaged.

As his men herd around him the 1,500 cattle they have captured in the fighting, their cheering and delight mock him.

Is this war against Moorosi really worthwhile?

Quthing — Saturday, March 22, 1879

The war has become as real for Moorosi as for Lerothodi.

Four of Moorosi's sons and two of his grandsons were among the 30 killed in the skirmish with Lerothodi. Even this hardened man, who has seen much warfare over his 80 years, is bowed down by the suffering, particularly as it came at the hands of a man whom he thought was a brother.

Now he knows without doubt that he and his people are alone in their fight against the white invaders. Lerothodi has turned on him.

But that realization serves to make him more resolute. He will fight to the finish. And he and his people will win.

Even though the big guns that should have been sent by Brabant have failed to arrive and no word has been received from him, Griffith remains determined to waste no time.

"We need to move now," he tells Native Affairs Secretary William Ayliff, who has joined them in Quthing. "Our scouts report that Moorosi has fled to his mountain. We are likely to encounter skirmishes, such as the one yesterday, as we clear out the rebels trying to hold their positions between here and the mountain. But before long we will be at the mountain."

Ayliff suggests that Griffith wait for a report from Brabant and for the guns to arrive. The stronger the force, the better the chances for a quick victory. "The longer it takes, the more it will cost the government," he tells Griffith. "Already your need for supplies and ammunition and the men's pay is making inroads into our treasury."

"I agree," Griffith replies. "That is precisely the reason we should *not* wait for Brabant. The longer we delay, the more we give Moorosi a chance to settle in and defend his position. And the more costly the war becomes. If we leave today, we should reach Moorosi's Mountain in a day or two. If we leave only when we know Brabant is at the mountain and when the guns arrive, we will have lost that many days simply waiting here.

"We will set off at first light tomorrow."

Quthing — Sunday, March 23, 1879

At 5 a.m. Griffith sets off with 300 yeomanry and 100 pro-government Mfengu, who have travelled from the Eastern Cape to join his forces. They have not gone far when a scout reports that about 60 Baphuthi under Ratsuanyane have gathered in caves in the hills along the Silver Spruit River, many with their families.

Griffith calls for volunteers to storm the caves with Lieutenant Badger and Captain Nesbitt. Ten step forward. At 8 a.m., Griffith, seated on his horse, takes up a position on a hill opposite the caves. The day is clear and he has a good view. He waves his sword in the air and orders an advance. The yeomen, all mounted and armed, descend to the valley in the strict formation that reflects their British-based training. They ride up the hill, toward the caves. On an order from Griffith, they raise their rifles and shoot toward the caves. Puffs of smoke fill the air.

The Baphuthi emerge from hiding, move down the hillside and respond with their own fire. Soon a battle is raging in the valley below the caves.

After two hours of firing, Griffith's forces capture 27 horses and kill three of the Baphuthi, but are unable to get close to the caves.

Griffith gives the order to retire. They are to rest for a few hours and return to the attack in the early afternoon.

More volunteer for the second round of fighting. Among them is Sergeant Thomas Muldoon, with Southey's yeomanry group, who declares his determination not only to fight, but to lead the way. "I will show those black savages who are the superior fighters," Muldoon says. "You will not find me wanting, sir."

Griffith thanks him. "Now that is the sort of spirit I want to hear and I want to see demonstrated this afternoon," he says.

At three o'clock, the yeomen gather in formation and prepare to attack once more. Griffith waves his sword.

The men advance.

The Baphuthi are ready.

As shots ring out on both sides, Muldoon moves faster than his fellow yeomen, leading the charge on horseback up the slopes to the caves. He waves his sword, yelling to his fellow troopers to follow. The Baphuthi warriors, who have moved out of their caves once more, fire on the approaching men.

Seeing a Baphuthi ready to throw his spear, an excited Muldoon jumps from his horse and runs toward him. The yeoman stops, raises his rifle and loads it. The warrior hurls his spear and Muldoon has no time to fire. The spear strikes him in the side, tearing a gash just under his heart. He falls.

As the skirmish continues, the Baphuthi slowly give way. Eventually they flee, leaving about 30 bodies lying on the hillside.

The yeomen capture 64 horses, sheep and goats. They climb up to the caves where they find some 50 unarmed women, whom they release.

By the time the Baphuthi have fled and his compatriots reach him, Muldoon is bleeding profusely. He has no strength to staunch the wound with his clothing.

He raises his head slightly, mumbles a few unintelligible words before allowing his head to fall to the ground.

He is the first colonial casualty of the war.

⚜

The messenger arrives at the mountain to deliver the news to Moorosi.

"Two of your grandsons were killed, one of your sons was shot and 27 of our people were killed in a battle in the caves on the Silver Spruit River today," he tells him. "It was not a good thing to see. Seeing the bodies lying there made me feel so sad that I still am sick from it," he says.

Moorosi's eyes fill with tears.

"Let my people come here, to the mountain," he says. "They will be safe here. The white soldiers will not be able to defeat us here."

Quthing — Monday March 24, 1879

After spending an uneasy night camped on the battlefield that saw Muldoon fall, Griffith's yeomen awaken to a cloudy morning. Taking turns, they dig a shallow grave on the side of the mountain where they lay their colleague's body to rest.

"This shall henceforth be known as Muldoon's Place," Griffith says. "Now, let us move on to revenge his death and destroy these men who dare rebel against the Queen and everything for which she stands."

Spurred on by revenge and Griffith's encouragement to kill more of the enemy, the men wave their swords and march in formation across terrain that never has suffered the sounds, the smells and the savagery of modern warfare. Until now.

A mile away, the soldiers reach a village, now deserted. Using similar tactics to those employed against Sarhili, Griffith instructs his men to seize food supplies, capture sheep and goats and destroy the community. The soldiers cheer as the thatched roofs catch fire, sending bright orange plumes into the morning air.

By the time they move northward, the village, until a few days ago home to a contented extended family community, is little more than a circle of blackened stones.

Griffith tells Colonel Minto, commanding officer of the 3rd Yeomanry, and Captain Davies, leading the Basotho contingent, to move northward. The yeomanry under Southey will accompany him on the road and they will meet at the mountain.

Quthing — Tuesday March 25, 1879

Leaving Ratsuanyane's deserted village where they camped for the night, Griffith's 400 men, with their tents, food and ammunition, move north.

Track to mountain on steep hillside.

Here the road is little more than a rough track along the side of the hills. The sharp curves and the steep slopes render it treacherous for the heavy loads of the colonial troops. Should any wagon veer off the narrow path it stands the risk of rolling 500 feet downhill and crashing into the river.

Many of the supplies have come a long way. They were first delivered to the nearest railhead at Queenstown, 150 miles away in the Cape Colony. Now, in the last stretch to Moorosi's Mountain, the wagons slow to less than a walking pace.

After some hours of travel, they reach

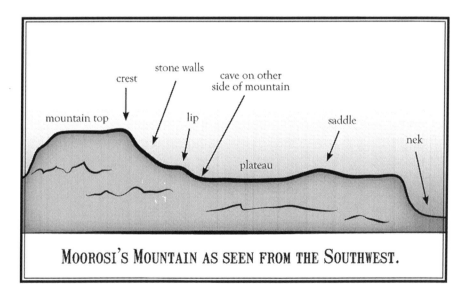

MOOROSI'S MOUNTAIN AS SEEN FROM THE SOUTHWEST.

Thomas's now-deserted shop. The two brick buildings — Thomas's house and his shop — will be converted to a hospital and quarters.

They drop off supplies at Thomas's Shop and Griffith leads a contingent to Moorosi's Mountain, encountering no resistance on the way.

"I want you to set up camp here," Griffith tells the men. "Pitch the tents on this side of the mountain. When the others arrive, they will camp on the other side of the mountain so that we surround it and prevent all chance of the enemy's escape."

⚜

"Look how flat it is on top," Peter Brown says to his colleague Robert Scott, as he looks up at the 1,200-foot mountain. Both have just arrived with the Cape Mounted Riflemen from Palmietfontein, summoned by Griffith who reasoned that, having made good progress against the Baphuthi, it is no longer necessary to keep the additional troops there; he will need them at the mountain.

"You could put a whole village up there," responds Scott. "The flat part must extend for more than half a mile."

"Moorosi and his men are up there," Brown says. "You can't see them from here. But, wait a minute. Right at the top you can see a rectangular shape that looks like a stone hut. There, on the right, near the end of the flat top. It looks small from here, but it must be fairly big."

"Can't say that I can see it," says Scott. "You must have better eyes than me.

"The story is that the top of the mountain, which we can't see from here, is crowded with cattle, sheep and goats, stocked with grain, small arms and ammunition and is defended by at least 300 men," replies Scott.

The men's eyes follow the outline of the mountain from the top to the right to where it descends 600 feet from the crown in a series of ledges on which stone-and-earth walls have been built before levelling out into a hollow that the men dub "the lip."

From the lip, a plateau extends to the right for about 1,200 feet to a large rocky outcrop they call "the saddle" — because it looks like one. From the saddle, the mountain dips down again to the right to an area they call "the neck" (or "nek" in Dutch) because it lies between Moorosi's Mountain and another mountain on the right that rises 500 feet.

From the edge of the plateau above them, the mountain slopes 600 feet down to where they are standing.

"I know they say these natives are an uneducated bunch of ruffians, but they have built up their defences on that mountain quite well," says Brown, casting his eyes back on the flat mountain top.

"I have to admit that it is impressive."

"It certainly is," replies Scott. "The other sides of the mountain are almost perpendicular and impossible to climb."

"Looks like the only way we can get to the top is from the right, along the plateau to the lip and up between the ledges," says Brown. "I assume there is a passage that goes up among the rocks on the slope to the top."

"There must be," replies Scott.

"Moorosi and his people must be climbing up and down there all the time. If they can do it, so can we."

Quthing — Saturday March 29, 1879

To clear the north-eastern part of Quthing, Captain Wood and his men have been moving southwest from Ongeluk's Nek, capturing cattle, sheep, goats and horses.

Where they encountered resistance, they fired at the rebels. In almost all cases, they eliminated the resistance; in several cases they killed men whom they believed were among Moorosi's leading supporters.

The only Baphuthi left are hiding in deep ravines.

In their sweep south they have captured 2,900 cattle, 6,000 sheep and goats and 490 horses reducing the Baphuthi wealth in northern Quthing, counted in cattle, to a fraction of what it was.

In the south-western part of Moorosi's territory Lerothodi's forces have captured large amounts of livestock from the Baphuthi and the area appears deserted.

"It seems many have fled across the Orange River into Kornet Spruit," Griffith tells Maitin. "With Wood's men sweeping the area from the northeast and Brabant eliminating resistance on his way from the southeast, the main concentration of rebels is on this mountain. Our job now is to oust them from it. For that, however, we need the big guns.

"Come to think of it, where are the field-guns? Did Brabant send them through Palmietfontein as I requested? If he did why are they not here yet? And where is Brabant anyway? How long does it take for him to get here? Will he ever reach here? We need to complete this operation as quickly as we can. Every day is costing money yet we cannot launch an attack on the mountain without the guns."

Maitin suggests that the men might find it difficult to bring the field-guns along the steepest part of the track leading to Thomas's Shop.

"An excellent point, my dear Mr. Maitin," says Griffith, controlling himself after what he realizes might have been an unreasonable display of emotion "Will you kindly send word to Sofonia Moshesh, who has 300 men of the Basutoland Native Contingent with him here, that I would like him to send his men to widen the road so that the guns can be brought along it."

Quthing — Tuesday, April 1, 1879

The 50 white triangular tents dot the slopes at the base of Moorosi's Mountain like sentries on guard. Men move among them drinking coffee, eating biscuits and talking of their anticipated attack. Now and then laughter and loud talk from one group attracts others. The joking helps reduce the tension as the men await the first attack any of them have made on a stronghold so well defended.

The men also have their complaints. Rain over the last few days has caused their tents to leak and some who have blankets have to resort to using them as shelter.

Below the mountain are two troops of Cape Mounted Riflemen under Captain

James Murray Grant; two regiments of Cape Mounted Yeomanry, one under Colonel Southey and the other under Colonel Minto; and 100 Mfengu from Herschel under Captain Hook and Captain Davies. Nearby, 1,900 Basotho under Lerothodi camp in the open or in huts vacated by the Baphuthi.

All the fighting men fall under the command of Griffith. His first move has been to establish a sentry on the saddle facing Moorosi's Mountain.

Griffith outlines his thoughts to Ayliff, who is staying at Thomas's Shop and is visiting Griffith today. "I believe I have the troops to do the job," he tells the native affairs secretary. "But I have to devise a way to break through these stone-and-earth walls. As we approach the walls, Moorosi's men will fire on us and be able to see us before we see them."

"How will you stop them from doing that?" Ayliff asks.

"I will need to precede the storming of the mountain by using the two seven-pounder cannon and rockets I ordered. They can break down the stone walls, causing them to topple, and also hit the Baphuthi hiding behind them. Without them, we will be unable to break through the stone walls. With them, victory will be ensured."

"I leave the prosecution of this war in your capable hands, colonel," Ayliff says. "But I must urge on you the importance of bringing this war to a speedy end."

Griffith calls Hook, the colonial captain in charge of the Mfengu contingent, into his tent. "We cannot waste any more time. We must have those seven-pounders Brabant is supposed to have sent through Palmietfontein. We cannot launch an assault on the mountain without them. I want you to travel south and find the guns. Once you find them, bring them here by forced marches. I need the guns. And I need them now."

Quthing — Wednesday, April 2, 1879

On his mountaintop, Moorosi is angry when he learns from scouts that so much of his people's stock has been captured, either by Lerothodi or by the colonial troops. The cattle represent considerable wealth to the Baphuthi people and a reserve food supply. But he is confident the losses can be reversed.

"Once we defeat the invaders, we will get our cattle back," Moorosi tells his people who are gathered outside his hut behind the mountain crest. "Our task now is to protect the cattle we have here on the top of the mountain, preserve our food, and see that the colonial soldiers do not climb this mountain and take us captive."

He stretches out his hand, symbolically embracing the mountain top.

"We can drink from the water in our two wells. We can survive for a long time on the corn we have stored here. We can drink milk from the cows we have driven up to the mountain top. We can slaughter some of them to eat. And we can climb down the mountain at night, when the white men are sleeping, and gather more food and cattle when we need it."

His listeners express their approval.

"I will sit now and then in my chair on the far side of the mountain where I can see the soldiers below."

Mountain top today, facing north, shows remains of stone huts built by the Baphuthi in the foreground. Many lived in caves in the rocky outcrops on the mountaintop, in the background.

Mountain crest, with highest stone wall in the foreground [contemporary sketch by Arthur Pattisson, using a telescope.]

Eastern slopes of Moorosi's mountain, showing length of mountaintop. Crest is on the far left, Moorosi's "chairs" on the far right.

His listeners smile. They have seen the natural indentations on the cliff top on the western edge of the mountain that provide two seats like legless chairs. Many have climbed down to sit in the "chairs," where they can look some 600 feet straight down to the river bank below. For some, sitting in the chair makes them giddy as they look down the steep slopes. They shudder to think what it would be like to slip and fall. This slope is the most sheer around the mountain.

"But, although we must be patient and wait," Moorosi says, "you also must know that soon we will be called upon to fight. You have seen the white tents down there. They will try to drive us from this mountain.

"We are not sure when they will attack. So we are going to have to be ready and watch for them. You all have weapons. Other rifles and all the ammunition you will need is stored in that hut." He points to a rectangular stone structure, about 20 feet by 10 feet, which also has food supplies.

Moorosi turns and faces southeast, looking toward the crest of the mountain immediately behind his hut.

"Raisa will appoint men to take turns to stand at the top of the mountain, over there, where they can see all that the colonial troops are doing. They will warn us when an attack starts.

"When the colonists attack, we will take up positions around the mountain top and behind the stone walls. I will assign the positions."

"I will assign men to positions along the walls. Some will roll rocks onto our attackers. Others will shoot over the walls or through the holes in them at the invaders. Don't wait for them to get close. Shoot them as soon as you can reach them with your rifles.

"We will use our rifles because they can reach across the plateau from where the white men will attack.

"We will use our spears only if we cannot stop them with the rifles and they get close to us.

"The best shooting position will go to Maketa."

Moorosi points to a short man with a colourless face. An albino, he has the facial features of his people, but does not share their skin tones. His skin is devoid of all colour, his hair off-white and his eyes grey.

Maketa has been accepted as special among his people.

Although many albinos cannot see well, Maketa's sight is exceptional. Since he reached the age at which he could aim a gun he has been honoured for being the best shot among all the Baphuthi people. So much so, that Moorosi presented him with a Winchester repeating rifle, the best of all the people's firearms.

Now Maketa is ready to use his skills to defend the only way of life he knows and the king he respects because he does not judge people by their looks.

Quthing — Sunday April 6, 1879

Cheers surround them as Hook and Lieutenant Best arrive shortly before sunset with the two seven-pounder muzzle-loading guns sent by Brabant.

Griffith calls his senior officers to his tent. "We have been camped here for nearly two weeks," he says. "Now that we have the seven pounders and the rocket launchers, there is no reason to wait for Brabant to reach here. Also, another troop of Cape Mounted Riflemen arrived a few days ago. We are ready to go forward.

"Here is how I will launch the attack."

15

Quthing — Monday April 7, 1879

Shortly after dawn, Griffith calls his men together on the grassy parade ground at the foot of the mountain. He outlines his plan of action. Scott and Brown join their colleagues, wondering whether Granville, still stationed in Palmietfontein, is wishing he were with them at the scene of the action.

Also listening is Secretary for Native Affairs William Ayliff, who has ridden to the mountain from his quarters at Thomas's Shop to watch the attack.

"We estimate Chief Moorosi to have 200 to 300 followers with him on the mountaintop," Griffith says, standing with his back to the mountain. "The mountain, as you can see, is inaccessible on three sides. We are calling the face behind me, the only accessible part, the 'attacking side.' It is steep and consists of a succession of three ledges, or tiers, one above the other. The Baphuthi have made excellent use of these natural ledges by building flanking walls on them.

"The walls are constructed of stone and earth and have been arranged with great skill. From this distance, they appear to be three to four feet high, but stand on ledges that vary from five to seven feet high. So we are faced with three tiers, one behind the other, each of which has a total height of nine to 12 feet. As you have no doubt observed, Moorosi's men are well armed and some are positioned behind the ledges.

"It would appear that these fortifications cannot be taken by straightforward assault without a great loss of life. As a result, I made up my mind when we arrived to invest the place to await the arrival of the two seven-pounders. They will be able to break down the walls and expose the enemy before we assault the mountain.

"In the meantime, while retaining the investment here, I have posted pickets day and night around three sides of the mountain, as many of you know who have been assigned those duties. I did not assign anyone to guard the far side as it consists of a perpendicular *krantz* that no one can climb.

"Let us remember, too, that the men on the mountain are not the only rebels. Until recently, others remained scattered around the countryside, hiding in caves and in the steep mountain valleys.

"So I have in recent days sent out patrols of mounted Basotho in different directions to scour the country and harass the rebels wherever and whenever they can be found. These patrols have succeeded in capturing 2,000 head of cattle, 2,000 sheep and goats and 400 horses."

The men cheer.

"On the west bank of the Orange River, the chief Lerothodi captured 2,000 head of cattle and 100 horses at a cost of two men wounded. He has also sent in six stands of arms, taken from rebels who surrendered. Six of the rebels were killed. I must also mention the good work of Captain J. G. Wood of the First Yeomanry. He and his men captured 700 head of cattle, 1,000 sheep and 50 horses with no casualties.

"Captain O'Connor has been working for 50 miles up and down the Orange River, clearing the country of rebels. In some cases they dislodged the rebels from strongholds capable of holding 500 men. They found large preparations for a siege.

"Essentially, therefore, the territory has been cleared of rebels. Now we are about to complete the task with an assault on the mountain stronghold here.

Seven-pounder mountain gun

"It has been a rather tedious and trying duty to invest the mountain over the past 12 days, but, as I am sure everyone here knows, the two seven-pounders arrived yesterday, brought here by Lieutenant Best. Now we can execute our plan of attack."

Griffith points to a cleared position among the tents. "About noon today, the field-guns, mounted on the same carriages on which they were towed here, will be drawn into position on this cleared ground, just out of Baphuthi rifle range, but close enough for the shells to reach the stone walls.

"Tonight we will fire eight rockets on to the mountain fortress. That will soften the enemy and warn the Baphuthi of the kind of attack they can expect.

"Later tonight, under cover of dark, the assaulting party — number 4 and 5 troops of Cape Mounted Riflemen under Captain Grant, assisted by Captain Surmon, numbering about 60 men, and about 100 members of the 3rd regiment of yeomanry under Colonel Minto — will move into a cave at the base of the mountain. You cannot see it from here, but it is near the first line of defences," he adds, turning and pointing behind him. "It will be under cover from the enemy's fire."

Brown, who is with No. 5 Troop of the Cape Mounted Riflemen, turns to Scott. "Hear that? That means I'll be joining them in the cave," he says. "I'll be among the first to storm the mountain." He smiles with pride.

"Better you than me," replies Scott.

Griffith continues. "The storming party is to wait in the cave till the fortifications have been well shelled. Their advance will be sounded by a bugle call.

"The supports will be three other troops of the Third Yeomanry under Colonel Southey. They will take up position on this side of the plateau. They will shelter from Baphuthi fire under the rocky overhang before I give the word for them to join the Riflemen who by then will have emerged from the cave, marched on to the plateau and headed toward the stone walls.

"In addition, I am ordering the 2nd Yeomanry to furnish three troops as supports and three more as reserves to Captain Grant. They will take up their positions on the knoll, or saddle, on which we have set up the picket.

"The Basotho under Lerothodi will take up position on the western side of the plateau, not far from our tents.

"To summarize: At sunrise tomorrow, around 6 o'clock, we will start pounding the mountain with the guns. Once these formidable weapons have subdued the enemy and opened a way for us to attack, the men in the cave under Grant will rush forward on to the plateau and up the path to the top, to be shortly followed by those troops who are on this side, on the knoll and west of the plateau. I suspect that most of the rebels will flee ahead of you. Your march to the top should be relatively easy.

"When you reach the top, you will take prisoner all who surrender and you will find and arrest Moorosi.

"I see no reason we should not be able to accomplish these tasks in one day. We could even be having breakfast with Moorosi tomorrow.

"As a result, we will end this siege before the Easter festival which starts on Friday. I cannot promise that you will be home for Easter; but I am confident that you will be on your way home by then."

The men arranged before Griffith are quiet. Scott shakes his head, but to most of the men, the plan seems a sound one.

In any event, it is not their place to question their commander's strategy, but simply to carry it out.

"I suggest we assemble in small parties to discuss the arrangements for the attack in more detail. After that, we will retire to our quarters and rest for what will be a concerted and successful action," Griffith says. "Oh, and I would strongly discourage you from drinking anything but coffee in the next day or two," he adds. "When we are victorious, there will be plenty of time to celebrate."

The men, grumbling in response, make their way back to their tents.

"We're going to trounce them," Brown tells Scott, increasingly excited at the opportunity to see action.

"Those savages might be good at piling up stones, but after our big guns destroy their walls, they will be exposed like naked people. I will have great fun shooting them. To me, they are little more than dogs, wild rabid dogs, who serve no good purpose and deserve to be put down."

Scott is sceptical and unimpressed with Brown's bravado.

"I'm not convinced it's going to be that easy. Have you looked at those walls through spy glasses? Do you realize how many there are? They look fairly thick. It must have taken them months, maybe years, to build them. You think we can destroy them in a few minutes?"

But Brown remains confident. "We've seen nothing moving on that mountain, beyond a few goats and horses, for days now.

"When the shells fall on the walls, the only reaction is a cloud of dust.

"In any event, we don't have to destroy them all. We have only to pulverize them enough to make those poor miserable scoundrels run for their lives. They will be so scared. It will be great fun to pick them off with our rifles."

As they walk back to their tents, the men notice a trooper sitting alone on a rock near the camp.

Sketch of mountain assault [reproduced in *Capture of Moorosi's Mountain 1879* by Major G. Tylden in the *Journal of the Society for Army Historical Research*, 1934]

"Who is that?" Brown asks.

"I hear his name is John Brome," Scott replies. "They say he is a volunteer farmer from Komgha who signed up recently. He never talks with anyone. He just sits around looking sullen and morose."

"He doesn't look excited about storming the mountain," adds Brown. "I'm so excited that I'm not sure I will able to sleep."

Quthing — Tuesday, April 8, 1879

Shortly after 3 a.m. Grant leads the main attacking group along the neck between the saddle on Moorosi's Mountain and the mountain opposite.

The troops, armed with the carbines with which they have all been issued, trudge over the uneven ground and, after crossing the neck, turn left toward the mountain, headed for the cave. They move as quietly as possible. As far as they are aware, they have not been detected by Moorosi's men who, they assume, are still asleep.

When they are about halfway to the cave, the moon rises over the surrounding mountains, lighting the scene and making it easier for the men to find their way.

A stone slips under a boot and clatters its way down the slope. The men pause, as if doing so will prevent the sound being heard. But that does not help. The sounds have alerted the

Carbine used by Cape Mounted Riflemen

Baphuthi to the soldiers' advance. Aided by the moonlight, the Baphuthi roll rocks down the mountain toward them.

"Run for the shelter of the cave!" Grant shouts.

Many stumble as they run through the grass and over the rough rocky ground. When they reach the overhang, they huddle together. Here they will wait, ready to storm the stone walls as soon as they hear the signal.

Grant counts those who are with him. Thirty-three, including Brown, Captain Surmon and Lieutenant Mitchell, are from the Riflemen and 13, including Captain Smith, from the 3rd Yeomanry. Colonel Minto is absent.

Brown has noticed that Brome, the sullen man, is among those who failed to join them. "Where are the rest?" he asks. "About 160 were supposed to have been here, now there are only 46. Why aren't they here?"

"They will join us later," Grant replies, unsure of the reason.

Cut to a third of their appointed number, the men feel a sudden sense of foreboding and loneliness; so few for such an important task.

Cape Mounted Riflemen field dress

As the first rays of sunlight creep across the mountain, four more men scramble across the ground to the cave, bringing the number to 50. "We must perform our assigned duty without the rest of our troops," Grant says.

At dawn, as the artillery men move into position, Griffith stands on the saddle overlooking the plateau. In an attempt to identify with his troops, he is wearing a regular trooper's uniform rather than an officer's dress.

At 6 a.m. Griffith signals to Lieutenant Best to begin the firing. A soldier loads a shell into the muzzle of the first gun, another rams it down and a third pulls the lanyard that ignites the primer, which, in turn, ignites the powder in the shell and shoots it 500 yards across the plateau and at the mountain. The fourth man in the team stands back, ready to assist.

The explosion — deafening to those who are close by — is followed by a cloud of white smoke that temporarily hides the path of the shell from the men firing the cannon. As the smoke clears, Best raises his spy glass to examine the walls. The shell has fallen short.

The second cannon ball also fails to reach its target.

Best adjusts the guns' tilt. The men clean the

barrels before firing them again.

After several adjustments and several volleys, the shells pound into the walls.

"Think of it as a cricket ball," Best tells his assistants. "You do not want to bowl a fast ball that has a flat trajectory, but a slow ball that rises into the air. You want to lob it high so that it falls both on the walls and on the men behind them."

The men, working with clockwork precision, continue firing each gun alternately, sending an average of three to four shots into the stone walls every minute.

Cannon impact on rock behind trench and stone wall

The Baphuthi stay in their positions behind the stone walls, watching as the cannon balls fly toward them. Moorosi has stationed himself in the front schanzes. Several of his sons take up positions behind the walls on the western side.

The noise of the gunfire, the smell of gunpowder and the white smoke drifting toward the mountain alarm the warriors. It hurts their ears, offends their senses and represents a new form of warfare. It is loud and comes in waves. When the first seven-pound shells slam into the walls and nearby rocks, shaking the ground like an earthquake, they feel fear.

But, after a while, they note that the damage is limited. In the time between volleys the men crouch down and run to pick up shell fragments. They return to their posts and examine this new type of fire power that spies have heard the colonists refer to as the steel guns.

"Let them fire their large guns with the smoke and noise," Moorosi says. "They will not harm us. Our defences are strong. If you see part of a wall that has been damaged, repair it, but make sure you are not hit by another shell." The chief adds that his men should hold their fire; those operating the guns are out of range.

The shelling continues for what seems like hours. Each time a hole is punched in one of the walls, the Baphuthi rush to repair it.

After firing about 100 rounds, Best orders the artillery to stop. Griffith, having noticed a number of Baphuthi scurrying up to the top of the mountain, is convinced the cannon fire has driven the enemy from their positions behind the walls.

At 8 a.m., Griffith gives the order to sound the advance.

As the bugle sounds, Grant and Surmon instruct the men to line up outside the cave where they are still out of range of Moorosi's rifles. From there, they are to march toward the point from which they will advance on the stone walls. The troops line up in rows.

From a distance, they look like toy soldiers: black velvet corduroy trousers, blue jackets with white sashes and brown helmets with the golden royal insignia. Each carries a Martini-Henry rifle. At their head, a soldier holds high an embroidered flag that reads, "Onward to Victory."

"Let's show that old chief and his followers their time has come," Grant shouts.

"Go, Cape Mounted Riflemen! Go, Yeomanry! Storm the mountain!"

The men set off in double time, their ankle boots crunching the ground below, sending stones scattering.

They advance in formation, but yell freely. Some shout "hurrah for the Queen" while others scream obscenities at the enemy. They have 250 yards of ground to cover to the first tier of stone walls. After 50 yards, they come within direct range of the Baphuthi rifles.

Moorosi cannot believe his eyes. These crazy white soldiers, dressed in outlandish costumes that make them ideal targets in the early sunlight, are advancing toward

View of the plateau from behind the stone walls. In this recent photograph, remnants of the walls are in the foreground; the saddle in the background. The trees were not there in 1879.

his warriors as though they want to die.

They don't duck or weave, but keep in formation. "Look at me," they are saying, "Here I am. Shoot me please."

He is only too pleased to oblige.

"Keep firing," Moorosi shouts as he and his best marksmen maintain a barrage of fire. He calls the men in the tiers above to join in.

There is no need for them to remain farther up the mountain as a reserve force. Maketa, the albino, aims his Winchester and scores his first hit.

⁂

The Mounted Riflemen march on undeterred. But as they approach closer to the walls the bullets begin grazing some and piercing others through their clothing. One shot knocks Surmon's revolver away as it enters his side. He falls. As the 57-year-old captain, blood oozing from his side, struggles to claw his way back to the safety of the cave, the rest ignore him, retain their formation, and march relentlessly forward.

As they get closer not only bullets but also stones, rocks and even huge boulders bound toward them down the mountainside.

Grant sees 100 of Minto's yeomen appear on the plateau from the direction of the saddle and he beckons to them to join the assault. It now becomes clear to Grant what happened; rather than move on to the cave early this morning, Minto instructed his men to hold back until the order was given to storm the mountain.

Grant's men cheer at the sight of reinforcements, but soon Minto's men come under intense gunfire. Unlike Grant's men, who are approaching from the side, Minto's men are moving directly toward the walls and well within rifle range. "The bullets are whizzing about us like hail," one yells.

Leading Minto's yeomanry, Lieutenant H.A. Reed moves out ahead and looks back, urging the men to follow him. He has not moved more than a few yards when a bullet fired from a stone wall strikes his face, penetrating behind the right eye. He collapses.

Seeing him fall, most of the men hold back, but about 15 continue to advance undaunted, leaving Reed lying where he fell. Moments later, Sergeant John Edwards and Private John Paschke are also hit. The two injured men scramble behind a lone rock, some 40 feet from the stone walls.

Unaware that the yeomanry under Minto are being gunned down, the soldiers under Grant arrive on the plateau in front of the walls. Grant instructs them to change to a wide shoulder-to-shoulder line, facing the enemy.

"On to victory," Grant shouts. "Advance to the walls and climb them! Go, Riflemen, go!"

The men, now facing the Baphuthi head-on, rush forward. The firing is intense. Many scream as they are hit in the arm, chest or leg. Some fall; others stumble in an attempt to find cover. Brown dodges from side to side, trying to make himself a difficult target.

Above them, the soldiers see an array of gun barrels poking through loopholes in the stone walls, filling the air with smoke and the acrid smell of gunpowder. Some consider firing into the walls above them, but they realize that stopping to load and aim their rifles will make them even better targets.

Baphuthi rile

A side group led by Grant works its way up to the rocks at the north end of the stone walls where the walls are shorter and easier to reach. Climbing the rocks, they reach the base of the first tier and soon are staring directly into the loopholes.

The Baphuthi stab at them with spears through the loopholes and throw rocks over the top of the walls. The colonial soldiers fire at them with their pistols.

Private George Rogers clings to the face of a rock, waiting for the opportunity to fire his pistol through one of the loopholes. As soon as the spear is removed, he determines, he will fire through the hole.

Suddenly a shot comes from a point farther down the stone wall and Rogers falls, pierced by a bullet in his right eye.

Corporal Charles Martindale jumps down and picks him up in his arms.

As he carries Rogers to safety, Martindale is shot in the leg and collapses, bleeding profusely. He drops Rogers, who is now close enough to drag himself to safety among the rocks.

From there, Rogers watches in frustration as the man who helped him tries to drag himself to shelter, but is unable to do so.

※

On the plateau, the rest of Grant's men break formation and run forward to the closest cover — the ledge below the first stone wall, where they can shelter.

From under the ledge, the men realize that the wall — built above the ledge — is a lot higher than it appeared from a distance. And the walls, intact in spite of the cannon fire, are bristling with men brandishing spears, some being thrown in front of them. Bullets, rocks and stones add to the onslaught, making it highly risky to move out from the ledge.

If they hunker down under the ledge, they are safe. But any attempts at venturing out are met with gunfire and more rocks.

"We can't climb this wall," Brown yells in frustration. "We're trapped. These men are crack shots. And they all fire one after the other, leaving no time between bullets. As one set of men load, the others are shooting."

A soldier, running from under the ledge closer to safety, is met with a hail of gunfire that creates so much dust that the soldier is temporarily hidden.

He makes it to safety, but no one follows him.

The men assess the situation. They count 12 wounded among them and a couple of men lying in the open — likely dead and at the moment not retrievable.

The men still able to fight are caught in a situation from which it seems impossible to escape without exposing themselves to extreme danger.

⸙

Aware that he probably has crossed the border into Quthing, Brabant is on the watch for rebels. So far, he and his group of 137 have seen no signs of them. The valley has begun to widen more, making the going easier. The weather is clear. Brabant insists the men need to move as fast as possible to meet Griffith at the mountain.

They are making good time when the men, hungry for meat after living on sparse rations, find a wide and deep cave filled with 200 sheep and goats. The men seize some of them. "These will supply us with meat," one says.

As they return, Brabant notes, "Because we are tired, let's spend the rest of the day and the night here where we can defend ourselves. But we must press on early tomorrow."

⸙

When Lerothodi sees the colonial soldiers falling to the enemy fire, when he sees the Baphuthi keeping the white soldiers at bay, and when he sees the futility of scaling the stone walls, he realizes that joining in the assault would be folly. He tells his men to stay where they are and not to join the storming of the mountain.

Although he is still angry at the Baphuthi people for killing his uncle, Lerothodi is having second thoughts about fighting with the white government. He still feels empathy with Moorosi and the king's attempts to preserve his people's way of life and to prevent the government taking over the running of his country.

Although Griffith is a fine man and speaks well to him and his father, he watches with concern as Griffith leads his white colonial soldiers in this fight against an old patriarch whose main concern is for the freedom of his people.

"This is a different Griffith," he thinks to himself. "He was a man we all admired. Now he is waging a war against our brothers."

⸙

The reserve troops stationed below a ridge at the southern edge of the plateau are in disarray.

As they watch the main advance become pinned down by surprisingly accurate enemy fire, they break ranks and scatter to avoid being told to join in the assault on the mountain.

Soon no officer can say he has the troops under control.

⸙

The two wounded troopers sheltering behind a rock on the open plateau — Edwards and Paschke — lie in pain, grateful that they are still alive, but uncertain how they will be able to make it back to safety.

There is scarcely enough room for both men to fit behind the rock. Paschke's right leg, struck twice by Baphuthi bullets, is exposed. He pushes toward the centre of the rock, pulling in his leg but causing Edwards to push out his leg on the other side, making it visible to the Baphuthi marksmen.

"Pull in your leg," says Paschke. As Edwards does, a bullet strikes the ground in the spot where his leg had been.

They sit huddled together, fearful of moving without risking their lives.

After two hours, Edwards and Paschke become desperate. Both men have staunched their wounds, but they have been able only to lessen the flow of blood and not stop it completely. Dehydrated and drained of strength, they continue to lose more and more blood. Their wounds need treatment urgently.

They decide to move out and try to make it to safety.

"I'll go first," Edwards says, dragging himself out from behind the rock. He screams as a bullet strikes him in the arm. He seeks the shelter of the rock once more. Now he is nursing two wounds. One in his leg suffered when he first was hit on the open plateau, and now another in the arm.

"I thought the firing had stopped," Edwards tells Paschke, talking slowly and carefully as the pain from his new wound starts to make itself felt. "But they are still there. What can we do?"

Edwards pulls himself up, catching a glimpse of the men hunched together behind the ledge, but collapses. A bullet whizzes over his head.

"The others are trapped under a ledge and we are trapped here."

The men realize they have nowhere to turn.

Edwards winces in pain as he looks down at his leg and sees flies settling on the caked blood. "The only reason Moorosi's men have stopped firing," he says slowly, gasping for breath, "is that no one is in their line of sight. As soon as we move, they will fire on us. And they are good shots."

Paschke, blood still oozing from the wounds to his side and his leg, lies quietly next to him. "I feel weak," he moans.

"We'll die here if we do not have a doctor and water," Edwards says slowly, the pain from the two wounds also sapping his strength. He has torn off his shirt and bound it around the deep bullet wound in his leg. The shirt is saturated in blood. He fears he is in danger of passing out from the loss of blood and dehydration.

"Do you have water?" he asks.

"No," Paschke replies, barely able to speak.

"Send a doctor!" Edwards screams toward the ledge,

"It's too dangerous," a yeoman yells back.

"Then bring us water," Edwards yells. "Water! We'll die without water."

Paschke is quiet. His face is drained of colour and he is fading fast. Edwards must try to save him — and himself. Summoning all the strength he has left, he screams again for water.

The soldiers under the ledge hear Edwards's screams. They ignore them. They cannot afford to risk their lives because someone needs water.

As more hours pass by, the men sheltering under the ledge turn to their task, which remains to scale the walls. Cowering here will accomplish little. They become restless, feeling guilty about failing to fulfil their duty, but afraid of being killed. As they discuss how to storm the wall, they note that the firing appears to have stopped. They need to resume their attack.

Corporal L.W. Bean volunteers to lead the way.

He steps out from the safety of the ledge and turns to face the wall. Using indentations in the rock face, he clambers upward. As he reaches the bottom of the stone wall, he grabs the muzzle of a Baphuthi rifle protruding from a loophole. But the rifle is wrenched back, out of his grasp.

A rock hurled over the wall hits Bean, causing him to fall backward, to the ground. He creeps under the protection of the ledge once more, telling his fellow soldiers what he did.

"That's not the way to do it," says Private William Braine. "We must get up there and get them where they are hiding behind the walls before they see us. If Bean can grab a rifle, it must be possible for us to make it over the wall."

Before anyone can stop him, Braine adds, "I am going up there."

He runs a short distance away from the rock face on to the open plateau, turns and hurls himself toward the wall.

He scrambles up the rock face, clinging to hand-holds. With a supreme effort, he pulls himself up and over two intersecting walls, trying to push them down as he does so.

Braine is lost from sight to the men below. For a moment they believe he might have succeeded. An outburst of firing behind the wall convinces them, however, that he likely has not. When he does not return, they are sure of it.

Corp. Charles Crole — more senior than those around him — suggests doing it differently. "We need to move out where we can see the walls, and fire at the men above us," he says.

"Private Braine has shown us that we can scale that wall if we are really determined. But we need to suppress the enemy fire first."

The men weigh up the suggestion. Having come under the fire of the enemy, they are unwilling to expose themselves to it again.

"They will not only fire on you, but will hurl down spears, rocks and stones on you," Trooper Peter Morley ventures. "I am ready to do what I can do to follow orders, but we will achieve nothing by being killed."

Others agree.

"If we all go together, we will not all be killed," Crole says. "I will show you how it can be done, just follow my example."

Trooper J. Broad tugs at Cole's arm and stops him. "You stay here," he says. "You already have suffered a bullet wound to your arm. Let me go."

He cocks his rifle and walks forward, away from the safety of the ledge. Before he can turn around and aim toward the walls, a sharp crack of rifle fire emanates from above him and a bullet strikes him in the side. He collapses.

Morley and two other men run forward and drag Broad back to safety. The bullet has torn a hole in his chest. The men bind up the wound and make Broad as comfortable as they can under the ledge. But they doubt he will survive the loss of blood without medical help. And where will he receive such help now?

No one suggests venturing out into the open again.

❦

It is approaching noon. Edwards's screaming from behind the rock starts up again and becomes more intense.

Peter Brown

Brown shown assisting Edwards and Paschke in a fanciful contemporary sketch.

"Water. Water. We need water," he screams. "We'll die without water."

He repeats his plea, fuelled by delirium.

"Water. Water. We need water. Water, water, water."

He shouts, over and over again.

"I can't stand this any longer," says Brown. "Those men need our help. Has anyone got water?"

A trooper hands him a half-filled canteen. "Here, you can have my water. But I wouldn't go there if I were you," he says.

Brown ignores the comment, drops his rifle and darts into the open. As he runs across the 40 feet of open space to the rock, the gunfire erupts once more and stones are pelted toward him. The men watch as he reaches the rock.

"Give Peter the water first," Edwards says. "He needs it more."

Brown bends down alongside Paschke. He shelters partly behind the rock, although his back can still be seen from the mountain.

Paschke drinks it all.

Brown takes a big breath and tears back to the shelter of the ledge. "Does anyone have more water?" he asks. "I need to help the other man."

"Here," says one of the troopers.

Once again, Brown runs across the open ground. This time he kneels alongside Edwards, exposing himself to the gunfire.

As the bullets fly past him, he

pours water into the trooper's mouth.

Edwards is still drinking when a bullet strikes Brown in the right arm, smashing the bone and knocking the canteen out of his hand. Brown picks up the canteen with his left hand before the liquid spills and pours more water into Edward's mouth.

Dr. Edmund Hartley

He has almost finished when another bullet punches a hole in the canteen, spilling the water on the ground. Almost immediately afterward, another shot hits Brown in the thigh, knocking him back. He pulls himself up once more and, narrowly avoiding being hit again, limps back to the safety of a different ledge, closer to a path of escape.

When he sees Brown's plight, Sergeant Major Edmund Baron Hartley responds. At 32, he's an accomplished surgeon and runs the hospital at Thomas's Shop. After arriving from Britain five years ago and serving as a district surgeon in Basutoland from 1874 to 1877, he was appointed surgeon to the Cape Mounted Riflemen.

Hartley creeps under the ridge to the north of the plateau, ducks behind a sheltered rock and back under the overhang until he reaches Brown. He dresses Brown's wounds as best he can.

"Are there any more wounded?" Hartley asks.

"There are a number of wounded where I was under the ledge," replies Brown. "And there are two unfortunate souls sheltering behind that rock," he adds, pointing out their position. "I received my wounds when I carried water to them. I fear that they might not survive unless they are rescued soon. But you're our surgeon and I don't think you should risk your life trying to reach them."

Hartley nods. "We should get you to camp as soon as possible."

Together, the men scramble down the hill. Edwards' renewed groans and cries of "Water, water, water" slowly fade into the distance.

As Hartley binds up Brown's wounds, Scott strides up, relieved that his friend, although wounded, is safe and appears likely to recover. "Why are the others still there? Why didn't they follow you out?"

"It is hell out there, Robert," Brown replies, pausing to regain his breath. "I came out a different way. They would be risking their lives by trying to do the same. Those savages are good shots, particularly the albino."

Brown tells Scott how he risked the fire power himself when he took water to the two injured men trapped behind a rock. "I nearly lost my life," he adds. "I suppose it was a foolish thing to do. But someone had to help them. "

※

It is afternoon when Southey, whose reserve troops have seen no action today, approaches Griffith on the rocky outcrop. "If you feel it is expedient for me to do so,

I will lead my reserve troops in support of the men trapped under the wall," he says.

Griffith thanks him, but turns down his offer. "It's just too dangerous right now," he says. "But I might take you up on that offer a little later. I have an idea that I need to discuss with some of my men. I believe it just might help us to gain the upper hand and enable your troopers to resume the assault on the mountain."

So far, Moorosi's defence tactics have worked flawlessly. The heavy stone walls have proven an effective barrier, both against bombarding from the seven-pounder cannon and from attempts by the soldiers to scale them. His men have fired well, killing a number of the enemy, pinning two behind an exposed rock, and trapping many more under the ledge.

This battle is proving to be easier and less painful than he had feared.

He walks down a path and along a trench where two walls intersect. In front of him lies the body of Braine, riddled with shots. The men leave the body where it has fallen, stepping around it to assume their firing positions.

"We will remove the body when the battle ends," Moorosi says. "I know that will be soon. The whites cannot do anything against us now. They're too afraid."

He addresses a number of the men behind the wall. "You are doing well," he says. "Maketa, your shooting has been good."

He turns to Lehana. "How many of our people have been hurt?" he asks.

"Only one or two," replies Lehana. "No one has been killed and the injuries are only slight. They are easily treated."

The casualties are nothing like those his people suffered in earlier clashes on open ground, when they numbered the dead in the twenties and thirties.

"We are winning," replies Moorosi. "Many among the enemy are dead. And the cost to our people has been small. I chose well when I chose this mountain to make my people's fortress."

It's mid-afternoon as Griffith outlines his plan to his special assistant Arthur Barkly, who normally serves as the magistrate at Mohale's Hoek. "I would like your assessment of my idea," he says. "First let me outline the background. Our problem this morning was that we were unable to lob the shells right into the enemy. We need to drop the shells behind those stone barricades where the enemy is."

"You might have to adjust the trajectory," says Barkly.

"Our men tried several times this morning to do that, but without any real success," Griffith responds. "Part of the problem is that we

Arthur Barkly

are too far away to aim the guns accurately."

"Are you proposing moving the cannon forward?" asks Barkly. "That would be dangerous. It would expose the artillery crews to the gunfire."

"No, I am not suggesting that, Mr. Barkly. Here is my idea. We take the time-fuse shells and use them in the same way you would use hand grenades. The men could run up and lob them over the walls. The shells will explode behind the walls and the shrapnel will cause severe injuries."

Barkly's eyes light up.

"That would silence the enemy gunfire, at least for a while, and give our men the chance to climb the walls," he says.

"Indeed."

"But surely the men lobbing the shells will be exposed to gunfire when they rush the walls?"

"That is the risk we have to take," Griffith responds. "Would you kindly ask Lieutenant Best whether this plan is feasible? He understands the guns and the shells better than I do. If he says it is, obtain some men who will serve as volunteers to carry it out."

Best confirms that the plan is a good one and says he will explain it to the men. He walks to the men who were to have been the second and third assault waves.

"Here's the plan," he tells them.

Scott, who has joined his fellow reserve troopers, listens carefully to Best's plan. He recognizes it as an opportunity to play a meaningful role in the battle just as his friend Peter Brown has done. The first to volunteer, he moves forward without hesitation.

"I will go," he says.

Three others follow his example. The men walk to the cannon where Best hands each two ready-fused seven-pound shells.

"Once you reach the walls, you will need to light the fuses," he explains. "The shells will explode nine seconds after you light them. Hold on to them for about five or six seconds and then throw. Those villains won't know what has hit them. Each of you should hurl your shells in different places. With six explosions along the line of fire, we should be able to make a big dent in the enemy ranks."

Barkly adds his advice. "Obviously you are going to come under heavy fire as you approach the walls," he tells the men. "I suggest you run as fast as you can and zigzag as you go. The quicker you can cover that ground, the less likely you are to be hit. You will have the advantage of being a moving target. Run fast enough and by the time you have reached the walls they will be only loading their rifles.

"You should get as close as you can; even climb at least some way if that is possible so you can land those shells right in the enemy's midst. Get as close as you can as quickly as you can.

"Sergeant Scott, you are the leader. The rest of you should follow his instructions. When he tells you to run, run. When he tells you to throw, throw.

"Now go. Good luck to you all."

Scott is aware the mission has extreme risk. He will have to avoid Baphuthi gunfire until he reaches the safety of the ledge where he can light the fuse, then step out, climb the ledge, and throw the shell high enough to get over the wall.

"I want you to take cover to avoid injuries from any premature explosions," he tells the men who have been assigned him. "I will go first. Remember that even though we might be hit we can still lob those shells. We are risking our lives for our fellow soldiers. If we can succeed, they will be able to complete the mission."

Scott places the two shells in a bag slung across his chest. He sprints across the open plateau before reaching the wall. He has not gone far before the firing starts. The Baphuthi are able to load their rifles quicker than he thought. He wonders what kind of firearms they are using.

A bullet hits the ground alongside him; too close, he reckons. His fear gives him added speed. Even though the weight of the shells slows him, he reaches the wall in good time. And without being hit.

The soldiers sheltered against the rock wall to the right stare in amazement as Scott runs toward them. "What is he trying to achieve?" asks one. "He doesn't even have his carbine with him."

"Maybe he is a negotiator and we are going to have a cease-fire," suggests another, enlisting a chuckle from the men.

"I'm amazed he hasn't been hit," adds a third. "He's a lot braver man than I am."

Panting from the run, Scott pauses under the ledge to regain his breath.

He turns to the soldiers. "I'm going to lob shells over the schanzes," he says. "Others will follow me. We'll cause panic up there and the enemy will scramble up the mountain for their lives. Once that happens, you will be able to storm the walls. But, for now, I need you to move further down the ledge to avoid the effects of the explosion."

The men, filled with a mixture of admiration for Scott and apprehension for themselves, move lower down. They fear that, even should the shells remove the gunfire threat, it will not prove easy to scale the walls. Yet they remain committed to carrying out their assigned duties if it is possible to do so.

"Now for the tough part," Scott says to himself, aware his every move is being watched by the three other volunteers with shells and by the men who will assault the walls.

He removes the first shell from his bag and lights it. Holding it in his right hand, he finds a protrusion on the rough wall. He counts slowly to seven as he pulls himself higher and places his feet in niches in the rock wall so that he is in a higher position to lob the shell over the schanzes above him. "..five, six, seven," he says to himself.

He lobs the shell in the air, watching as it flies over the stone wall above him. When he hears loud shouting from the Baphuthi above him he knows the shell has landed in the intended spot.

⚜

The Baphuthi are mystified as to Scott's intentions when they see the trooper running toward them. "He has no gun," observes Maketa. "Why is he running here?"

Only when Scott lobs the shell and it makes a fizzing sound as it flies over the wall, do the Baphuthi realize what Scott is doing.

"Out of the way," Maketa yells as the shell lands alongside him. He recognizes what it is and starts to run in the opposite direction. Before he has moved more than a few paces, he looks back because the shell has not exploded.

Maketa runs back, seizes the shell, and tosses it back over the wall.

※

Scott watches as the shell is thrown back. He runs forward and picks up the shell, determined to lob it back before it explodes.

"Watch out," he screams, running back toward the ledge with it.

The men, frozen with fright, brace themselves for the explosion.

Scott looks down at the shell and stops. As he reaches the safety of the ledge, he removes the fuse. He shows it to the men. "It failed to fire," he says. The soldiers breathe a sigh of relief.

Scott reaches into his bag for the second shell.

This time, he will count to seven, pause slightly, and then lob the shell. The closer he can get to having the shell explode exactly as it hits the ground the less chance the Baphuthi will have to throw it back.

In case he did something wrong last time, Scott makes sure he lights the fuse correctly.

He grabs on to the rock wall and starts hoisting himself up it.

As he does, Scott looks at the shell in his right hand and realizes too late that the fuse is defective. Suddenly the shell explodes in his hand, instantly shattering it. The cap on the shell bursts off, puncturing his left leg. Other pieces of shrapnel cut into his body.

Pieces of the shell fly toward the soldiers under the ledge. Several hit Trooper Morley, who failed to move lower down as Scott requested. He screams in pain and falls. His fellow soldiers run to assist him.

The explosion not only has severely injured Scott, it has caught his shirt on fire. He falls to the ground, slapping at the flames with his left hand in an attempt to put them out.

Horrified by the turn of events, the other three bomb carriers run forward to take his place.

"Stay there!" Scott shouts to them.

Although the firing has stopped as the Baphuthi on the ledges above watch in amazement at the flames surrounding him, Scott is aware that the firing could resume at any minute and be directed at the others, who continue to run toward him.

Summoning every ounce of strength he has left, Scott barks at them: "I am ordering you to stay there!"

As the men — unwilling to disobey an order — hesitate, Scott remembers the drill he had been taught should his clothes ever catch on fire, something he had considered highly unlikely at the time. He drops to the ground and rolls over and over, setting fire to a patch of grass. The flames go out, but in his manic effort, Scott continues rolling. He does not realize how close he is to the edge of the plateau. He rolls over an incline and falls 25 feet to the valley below.

Griffith is dismayed. His plans have gone awry. How many times in the past had he not made similar plans and seen them carried out? True, now and then there were hitches. Not every plan works right. But never before had they all gone wrong.

He looks across at the Basotho under Lerothodi who fired their rifles from a distance, but did not get within range of the enemy. It is clear that they were reluctant to get involved. That was only one disappointment on this unfortunate day.

Yesterday, as he planned the attack, he was convinced the big guns he so desperately needed would blast their way to victory. Now he knows they could not do so.

Yesterday he visualized his men assaulting the stone walls, overwhelming the Baphuthi fighters and climbing relentlessly to the top of the mountain. Now he has 50 soldiers pinned under a ledge, two seriously wounded men sheltering behind a rock, an unknown number killed, and a Basotho fighting force unwilling to fight.

Yesterday he was convinced his men's bravery and ingenuity would gain him victory. Now even a brave act by a sergeant has fallen flat.

Yesterday, his men were fit and eager to fight. Now even the men being held in reserve are in a state of panic.

Yesterday he told his men they would take the mountain and cause the Baphuthi to flee. Now his men are the ones on the run.

Griffith had no idea it would be this tough. True, his men fought bravely. They showed extreme courage. But the task was too great for them.

Enough recriminations, Griffith concludes. They can wait. Now he must rescue the situation. He must engineer a withdrawal before more lives are lost.

He is considering how to effect that withdrawal when Grant climbs the saddle to speak with him. "I have to report that the attack we launched from the cave has failed," he says.

Griffith simply nods. He does not want to speak out of fear that his emotion will show in his voice. Grant stands silently alongside him, unsure whether to continue speaking. Griffith's disappointment, anger and humiliation are apparent in spite of his attempts, in true British fashion, to hide his emotions.

Griffith gathers his composure. His task now is to save his men pinned under the ledge. He asks Grant to instruct Best to resume firing the cannon. "The men need to be withdrawn," he says. "We have to provide them with cover so that they can retreat. If we wait until the sky starts to darken and we fire the cannon then, it will be more difficult for the enemy to see and fire at our men. Not only will their sight be limited, but as we fire the cannon in the failing light, they will also be disoriented."

He desperately hopes the manoeuvre will work.

Scott moans in pain as his fellow bomb carriers reach him. One bends down to examine him.

"He is alive," he says. "I don't know how he did it, but he is alive." The man looks up at the cliff and shakes his head in amazement at Scott's ability to survive not only having his hand blown off, his thigh torn apart, and his clothes catch on fire, but also plummeting down the mountainside.

The men lift him up gently and place him on a blanket. They lift the blanket and carry the injured soldier over the stone-covered ground toward one of the tents where the surgeon, Edmund Hartley, is waiting.

⁂

It is growing dark as the commander's final battle plan of his disastrous day takes shape.

Griffith has decided that not only should they shell the stone walls, but they should keep up a steady rifle fire as well. He places the reserves in position.

"It is not important whether you hit the enemy," he tells them. "I know that is almost impossible to do from this distance, particularly as they are hiding behind the walls. Your job is to keep firing, one after the other in quick succession, so that they are distracted. At the same time the cannon will be fired. That, combined with the failing light, should draw their attention away from the ground in front of them so we can get our men to safety and bring down the wounded."

Close to 7 o'clock, as the sun dips over the mountains, Griffith gives the order to start firing. The hills echo with loud explosions interspersed with the pop of rifle fire. White smoke drifts across the plateau as the men scramble down the mountainside in small groups. The Baphuthi taunt them to return.

"Come and get us."

"Here we are."

"Why are you running away?"

Grant, looking worried, strides up to Griffith.

"I must report, colonel, that Sergeant Edwards and Private Paschke, who are both badly wounded, are still lying under cover on the plateau," he says. "I think it is safe to bring them down now that it has become dark. Unless you disagree, I will give orders that it be done.

Griffith nods. "Go ahead."

"Also, I need to report, sir, that Captain Surmon is missing," Grant adds.

"He is one of our finest men," responds Griffith. "A great leader and popular among the men. When last did you see him?"

"He was among those who stormed the mountain at dawn; he was the senior officer who led the men. But we lost sight of him in the fighting. Perhaps he is among those sheltering against the wall, although no one has reported seeing him there."

A Basotho man runs up to the camp. "My master is lying badly wounded in a cave," he says, pointing toward the side of the plateau. "I'll show you where to go."

A group of volunteers follow the Basotho man, who has remained faithfully at Surmon's side for the entire day. The captain, badly wounded, can barely speak. The men carry him carefully to a tent that has been set up as a field hospital.

As darkness sets in, with the heavy firing still under way, Griffith orders the unhurt men to return to the ledge and to bring down the wounded. Many are suffering from gun wounds; those unable to walk are carried down the mountain slope while the others are assisted over the rough terrain.

By half past eight all dead have been brought down from the mountain, except Braine, whose body still lies behind the stone walls. Also left behind on the plateau is a tattered flag, trampled under foot as the men scrambled to save their lives. The words, "Onward to Victory" are barely discernible in the dirt.

Griffith orders the shelling to stop. Best reports that 125 shells were fired during the day. "That is more than I fired during the whole Gcaleka campaign," Griffith says. He adds, to himself, "and that campaign I won."

As lanterns flicker in the tents, and the men huddle outside around fires to counter the cool temperature that has set in, the mood is sombre as the men reflect on the lost battle. Tired and sore, those not injured sit around drinking coffee, relating to their fellow soldiers how tall the ledges and stone walls were, how it was impossible to climb them and wondering how they will ever take the mountain.

"We failed," says Thomas Reeves, a member of the Cape Mounted Riflemen who spent the day under the ledge. "They are calling it a check and a 'slight repulse,' but I say we should look at it for what it was. It was a failure."

"Perhaps," replies James Gorman, one of the reserves. "But we were not disgraced. We didn't turn and run. We did what we were told to do. We did it as best we could."

"But no amount of bravery can take away the fact that we failed," says Reeves. "Imagine what the people in the rest of South Africa are going to say about this. Think what the Basotho people are going to think of us. We failed. It was a grand failure that will have repercussions around the country. If not the world.

"Just look at what has happened. We and another 500 of us sat here for 12 days, doing nothing but waiting for those useless toy guns to arrive. In the meantime, the enemy on the mountain were adding to their stone walls. They saw us down here. They knew what we were going to do. When we attacked they were ready for us.

"And then what do we do? Do we shell the walls for a full day? No. We fire a few shots into those stone walls. They have no effect. And then we stop firing. Instead of us advancing under a cover of heavy fire, not a shot was fired after we came in range of their fire. Our officers were much more surprised than we were at the resistance offered. We underrated the enemy and the usual consequences followed. And we didn't do it on the cheap. I hear £200,000 was spent on keeping us here before the cannon arrived."

A third trooper joins in. "I want to know why the Yeomanry didn't join us. We had to rush through that hail of gunfire while they sat back. Group of cowards."

"You can't blame them," says Reeves. "They saw what was happening to us. Apparently they were firing over our heads and I am sure that helped when we stormed the mountain. If it had not been for them, maybe none of us would have been alive to sit around this fire tonight. If they also had stormed the mountain, there would have been no fire from below to cover their charge."

Not far away men of the Yeomanry also gather to discuss the day's events.

Comments one, "I know they're saying we're cowards. I am not a coward. I would have stormed that mountain if I had been ordered to do so. I thirsted for blood and I would have thought no more of shooting a native than I would a dog."

"Perhaps you would have," another replies. "But I don't mind admitting I was a coward. I tell you I'd rather be a frightened Peter than a dead Peter."

❧

Senior officers, all on the front line in today's fighting, sit around their own fire, holding their own post-mortem inquiry into the day's events.

"I think Colonel Southey should have been in charge," says Captain Fincham. "He has the confidence of more officers and men. I've seen him in action and he is always cool, cautious and observant. He stands up solidly in the face of danger and he has undaunted courage."

"You're right," says Captain Leach. "He is quick to notice opportunities and to avail himself of them."

Fincham continues, "The problem with Griffith is that he has worked among the Basotho so long that he has inoculated himself with the Basotho nature. He has become like them, and I don't think he really wants to fight them.

"His old fire is quenched; instead of acting quickly, he has become deliberate. It is almost as though he is doing what he must do and not what he wants to do. He is cautious and slow. He lets opportunities slip past him."

"I agree," says Leach. "He's impassive. It's excessively annoying — and I might add discouraging — when you're dealing with him."

"He's excellent as a political chief," says Fincham, "but a worse selection could not have been made for the military chief. He never really allowed the guns to do their work of breaching the walls.

"He didn't acquaint himself with the task that he required the force to execute. If he had, surely he would have realized it was nothing short of stark madness to order men to charge up the face of a hill at those stone fences. It was worse than foolhardiness to send the men there only to discover that the enemy position was unassailable. It was a foolish sacrifice of valuable lives, to say nothing of those who were injured."

As the officers continue their discussion, Brome, who is thankful that he was not ordered to take part in the assault, leaves his fellow soldiers and wanders down to the temporary morgue. Among the bodies in it is that of Paschke, who died shortly after being brought down from his spot behind the rock.

Brome walks to a series of tents in which some 25 men lie with wounds. In one tent, four are from the ranks of the Cape Mounted Riflemen who stormed the mountain: Trooper J. Broad, Sergeant W. F. Cole, Corporal Charles Martindale and Captain James Surmon, who is suffering from a serious gunshot wound to the lung. Edwards, who sheltered behind the rock with Paschke, is also there. They appear to be the most seriously hurt.

Brome feels their pain as if it were his own. He watches Hartley, the surgeon, tend to the men. When Hartley is done, and leaves the tent, Brome inquires of the men's condition.

"I don't like to say it, but the men in this tent are not expected to survive," Hartley says. "We will still fight to save their lives and I have instructed that, if possible, three of them be taken to the hospital we have set up at Thomas's Shop. But Surmon is too seriously injured to move. I have instructed that he not be disturbed.

"Most of the wounded in the other tents are expected to survive. They are suffering from gunshot wounds to the legs, arms and face. Three were struck in the head by rocks hurled from the mountain.

"I'll have to amputate the limbs of three of the men in the morning when it is light. One of those is Scott, whose right hand is too severely injured to save."

With Brome following close behind him, Hartley enters another tent and crouches at the side of Brown's stretcher. "Your body will heal, but I am sorry to have to tell you that you will not be able to use your right arm again," Hartley says. "Your fighting days are over. Your age of 45 counts against you, too. I suggest you retire on pension."

Brown, tired and suffering severe pain, has learned that war is less than the adventure he remembers from earlier years. Killing barbarians proved not to be that exciting or rewarding.

"I will accompany you and some of the other wounded men to Aliwal North where you will be cared for at the hospital," Hartley says.

Brome lingers at the entrance to the tent after Hartley leaves. Brown, looking for someone to blame for his suffering, calls to him, recognizing him as the loner who spoke with no one.

"Did you ever become involved in the assault?" he asks.

Brome is quiet for a moment. "No. I was not ordered to do so."

"You should have volunteered, to make up for those who were ordered to join us but did not do so," says Brown. "If we had more men we might have won. It's sad that so many of them were too cowardly to join us."

Brome does not respond. He has no answer. Perhaps he is a coward. If he could leave the camp and go home now, he would. When he signed up as a volunteer, he regarded it as his patriotic duty. He told his wife it would be an honour to serve in the military, to protect his fellow men and to defend their farms and settlements from native attacks.

But what he once thought would be little more than a police patrol has become a death mission. Although he cannot bear to see his fellow soldiers suffering, he realizes he is pleased he did not volunteer to join in the assault.

"I'm sorry. I hope you get better," he mumbles.

He pushes open the tent flap and leaves.

Brown calls out to him.

"I am sure you'll get another chance. We're not going to stop until we win. Get out there and kill those rebel good-for-nothings. Do your duty to God and country!"

⚜

Griffith walks in and out of the tents of the wounded men, commiserating with them and thanking all for their valiant efforts.

He walks across to the group of Cape Mounted Riflemen. "I have never seen anything quite like the way you stormed that mountain," he says to them. "Observers from the colony tell me they would have travelled 200 miles to see that sight. You are a brave and honourable group of men and I am proud of you.

"But, as I am sure you have concluded, storming the mountain without heavy artillery does not work," he says. "The seven-pounders were ineffective, mere toys. The ascent is more difficult than one would have thought from looking through even good glasses from the bottom of the hill.

"So my plan now is to starve out these people. They will not be able to survive for long without food and I am not sure how much water they have up there."

The men wonder why they had to endure so much pain and death before Griffith came up with that plan. And they wonder whether such a plan will ever succeed.

16

Quthing — Wednesday April 9, 1879

Scott lies in the tent. He must face a cruel reality, he says to himself. He has lost a hand. He will never be able to use that hand again. Never again. This wound, unlike others, will never heal.

In addition, his leg is throbbing and he wonders how that will heal or whether it, too, will have to be amputated, a routine procedure for severe leg wounds.

Yesterday he was proud to be strong and energetic; today he feels a quarter of a man. He cannot help thinking he is suffering because he volunteered to undertake a duty that should never have been attempted. He thinks of the other sufferers in the assault, men who also were the victims of an ill-considered assault plan. They did not trust Griffith's battle tactics on the eastern frontier; they should have known better than to trust them here.

Running through his mind are the words of the poem *The Charge of the Light Brigade* by Alfred Tennyson, written to commemorate a similar crazy mission undertaken by the British in Crimea in 1854. One verse in particular comes back to him.

Someone had blundered:
Theirs not to make reply,
Theirs not to reason why,
Theirs but to do and die.

When he had learned them by rote at school the words were little more than a cascading rhyme. Now Scott finds himself thinking for the first time of the meaning behind those words.

Someone had blundered.

Griffith, perhaps? He had rushed without thinking into the battle, refusing to wait for Brabant's forces. Would it really have been so bad to have waited a day or a week? Or did Griffith want to take all the glory?

Theirs not to make reply

No one could question whether Griffith had looked carefully into the battle plan, whether he was sure that the walls could easily be scaled, whether he had even taken time to consider what he was doing.

Theirs not to reason why

They had rushed into battle, like madmen, into a storm of gunfire.

Theirs but to do and die.

At least he is not dead.

❧

As he continues to assess the results of yesterday's assault, Griffith notes the death toll has reached four — so far — and the wounded 17, four of whom might not survive. The casualties, killed and wounded, amount to almost one-fourth of the hundred or so men who stormed the walls.

"We will have to arrange a burial for the dead," he tells Barkly. "I am sure you can find a chaplain to conduct the service. Choose a site for a cemetery."

Griffith prepares a report for Prime Minister Sprigg in Cape Town, including a request for the government to send as many men as it can spare.

He adds, "I have seen nothing of Colonel Brabant, who left Kraai River camp about eight days ago, and was supposed to be working his way down the Buffalo River to join me at this place."

Griffith also asks that a full hospital be established at Thomas's Shop Camp. Two more ambulance wagons are urgently required, he adds.

"I also require several hundreds rounds of ammunition, sent up without delay. Supplies for at least a month for eight or nine hundred men will be required."

Moorosi is proud of his men, of the way they fought and of the victory they achieved. He walks around the huts and the caves on the top of the mountain and ascertains the damages his men suffered. After listening to their reports, he summarizes the results.

"Motsapi, you were injured in the arm by a bullet when you were occupying the front position behind the wall; Mofullufullu, you were also hit in the arm by a bullet; Hlukana, you received a wound in your leg from a piece of a cannon shell that landed close to you in the trench behind the wall; Moshibidi, your hand was hurt by a cannon shell."

"These injuries are minor and they will heal. You all fought well and you killed and injured a number of white soldiers. I am proud of all of you. Maketa, I am proud of you, too. You shot well and accurately."

The albino man smiles.

"We won that battle, but the white men are still there," Moorosi continues. "Their tents are still there. You can all see them. The lion is still ready to pounce, and he is going to pounce on us again. But we are nimble antelope who will defend ourselves.

"Others of our people are hiding in caves along the rivers where they have defended themselves and are ready to fight in the way we have fought.

"When the whites eventually realize they cannot defeat us and give up and leave our land, we will join our brothers and sisters who are hiding in the caves and together we will take back our country and live in freedom once more.

"Now we must build up the walls where they have been damaged. We must make them higher and stronger so that when the next attack comes we will be able to repulse it as well as we did today."

Quthing — Friday, April 11, 1879

Brabant has travelled for more than three weeks, having led his men through swollen rivers, down the sides of steep ravines and across a high mountain that few people had ever crossed.

Now, having reached the headwaters of the Buffalo River, known to the local people as the Sibaphala, Brabant has picked up the pace. At noon, his men stop for a meal. One explores ahead and runs back to Brabant.

"We are only about five miles from the mountain," he reports. "I can see the tents around it." The men need no encouragement to pick up the pace and cover the five miles as quickly as possible.

❧

Late in the afternoon Brabant arrives at the mountain. Griffith comes out to meet him.

"I am pleased to see you," he says.

"Have the guns arrived?" Brabant asks. "I sent them through Palmietfontein."

"They have," replies Griffith. "They arrived on Sunday, we set them up on Monday. On Tuesday we fired them and stormed the mountain."

"You stormed the mountain? You didn't wait for me to arrive?"

"I believed we could scale those walls with comparative ease," Griffith responds. "I did not think your presence and any additional troops would have changed anything. My senior advisers agreed with me.

"It was only when our troops reached the spot just below the walls that we realized what we were up against."

"You found that the guns were ineffective, did you not?" Brabant asks.

"Yes."

"If you had waited I would have told you that Captain Giles is bringing a 12-pounder," Brabant responds. "That likely will be more effective against the stone walls and will make the job of the storming troops a lot easier.

"In addition, I have brought 140 men with me. Had you had them as well, you might have succeeded."

"I am not sure whether any number of troops would have helped. We might only have suffered more casualties. When the storming party reached the first line of schanzes, they found it was impossible to scale them or pull them down."

Quthing — Thursday, April 17, 1879

Ellenberger is taken by surprise at the hostilities at the mountain. When he saw the guns being transported past Masitise, he thought the battle would be some weeks off. Perhaps, he thought then, it could still be prevented. He knew more soldiers were on their way from Palmietfontein and he had heard that troops under Brabant were still to arrive.

When word reached him that a battle had already taken place, with loss of life and injuries on the government side, he was disappointed at being unable to negotiate a settlement. He realizes that more warfare probably lies ahead — unless he can step in and prevent it. He believes there is still hope for a peaceful settlement of the conflict, particularly in the wake of the failure of the attack on the mountain. Earlier, the government spoke confidently of defeating the Baphuthi, making them unlikely to seek any sort of settlement. Now they might be thinking otherwise.

So today he has come to the mountain to talk to Griffith to try to advance such a settlement.

"I am told that a number of Baphuthi people in caves and other hiding places want to surrender themselves and give up their arms," he tells Griffith. "Among them are a group who belong to Lehana's Ward and live up the river not far from my mission station at Masitise. They do not believe they have done anything wrong and do not want to fight against you."

As far as he can ascertain, Ellenberger adds, the stock under that group's control had originally consisted of 6,000 head of cattle, 6,000 sheep and goats and 700 horses. Of those, 2,000 head of cattle and 100 horses were captured by Lerothodi.

Griffith welcomes the news.

"Thank you for the information," he tells Ellenberger. "Thank you, too, for taking the time and effort to travel here to tell me. As you see, we have the mountain surrounded and we have a couple of guns in position.

"My plan now is to starve them out. They will become so hungry that they will be forced to surrender. This, I believe, is a more effective way of solving this problem and will involve less loss of life on both sides. But to do that I need more men and more fire power here and I am ordering that from the government."

Ellenberger nods. "Your approach might be the right one from a military perspective, but I believe that if you and the Baphuthi talked to one another and tried to understand each other we might avoid further conflict.

"As I said, several people in Lehana's district are ready to surrender. If you are prepared to reach a compromise with them, it is possible we could persuade more to stop their rebellion against the government. Offer them more autonomy, perhaps. You might have to give up something to achieve peace, but it'll be worth it.

"I wish once again you and King Moorosi could sit together on the Wodehouse bench as Colonel Bowker did. He was able to achieve a compromise solution and averted war.

"Perhaps you could talk and again achieve a compromise.

"The more you talk, the longer you keep the killing at bay and the closer you get to preventing more killing. Remember, as Christians, we are called upon to be peace makers, not war makers."

Griffith appreciates what Ellenberger is saying, but he remains a dedicated government official with the responsibility of carrying out his duty, which is to punish Moorosi, his family and his followers for rebelling against the government. But perhaps, as Ellenberger suggests, he could start with those hiding in the caves. They might be more amenable to compromise than Moorosi.

Before he leaves the mountain, Ellenberger visits the wounded men, including Captain Surmon. He prays for them.

Griffith suggests in a letter to Ayliff, who is still at Thomas's Shop, that Austen, who remains the magistrate of the Quthing district, be told of Ellenberger's statement that there are Baphuthi in the mountains who want to talk peace.

"Of course," he tells Ayliff, "all those who have taken a leading part in the rebellion will have to be tried for sedition. But many others have apparently only fled to the mountains from fear of their chiefs, and to get away from our forces.

"I think all the people who have not taken a leading part in the rebellion should be allowed to come in and give up their arms."

Quthing — Friday, April 18, 1879

Ayliff, responding to Griffith's suggestion, provides written instructions concerning those Baphuthi who wish to surrender that:

They hand over themselves and their arms to the government;

In surrendering, they are not exempted from trial should evidence be found justifying trial for any crime or aid in the rebellion;

If they agree to these terms, they should be placed in safekeeping and prevented from communicating with Baphuthi still in opposition to the government.

Quthing — Wednesday, April 23, 1879

Griffith has turned his attention to a cave along the banks of the Silver Spruit River in which a Baphuthi informant has told him that Lehana is hiding.

Lehana must be captured, not only because of his role in starting the war, but because he is undoubtedly helping to supply Moorosi on the mountain.

So it is that Griffith has sent 75 men under Captain Clough to seek out Lehana and his followers, charging them to use force only if Lehana refuses to surrender.

Today, after a march lasting most of the night, Clough, directed by the Baphuthi informer, is leading a party of men into a deep ravine called Quanatu. It is daybreak as Clough and his small band of troopers approach the spot. The informer points down the ravine. "That is where they are hiding," he says.

There, under a sheer rock face, 40 or 50 men led by Lehana have built a stone wall across the cave entrance. About a foot thick, it is loopholed in the same way as the stone walls on the mountain and has a narrow space at the top. Above this is another cave, a sort of second story, into which the men climb using a long pole set alongside the lower cave.

As Clough's party winds its way into the ravine, they see men watching them from the upper slopes opposite the cave. The watchers make no attempt to attack, even as the colonial soldiers commandeer a dozen horses and 16 sheep in the ravine.

As Clough approaches the cave, he divides his men into three groups. Two are to take up positions upstream and downstream, blocking the escape routes. He will lead the main party of 30 men toward the cave.

About 30 yards away from the entrance, Clough positions his sharpest shooters and waits, as arranged, for the arrival of Austen. "Mr. Austen understands the people and the terrain," Clough tells Captain Kemper. "I am waiting for his best judgment on whether I should launch an assault. I don't want to make the same mistake that was made in storming Moorosi's Mountain."

No one mentions calling on the Baphuthi to surrender.

The colonial soldiers wait with intense anxiety. They are talking nervously when a bullet is fired from the cave, striking the ground near one of the men. The soldiers dive for cover, from where they fire back, hitting two men who have stuck their heads out from behind the stone wall to fire more effectively. The injured Baphuthi duck behind the wall. Their heads have been grazed, but the injuries are not serious.

The Baphuthi continue to fire through the loopholes. After several exchanges, the soldiers are retreating as Austen arrives. He assesses the situation.

"I don't believe you should attempt to launch an assault on this cave," he tells Clough. "It is too well fortified. Should your men storm the lower tier of schanzes, they would be completely cut up by the men in the upper cave. They could destroy you." He, too, is afraid to see the disastrous attack on Moorosi's Mountain repeated.

"In addition, we have no medical men and no stretchers to carry the wounded," Austen continues. "This is one of the best-fortified caves that I have seen and I don't think we can take it. I suggest you withdraw."

Clough reluctantly agrees.

⁂

"We chased away the government soldiers," Lehana says. "All we had to do was to fire a few shots at them and they became afraid and ran away. We are safe here where we can stay until the war is over. We must get word to my father. He will be pleased."

Quthing, Thursday, April 24, 1879

Hearing that their father has been seriously wounded, Captain Surmon's daughters, Elizabeth, 24, and Evelina, 23, have arrived in camp. They are distraught. Their mother, Maria, died two years ago at the age of 41 when their family was living at Palmietfontein police station and they do not want to lose their father, too.

They ask directions to his tent where they promise they will watch over him and help nurse him to health in spite of the serious nature of his wounds. "He must not die," says Elizabeth. "He turns 58 on June 18th and we want to celebrate his birthday with him."

Cape Colony — Saturday, April 26, 1879

Debate on the failed attempt to storm Moorosi's Mountain has begun throughout the Cape Colony. Scapegoats are being sought. A loss cannot simply be accepted as a loss. Someone has to be held responsible.

To the white settlers, politicians and editorial writers, the explanation cannot be that the colonial forces were beaten by a better prepared force with a better strategy operating from a better position. It cannot be that the troops were out-shot and outwitted. It cannot be that Moorosi is a more wily fighter than anyone had thought. Surely, it cannot be that a native fighting force proved itself to be better than the Cape men trained in guerrilla warfare.

Yet the attack failed. There must be an explanation.

Under Secretary for Native Affairs Richard Bright, acting for Ayliff in Cape Town during the secretary's absence at the scene of the war in Basutoland, believes the blame lies with Austen for allowing Moorosi to build the fortifications at his mountain in the first place and not warning the government about them.

Aliwal North's *The Northern Post* also suggests the blame lies with Austen — not because he failed to warn about the stone walls, but because he shot two Baphuthi while on patrol.

"We do not wish to anticipate the results of an inquiry, which no doubt Parliament will institute, but we must say that Mr. Austen will have to show strong grounds for firing the two fatal and unnecessary shots, and for deserting his post so precipitately and without first warning the traders or giving the loyal and faithful people in the district an opportunity of declaring for the government.

"The question is: Could the rising of Moorosi, which has occasioned the loss of so many valuable lives, have been avoided by tact, prudence and courage; or did it break out in spite of the exercise of those qualities by the magistrate?

"For Mr. Austen's own sake, we trust there will be a searching investigation."

Others blame Griffith.

"The brave and gallant Southey was the proper officer to have had the command-in-chief," says the *Burghersdorp Gazette*. "He possesses the confidence of officers and men, and his conduct in action has shown him to be cool, cautious, observant; intrepid in danger and of undaunted courage; he is quick to notice opportunities and prompt to avail himself of them.

"New associations have metamorphosed Mr. Griffith and have inoculated him with the nature of the people he has been placed among...He is excellent as a political chief; but all parties agree that a worse selection could not have been made for a military chief."

A report in the *Queen's Town Free Press* also blames Griffith. It is written by a trooper who took part in the battle. "On the 8th one of the most grievous mistakes ever made in warfare in this colony was made by Commandant Griffith in ordering the attack on old Moorosi's Mountain. We had to own we had suffered a severe and humiliating defeat, without killing a single combatant on the enemy's side."

Argues *The Cape Argus*: "Whatever Mr. Griffith is, he is not a professional soldier. There could, therefore, have been no suppression in giving the chief command, when it came to military measures, either to Colonel Brabant or Colonel Southey, whichever may be senior, both being soldiers by training, and both enjoying more confidence than Mr. Griffith has lately been able to command."

The newspaper adds that "the military measures directed against the recalcitrant Moorosi have resulted in fiasco, while the attack upon his stronghold can only be described, in its own small way, as a disaster of serious moment.

"The result will doubtless shake the faith of those who have long held it as gospel that the colonial man, left to himself, will make short work of any African native who may dare to defy his arms."

To the missionary community, the blame lies with the disarmament measure pushed through Parliament by Sir Bartle Frere, a measure they vigorously opposed.

The missionaries are convinced the war with Moorosi was unnecessary and was caused by the disarmament act: "We would respectfully ask, even if it is not our duty to express our doubts in this momentous question, that the government should reconsider this serious question."

From his vantage close to the action, Native Affairs Secretary Ayliff has had time to ponder the effectiveness of Griffith's leadership in the assault on the mountain. He has concluded that Griffith conducted himself well. At no stage did he quarrel with Griffith's tactics. Some say Griffith should have waited for Brabant to arrive or that he should have ordered more powerful cannon or that he should have demanded that the soldiers climb the walls. Their suggestions, however, were all made after the fact. No one can conclusively demonstrate what would have worked.

Ayliff is upset at the casualties suffered in the attack. The latest death toll is seven, a figure that is too high. When added to the injuries suffered by nearly 20, some of whom have lost limbs, the battle was costly, both in men and money. Ayliff remains concerned at the mounting financial expense of the war effort. More men, more food supplies and more ammunition all cost money — and the colonial budget is far from overflowing.

But is the solution to take the command away from Griffith? Would someone else fare any better?

Starving the rebels out seems to be a reasonable approach. He will give the man another chance to prove himself.

Cape Town — The same day

Prime Minister Sprigg is fuming.

Before the attack, his officials had assured him there was little chance the attack would fail. Newspaper reports detail a disaster.

Sprigg grunts. "Coming on the heels of the Zulu defeat, this is extremely embarrassing," he tells Under Secretary Bright. "I can understand it — although not appreciate it — if a battle is lost against a bloodthirsty warrior with thousands at his disposal. But to lose to an old chief with a ragtag group of barbarians who live in the mountains...

"Now some are saying that we should withdraw; that we should let Moorosi go unpunished, that we should not complete what we started, that we should wave the white flag of surrender.

"I cannot accept that argument. One way or another, we have to remove Moorosi from that mountain."

Bright nods. "I cannot agree more," he says. "Imagine the impact a withdrawal would have on the Basotho people, and perhaps all the natives in South Africa."

When Sprigg suggests the fault lies with Griffith, Bright, as instructed by Ayliff, defends the colonel. "He is a fine man, a good leader and an excellent soldier," he says.

Sprigg pauses, thinks for a while, then adds, "In the meantime, however, I am inclined to follow your suggestion and leave Griffith where he is and to accept his plan of starving out the rebels. I will accede to his request for more troops, ammunition and guns to prevent the rebels restocking their mountain. I believe one must give a man the right tools to complete the job.

"Will you see his request is acceded to?"

Bright nods. "It will be my first order of business today," he says.

Quthing — Saturday, April 26, 1879

In the past few days, several Baphuthi have approached Austen in his temporary office near the Masitise mission station and offered to surrender.

So far the tally is 104 men, 119 women and 234 children. In addition, 52 women and 125 children who were living with the rebels in caves in the area have surrendered in nearby villages, leaving their men to continue fighting. Austen realizes that these numbers are only a fraction of the 5,000-strong Baphuthi people.

Quthing — Sunday, April 27, 1879

With an apparent stalemate reached in the war, Ellenberger goes ahead with the formal opening of his church. He had hoped that Moorosi would have been able to attend, but the king clearly cannot do so.

Among the special guests is Georges Steinheil, now 21, who recently joined the missionaries at Morija. He made this journey specially to see the new church inaugurated and visit with Frederic and Emma Ellenberger, even though he had been warned that war was being waged in the area. "It was worth making the visit, in spite of the dangers," he says.

"As I am sure you can see, things here in the south of the country are quiet," Ellenberger says. "Several Baphuthi here have surrendered. But I have had to close my mission station at Sibaphala, which is closer to the scene of the fighting — temporarily, I trust."

The men discuss the war, with Ellenberger explaining how he tried to avert it, but could not persuade Moorosi to give up his son Lehana, nor could he persuade the authorities to allow Lehana to surrender by offering him a lesser sentence.

"So am I to believe that this war is being fought because one man was sentenced to jail for advising people not to pay taxes, escaped from prison and now will not give himself up?" Steinheil asks.

"Yes, that is the immediate cause," replies Ellenberger. "But the real reason for the war is to determine who holds the power in Quthing. Neither side wants to cede ground and at this stage it is difficult to see how we can bring back the peace we had here for so long. But I will keep trying to do what I can to avoid more deaths on both sides."

"If anyone can do it, you can," says Steinheil. "They don't call you the fire extinguisher for nothing."

"But sometimes," Ellenberger responds, "the fire is too great for even the best extinguishers."

Quthing — Monday, April 28, 1879

The days on the mountain are punctuated by the pop-pop sound of guns fired by pickets whenever they see people moving around behind the walls. At times, too, when the soldiers move too close, the Baphuthi shoot back. For the most part, however, the firing back and forth, which has resulted in no injuries, is simply an indication that both forces are on guard.

The higher altitude on the mountain top means the nights are a little colder than in the valley below. Frost settles on the ground before the sun rises to thaw it.

In spite of the cooler temperatures, the Baphuthi work on the walls largely during the hours of darkness to avoid attracting fire from the colonial pickets. Using crowbars, they dig stones out from the ground on the mountain and build the walls even higher. Where the walls are weak, they strengthen them.

The Baphuthi have heard through informants that more ammunition is being sent for the cannon and they want to strengthen the walls so that it will be harder to break them down should the soldiers decide to use the big guns again.

Griffith has ordered the men to remain vigilant. He knows the Baphuthi are masters at slipping down the mountain and returning with supplies so he wants to prevent them doing so. But Brabant, settled in at the mountain and advising Griffith, is not convinced that starving out the Baphuthi is the best way. It will take too long, he suggests, and will cost the government too much. Brabant believes it is possible to storm the mountain again with the troops that they now have and remove Moorosi by force.

Griffith disagrees.

"With all respect, you were not here when we made that first attempt," Griffith tells Brabant. "We cannot storm the mountain unless we can breach the schanzes. The seven-pounder guns could not do it and I believe even the 12-pounder guns will be unable to do it. This mountain is such an extraordinary natural fortress it is almost impregnable. It would be hard to take even if we had many guns and unlimited ammunition."

But Brabant is adamant. "I believe that if we can get four big guns, or even three, into position on the heights facing the mountain, the fire will become too hot for anyone to live up there. Once the 12-pounders and the ammunition get here, we could start pounding them day after day. If we do that, we will ensure that nothing can live on the mountain. I feel certain of that."

"My strategy right now is to starve Moorosi out," Griffith insists. "But I will use the threat of force against him. I will dispatch a messenger to Moorosi to send down his women and children. I will tell him they will be protected should we use force against him again. In that way, we will reduce the population on the mountain."

Moorosi sees a messenger below the walls with a white flag. "Mr. Griffith wants you to send down your women and children," the Basotho man explains.

So that's it. He wants to take away some of his bargaining power. Two of paramount chief Letsie's daughters are married to one of his sons. By sending the women down the mountain into the arms of the government he will no longer have them to use as a lever against Letsie; no longer will they be exposed to government fire.

"Tell Mr. Griffith that I will not let any of my people leave their home here on the mountain," he says, ordering his men to make the walls even higher.

Quthing — Thursday, May 1, 1879

The only vulnerability Moorosi feels is his ability to survive on the mountain. A concern is that the grain supplies have been running low. Some replenishment has been possible from men who have slipped through the enemy lines and collected grain stored in villages and caves, but the amount that one man can carry is limited and even several men cannot carry the amount of food needed for what looks like being a long siege through the approaching winter.

As the corn and other food supplies dwindled during the summer, cattle became the group's main supply of food. But, in addition to those that have already been slaughtered for food, a number of cattle have been dying. Some that wandered too close to the edge of the mountaintop were struck by stray cannon shot during the bombardment and a few have been hit by bullets, but other cattle that should have been healthy have also died. He is unsure why.

Moorosi needs, therefore, to gather more cattle as well as corn. He does not want his people to starve when they have so successfully defended themselves.

Answers are at hand. It's approaching harvest time and corn should soon be in plentiful supply; the challenge is to get it up on the mountain in sufficiently large amounts to see them through the winter and into the next summer.

He knows, too, that cattle are available in the surrounding areas, even if they have to commandeer them. But the problem is obvious: The constant patrolling and pickets, who regularly open fire when they see any movement on the approaches to the mountain, make it challenging to bring corn and, more especially, cattle up the mountain path.

Indeed, a few men have been shot and some have died from injuries received in their attempts to herd cattle through the enemy lines.

Moorosi calls his senior advisers to him. "We need to find a way to gather more food supplies and particularly more cattle," he says. "You are all aware of our problem. We cannot get more than a few people off the mountain at a time and they cannot get the cattle past the soldiers. Does anyone have a suggestion?"

Lehana, who has joined his father on the mountain and who is coordinating the gathering of supplies, speaks. "We were able to get up here in the darkness. We mingled with Lerothodi's men, who sheltered us and then, when it was dark, we climbed up the side paths. We heard gunfire from the enemy, but we were not shot."

Moorosi agrees. "Yes, but herding cattle up here is a lot more difficult than moving people up here. Cattle don't understand that they have to move quickly. They don't know how to hide behind rocks and duck when the bullets start flying. They take their time and they are big targets.

"Another thing. Go yourself to the rock at the highest part of the mountain behind us here and look down. You will see there are more men guarding the mountain than before. It is becoming dangerous for our men to leave and return to the mountain.

The saddle today, from the back. The trees were not there in 1879.

Guards on the saddle [*The Graphic*, 1879]

They can do so only in small numbers. They can't bring enough grain and cattle to keep us going through the winter."

As the men continue to discuss the situation, a strategy begins to emerge. "I have a plan," Moorosi says. "I need 10 men to help me accomplish it."

Quthing — Sunday May 4, 1879

Picket duty on the saddle facing Moorosi's Mountain, particularly at night, is becoming a chore. As a result, many new soldiers, ordered by Sprigg to the mountain at Griffith's request, are selected for the duty to relieve those who have served many times. Among them is Alexander Granville, recruited in England two years ago to serve in the colony's police force, who has been sent north from Palmietfontein.

"This is one of the most boring things I've ever done," Granville says to Sergeant James Corfield who is already tired of the duty after serving a few times.

"You stand on that saddle and you look at the mountain and its stone walls. You cannot see very well in the darkness, particularly when there is no moon, so you rely on sound as well as sight to try to detect movement.

"Should you happen to detect someone moving around, you fire generally in their direction. Soon they disappear and all is quiet again. It is like waiting for a mouse to come out of its hole.

"It is deathly still up there. The nights are cold and you pull your coat around you. Below, hundreds of men are asleep in their tents. You cannot talk to the next picket as he is too far off and voices carry across the night air. I must confess I have dozed at times. It is dull, boring and meaningless work."

Corfield can offer no antidote. He wishes him good luck anyway.

Granville climbs the saddle where he and two others are on picket duty. Tonight's full moon provides them with a better-than-usual view of the stone walls. They are to stare at the ghostly grey barricades for the rest of the night — if they can stay awake.

✦

He guesses it must be around 11 p.m. and he is already starting to feel sleepy when Granville hears a noise behind him. He looks around. He can hardly believe what he sees. Lit by the moon, a Baphuthi man armed with a spear is moving toward him. Somehow the man succeeded in climbing undetected off the mountain and up the knoll behind the pickets and is now almost upon him.

Granville raises and cocks his rifle. He sees other Baphuthi climbing the knoll.

"Enemy upon us!" he shouts.

He fires into the warriors below, hitting one. He swings around and realizes more men are climbing up the hill from the front. He and his fellow pickets are being surrounded. They fire repeatedly, shattering the night stillness with the popping sound of gunfire, but the Baphuthi warriors keep coming.

A Baphuthi flings his spear toward Roger Warren, the soldier alongside Granville. The spear finds its target and Warren slips and falls over the edge of the knoll. Baphuthi men, holding their spears above their heads, run toward the spot where he has fallen where they plunge more spears into his body to ensure he is dead.

The rapid gunfire arouses the men in the tents. They tumble out of their beds, grab their revolvers and rifles, and head out of their tents toward the gunfire.

Best and his men run to the cannon, which are positioned behind the knoll. In the moonlight, they see men moving around on the plateau and can hear gunfire, but they are unsure how many men are attacking and exactly where they are coming from.

Best instructs his men to fire the cannon over the saddle on to the plateau, hoping to deter those who are there from moving forward.

But, taken by surprise and without clear direction, the colonial troops have difficulty deciding what to do in the chaos.

✦

The sound of gunfire puts Moorosi's plan into its second phase.

The first phase started three days ago when about 10 men began moving down the mountainside on their way to find grain and cattle in the nearby villages. They went individually, slipping out under cover of darkness.

For the past three days they have collected baskets of grain recently harvested and left in villages by people who surrendered or fled, or that were given them by villagers hiding in caves. They also have rounded up 50 head of cattle, which they are ready to herd up the mountain.

During the day, the men hid in places where they could not be seen by the colonial soldiers. Now, whistling and whooping as they herd the cattle ahead of them, the men push forward to a path up the mountain. They prod the cattle — many of them oxen laden with grain — to climb up the mountainside as quickly as they can.

Among the tents below, Griffith's staff officer Arthur Barkly, seeking to take charge in Griffith's absence, climbs to the scene of the action. At the base of the saddle, he comes across a soldier covered in spear wounds.

"It's private Charles Peterson," says a soldier. We shared a tent. Look at his injuries." He counts 10 puncture wounds. Although unconscious, Peterson is still alive. Barkly instructs some of the men to carry him to the field hospital.

The base of the saddle is swarming with soldiers firing at the Baphuthi, who are now fleeing toward the stone walls. Barkly orders them to give chase. "Line up here in skirmishing order," he says. "When I say 'advance,' move toward the walls."

The men line up, carrying their weapons at their sides, and march quickly forward. Approaching the plateau below the stone walls, the men, now visible in the moonlight, brace themselves for enemy fire and prepare to fire back. But the Baphuthi seem to disappear. Suddenly, the soldiers find they have no enemy to confront.

"They have fled," Barkly says. "We have trounced them and sent them scurrying away. Well done, men." He instructs his men to return to their camp. It is nearly midnight and quiet is returning to the mountain.

"That just shows you that once we have them in the open they become frightened and run away," Barkly says as the men walk back to the camp. "I am only sorry that Warren was killed and poor Peterson was so severely wounded. But I suppose that every victory comes with a cost."

As the Baphuthi men herding the cattle reach the top of the mountain, they are greeted with rejoicing. King Moorosi's ruse worked. The whites were thoroughly deceived. The cattle will provide them with meat for many weeks and the grain is sufficient to keep them going for two or three months.

About 4:30 a.m. the moon sets and darkness descends on the mountainside. The men who launched the attack on the pickets and have been hiding in the rocks at the base of the mountain return up the trail. They report that not one warrior was hurt and they killed one white soldier and possibly two.

The warriors join their fellow Baphuthi in packing the grain into a rectangular thatched-roofed stone hut where it will be protected from the rain and wind. The rest plan a celebratory feast tomorrow when they will slaughter an ox.

Moorosi smiles with satisfaction.

The whites will never oust him from his fortress.

17

Cape Town — Tuesday, May 6, 1879

When white settlers gather in homes, stores and town meetings in the eastern Cape, events in the Quthing War have become a central topic of discussion. As soldiers return with first-hand stories of the battle and observers arrive home to tell what they saw, they provide fodder for newspaper reports and add a new dimension to the debate.

They ask: Why is the disarmament law not being enforced to prevent rebelliousness like this? Why has Moorosi not been brought to book? Why is it beyond the powers of the colony's best soldiers to oust this old chief from his mountain fortress?

The settlers fear that if the battle against Moorosi is lost, the result will be outbreaks among the rest of the Basotho people, leading to a wider war and greater casualties than the wars on the eastern frontier.

The discussions centre not on whether the government's policies are right or wrong, but on what is wrong in implementing the policies, accepted as right.

Thus: The disarmament act is not wrong; it is the way it is being imposed that is wrong. "It was quite possible to have carried out the disarmament measure without forcing the natives into hostilities," writes the *Burghersdorp Gazette*.

Similarly, the war is not wrong. It is how it is being fought that is wrong.

Increasingly, Griffith, seen as ineffective and indecisive, is taking the brunt of the blame. Instead of procrastinating, he should have acted when Moorosi's people crossed the Telle River and confronted them in Palmietfontein, the editorial writer for the *Gazette* argues.

"Now that the assault of the position has failed, the force is to return to the waiting system. Mr. Griffith expects that the Yeomanry will wait before the mountain until the enemy are starved to surrender. We are surprised that he does not propose that they shall wait there until the mouldering hand of time shall remove enemy and barricades and all. It would be equally sensible.

"We are sure he might render the colony a far greater service by resigning the command and returning to his office of political agent."

The Northern Post of Aliwal North, which previously blamed Austen for the war, is now equally scathing of Griffith's command.

"The sad roll of five killed and 27 wounded speaks sufficiently to the losses sustained by our men, whilst, on the other hand, not one of the enemy is known to have been killed.

"The story, however, of Mr. Griffith's bungling does not end with the fiasco of the assault. In every other particular he was unprepared. No provision was made for the wounded, not a stretcher nor an ambulance was on the spot, not even a bed to lie the poor fellows on, nor a single 'medical comfort.' We have at our disposal all modern appliances of warfare, and yet we are absolutely reduced to confess our inability to take the mountain by force, and resort to starving the 'garrison' out...

"A few gallant men do not make a glorious campaign but one incompetent officer may ruin the prospects of the bravest army that ever took the field."

Quthing — Wednesday, May 7, 1879

One of those brave men breathes for the last time at 10 a.m. today. At Captain James Surmon's side are his daughters, Elizabeth and Evelina, who watch in desperation as the wound that pierced his lung and caused him a month of intense suffering eventually takes his life. He will not live to see his 58th birthday.

The women are handed a letter written to them by a Cape Mounted Rifleman: "Pardon me if I intrude on this your privacy on the occasion of your sad bereavement. I have long known you both and I could not conscientiously allow this opportunity to pass without expressing my heart-felt sympathy.

"Although I speak individually allow me to say that I convey the sentiments of the troop and many would fain express their wishes as I have done were they privileged to do so. Your father has endeared himself to many in this troop and most particularly in the gallant and soldier-like act on the occasion on which he met his death wound. May God in his providence overlook all for good in the humble prayer of your sincere friend."

Quthing — Monday May 12, 1879

The colonial camp at the mountain has settled into a tedious daily routine of manning pickets. An occasional patrol into the countryside relieves the boredom.

The lull gives Griffith the opportunity to catch up on his paperwork. He forwards Austen's response to Under Secretary for Native Affairs Bright in which Austen says he warned the government repeatedly about Moorosi and his fortified mountain. "I have faithfully kept Moorosi before the Government for more than 20 years, and pointed out the danger he was to the colony," he writes.

"This is the first example in our colonial warfare in which we have had to encounter such determined opposition and good engineering generalship. We were all, more or less, taken by surprise."

⚜

The Surmon daughters, having watched their father buried at the mountain, arrive at Masitise where they will spend a few days with the Ellenbergers.

Expressing his sympathy for their loss, the missionary vows to do what he can to bring the war to a peaceful end so as to prevent more tragedy — on both sides.

Quthing — Wednesday, May 14, 1879

Reports say that rebels led by Lehana have returned to their caves along the Silver Spruit River after fleeing to the mountain fortress following the aborted attack by Captain Clough three weeks ago. To ascertain the truth of the reports, Griffith dispatches a mounted patrol of eight volunteers under Lieutenant J.J. Dunn.

The men ride up the deep valley before off-saddling and tethering their horses.

Dunn walks about 300 yards to scout the area. He stops.

"Take a look at this," he says, indicating a footprint in the soft sand. "This tells me that a barefooted Baphuthi was here recently," he says. "He was almost certainly a rebel." Dunn instructs a soldier to return to camp and ask Sergeant Frost to join them with more men "as it seems to me this is a nasty place."

The man rides off. The others return to their horses to wait.

"I'm tired of waiting. I'm going further up the kloof to look for the savages," says trooper Frederick Von Brombsen of the Herschel Mounted Volunteers.

"You are to wait here until our reinforcements arrive," says Dunn.

"No, I am going on my own," replies Von Brombsen, walking off toward where the rebel stronghold is believed to be.

"I order you to return," Dunn shouts after him. "Come back this instant!"

Von Brombsen swings around and shouts back, "No savage has ever moulded a bullet to kill me."

Alone, Von Brombsen walks toward a cave across the valley. As he enters the cave, he is hit in the chest by a bullet. He collapses, yelling, "I'm shot! I'm shot!"

Five men following Von Brombsen at a distance fire at the cave. Their fire elicits no response and they retreat.

Shortly after they reach the place where the horses are tethered, Sergeant Frost arrives with reinforcements. After consultation, Dunn and Frost conclude it is imperative that they retrieve Von Brombsen's body.

"Cover us," Dunn tells the men. They fire round after round toward the cave as Dunn and Frost reach the body and carry it down the hill.

"I think our wisest plan now is to return to camp," Dunn says. "We have used up most of our ammunition. I am afraid the foolish actions of one of our volunteers who thought he knew better than me has led to the failure of this mission."

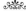

The death of another government soldier with no corresponding progress in the war reinforces Griffith's frustration. Not only does the mountain remain unconquered, but the Baphuthi appear to be reinforcing their cave hideouts in the surrounding countryside and even rebuilding new ones in areas that he believed to have been emptied.

He needs to turn the war around. He needs a victory, even a small one.

Griffith identifies three major centres of resistance. Obviously one is the mountain. Another consists of the near-impregnable rebel holdouts up the Silver Spruit where Lehana apparently is holed up. A third is a labyrinth of caves some 15 miles east along the Quthing River, in which patrols report an unknown number of rebels, led by Letuka and Raisa, are hiding.

Griffith's plan now must be to destroy the two other main centres of resistance while blockading the mountain. He will begin with the caves up the Quthing River, which appear more vulnerable than those occupied by Lehana.

He will send Brabant to subdue the rebels in the caves, giving him 85 of the best Cape Yeomanry, including Corporal Andrew Jones, and 100 Basotho under the command of Captain Henry Lee Davies and Inspector George Moshesh of the

Basutoland police. To provide every assistance, he will even let Brabant take one of the seven-pounders to blast at any stone walls. He assigns Lieutenant Best and seven men from the Cape Mounted Riflemen to ensure the gun is correctly used.

If successful, the foray will not only provide him with the victory he needs, but also serve as a warm-up exercise for an attack on Lehana's hideout.

Quthing — Thursday, May 15, 1879

Raisa walks out of a natural passageway at the entrance to the cave into the crisp air outside. He looks down the gorge where his fellow Baphuthi have built themselves strong fortifications at the entrances to a series of caves alongside the Quthing River.

He thinks back two years when it also was harvest time and Hope wanted to punish him for destroying MaLebenya's cornfield. When rumours of war became rife,

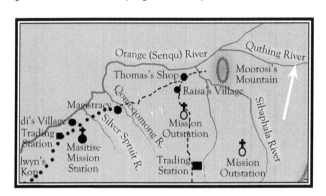

Raisa reflects, he feared he would be targeted by the government as a known opponent. So he and his family retreated to these caves for safety.

Letuka, Moorosi's other senior son, is living with his family in a cave on the slopes of the valley above them.

The people hoped the white government would not find them here, but, as Raisa looks toward the mountain tops today, he realizes those hopes were in vain. The white government has arrived and is about to find them.

❧

Reaching the mountain above the valley in mid-afternoon, Brabant realizes the rebel stronghold is much stronger than he had anticipated. Situated in a deep gorge, it is protected by natural rock surroundings, steep slopes and bush cover, as well as by fortifications.

As his troops pitch their tents for the night on a spot high above the river, Brabant sets out to reconnoitre the area, descending a narrow trail that winds down the slope of the gorge toward the river below.

The gorge, about 200 yards deep and 600 yards long, becomes narrower at the far end and its sides progressively steeper until the cliffs are almost sheer. Although the side of the gorge down which he is descending is wider and easier to follow, it is covered at the bottom by a large mass of boulders interspersed with bushes. Beyond the river are several cellar-like caves behind stone walls that the Baphuthi have built.

Halfway up the slopes of the gorge opposite him, Brabant spots a cave on a semicircular rise that appears to be the rebels' main holdout. Giving the appearance of a miniature version of Moorosi's Mountain, the entrances to the cave are fortified with loopholed stone walls.

The cave can be reached on only one path, which leads up the slope to a narrow rock platform, surrounded by several more small caves, also defended by stone walls and boulders. The way to storm the cave complex, Brabant decides, would be to rush up the slope and destroy the stone wall that closes off the entrance.

Brabant is struck by the quietness of the valley. Apart from the sounds of his men settling into their camp on the high ground behind him, he hears no voices or sounds of movement coming from the caves.

Best, who brought the seven-pounders by horse team from the camp at Moorosi's Mountain, descends the path. Brabant points to the defence complex.

"We are going to have to pummel these stone walls with the gun until they are damaged enough to afford us access," he says. "Then we will drive the rebels to the back of the caves, forcing them to surrender."

"I'll set up the gun in the morning," says Best.

"No, I think we should start shelling them now, before it gets too dark to see," Brabant replies. "You can be sure that they already know we're here. We need to hit them before they better their position or try to escape."

Best returns to the camp where, assisted by seven gun operators, he wheels the gun into position on a level spot opposite the main cave on the side of the hill. Soon they are lobbing shells into the stone walls around the cave.

Letuka's thoughts are shattered by the sound of the large gun. The blast echoes through the valley, breaking the afternoon stillness.

In the cave the children are crying, the women are looking worried and the men are reaching for the guns that they have stored there. He tells his people that they should not be afraid, and should not run outside. The shells from the big gun will not hurt them, the walls are strong and the government soldiers will not be able to get into their caves.

They failed to destroy the walls at the mountain and they will not destroy the walls here. He will see to it.

Quthing — Friday, May 16, 1879

In the morning, Best continues to direct his cannon fire at the caves on both sides of the gorge, pounding the stone walls. Brabant is hoping that the shells will break down the walls, but, as was the case yesterday with the cave halfway up the hill, there is no sign the shelling has any effect. The only alternative, he reasons, is to attack the cave directly.

"I would like you to storm the cave halfway up the hill by climbing as quickly as you can up the path," he tells the men. "Once there, you should punch a hole through the stone walls that guard the entrance. The men will be trapped inside and you will be able to force them to surrender and capture them, or, if they will not yield, kill them."

Carrying their carbines, the men clamber up the steep slope until they reach the narrow rock platform outside the cave, where they pause, ready to rush at the stone walls. They are surprised when they suddenly come under fire, not from people inside the cave, but from farther up the gorge, 250 yards away.

The men rush at the stone walls, pushing on them with their rifle butts in an attempt to topple them and also to get inside to escape the gunfire. But the walls cannot be pushed over. The only effective way to break them down would be stone by stone, starting at the top. But that would take time; and the men are being shot at.

Brabant, standing near the top of the path up the hill to the cave, takes in the scene. The rebels doing the firing are concealed behind rocks and bushes, providing them with cover, whereas his men are crowded together on a rock ledge fully exposed. Mindful of the loss of men to Baphuthi fire on Moorosi's mountain nearly six weeks ago, he orders his men to retreat.

⚜

Frustrated that he has achieved little since arriving here yesterday, and realizing the attack on the caves will be challenging, Brabant gives the rebels one more chance.

He decides that a woman taken captive after wandering close to the camp might prove useful. Her name is MaTsekelo, but Brabant dubs her "princess."

"I want you to return to your chief or headman and ask him whether he is prepared to surrender," Brabant tells her. "Tell him I am giving him one more chance to come out and cooperate with us before we attack the caves and destroy him and his people. He has until an hour after dawn tomorrow to let me know he is surrendering. If I do not hear from him by then I will order my troops to attack the caves."

"I will go with your message," she says, leaving as the sky darkens.

Quthing — Saturday, May 17, 1879

Letuka, ensconced in the cave halfway up the hill, laughs when he hears MaTsekelo's message, which she delivers shortly after dawn.

"He wants us to surrender?" Letuka says. "We fire at them and chase them away from our caves, they run away and slide down the mountain in their fear, and now they want us to surrender? Why would we do that?"

Letuka laughs again, even more loudly.

"I know these white men. They think it is easy to defeat us. They think they can show off with their big guns and their rifles and march around in their fancy clothes and we will obey them because we are afraid of them.

"But did it work when they marched on my father's mountain fortress? It will not work here either. Tell them we will not surrender."

⚜

"Very well," Brabant says when MaTsekelo conveys Letuka's response. "If that is the way he wants it."

Soon the seven-pounders are firing toward the caves once more. Shells arc into the air. Some hit the walls, but to little effect. More shells fired farther up the gorge have little impact. For most of the morning the heavy gunfire echoes around the narrow ravine. Shell after shell pounds the caves. Now and then Best adjusts the trajectory to make sure they have the strongest impact possible.

But, apart from breaking holes in some walls, the gunfire achieves little.

After several hours the shelling stops and the gorge is quiet.

At midday Brabant consults with his senior men. "What is our next move, gentlemen? How do we force these people to surrender? We have pounded their fortifications once again this morning, but I am afraid we have not created enough damage. And, in any event, we have run out of ammunition for the gun so we can make no further use of it. I need ideas."

"I have an idea," says Jones. "I have served in the Royal Engineers and we used dynamite. What I suggest is that we throw dynamite into the caves. We could start by throwing charges from above down the cleft of the rock into the cave on the side of the hill. That should effectively blast a hole in the wall."

Brabant turns to Best. "Did we bring dynamite with us?"

"A small quantity. We can obtain more from the main camp."

"Let's try it out before we send for more," Brabant says. "Corporal Jones, seeing you have experience in this type of warfare, why don't you climb to a point above the cave and do as you suggest?"

Carrying heavy charges bound in rags, Jones climbs to the top of the hill. He balances on a ledge and lights the first stick. He drops it toward the entrance to the cave. The dynamite fails to ignite. He lights the second stick, dropping it, too, down the cleft.

<hr/>

After the first stick of dynamite lands on the ground outside the wall, but fails to explode, the men in the cave move toward the entrance to examine it. They have just started to look at it when the second charge falls just within the wall.

Letuka sees that the stick is burning. Seizing it, he runs to a nearby bucket of water. As he places the dynamite in the water, the charge explodes, turning the bucket into shrapnel, hurling the men against the walls and to the floor of the cave.

The cave falls silent.

Letuka looks down at his right hand, which has been shattered. He cannot hear anything, nor can he feel any pain, but the wound is bleeding and his hand has turned into a mass of blood and bone. The men brace themselves for another blast. When it does not come, and the smoke clears, they try to ascertain the extent of the damage.

A man lies motionless on the cave floor. Letuka looks across at him. He is dead. Another six men have been wounded.

Letuka, still feeling no pain, stares at his hand. "This is a new kind of weapon," he says. "We have no answer for these kind of weapons."

Minutes later, as his hand starts to throb with searing pain, Letuka passes out, collapsing on the floor next to the body of his friend.

<hr/>

Jones reports to Brabant that the second charge blasted away part of the stone wall, but he has no way of knowing whether it caused any damage inside the cave.

"I am glad it worked," says Brabant, who has been giving Jones's idea some thought. "But before I proceed, I need permission from the government to use dynamite. I am concerned that we might not just break down the walls, but will kill the people behind them and that this kind of warfare might be frowned upon.

"Jones, take a message to the camp at Moorosi's Mountain. You are to go to Colonel Griffith and Mr. Ayliff, the secretary for native affairs, and ask them whether they will authorize the use of dynamite to blast our way into the caves," he says. "Explain to them that the caves here are protected by stone walls in the same way that the mountain is."

While he waits the several hours that it will take before Jones returns, Brabant, accompanied by a number of yeomen, clambers down the hill.

At the bottom he discovers a cave on the left of the entrance to the gorge that he had not noticed before. It, too, is well fortified.

Brabant instructs the yeomen to ascertain how many people are hiding in it.

As the yeomen approach the cave, the men inside, led by Raisa, fire on them. A small battle ensues, with neither side making any gains.

As he watches the action, Brabant calls his men together.

"I think it is clear that the way this cave and its fortifications are configured, it is all but impossible to gain entry with rifle fire," he says.

"We have to try another method.

"While we await word about the dynamite. I want you to assemble a group of men. They are to light a fire outside the cave. Dampen the branches if necessary so that they produce an abundance of smoke. Build it so that the wind will blow the smoke into the cave.

"Let's smoke them out."

As the smoke wafts down a narrow passageway that leads into the main part of the cave, it sets the men, women and children inside coughing and spluttering.

For a while, they are content to wait it out.

But soon dense smoke fills the front portion of the cave, forcing those inside to close their eyes and making it harder to breathe. They know that to move outside will invite the soldiers to shoot at them and is likely to result in their being seriously wounded or killed. Yet the only way out is through the entryway.

The Baphuthi move to the back of the cave, where it is easier to breathe. But they know they are trapped.

Raisa calls four men and a boy to him.

"Listen to what I tell you to do," he says.

Jones returns from the mountain carrying several sticks of dynamite. "Both Mr. Ayliff and Colonel Griffith agree that we can use the dynamite," he tells Brabant.

"Excellent work, corporal. We will tackle that task later. Right now, we are concentrating on this cave.

"We might have some success with this idea of mine to smoke the enemy out of his lair.

"Why don't you store that dynamite somewhere safe and then join us here? You are a man of considerable experience and we need you to help us here first before we use the dynamite again."

⚜

Four men and a boy emerge from the cave, shouting at the men not to shoot.

"We surrender," they say. "All our people want to surrender."

The soldiers drop their rifles to their sides, ascertain that the men and boy are unarmed, and arrest them. The men, now prisoners, tell them that the people inside are having trouble breathing, some are dying and they need help. The men move to the entrance of the cave and peer in through the smoke.

"Help us, please help us, we cannot breathe," Raisa cries down the passageway, between coughs. "We want to surrender, but you need to come in here and help us to come out as we are dying from the smoke and we can't see the way out. Please you must come and help us."

The colonial soldiers douse the fire with water. When the smoke has cleared enough to enter the cave, they do so.

Among the first in the cave is Jones, accompanied by one of the Baphuthi men, now a prisoner, who says he will show Jones where the people are and who among them needs the most help. The other soldiers follow Jones in single file down the narrow passageway.

"Those of you who can must come out and surrender," Jones shouts into the darkness as he enters the large interior of the cave. "You will be safe outside and you can —" A large stone hits him on the head. He falls to his knees. A bullet fired from the dark recesses at the back of the cave passes above him, hitting the man behind Jones in the eye.

Jones staggers to his feet, his head pounding, and fires back.

"They are not surrendering; they are shooting at us," he shouts. "It is a ruse. Get out of here! Now!"

As they lurch backward, tripping over one another, the men fire repeatedly to cover their retreat. Raisa and his followers fire back. For a few minutes, the bullets fly in all directions, ricocheting off the stone walls.

Outside, the soldiers curse themselves for falling for the trick. They angrily relight the fire, which takes a while to get going because so much of the wood was doused with water.

As darkness falls, and no more people emerge to surrender, the soldiers return to their camp, leaving the fire to smoulder. They will build it up again tomorrow.

Quthing — Sunday, May 18, 1879

The morning begins for Brabant when Davies enters his tent.

"I went to the caves early today — unarmed," Davies, who speaks the local dialect, says. "I said I came in peace and spent some time talking with the Baphuthi people. One of the headmen, Raisa, has offered to surrender with all of his people."

"His people did that yesterday, too," Brabant replies. "But it was a ruse. He wanted our men to enter his cave so he could fire on them. Ignore him."

"I don't think it's a ruse," Davies replies. "He and his people are coming out from the caves along the sides of the gorge, carrying their belongings."

"Why are they doing that?" Brabant asks. "We failed to oust them yesterday with the smoke and now they've suddenly changed their minds? I smell a rat."

"They told me that nine of Raisa's men were killed in the firing in the cave," Davies says. "Apparently one of them shot and killed one of his own men in the confusion. That, and the fear of suffocation that many of the people felt, apparently gave Raisa second thoughts. When I spoke with him and suggested it would be a good move to surrender, he decided to give up before more people die."

Brabant's demeanour changes. Without his having done anything this morning, other than wake up, victory is at hand.

"Well done, my good man."

Davies continues. "The Baphuthi people say that another of the headmen, named Letuka, also wants to surrender."

During the day, hundreds of Baphuthi stream out of the caves to an area the yeomen mark out. They are told they are prisoners and will be taken back to the camp at Moorosi's Mountain and, from there, to the camp at Phaladi's village.

Quthing — Monday, May 19, 1879

Before leaving the area, Brabant, determined that the cave fortifications will never be used by the rebels again, orders his men to destroy the stone walls with dynamite and dismantle what is left by hand. He also orders them to gather all the Baphuthi grain.

A count reveals 15 Baphuthi were killed during the skirmishing in Raisa's cave, and by the dynamite thrown into Letuka's cave. In addition, 82 fighting men, of whom 10 are wounded, 18 youth and 310 women and children are taken prisoner. In addition, 13 horses, 207 sheep and goats, 49 stand of arms and 40 spears are seized. A large quantity of tobacco and thrashed-out grain are destroyed.

Looking at the prisoners and the booty, Brabant realizes the cave fortifications were far more extensive than he had thought. If the Baphuthi had not surrendered, he could have faced a long siege.

The 400 prisoners are escorted by the yeomen back to Moorosi's Mountain.

"I am sure this capture will materially affect the war," a triumphant Brabant says to his men. "I strongly expect that Moorosi will offer his surrender when he learns what has happened here." What he does not notice is that, as the group nears Moorosi's Mountain amid great excitement from the men at the camp, Letuka and Raisa — accompanied by a few others — slip quietly away, heading for a path up the mountain.

Quthing — Saturday, May 24, 1879

The cool autumn nights are starting to make themselves felt at the mountain and William Ayliff, the secretary for native affairs, says he will leave for Cape Town on Monday to attend to matters that have been accumulating in his absence.

He tells Griffith that, although he is satisfied with his decisions, it is imperative that victory be achieved as soon as possible.

"The war is proving costly," he says. "The 600 men camped here have to be supplied and fed. The ammunition costs are growing.

"Colonel Brabant thought his victory up the river would lead to surrender at the mountain, but that has not happened and is unlikely to do so. I know you believe your plan to starve out the rebels will work in the long run, but it will bring with it a heavy toll in monetary costs and the government is reluctant to bear that burden. We are growing impatient.

"So I have to urge you to consider the value of time. Your forces have been increased and once they are at their full strength I must ask you to move as quickly as possible to destroy the rebel strongholds, both here at the mountain and any remaining in the surrounding countryside."

Griffith weighs his options. It is unlikely that another assault similar to the last one would be successful. It also is clear now that starving the rebels out will take too long; they keep mysteriously adding to their supplies and do not appear to be likely to run out of grain and cattle any time soon.

Before he tackles this problem, Griffith must put together a force to clear out the other remaining major centre of resistance: the fortress that Lehana has constructed on the banks of the Silver Spruit River.

Quthing — Sunday, May 25, 1879

The weather this morning is bitterly cold, with frost covering the ground. Hundreds of colonial soldiers gather on the parade ground among the tents for a Sunday service at 11 a.m. to be conducted by the Rev. Joseph Start, a Wesleyan minister from the Eastern Cape. Start arrived in the camp just as it was getting dark last night. He had stayed overnight with the Ellenbergers at Masitise and had visited the injured men, including Scott, at Thomas's Shop yesterday afternoon.

The men sing several hymns, including "Rock of ages, cleft for me," "Oh, for a thousand tongues to sing," and "Jesu, lover of my soul." Every now and then the singing is drowned out by the sound of cannon fire, but the firing is stopped for the minister to deliver his sermon.

As his text, Start has chosen Acts 26:18, "To open their eyes, and to turn them from darkness to light, and from the power of Satan unto God, that they may receive forgiveness of sins, and inheritance among them which are sanctified by faith that is in me."

Presenting the war as a battle between Christianity and heathenism, he prays that the Baphuthi might turn from their sinful ways. He prays, too, for strength for the colonial soldiers, never questioning that what the men are fighting for is right and true and that what the Baphuthi are defending is heathen and wrong.

꧁꧂

The sounds of singing through the brisk morning air attract the attention of the Baphuthi.

"It's a church service," Moorosi says. "They are singing to God."

"Is God on their side?" asks Letuka.

"I have heard the missionary say that God is a loving God," Moorosi replies. "They say He is not the God of the white people only. He is the God of all people and so He is the God of the Baphuthi people, too. We might look different on the outside, the missionary told us, but we are the same on the inside. He loves us as much as He loves them and He does not want us to be hurt."

"Do the white people think God will help them and not us?"

"They think God is on their side and not on ours," Moorosi replies. "But I think God will help us."

He walks back to his hut and digs among the amulets he has gathered over the years — a baboon's foot, an ox tail, a bone from an antelope — to find a leather-bound Bible given to him by Ellenberger. He pages through the Bible before placing it on the ground once more, alongside the lucky charms. Together, they will strengthen him and his people.

❦

Now that the cave complex on the Quthing River is cleared of rebels, Griffith sets his sights on the other major rebel resistance apart from the mountain: Lehana's holdout along the valley of the Silver Spruit River. He has selected Colonel Southey to lead 80 men from the 2nd regiment of Cape Mounted Yeomanry, a mountain gun under Best and about 100 Basotho and Mfengu fighters to attack Lehana's caves.

"If Brabant can do it, so can you," he tells the colonel." The force I am sending with you is similar in size."

Quthing — Tuesday May 27, 1879

After spending most of yesterday reconnoitring along the Silver Spruit River, Southey has determined that hundreds of Baphuthi, presumably led by Lehana, are hiding at the end of a deep ravine in six caves, linked with one another by a passageway behind a series of stone walls.

The caves lie below a 50-foot rock face and are covered by thick bushes. Access can be gained only by climbing large rocks.

The attack, Southey determines, will start today and will be similar to that used by Brabant, without the dynamite. He instructs Best to fire cannon shells at the walls to unnerve those hiding inside and to deter them from firing back.

With the gunfire backing them, the colonial soldiers, lined up shoulder to shoulder in a wide arc, advance on the fortress, firing as soon as they are within range. Southey directs the men to attack the smaller of the caves first. When the men advance on the holdout, he orders Best to cease the cannon fire, afraid that the shells might hit his own men.

The men climb the rocks, manoeuvre through the entrance in the stone wall, and enter the cave.

Holding their long-barrelled rifles on their shoulders, they wait to allow their eyes to become accustomed to the dim light before advancing more deeply into the cave. Soon they realize it is empty.

Lehana's cave — in this sketch, by Arthur Pattisson, magistrate John Austen is shown standing on a rock on the left and Capt. James Surmon on the right.

As they move from cave to cave along the passageway between them, they find each new cave is empty.

Eventually only one cave — the largest — is left. As they approach it, the men are blasted with a volley from behind the stone wall guarding it. They retreat, climbing down to the valley below.

"They are all in that one cave," Southey tells his men.

He orders Best to bring the gun closer and to use it to break down the walls while the yeomen keep up their firing to prevent the Baphuthi rebuilding the wall.

This time, perhaps because of the short range, the cannon fire is more successful. In places the shells knock down the tops of the outer stone wall.

The Baphuthi try to repair the damage, but heavy firing from the yeomen prevents them from achieving much success. Nevertheless, the Baphuthi continue to fire from behind the walls, turning every advance by the yeomen into a retreat as they are forced to find safety.

The result is a stalemate.

By nightfall, the yeomen are tired and hungry after fighting furiously during the day, yet gaining little ground. Hundreds of Baphuthi are still in the cave.

Southey orders his men to withdraw, but stations two sentries outside the cave, ordering that a fire be burned at the entrance. He learned the tactic from Brabant, but applies it with a difference. Concerned that the inhabitants might leave during the night, Southey reasons that blocking the entrance with fire will keep them from doing so.

Under cover of darkness, the yeomen gather logs, building a huge fire in front of a gap in the stone wall that is the only way out of the cave.

"Keep the fire going all night," Southey instructs the pickets. "They will not be able to get out without being severely burned. Tomorrow we will enter the cave."

⁂

The heat from the fire permeates the first few feet of the cave and the blaze lights up the interior. Lehana assesses the results of the day's fighting. Five men are dead, three struck by colonial fire over the top of the damaged wall, and two struck by stones loosened by the cannon fire. Another two men lie badly wounded.

In the recesses of the cave 300 men, women and children huddle together. Some have lived here for weeks; others came from adjoining caves when the war began. The cave is stocked with grain and pumpkins that will keep them fed for months. The 10 horses in the cave appear to be in good shape, being kept at the back of the cave, away from the gunfire.

"The enemy forces have left two men to guard the cave," Lehana says to his warriors. "They have built a big fire to stop us going out and returning. I want you to continue firing at those two men during the night. I know it is difficult to see them in the dark. But you must keep firing, even if you use up a lot of our ammunition.

"I need another set of volunteers. Come here and I will show you what to do."

Quthing — The same day

The heavy firing from the cave echoes around the steep-sided ravine throughout the night, amplifying its sound and keeping Southey's men awake until the early hours of the morning when they fall asleep through sheer exhaustion. The two sentries fire back occasionally, but the Baphuthi bullets fall some distance in front of them.

Shortly before dawn, the firing stops. An eerie silence descends on the ravine.

As the early dawn glow turns into the light of day, the soldiers douse the fire and Southey walks carefully to the cave entrance. Several men accompany him, rifles at the ready. They encounter no gunfire, however, and enter the cave.

Inside, Southey finds three bodies and two badly wounded men.

Five men emerge from the back of the cave, holding their hands high in a sign of surrender. Soon they are followed by scores of women and children. The yeomen accompanying Southey take them into custody and escort them to the camp.

Questioned by Southey, the men say the rest of the men in the cave fled in the early hours of the morning, accompanied by 18 who were wounded but are able to walk.

They point to a break at the far end of the wall, away from the fire and out of the sentries' sight, explaining that the men, led by Lehana, were able to take down the stones without being heard because of the sound of the gunfire. It took time to demolish a section of the wall, but they left before daylight.

"Where did they go?" asks Southey.

The men point up the ravine and over the mountains. Spotting a group near the top of a mountain, Southey dispatches several yeomen to pursue them.

⁂

The yeomen return to the camp in the afternoon. They report that they chased the rebels for seven miles, trying to cut them off. They shot and killed two, but the rest scattered in all directions. They turned back because the horses were exhausted and the terrain too mountainous.

"We need to abandon our attempt to hunt the enemy," Southey tells the men. "Not only has our meat supply run out, but I also have received a note from Commander Griffith telling me to return to camp as soon as possible."

Quthing — Thursday, May 29, 1879

Shortly after midnight, in the dim light of the half moon, 150 Baphuthi silently creep down the south-eastern path on their mountain fortress.

They have no need for more light than the half moon provides; they know the area well and are able to find their way over rocky outcrops, through the long grass and among the bushes with comparative ease.

Leading them is Letuka, Moorosi's son, who, having escaped from Brabant, is living on the mountain. The gnarled stump at the bottom of his arm, left when his hand was blown off 11 days ago by the stick of dynamite, has begun to heal but is still painful.

Indeed, the pain spurs him on; it was a major reason he agreed to lead this group, whose mission is to attack the colonial soldiers camped at the junction of the Orange and the Quthing River. His injured hand means he will be unable to shoot or throw a spear, but he will lead his fellow Baphuthi, who are dressed for war and carry spears, shields and guns.

Moorosi has told them that attacking the isolated camp would be revenge for the attack on Letuka and Raisa in the caves and would serve as a warning to the colonists not to venture on such sorties any more.

Watching from the rock "chair" on the northern edge of his mountain top, where he can look down a vertical incline to the area where the Quthing and the Orange rivers meet, the king saw the soldiers set up their camp four days ago.

The soldiers make a good target.

Not only are they relatively few in number, but their distance from the main camps means help would take some time to arrive.

The warriors cross a low point on the Quthing River, turn south and walk toward the Orange River.

Ahead of them white pyramid-shaped tents, lit by the moon, stand starkly against the dark background of the night sky.

They move closer under cover of the bushes, which are thicker and taller near the river bed.

Four sentries are standing in a trench behind a short stone wall 15 yards up the mountain from the camp and 60 yards from the Orange River.

The Baphuthi stop.

As planned, a group breaks off and climbs the slope behind the camp.

Looking down, the scouts obtain a good picture of the camp layout.

Now and then they hear the sentries in the trench behind the stone wall talking. One

Above: View of camp site from Moorosi's "chair." Below: Path below mountain leads to river.

laughs, another lights a cigarette, a third sips from a mug of coffee. Their guns lie alongside them. They appear relaxed.

The scouts return to the main body of fighters. Together they move away from the camp until they are out of hearing of the soldiers.

After hearing the scouts report on what they have seen, Letuka instructs the fighters to continue on the path that runs along the river and to attack the sleeping soldiers.

The warriors creep forward, their bare feet silent on the rock-strewn path leading to the camp.

18

Quthing — The same day

Trooper C. F. Meyer, one of 12 sentries, reckons it must be around 2:30 a.m. Four more hours to go before the bugle announces the end of his duty. He cannot see the other sentries, but he assumes they are as bored as he is, wishing they could be asleep in their tents as are the other men in the 48-strong regiment posted here four days ago as one of the forces around the mountain, charged with isolating the Baphuthi on the mountain and ensuring that help does not reach them from Kornet Spruit, just across the river.

Thirty minutes ago, his commander, Captain A. L. Chiappini, had checked in with him, saying he was about to go to bed and wanted to ascertain that all was quiet. Meyer assured him it was.

Meyer reaches into his pocket for a cigarette. He puts it in his mouth and prepares to light a match when he hears the sound of a breaking bough. He looks behind him, near the river bank. It is probably an animal, a jackal perhaps. Another noise follows, this time the swishing of branches. In the pale moonlight, he makes out a movement in the bushes. It must be a fairly large animal.

Then he sees it's no animal. A hundred to 200 men, most carrying spears and some bearing guns, are running from the bushes along the river toward the tents.

At first, he cannot comprehend it. The moonlight creates a ghostly picture and he thinks he must have fallen asleep and is dreaming. But, as the scores of Baphuthi continue to rush forward, his mind stirs itself into action.

Meyer fires in their direction. Realizing he cannot achieve much with one rifle against a horde, he runs the 100 yards down to the camp to waken Captain Chiappini. He reaches Chiappini's tent, which is closer to the stone wall than the others, at the same time as the Baphuthi arrive at the first row of tents.

"We're being attacked by natives," he shouts. "Hundreds of them!"

Chiappini rolls out of bed, shaking himself awake. Perhaps, he thinks for a moment, Meyer is wrong. Perhaps these are the friendly natives, the Mfengu, moving through the camp site on their way elsewhere.

But as he leaves his tent, his doubts end. He is glad he ordered the men to sleep with their arms loaded.

"Out of your tents!" Chiappini screams toward the tents not yet attacked. "Go to the schanz!" referring to the stone wall.

The men awaken, instinctively grab their rifles, and scramble out of their tents, some dressed more fully than others. Chiappini orders them to run. "Get to safety, go to the schanz," he repeats, running for cover himself toward the stone wall.

For more than 20 of the men in the tents attacked first, the order comes too late. The Baphuthi surround their tents, cut the guy ropes and spear the men trapped in the collapsed tents.

From the stone wall breastwork, 16 men raise their rifles and fire toward the attackers. The Baphuthi, wearing few clothes in spite of the night cold, are not only difficult to see, but are also moving constantly. The soldiers fire again and again toward the warriors, being careful not to direct their fire into the tents themselves. Now and then a scream confirms they have hit a Baphuthi.

The warriors continue to plunge their spears into the side of the tents, which are now stained red with blood. Even as they fire, the yeomen of the 3rd regiment watch in horror as their comrades are slaughtered.

After intense, seemingly endless, stabbing into the canvas, the Baphuthi — satisfied that no one can be alive in the tents any longer — run toward the stone wall, flinging their spears, many now covered in blood toward the soldiers. The spears reach the trench, striking and wounding some of the soldiers.

The persistent fire from the yeomen finally forces the Baphuthi back. After a while, they regroup and rush forward again, but are repulsed and driven back once more.

The chaotic noise arouses the Burghersdorp Troop, a group of volunteers from the Cape Colony camped on the opposite side of the Orange River. They run to the banks of the river; a soldier with a bugle sounds an advance.

"Listen, the bugle is blowing and help is coming," Letuka says. "We have done enough. Let us return to the mountain."

The warriors abandon their attack and follow the path along which they came. Some are carrying wounded fellows. One carries the body of a warrior killed by a soldier's bullet. They move as fast as they can toward the mountain.

⁂

Joined by the Burghersdorp volunteers, who have crossed the Orange River, the men under Chiappini hunker behind the stone wall. They remain for several hours, afraid that the Baphuthi will return, perhaps in greater numbers. They make no attempt to go to the destroyed tents; they are convinced none of their colleagues could have lived through the slaughter they have just witnessed.

⁂

The birds are the first to greet the approaching dawn, doing so with a cheeriness that mocks the scene of destruction around them. Soon they are followed by the chirping of insects and the buzzing of flies.

As the first rays of the sun light up the scene, the men of the 3rd Yeomanry Regiment are greeted with a horrific sight.

Tents attacked by the Baphuthi are in shreds, covered in pools of blood. Bodies, some half covered in canvas, lie at angles, some crouched in a foetal position to which they turned as they tried to avoid the spear thrusts. Broken spears, guns, blankets, clothes, pots and water bottles are strewn in a circle of chaos.

As the yeomen peel away the canvas, they hear groans. "Some of these men are still alive," says one.

Chiappini springs into action. "Get these wounded men some help," he says. "On the double!

"Also, we need to know how many men we lost and how many have been injured."

As Chiappini picks his way through the debris, he sees teeth scattered about and wonders whether they came from his men or the Baphuthi attackers. At the edge of the scene of carnage he spies drops of blood on the ground. A bit farther on he notes more. He calls to a couple of his men. "Follow the blood trail," he says.

A man reports back. "We have six men dead and fifteen wounded, seven of them seriously," he says. "Three of the wounded are in dangerous condition.

"We also found the bodies of three Baphuthi."

"Get our wounded men to the hospital tent as soon as possible," Chiappini replies. "Leave the bodies of the Baphuthi here. They are likely to come and retrieve them once we have moved out. We will take the bodies of our men back to the main C.M.R. camp for a decent burial.

"Once you have seen to all of that, break up camp and clean up as much of this mess as you can."

Top: Site of mass grave below mountain of those killed in the attack on the Chiappini camp. Below: Gravestone, corrected, reads: "Troopers killed during the Moorosi war May 1879, repaired by C. Geyer July 1904." [Photographs courtesy of Mick Jones and Peter Millin.]

Quthing — the same day

In some ways, the order — sent by telegram to Palmietfontein and brought to Thomas's Shop by express post overnight — comes as a relief to Griffith. It informs him that he is to hand over his command to Colonel Brabant tomorrow.

No reasons are given, but Griffith knows what they are. He has been roundly condemned for the failure of the attack on the mountain. He has made only limited success in ousting the rebels from their cave hideouts. His plan to starve out the rebels is showing no signs of progress; the men keep supplementing their supplies. As a result, the government has lost faith in his ability to end the war.

The only real success in this war has been Brabant's taking of the cave stronghold up the Quthing river. So why not give overall command to him?

Griffith accepts the verdict, although he doubts whether any other officer could have done better.

His day is about to become worse. A trooper brings him the news of the attack on the Chiappini camp.

Griffith is devastated. Not only is the news of the deaths and wounding of the yeomen in the early hours of this morning itself horrifying, but he suspects that, although he was not there and had placed Brabant in charge, he will bear responsibility for the attack. After all, he was the commander who instructed the camp to be set up there.

This attack will be seen as another reason to consider Griffith's work at the mountain a failure.

⚜

Returning from Thomas' Shop to the mountain, Griffith hears more details of the vicious attack. He orders a court of inquiry to look into it.

The court, he stipulates, should begin its proceedings tomorrow morning, minutes after he hands over command to Brabant. He appoints Captain J. T. O'Connor of the Cape Mounted Riflemen, now stationed at the mountain, as the president of the court, and recently arrived Captain George E. Giles and Captain Howard Sprigg as members.

He is confident that the proceedings will clear him of blame.

Quthing — Friday, May 30, 1879

Members of the court of inquiry gather in a sombre mood. As they do, they learn that Andrew Johnston, wounded in the attack, died last night, bringing the death toll to eight.

First to give evidence is Chiappini, who says he received orders from Captain Minto on Sunday, the 25th of May, to form a camp at the junction of the Quthing and Orange Rivers to assist in the blockade of Moorosi's Mountain.

"I pointed out to Colonel Minto at the time that it was a dangerous position on account of its isolation, and also because there was no favourable site for a camp," Chiappini says. "Colonel Minto told me that it was the commandant's order that a camp should be formed there."

Chiappini outlines the attack. He is followed by Meyer and two yeomen.

In his evidence, Minto, commander of the 3rd yeomanry, says Griffith instructed him to send a detachment of his regiment to set up a permanent camp at the junction of the Orange and Quthing rivers to guard entry to and from the mountain. He therefore dispatched the group under Chiappini.

"Owing to the rugged country, the enemy were enabled to come quite near the pickets before they were discovered, and rushed on to the camp at once, stabbing into the tents with their spears," he says. He praises the stand taken by the men as "most heroic."

Griffith asks to be heard. "If the men had not been sleeping in tents they would not have been as vulnerable to attack," he says. "I do not know why the men were sleeping in tents. I gave no orders that tents should be used."

Minto disputes Griffith's statement: "Commandant Griffith told me that tents were to be erected on the site. It was, after all, a permanent site."

"But I gave no order that tents should be erected," replies Griffith.

"Yes, sir, you did."

O'Connor, as president of the court of inquiry, intervenes. "Colonel Minto, do you recall Colonel Griffith using the word tents?"

After thinking deeply for a moment, Minto slowly replies, "I recall him giving instructions that a permanent camp was to be established on the site," he replies.

"But did he use the word tents?"

Minto ponders the question for a little longer. "The order from the Colonel-Commandant of the Field Forces to me about forming a camp was a verbal one. In the course of the conversation on the subject I was told the camp was to be a permanent one. And the men were to be made as comfortable as possible."

"I must ask again," says O'Connor. "Did Colonel Griffith use the word tents?"

"Although I cannot be certain that tents were actually mentioned, the impression on my mind was that tents were to be taken, and I accordingly gave the order that they were to be taken."

Griffith is satisfied. As far as he is concerned, Minto has conceded that he took it upon himself to use tents.

O'Connor asks Minto to put his account of Griffith's order in writing by Sunday, when the inquiry will issue its report.

Quthing — Saturday, May 31, 1879

George Whitehead steps down the path to the Orange River, pulling his coat around him. A member of the Cape Mounted Riflemen, he was ordered to join the troops at the mountain two weeks ago as part of a new supplementary force of 300, consisting of Riflemen as well as members of the Cape Mounted Yeomanry, authorised by Prime Minister Sprigg.

Since his arrival Whitehead has found the days becoming cooler and the nights intensely cold as autumn sets in. The tents offer little protection from the freezing temperatures, although they afford shelter from strong winds that whip through the valley.

The thick layer of frost that formed overnight crunches under his boots as Whitehead approaches the river, flowing slowly now that the summer rains have stopped.

A soldier standing at the river introduces himself as William King. A farmer in the Cape Colony who volunteered for duty in Basutoland as a member of the yeomanry, he also arrived two weeks ago. He and Whitehead talk as they stoop down to the water, washing their faces between words.

"We were supposed to relieve other members of the yeomanry who wanted to return home," King explains. "But when we arrived here, Griffith didn't release them and when Brabant took command yesterday he told them they must stay on.

"I hope that means we'll see action soon. Ever since we arrived here we've had nothing to do. If we continue sitting around like this, the enemy will come off the mountain and attack us in our tents the way they did those men up the river."

⁂

At the headquarters camp, Maitin concludes that his work is done at the mountain. He held an important position as Griffith's aide; now he will go back to being a clerk and translator. He will return with Griffith to Maseru.

During the campaign, Maitin felt it was his duty to stand by Griffith, just as he had stood by Hope, in spite of everything, and later by Austen.

As the situation changed from confrontation to colonial obsession with winning the war, Maitin saw Griffith change. The senior magistrate, once so proud, so efficient, so calm, and so dedicated to impartial justice, stumbled as a commander. Losing the assault on the mountain unnerved him. He lost his way. He lashed out at others, determined to be shown to be right, even when he knew he was to blame.

He watched as Griffith moved from being an administrator and a peacemaker, a task at which he excelled, to being an army commander and a war maker, at which he failed. Griffith had left his area of competency for a position for which he was not suited. That was why, Maitin assumes, he had heard unfavourable reports of Griffith's leadership on the eastern frontier where he also had been called upon to be a destroyer, not a diplomat.

Had it not been for Griffith, for whom he will continue to work in Maseru, Maitin might have quit Quthing months ago when he became disillusioned with the war. But, not one to voice his opinions against those in authority, he said nothing then and will say nothing now.

Yet his unvocalised views on the conflict run deep. The son of French missionaries and born and raised in Basutoland, Maitin understands the Baphuthi people. He knows how they think and what they believe. He understands that Moorosi's resistance runs deeper than his desire to remain king. It is driven by the powerful force of culture and the duty of leadership his culture has bestowed on him. Rooted in land, language and custom, the Baphuthi culture, like all cultures, cannot be changed by decree, by force, or by self-will. It is the very essence of who the king and his people are.

That base can be modified, but it cannot be eliminated. Their customs and ways of thinking and their languages will continue to direct their lives no matter what they do or where they go. Their culture might change over time through interaction with other groups, or even through a desire by the people to remake their own culture, but such change can take generations and even then would not be complete.

Indeed, the colonial people also have their culture and would strongly resist any attempts to change it, particularly by force, were the roles reversed.

Of course, Maitin knows the colonists' real aim is to take over the Baphuthi people's land and use the people as a ready form of cheap labour. But, to put a moral face on it, the government says it wants to bring a civilized way of life to people who lack it. The Baphuthi people, the government says, would be uplifted materially and morally by having to follow European standards and later, having learned the European ways, would adopt those standards as their own. Light would be brought into the Baphuthi darkness. The Baphuthi would become Europeans in black skins.

That motive assumes that European culture is superior to Baphuthi culture. Maitin does not share that belief. One is not better than the other; they are simply different.

But Maitin knows, too, that even were such a motive genuine, cultural change is impossible to achieve through force.

The ideal outcome would be to establish a joining of cultures as equals, each understanding and respecting the other, sharing what they have in common and recognizing and honouring what is different between them and what neither can change. They will compromise, seek a middle way and combine the best of their two cultures. They will not seek to destroy or to dominate. It will not always be easy, but it will be fulfilling and, above all, peaceful.

But that will not happen here in Quthing. Not between these two peoples. This is a clash, not a drive for collusion. One side will win the battle for the land and the control of the people living on it.

Should the Baphuthi win and the colonial government leave, the conflict will be gone and the *status quo* restored. One language, one land, one way of life. Peace.

Should the colonial government be the victor, however, and attempt to impose its cultural norms and way of life on the Baphuthi people, they will have to dominate them by force as the Baphuthi's culture can never be expunged by the orders of white magistrates or the spoils of war. Unless the Baphuthi people are annihilated — an outcome too horrible for Maitin to contemplate — the cultural clash will remain. A colonial victory will only smother it until it resurfaces later.

Maitin hates what is happening in Quthing. He will be pleased not to be directly involved in the war any longer.

⁂

The attack on Chiappini's camp has made Brabant, on his second day in command, even more determined that the war should be ended — soon. That is the reason he was chosen to take over from Griffith and he will make sure that he does not disappoint the government.

Brabant, 40, is a man of fortitude. A couple of months ago he led his men through almost impassable rivers and deep ravines to reach Moorosi's Mountain. And, while Griffith sat at the mountain, Brabant completed a successful mission against hundreds of Baphuthi hiding in caves along the Quthing River.

His record shows he knows what needs to be done, he is not afraid to do it and he knows how to achieve it. He must act now. He does not have the options Griffith had. The cost of doing nothing has risen — and not only the political and economic costs. The winter cold has set in and it may snow in coming weeks.

Brabant's troops are at full strength and he does not see any purpose in sitting around and waiting for the Baphuthi to become hungry and surrender.

"I plan to storm the mountain again as soon as additional ammunition arrives," he tells his officers. "This time we will employ a 12-pounder M.L. R. Armstrong, which is on its way here, as well as the 7-pounder M. L. R. mountain guns. And I intend to use them as they are supposed to be used, with strong and sustained bombing.

"They will blast the stone walls so effectively that the way will be cleared for our men to reach the top and declare victory.

"In the meantime, we need to be ready. I could make the decision to move as soon as the big gun arrives. Before I do, however, I need a group of men to patrol as close to the stone walls as they can and report back to me on the most practical way to attack the walls. Do I have any volunteers for this mission?"

Newly found friends Whitehead and King are among five who step forward.

Quthing — Sunday June 1, 1879

Griffith spends the morning preparing his report on the court of inquiry. Although he addresses it to Brabant, it will form a part of the official record of events and will be sent to the government in Cape Town and eventually to London.

"It appears that the picket in question was taken by surprise, in consequence of the sentry or sentries not having given the alarm in sufficient time to allow the men to turn out of their tents," he writes. "It is also my duty to bring to your notice the unheard-of proceeding upon the part of the officer commanding the 3rd regiment of yeomanry in allowing the pickets to take tents with them.

"The mere fact of pitching tents, of course, exposed the position of the picket and gave the rebels the opportunity either of invading or attacking it, and it appears they were not slow in taking the latter course.

"I was absent from the camp and was therefore not aware that the picket in question had taken their tents with them, which, had I been aware of, I should most certainly have not allowed."

That should do it. He has resorted to his favourite tactic — a legalistic, exact interpretation of his words — to clear his name and is ready to return to Maseru to resume his former post. He has had enough of this war.

Quthing — Monday, June 2, 1879

Shortly after the sun sets, but before it becomes too dark, Whitehead and King, accompanied by three other members of the Cape Mounted Riflemen, set out on their assigned task. With Whitehead in the lead, the five men creep up the hill toward the stone walls. They approach from the southwest, hoping to be either out of sight of the Baphuthi or out of range of their gunfire should the warriors see them in the light of the dusk and the quarter moon.

Their plan is to shelter under the ledge and follow it eastward, stepping back now and then to view the walls above.

Drawing closer to the walls, the men instinctively walk more quietly. Coming within range of the Baphuthi rifles, they are bracing for a possible shot.

They reach the ledge without incident and begin to step out into the open to look up to examine the stone walls.

They see the occasional Baphuthi above them, peering at them from above the walls. But no one shoots.

Gaining more confidence, the men edge farther into the open. They estimate the height of the walls, the loopholes and the occasional breaks between them, envisioning how and where the walls can be destroyed or overcome.

The Baphuthi watching them remain unmoved.

The men's inspection reveals embankments of solid earth with heavy stones placed in front of them. Most have a double row of loopholes, near the base and near the top. The men conclude that should the outer facing of the walls be knocked away, the Baphuthi would still have earth behind which to shelter.

Satisfied they have made a careful inspection, King suggests moving off.

"Before we go, let's make sure we have seen all we need to see," Whitehead, emboldened by the lack of Baphuthi response, tells the soldiers gathered around him. "Do you see how we could climb up the rocks, scramble over the walls, which will then be in a state of disrepair after being hammered with the 12-pounder, push our way through the earth embankments and get into the trenches behind the walls?"

"It will be difficult, but not impossible," responds King. "We could — "

He stops in mid sentence as a spear swoops past him and embeds itself in the heart of Peter Ferreira, a member of the Cape Mounted Riflemen standing next to him.

The air is filled with yells and whooping as a group of Baphuthi rush out of the semi-darkness on their right, heading directly toward them on the plateau, firing and throwing spears.

The men realize that while they were looking at the wall structures, the Baphuthi had come down from the mountain almost alongside them. Now it is clear — too late — why the warriors behind the walls made no attempt to fire.

Once again, the "ignorant barbarians" have outwitted the colonial forces.

The white soldiers turn and run, leaving Ferreira lying on the ground. They have no doubt he is dead.

"Run to that ridge ahead of us," Whitehead yells.

"Get behind it, load your rifles and give these natives what they have coming to them."

The soldiers have a 20-yard lead over the Baphuthi, but the fleet-footed warriors are shortening the distance and flinging spears toward the men.

As he runs, King turns to see how far off his pursuers are. In doing so, he fails to see a rock ahead of him. He strikes it with his boot, loses his balance and falls forward. The others continue running toward the ridge, unaware King has tripped and fallen.

King pulls himself up. A sharp pain in his knee tells him he is injured, but he is determined to make it to safety behind the ridge.

His four-and-a-half foot long Snider still in his hand, he slowly pulls himself up on to his legs, in spite of the pain.

He staggers only a few feet forward, however, before three Baphuthi surround him. They seize him, grab his rifle, and hold his wrists behind him.

"You will come with us," they say. "You are our prisoner."

Quthing — Tuesday, June 3, 1879

The wagons carrying the ammunition roll into camp. The men cheer. They know the ammunition is key to their next moves against Moorosi — and they are ready to seek vengeance on the Baphuthi. Their vindictiveness has been spurred by the attack on Chiappini's camp, and strongly advanced by King's seizure.

"We will move at first light on Thursday," Brabant tells his officers.

"We will pummel the stone walls with intense bombing for 48 hours until we have

12-pounder cannon

evidence that the cannon are having an effect. We will accompany the bombing with sustained volleys of rifle fire.

"In fact, I suspect that the rebels will scamper to higher ground as soon as the walls start to crumble and they find they cannot rebuild

them under the withering fire both from the cannon and from our rifles. Then we will rush the fortress.

"Sergeant Whitehead led a group of valiant men to a position just below the stone walls yesterday. He was able to confirm that it is possible to storm the enemy's position once we have destroyed the walls with cannon fire.

"The foray was not without incident. As I am sure you know by now, the men returned with valuable information, but a soldier was killed and another taken prisoner by the enemy."

The men are interrupted by shouts from the mountain.

They look up to see a pole sticking up from behind the walls. On the end is King's severed head. As they watch, King's headless body is thrown over the wall to the ground below.

It is one thing to watch a friend die in battle. In a sense, it is part of the high-risk game that a soldier knowingly plays, the rules of which are etched out in a mutually agreed code. You try to capture us; we try to capture you. You shoot at us; we shoot at you. You stand to die if we succeed; we stand to die if you succeed. Severing a man's head breaks the rules.

"We will remember this when we finally get to attack them," Whitehead vows, tears welling in his eyes when he recalls the friend he had known for only a couple of days but with whom he felt he had shared a year's worth of adventure.

The Baphuthi no longer are simply an enemy. They are now a hated enemy.

⚜

Moorosi is proud of what his people have achieved in the last week.

First, there was the victory his son Letuka won in the attack on the camp at the junction of the Quthing and Orange rivers. As he looks down from the northern end of his mountain home, Moorosi notes that the tents are gone.

"You avenged the deaths of our people in the Quthing River caves," he tells Letuka. "The white men showed in that attack how cruel they can be to our people. They tried to smoke our people out of their caves and they threw an explosive at you and caused you to lose your right hand and other people to be killed. Even now your hand is healing only slowly, and will never be right. It will forever be a reminder to you of the cruelty that the white people show toward us."

"I am angry at the white people for what they have done," Letuka says, "not just to me but to our people. At least I survived. Others did not. But I am pleased that I was able to lead my people to one of their camps and to show them how it feels when you are attacked, how your people die and how you grieve for them."

Moorosi agrees. The attack on the camp was not their only recent victory.

"After we captured one of their men last night, we showed them today what it means to fall into our hands," Moorosi continues. "We showed them what we think of the people sent here to kill us."

Moorosi calls his people to him.

"We have killed some of the men sent here to kill us," he says. "We have killed many of them as they lay sleeping in their tents. We have cut off the head of one of them who tried to spy on us and killed another with a spear. But we cannot rest. I see that the government people have brought a bigger gun to their camp. I see the men marching around.

"They are about to attack us again. They will aim that bigger gun at our defences. We are to build up the walls if they are damaged. And if they are foolish enough to try to storm our walls again, we are to shoot at them as we did before.

"I want those who are guarding the walls to be on watch all the time. No one is to return here to the top of the mountain at meal time. The women will bring the food to you. You are to stay on watch continuously. When it is time for you to be relieved so you can sleep then someone else will take your place.

"Now, those who are not watching on the walls must get some sleep tonight because our spies tell us the government people will attack us tomorrow."

As the men move toward their huts, the mountain shakes from the pounding of the 12-pounder gun. "They are attacking sooner than I thought," Moorosi shouts to his men. "Forget what I said about sleep. Everyone, to the walls!"

19

Brabant plans to pound the stone walls, or schanzes, for a couple of days using the two 7-pounders as well as the stronger, more effective 12-pounder Armstrong gun until they have been destroyed.

After pounding the walls for several hours, the 12-pounder proves its worth. It shatters parts of the first tier, which consists of two parallel stone walls with earth between them, causing the stones to tumble on both sides, some rolling down the mountainside. By 1 p.m. many of the stone walls are in ruins, prompting Brabant to order the firing to continue until dark and to resume tomorrow.

But, after 87 rounds have been expended, the firing from the 12-pounder stops. Captain George E. Giles, who brought the gun with him and is now in charge of the artillery in the field, wants to know why the men have stopped firing.

"The copper lining of the vent has become bulged up and that is impeding the firing," they report. Giles examines the vent, which must be clear if the firing is to be at full force. "Keep firing and make every effort to keep the vent clear," he says.

The men fire several rounds, but each successive discharge closes the vent even more. "Stop firing," Giles says. "It seems only to be making matters worse. Let's do all we can to clear this vent."

The men work on the vent all afternoon. By the evening it has been partially cleared — enough for the firing to be effective — but the lining is severely bulged and cracked. "I'm afraid that damage might be done to the gun if we continue to fire it before it is re-vented," Giles tells Brabant.

"Well, re-vent it then and let us get on with the firing at dawn," Brabant replies.

"We cannot do that without the proper tools," Giles replies. "They might have them at Thomas's Shop Camp. If they do, repairing the gun will mean a delay of a day or two. If not, we might have to wait for them to come from Aliwal North."

"We cannot wait that long," Brabant replies. "We have made considerable progress in tearing down the walls and, if we stop even for a day, the enemy will rebuild them. No, Giles, we must keep pounding those walls. Even if it damages the gun, we need to continue firing at first light tomorrow."

Brabant doubles the picket on the saddle and orders constant carbine fire should they see the enemy attempting to repair the walls. The full moon will help them see until it sets during the early hours of the morning. He is confident his plan will work.

Quthing — Wednesday, June 4, 1879

At dawn, Brabant discovers that the Baphuthi have been busy in the night rebuilding the walls, most of which have been restored to their former strength. He will have to destroy them again.

Working during the night, Giles' men have removed the copper lining of the vent in the 12-pounder, making the gun useful for the time being although the problem with the vent is still causing a long delay between firings. Brabant orders him to pound the mountain during the whole day and into the night, using the 7-pounder under Best in addition to the 12-pounder.

Impact of shells from 12-pounder cannon.

"Tonight, we will again direct a heavy volume of small-arms fire at the schanzes," Brabant adds. "After the moon sets, you will use the 7-pounder to lob star shells to light up the walls and enable the men on picket duty to see their targets and prevent the enemy from rebuilding them. I will order the attack at dawn tomorrow."

Although less accurate now, the 12-pounder is able to fire 170 rounds of segment shell during the day, breaching the walls in several additional places and adding to the damage that the Baphuthi were unable to repair during the night. Some of the flanking walls are almost destroyed.

The success of the guns gives Brabant confidence. As he gathers his officers in the late afternoon, he explains that he will send groups to act as feints on either side of the mountain, diverting the enemy's attention. As the enemy moves to the sides, the main group will storm the centre.

Brabant assembles the men into three groups of 150 each.

The first group is to move up a gully on the south-western, or left, side of the mountain. "Your attack will be a feint," he says. "You are there to divert the enemy's attention. Only should the opportunity offer, should you launch a real attack."

The second group will undertake the other feint attack on the slopes on the south-eastern face, or the right side, from where Baphuthi have been seen emerging, Brabant says. He is convinced there's a hidden route to the top unguarded by stone walls; he wants the men to find it and advance as far as they can. For this attack he orders troopers from the Cape Yeomanry to take the lead and Captain Henry Davies to follow with 500 Basotho. "You will be covered by one of the seven-pounders," he tells the men. "We will aim the fire above and ahead of you.

"I want you to advance as far as you can, but your goal is not to take the mountain. That is the purpose of the men who will storm the main walls. Your role is to make the enemy think your advance up the path is our main attack. Once the two diversionary groups have successfully attracted the enemy's attention, we will send the main body across the plateau to scale the walls and take the mountain."

Addressing the third group, Brabant says, "You are my main body of troops. I have chosen you to attack the schanzes. You will not be called upon to attack them without help. The walls will have been so weakened by the cannon shells we will fire today that they will be lightly manned by the enemy."

He turns to face all 450 soldiers. "All of you in all three groups will parade at 6 a.m., just before daybreak. We set off at dawn."

Whitehead, selected for the main attacking force, is nervous. He has heard from Scott and Brown what good shots the Baphuthi are. He also experienced a stealth attack from the Baphuthi two days ago in which he narrowly escaped with his life.

He shares his fears with Corporal Andrew Jones, who threw dynamite in Brabant's attack on the caves, and also has been chosen for the main storming party.

"Don't you worry," Jones replies. "Remember how you were taken by surprise the other night when you surveyed the stone walls?"

"How can I forget? I am afraid we will be facing the same thing here."

"Well, it will be the same thing, only the opposite," Jones says. "Just as you did not expect those men to attack you from the side, so the Baphuthi will not think we are attacking from the front."

"I hope you are right."

"I know I am.

"Also, we will have the larger gun pounding the walls. They will not be able to simply stand there and fire at us as they did last time. As for me, I will be protected by more than the cannon; I have my lucky rabbit's foot charm with me." He pats the outside of a pocket and smiles.

Brome, lingering in the background when selections are made or volunteers are called for, is pleased that he is not chosen for any of the groups. For now he is happy to be on the sidelines.

Quthing — Thursday, June 5, 1879

As dawn breaks, the cannon resume their blasts on the lower tier of stone walls, large parts of which remain breached as the Baphuthi were unable to rebuild them effectively during the night.

Amid the screams of shells and mortars, concussion of explosions and whistle of rockets, the men in the diversionary force on the right, or south east, led by Davies, reach the base of the mountain and find the path to the top.

It starts out smooth, but they soon find the going steeper than they had thought. Taking big strides, they climb up jagged rocks that form a series of irregular steps. Soon they are winding up the mountainside in a zigzag pattern, heading north, then south and north again as they climb upward.

Above them, the cannon shells crash against the rocks, sending stone splinters cascading around them and overriding the sounds made by the men as they climb in single file.

Unopposed, the men make good progress.

Soon they can no longer see the crest of the mountain as it is hidden from their sight by a ridge above them. After about 30 minutes of climbing, the men hear gunfire and see puffs of white smoke above them as bullets fly over their heads.

They press on, acting as targets to divert the Baphuthi attention. Now and then they stop to fire above them, another means of drawing attention away from the stone walls in the front.

⚜

The men charged with advancing up the gully on the western side of the mountain are unable to progress far. The ravine is steep and when the Baphuthi hurl boulders down the gully, they return to their starting point. As they do, they fire repeatedly, trying to divert the attention of the Baphuthi toward them.

⚜

Forty minutes after they began their climb, the leading men on the right reach a level 40 yards from the first tier of a series of three sets of stone walls above them. But their path, which now leads north, is only two feet wide, with an almost perpendicular rock face on their left and a precipice on their right.

The Baphuthi, who have now realized the men's presence, roll boulders down the path toward them and fire in their direction. Two of the 3rd Yeomanry troopers, who are leading the Basotho, are struck by bullets. William Hannan is hit in the stomach and Henry Leonard in the right thigh. Seized with pain, they lie in the path, unable to move. Some of the yeomen move forward to try to help the wounded, but they can do little in the face of the fierce fire being directed at them.

The other members of the yeomanry fall back, urging the Basotho to go ahead of them. As the firing intensifies, Mphelekane, one of the 500 Basotho who had formed the main part of this attack, is struck by a bullet; he dies within minutes. Gunshots strike Musi in the right arm, Mekwane in the knee and Penoki in his chest.

The sight of the men being hit is too much for the remaining Basotho, who turn and flee. Halfway down, they stop and fire every round of ammunition they have above the heads of the yeomen on the path above them. Their hearts were not in this mission — and now their lives are in danger. Promises of keeping the cattle taken in the war and their arms appear hollow. This war is real. They could die. It is not a game.

With the Basotho gone, the yeomen move slowly forward on the path, firing repeatedly ahead of them. The Baphuthi fire back, retreat and disappear around a curve. The yeomen follow. Ten yards past the curve they see Baphuthi pointing their loaded rifles at them from behind a stone wall ahead of them.

⚜

Brabant sees smoke from gunfire emerging above the gully to his left and to the right. The sound of continued firing to the right suggest his plan is succeeding.

He directs his senior officers to ready the main assault troops. They gather 70 of the 150 selected for the first wave. The other half will follow once the walls are taken and will help in the final push to the top.

Now and then Brabant catches a glimpse of Baphuthi at their posts behind the centre stone walls, but he assumes most are diverting the forces on the right and left.

⚜

The 70 troopers, under Captain J. T. O'Connor, are assembled behind the saddle. Among them are Whitehead and Jones.

"You are the advance force," O'Connor tells them. "Once I give the signal, Captain Pope will lead you to the plateau. You will rush 500 yards to a ridge of rock running parallel to, and 25 yards from, the first stone wall. There you will wait a few minutes before gathering your breath, sizing up the scene, and making the final rush for the schanzes.

"Those at the forefront of the advance will be able to make use of a scaling ladder that will be carried there by two of the troopers. They will be able to climb up it, confront the enemy, and clear the way for the rest to follow.

"Judging from the appearance of the walls, we hope to be able to take the schanzes without much opposition.

"Once you have taken the lower schanz, the next force, consisting of 80 men, will follow you with more ladders and climb the walls up to the next level. From there you will advance higher and eventually take Moorosi himself."

The men line up, rifles at their sides, and edge forward still behind the saddle. Their view directly ahead of them is blocked by the saddle, but they can see the smoke and hear the shooting from the right side of the mountain where their comrades are fighting on the cliff trail.

At 8:30 Brabant orders the first wave of the main storming party to advance. "Onward to victory!" he shouts. The men hesitate. O'Connor is about to repeat the order when the cannon fall silent.

Brabant calls to an officer. "Tell them I need them to keep up the firing," he says. "We have to cover our advance."

The officer returns in a few minutes.

"The guns have broken down," he says.

"What? Both of them?"

"Yes, sir. The carriage of the 7-pounder is totally disabled and ammunition for the 12-pounder is running low. Captain Giles wants to reserve the ammunition for any further advances that might be made later in the day."

❧❦❧

Moorosi moves from group to group in the trenches behind the stone walls, encouraging his warriors to keep up the firing and not to be distracted.

"They are trying to attack us from the sides," he says. "We can hold them off. Stand in the places that I gave you and don't go anywhere else."

❧❦❧

"Why do you think they've stopped the cannon fire?" Jones asks Whitehead.

"They likely have broken down the walls enough for us to make it through," Whitehead replies. "They don't want to fire into the walls when we're scaling them."

O'Connor again gives the command to advance. The men emerge from behind the saddle and line up in a broad wave that stretches across the plateau, with their leader, Captain Pope, on the right flank. They stride forward, rifles at the ready.

They have advanced only a short distance when they run into a hail of bullets. They press on, but have covered only 100 yards of the 500-yard-long plateau when Pope is shot through the forearm. With flesh ripped off his arm and the bone exposed,

Ridge behind which the soldiers sheltered is on the left.

he turns back toward the saddle. A number of volunteers also turn.

Jones and Whitehead, on the far left flank, are unaware of what has happened to Pope. They move at a slight jog across the bare rock with the rest of their group, making good progress. They hear rifle fire but are unsure at first whether it is coming from the pickets on the saddle behind them or the walls ahead of them. Soon they know it is from the walls as bullets kick up the dust around them.

Some of the soldiers stop, load their rifles and fire back. But they soon realize they present better targets when they stop, so they press forward. As they proceed into the teeth of the heavy and accurate rifle fire, a number are hit.

Unwilling to continue against the withering fire, many of the men turn and head back toward the saddle. No amount of persuasion or degree of command will convince them to return to the plateau.

Others, including Jones and Whitehead, continue forward, heading, as instructed, toward the shelter of the ridge 25 yards from the walls. As they get closer, fire directed at them from all the lower schanzes, including those that appeared to be demolished, gains in intensity. This was not supposed to happen. The Baphuthi were supposed to be thinned out. Yet, the troopers are finding, the warriors' fire power is severe, scathing and spot-on.

As more men are hit, any pretence of a marching order is gone. The men scatter, some running back to the saddle and others darting for the ridge ahead.

Not all reach the ridge. A few yards away, Sergeant J. Robinson, of the 2nd regiment of Cape Yeomen, falls, shot dead through the heart.

Behind him, Whitehead and Jones evade the bullets, and keep moving forward. "No good turning back now," Jones says. "We can make it to the ridge. Imagine the natives' surprise when we show up right in their midst. They will —"

Jones falls to the ground, struck by a bullet to the head. As Whitehead leans down to tend to him, a bullet whistles past his ear. With bullets flying around him, Whitehead calls to those already behind the ridge for help.

⚜

The soldiers on the cliff trail on the mountain's right side stop in their tracks as they see the Baphuthi behind the wall ahead of them ready to fire. "Enemy ahead!" the yeoman leader yells to the men behind him. "Fall back!"

The men scramble back, still in single file. They hear the crack of rifle sounds and, seconds later, see puffs of smoke drifting into the air ahead of them. Turning and heading downhill, they recall Brabant's words, "You are essentially a diversionary tactic, not a main advance force."

Clambering back down, the men reach the next set of rock steps. They kneel and fire toward the warriors who are now sheltering behind the rocks at the other end of the path.

The two groups of fighters, each behind rocks, size one another up. Neither group wishes to move forward or backward. Occasionally a shot is fired.

They can hear the sounds of a blistering fire fight coming from the plateau.

⚜

Whitehead remains fully exposed to enemy fire as he kneels to help Jones. He tears off the bottom of his shirt and uses it to try to staunch the blood from the wound on Jones' head. His efforts meet with little success.

"You can make it," he pleads with Jones. "Don't leave me now. We have been together too long for you to leave now."

"Get to safety," Jones replies, breathing deeply. "Take care of yourself."

"I will stay with you," Whitehead says. "I will see to it that you get help."

A shot scrapes Whitehead's trousers and strikes Jones in the arm.

"Go on," Jones pleads, intense pain coursing through his body. "Don't lose your life because of me."

Whitehead looks back toward the ridge; no one is responding to his calls for help. He shouts, "Is there a doctor there?"

Surgeon-Major Edmund Baron Hartley, who made it to the ridge with the initial wave of men, looks up from tending to the wounds of a man resting against the ridge. "Yes. I am a doctor," he shouts.

"A man is lying out here, badly wounded," Whitehead responds.

Hartley quickly secures the bandage to a wounded man under the ridge and runs zigzag 20 yards across the plateau toward Jones.

Whitehead, realizing he can do little more to help Jones, runs toward the ridge, shouting back, "You are in good hands, my friend. I will see you again soon."

With bullets flying on either side of him, Hartley staunches the blood, stretches into his side pack, retrieves a bandage, and winds it around Jones' head. Jones, who is losing a lot of blood, needs to receive more medical help soon.

Hartley picks up Jones and staggers back toward the saddle, across the exposed ground over which the men were so recently marching. A bullet strikes Jones as he lies in Hartley's arms. This time it hits his leg.

After carrying Jones for 200 yards, Hartley moves out of range of the enemy fire and behind the shelter of the saddle rock where stretcher bearers take Jones back to the camp.

Aware that his services are needed behind the ridge where several men are lying wounded, Hartley turns around and runs back across the plateau, successfully avoiding the bullets directed toward him, returning to the ridge.

Hartley carries Jones [*Heroes of Our Day,* 1900]

There, he dresses the wounds of eight men hit on their march to the ridge.

Most seriously wounded is Trooper C. Lewis of the 1st Cape Mounted Yeomanry who, Hartley realizes, is in imminent danger of bleeding to death from a wound in the arm. He makes Lewis as comfortable as he can, hoping he will survive.

Hartley cannot risk carrying another man across the plateau as he did Jones. Not only would he risk being hit himself, but his experience with Jones has taught him that the man he is carrying could himself be hit.

⚜

"You are doing good work," Moorosi tells his men. "We are keeping them from reaching the walls.

"Maketa, your shooting has again been accurate. How many have you shot?"

"I am not sure, my king, but I have hit a lot of them."

"These people are not very clever. What are they thinking when they run at us? Do they think we will not shoot them? Do they have herbs that they think will stop the bullets from entering their bodies?"

Moorosi laughs.

"The white people believe they can do anything," he replies.

As he moves among the men crouched in the trenches behind the stone walls, Moorosi checks on how many have been injured.

Some have been struck by exploding shells and a few have been grazed by bullets, but the injuries are not serious and no one has been killed.

"Keep watching," he says. "We do not want to drop our guard at any time. Even if they are not moving now, they might decide at any time to rush at the walls again. We must be ready for them."

"We were instructed to move from here and storm the walls," Whitehead says to the men crouching behind the ridge. "But to do so, we will have to cross the 25 yards ahead of us. We will be completely exposed to enemy fire.

"It is inviting death. They fire with great accuracy and they seem to be familiar with every inch of ground between the saddle and the schanzes. Almost every man that tried to make it to this ridge was fired at. Now that we are closer to the walls, it will be worse."

"We've had to run the gauntlet," says Private Andrew Hemple. "I don't want to do that again."

"Look at what happened to Robinson," responds another. "Shot dead just as he was about to reach here."

In spite of the blistering attack from the walls, Captain O'Connor orders the second wave of 80 men at the saddle to advance. But most refuse to move, willing to suffer the consequences of disobeying orders rather than face death.

Believing that he should lead by example, O'Connor moves out on the plateau.

"Follow me," he says, waving at them with his hand. But only a handful do. O'Connor leads them across the plateau, evading the Baphuthi gunfire. Incredibly, they make it to the ridge, where they join those already there.

O'Connor completes a quick head count. Of the 150 men in the two waves, only 78 — the bulk of them from the first wave — have reached the ridge. But a number of those are injured and unable to fight.

As the highest ranking officer with the men behind the ridge, O'Connor takes command. He asks for volunteers for the attack on the walls that lie just 25 yards ahead of them.

"I would be prepared to go," says Captain Douglas. "But only if I had a strong force of men with me."

O'Connor ponders issuing an order for all the men to storm the walls, but fears most would refuse to do so. As he is thinking, three troopers from the Cape Mounted Riflemen volunteer to creep closer to the wall. "We may be able to gain some information," says Sergeant Graham. "Or we may be able to get a shot at them."

"I am not ordering you to go at this stage," says O'Connor. "But if you are prepared to do so, I will not stop you."

Accompanied by Private Jones (a brother of Andrew, the corporal shot earlier in the head), and Private J. R. Handyside, Graham moves ahead. Near the wall, a shot blasts Handyside in the foot. He reaches down, grabbing at his foot with his hands. "Help," he cries. "Please help me."

Captain Dalgety, using the ladder carried to the ridge, climbs to the top of the ridge, and helps Handyside down, narrowly escaping being hit by bullets.

As the men return to safety, O'Connor decides he has had enough for now. "Under these circumstances, I deem it best to abandon further attempts at assaulting the mountain at this stage," he tells the men. "Any further attempts will only result in great additional loss of life, without achieving any real advantage. We'll wait here until one or both of the assaults on the left and right prove successful. Then we can make a rush at the stone walls, which by then should be empty."

As the rifle fire near the front of the mountain dies down, the members of the distraction force on the right assume the main assault has been a success and therefore that their job as a distraction force has ended.

Slowly, the soldiers move back down the path, all the while holding their arms at the ready. The Baphuthi do not follow them.

The men pinned behind the ridge, tired, dejected and disillusioned, also note the silence and wonder what has happened in the distraction attacks on the flanks of the mountain.

Shortly after noon a Basotho messenger, who has succeeded in braving the gunfire, hands a note to O'Connor from Brabant. In it, he asks how many casualties his group has suffered and asks about the feasibility of storming the mountain stronghold after dark.

O'Connor retrieves pen and paper from his pack. "In addition to the wounded who have already left with Dr. Hartley, there are three yeomen and two Cape Mounted Riflemen lying wounded behind the ridge, and Sergeant Robinson is dead," he writes. "I consider the attack at this point to have failed as so many of the stormers are still behind."

The Basotho messenger is soon back with a reply from Brabant: "I order you to retire as quietly as possible after it becomes dark. Send the dead and wounded down first. I regret our casualties and I would not feel justified in risking further loss."

As darkness descends, Giles orders the 12-pounder to resume firing to cover the retreat from the ledge. The ammunition is dwindling, but it is more important now that it be used to enable the men to return to the camp.

With the 12-pounder firing, O'Connor signifies that the men can retreat, warning them to be as quiet as possible. But their movements soon attract the attention of the Baphuthi who, assisted by the light of the moon, open up an insistent fire. When he realizes what is happening, O'Connor orders the men still behind the ridge to fire on the stone walls to cover their comrades' retreat.

One of the men still under the ridge, William Sluyter, who left his farm at Beaufort on the eastern frontier a few weeks ago to join the yeomanry, looks across at Robinson's body lying just yards away. He seethes with anger when he sees what the natives have done to his fellow farmer.

With only the light of the moon to aid the Baphuthi shooters, Sluyter feels now is the time to help in some way. He moves from the shelter of the ridge, runs to Robinson's body and picks it up, determined to carry it back to the camp.

Struggling to hold the dead weight in his arms, his knees buckling under the strain, Sluyter carries Robinson's body down the slope. He has not gone far when he is struck in the back by a bullet. He staggers forward, dropping Robinson's body, and falling to the ground.

The one casualty has become two.

The remainder of the men make their way as quickly as they can down the mountainside, back to their camp. As they do, Baphuthi jump down from the walls and run toward the ridge, stopping now and then to fire in the direction of the departing men.

When the colonial soldiers are about halfway down the mountainside, they hear shouts behind them. They turn around to see the Baphuthi warriors, standing in front of the stone walls, dancing and chanting victory songs.

Quthing — Sunday, June 8, 1879

They bury their comrades in a graveyard by the Orange River with a view of the mountain on which they died. They chisel crosses and names on stone slabs and set them up as gravestones.

The lines chiselled below a cross on one of the gravestones sum it up: "Corp. A.

P. Jones, No. 1 Troop C. M. R., Wounded June 5, Died June 7, 1879."

After digging the grave, placing Jones' body — and his unlucky rabbit's foot alongside it — in a crude coffin, and covering it with earth, others help Whitehead raise the heavy gravestone. They repeat the procedure for three others and ask a soldier to say a prayer to serve as a funeral service.

They have done all they can for the men who served alongside them, who took the bullets that so easily could have hit them. Perhaps these men even died in their place. "Had I been on the right side of him and not on the left, I — not Jones — would have been hit in the head," Whitehead says ruefully as he stares at the slab.

"I will not forget him; he was a fighter brave enough to admit he was afraid and courageous enough to overcome his fear."

But being brave did not rescue these men from death. And their deaths did nothing to gain victory. Did these men, therefore, die in vain? It is difficult for the survivors to come to any other conclusion. They walk silently and slowly back to the camp. There, in a tent, the leading officers, conducting a post-mortem, admit the storming of the mountain two days ago was, like the first, an unmitigated failure. They achieved nothing; they got nowhere; they set back their cause.

At last count, 10 died. Not counting the wounded, the assault was more bloody than the first, in which seven died. The war is worsening, not improving.

Slowly, the colonial troops are being forced to concede that they seriously underestimated their enemy. The Baphuthi are smarter than the whites imagined. They have better rifles and are superior shots. They understand the terrain better. Their fighting tactics work better in the mountains of Basutoland than the colonial troops' British-style military methods. Moorosi is proving to be a shrewd fighter, hunkered down on a virtually impregnable mountain fortress.

What can be done?

Discussing the events with the senior officers in Brabant's tent, O'Connor, leader of the storming party, is dejected. "We all hoped this would be a success," he says. "Indeed, it plainly appeared to promise success."

He pauses. The words are difficult to say. "I sincerely regret that it failed."

"Why do you think we failed?" asks Brabant. "Was it the quality of our men, many of whom were found wanting when it came to acting bravely under fire? Or was our strategy at fault?"

"The men lacked training," volunteers Southey. "I think that is one of the major causes of the disastrous failure. They failed to obey orders, they were undisciplined and untrained."

"I agree," responds O'Connor. "Almost half of the men under my command simply refused to march across the plateau and take the mountain. Had they all obeyed orders we might have succeeded. I think that nothing short of a regiment of steady, well-trained soldiers will succeed in capturing this mountain stronghold.

"The ascent is difficult, steeper and more challenging than we had thought. The fortifications that the mountain offers in its natural state are in themselves formidable. Even without the stone walls, the enemy has the advantage of being able to fire down on the troops below and they can shelter behind the rock formations. The vast towering height of the mountain effectively becomes visible only from the ridge behind which we sheltered. There you gain a different perspective on just how massive it is, how strong the fortifications are, and how difficult it is to ascend.

"Any attempt to take the place by storm must result in a more or less serious loss of life. That is all there is to it."

Brabant sighs. "I thank you for your perspective, with which I agree. Here's my view, which is similar to yours. I believe that the mountain is so strongly defended that nothing but a considerable body of regular troops — not yeomen, not volunteers, but regular troops — provided with heavy guns, in good condition, of course, and proper siege material would have any chance of taking it.

"We have found in this attack that irregular troops, such as volunteers, can seldom be relied upon for the attack of a strongly fortified position like this mountain."

For now, Brabant decides, he has to revert to Griffith's tactics of keeping Moorosi and his followers besieged atop their mountain. He must ensure they do not sneak in any food, that they have no access to the springs at the base of the mountain and that they do not launch any further attacks. He will maintain a ring around the mountain that watches Moorosi continuously and may help to drive him into eventual surrender. The old man cannot last there indefinitely. Can he?

Brabant believes he must also continue Griffith's strategy of ousting other rebels from their mountain holdouts.

"Every one of those cave strongholds is a supply depot for the mountain," he adds. "We must visit them and persuade the people to surrender and seize their grain and other food supplies or we must blast them out."

In a telegram relayed from Palmietfontein, Ayliff is adamant that the second failure to take the mountain should not deter the government to oust Moorosi from his mountain. He remains determined to win the war at all costs.

He writes to Brabant to tell him that the government's idea is "that you keep possession of the country and that you do not withdraw one inch from the position taken up...In case of communication with the rebels being opened up, and terms asked for by the rebel chief, his sons, or subordinate chiefs, those only admissible by the government will be an unconditional surrender."

To help implement Ayliff's instruction to hold his ground, Brabant requests an additional 300 Cape Mounted Riflemen from the frontier districts of the Cape Colony to supplement and enlarge the troops at his disposal. Using the additional men, Brabant will be able to rotate the troops regularly, preventing them from becoming bored, and have about 450 men in the field at any one time.

Another action Brabant will take is to consult the colony's top military planners in Cape Town and ask them for a strategy to oust Moorosi from his fortress.

Those steps are the best he can take right now, particularly with winter approaching.

London — Tuesday, June 17, 1879

The mounting cost of Moorosi's War is straining the Cape Colony's deficit and the British will to fund it. In isolation, it would not have raised as much concern, but it comes on the heels of the eastern frontier wars of the past two years and the Zulu war this year.

These adventures bring little direct benefit to Britain. Not only are they costly, but they have bogged down the move to confederation, aimed at moving the colonies to unity and self-sufficiency so they will no longer rely as much on Britain for financial help.

Sir Michael Hicks-Beach, British colonial affairs secretary, writes to the British-appointed Cape Colony Governor Frere, insisting that the matter is urgent. A major reason is money.

"This country, which has already in various ways borne a large part of the cost of the proceedings which have resulted in the acquisition and pacification of these territories, without receiving any direct benefit in return, cannot be expected to undertake the responsibility of their future government and defence," he writes.

Cape Town — The same day

The colony's own financial situation is a more important issue to the colonial government than that of Britain. The preliminary figures of expenditure for the colony over the last financial year, which will be released publicly in the next few weeks, reflect a loan of £650,000 for an item marked as "native rebellion."

"This figure is a third — yes, a third — of our total debt of £2 million," Prime Minister Sprigg tells his cabinet. "And almost all of it is being spent on the war against Moorosi.

"This loan is a big jump — something like 32 percent — from the £490,000 we borrowed for native rebellions in the last fiscal year," the prime minister continues. "And may I remind you that last year we were fighting wars on the eastern frontier.

"We must conclude this war before it swamps us in debt that will never yield us any returns.

"For now, we can at least make up for it to a small degree by making the people of Basutoland pay toward the war. After all, it is their people who rebelled and forced us to wage it."

Sprigg orders the government to send a telegram to the accountant in the magistrate's office in Maseru, instructing him to transfer £12,500 from the Basutoland Treasury to the colonial government.

Cape Town — Saturday June 21, 1879

Sir Bartle Frere, opening the first session of the sixth parliament of the Cape Colony, is blunt: "I deeply regret to be unable to announce to you that peace reigns upon our borders and in the neighbouring colonies," he says.

"The Colony of Natal is still passing through a period of great anxiety. A war of considerable magnitude is being waged against a barbaric power, which has for years silently but steadily grown in strength, until that strength has become seriously and actively dangerous to the peace and prosperity of South Africa.

"I regret to have to state that military operations are still rendered necessary by the attitude of certain chiefs upon the northern border of the colony, and by the rebellion of the long discontented Baphuthi Chief Moorosi, in Basutoland. In both cases the operations are being carried on solely by colonial forces, of whose gallantry the colony may be justly proud.

"The colony has to deplore the loss upon the northern border and in Basutoland of some of her bravest sons.

A speedy termination of hostilities is expected; but it will be necessary to make permanent provision for the defence of that part of the colony to ensure the maintenance of peace in the future."

Quthing — Wednesday, July 2, 1879

Favourite son and escapee Lehana has become the leader of an underground ring that maintains communication with Moorosi and supplies the king with food on the mountain. He travels regularly between the mountain, villages and cave holdouts.

Everywhere he goes, he hides his presence as best he can, aware that there are those who will disclose his whereabouts to the government. He remains elusive, determined not to let his guard fall.

Lehana is part of Moorosi's overall plan to hold out until the government gives up its siege, which he is confident must happen before too long. As the government troops withdraw, Moorosi will follow them and chase them off his land. He will then link up with those living in the caves. In that way, the Baphuthi king will be able to take over his land once more.

Zululand — Friday July 4, 1879

Although Sir Garnet Wolseley, sent by sea from Britain, is said to be on his way to take over command in Zululand, the commander of the South African troops, Lord Chelmsford, has decided he will not allow Wolseley to take over, and claim victory.

So it is that Chelmsford and his force of thousands have been advancing steadily on Ulundi over the past few weeks and are only a day's march from the Zulu capital when today they are attacked by 20,000 Zulus armed with spears.

As the Zulu impis descend on them, the soldiers hold them at bay with their rifles. The British soldiers fire into the waves of advancing warriors, preventing the Zulus from reaching close enough for spear-to-bayonet combat.

The Zulus run over the bodies of their fallen comrades in an attempt to get close to the soldiers, but are repulsed.

Eventually, they retreat and the British, cheering wildly, move on to Ulundi, where they find the great kraal deserted.

Although parts of Zululand remain unconquered, the taking of the capital means the British have won the war.

News of the Zulu defeat will renew the confidence of the whites in the Cape Colony that the back of the black resistance can be broken.

Quthing — Saturday, July 5, 1879

For some time Brabant has been trying to devise a way to keep the men on sentry duty warm at night. The cold is intense and a sentry cannot stand by a fire. It would make him a target and it would dull his night vision, which needs to be firmly fixed on the mountain. But the sentries are complaining bitterly about the cold.

Brabant issues them extra rations of rum, confident that the alcohol will help warm their bodies. But the complaints continue.

One of the men offers the commander a suggestion, one that he had heard some years ago while serving in winter conditions on the eastern frontier. "I have heard that onions are useful in warding off the cold," he says.

"Really?" Brabant responds. "It so happens that we have just received a large supply of onions from the colony. I suppose there is no harm in trying it out."

Brabant issues a large onion with the regular supply of biscuits to every man on picket duty. It works. The onions, he finds, supply the warmth the rum failed to do.

Quthing — Sunday July 6, 1879

After conducting the regular Sunday service at his new church, Ellenberger sits down with the Baphuthi Christians who help him run his mission station.

"This war and the deaths that have resulted have me extremely worried," he says. "I have temporarily closed our outstation along the Silver Spruit river and invited the Christians living there to move here. I am afraid that they will get caught up in the war, even though I know that Moorosi has no quarrel with them. Here they will be safe."

One of the Baphuthi Christians, Philemon Seboka, says he cannot understand why the whites, who are a Christian people, are fighting a war against them.

"As our wise king Moshoeshoe said many years ago: Before the white people came, we fought because we had no other examples than the wild animals. When we first heard the Gospel we put away our weapons because we thought war would not be possible by people who call themselves Christian.

"But now we see those who profess to be the children of Him who said, 'Love your enemies,' taking pleasure in fighting.

"They work this evil without anger, mixing wisdom with it.

"I can make no sense of it except that war must be a rod that God does not choose to break because He will make use of it still for the chastisement of men.

"The great chief wished peace. He said he knew war could produce no good. That is what Moshoeshoe said and I myself see it happening now in our land. I can see what he said is true."

"The wise Moshoeshoe was right," Ellenberger says. "And you are right, Philemon. Jesus told us that we must be peacemakers, that we must love our enemies. That is one of the most important commands he gave to us.

"It is so very sad to watch the people who profess to be Christians failing to follow what Jesus said.

"But you must not stop doing what Jesus said because you see a bad example.

"It is as important to be peacemakers when we are dealing with our family and our friends as it is between us and other people who are different from us or who disagree with us.

"Even if they hate us and are sent to kill us, we must still love them."

Seboka shakes his head in disbelief.

"But they are not following what you say. This shedding of blood is no good." His eyes pleading, he asks, "Can you not stop it?"

Ellenberger explains that he talked with the government people in an effort to prevent the war.

He says he was critical of the colonial authorities for their action, which he regarded as hasty and precipitous. He had even tried to get the government people to sit down with Moorosi and try to find a compromise that could achieve peace. He had offered to serve as a negotiator.

"But I was unsuccessful," he says. "Now there have been two attacks on the mountain and many attacks on the people hiding out in caves. Many lives have been lost on both sides and still no peace is in sight. Perhaps it is a good time for both sides to see reason.

"If I can get the king and the leaders of the colonial army to sit down on the Wodehouse bench and even if we have to talk for days I am sure we can get them to agree on many things and to stop fighting. Each side will have to give up something, to make sacrifices, but that is the only way we can have peace."

His listeners nod in agreement. They have come to respect Ellenberger's ability to bring about peace between feuding people, having seen it work in their lives and in the lives of those around them.

"It would be good if you could stop the war," Seboka adds.

"Now I know that, much as I would like to do so, I am unlikely to get them to come here to Masitise and actually sit on the Wodehouse bench," Ellenberger continues. "But I will talk once more with the people on both sides and encourage them to come to some sort of compromise.

"Before I speak with the government, I would like to talk to King Moorosi about what compromises he is prepared to make and what he can do to try to achieve peace. Can anyone help me to speak with King Moorosi? The mountain is ringed by the colonial army, but I know it is possible to get up the mountain to see the chief. Does anyone know how I can do that?"

"I do not think you must go on to the mountain," Seboka says. "It will be too difficult and you will put yourself in harm's way. But I can get a message to King Moorosi through one of my people.

"What should I tell him?"

After outlining his proposal to Seboka, Ellenberger sets off for the mountain, where he hopes to be able to talk with the colonial military leaders about the same time that the message is being conveyed to Moorosi.

Quthing — Tuesday, July 8, 1879

Brabant is preparing for an early-morning troop inspection when a sergeant-major looks into his tent. "The missionary from Masitise is here," he says.

"Send him in."

"Thank you for agreeing to talk with me," Ellenberger, carrying a large leather-bound Bible, says. "I would like to talk to you about a compromise to end the war."

"Compromise?" Brabant responds. "You missionaries always take the side of the natives against the government. I suspect you want us to surrender, not settle."

"That is not what I am suggesting," Ellenberger responds. "I know it is difficult to talk about settlement in the middle of a war. The issues are forgotten; people want only to fight to win and nothing else. They do not remember why the war started in the first place, nor do they try to understand the enemy's motivation. Or even their own motivation for that matter. They want only to win.

"Neither side wants to back down and be seen as losing. Honour and pride are at stake. I understand that. But now you have lost two assaults on the mountain and lives have been lost. The war has caused much suffering.

"I am sure the government wants the war to end. I am sure King Moorosi wants the war to end. We all want the war to end. And I think the way to end it is through a negotiated settlement. I think you might find that Moorosi might meet you somewhere in the middle. You might have to give up something, and Moorosi might have to give up something, but you will both gain an end to the war, which is what we all want."

"Reverend Ellenberger, I am not the government," Brabant says. "I only work for the government. My duty is to obey orders, to carry out what the government decides. The government minister, Mr. Ayliff, has told me that we will accept nothing but unconditional surrender from Moorosi. The government wants us to defeat Moorosi. And, I assure you, we *will* defeat Moorosi. That is how we will bring about peace."

"But there is another way," Ellenberger counters. "Mr. Bowker, as you know, was able to work out such a compromise in a previous confrontation between the government and Moorosi. He did so with wisdom and tact and prevented the outbreak of hostilities."

A look of urging in his eyes, he pleads with Brabant. "Does it not make sense to talk to Moorosi again and to reach some sort of agreement that can prevent more people being killed on both sides? Can I ask you, instead of continuing this war, to at least try to seek a negotiated agreement as Mr. Bowker did?"

"What did Bowker achieve in the long run?" Brabant asks, a hint of anger in his voice. "He was an appeaser and didn't solve the underlying problem. Once Lehana was released, he was up to his old tricks again, spurring on people to rebel against the government. Bowker should have punished Lehana and Moorosi properly. Then the rebellion would have been squashed and we would not have had to go to war.

"In any event, as I said, you are speaking to the wrong person, reverend. I am doing what I was instructed to do. I am a soldier first, and an honourable one at that. I and the men I command are fighting for our country, our Queen and our God."

The statement touches a nerve in Ellenberger. "Queen and country perhaps. "But God?"

"Yes, these people are unchristian and heathen, reverend. Surely you, of all people, understand that? They are a mass of savagedom. They are lazy. They are thieves and, like the other black people in this country, are incapable of acquiring civilization.

"They have no redeeming qualities. If they refuse to listen to us, if they won't obey us, it is our duty to fight against them for our country, our Queen and, yes, our God."

Ellenberger stands and takes a few paces to his left as an effort to subdue his emotions. When he hears people say they are fighting in the name of God, he bristles with righteous indignation. How dare they abrogate God to their side? What possible reason would God favour them? How can they ever justify going to war against any people in the name of God? As he strides back to face Brabant again he feels he has been able to control his anger sufficiently for him to speak in careful, measured tones.

"Even were the Baphuthi heathens and savages, which they are not," he tells Brabant, "that would be no reason to set out to destroy them in the name of God.

"Even though you see them as rebels against colonial rule, that is no reason to annihilate them in the name of God.

"Even though they might want to drive you out of their land, which you have invaded, that is no reason to take up arms against them in the name of God.

"Even though they might hate you and despise you, that still is no reason to seek vengeance on them in the name of God.

"No matter what they say about you, no matter what they do against you, there never is any reason to send your people to kill them in the name of God.

"Never.

"You see, they, too, are children of God.

"Because they are children of God, our Lord wants even more from us than simply to refrain from fighting against them.

"Jesus instructed us to love our enemies — not to tolerate or ignore them, but to love them.

"Do unto others, he said, as you would have them do unto you.

"If you live by the sword, he said, you will die by the sword.

"If you are attacked, he said, you should turn the other cheek.

"Peacemakers, he said, are the true heroes of this world.

"Love crosses cultural boundaries, he said, citing the Good Samaritan as an example.

"Everything Jesus did and said spoke of loving others, not hating others — and certainly not waging war on them.

"So I do not think it is right for you to say you are fighting for God."

Brabant is subdued as he ponders Ellenberger's comments. After a while, he responds: "God helped the children of Israel win their wars against the heathens surrounding them. And let me tell you that the bishops of the church support us in this war. They have even come here to encourage us. *They* believe God is on our side. They understand that these people are infidels, that they have rebelled against the Christian government and they must be brought to justice. They say this is a just war, a war of good against evil."

Ellenberger opens his mouth to disagree but lets the colonel continue.

"They agree that the noblest thing you can do is to fight — and die if necessary — for your country," Brabant adds. "That is what we are doing. What we are doing *is* noble. You say we should negotiate with these barbarians. But if we let them continue their rebellion through some sort of compromise or settlement, as you suggest, they will rebel another time, again and again. They will continue to refuse to obey us. These people are rebels, they are traitors. They are cruel and they are vicious. They want to wage war against us and we have to defend ourselves. They will kill us if we give them half a chance."

"I do not think they would wage war on you if you did not wage war on them," Ellenberger says. "They, in turn, want to protect themselves against you, whom they see as invaders sent here to kill them. Perhaps they believe God is on *their* side. Surely God loves them as much as he loves you.

"War is the most uncivilized of human pursuits and the most unchristian way of trying to solve problems. Anyone who says he is a Christian and goes to war is not following the clear instructions from Jesus. It's as simple as that. By fighting against your enemy you are disobeying Jesus. Even now, at this late stage, surely a peaceful settlement is the best outcome.

"You still can solve this problem in a civilized and Christian way through compromise. If you do, you will be a hero, colonel. You will have achieved something of which you can be truly proud.

"Let me appeal to you: If the chief comes with a proposal aimed at you allowing him a conditional surrender — a compromise — would you please consider it, not just for his sake, but for your sake, for the sake of peace, for the sake of your country, for the sake of your Queen and, yes, for the sake of God?"

Brabant sighs. It seems the only way he can get rid of Ellenberger is to placate him. "Very well. Should that occur, I will consider it, as far as I am able to do within the confines of my jurisdiction, but I don't believe Moorosi will concede anything."

Ellenberger persists. "All I ask is that you listen and that you weigh carefully the alternatives — continuing what looks like a war that will drag on for a long time without resolution, costing more and more in lives and money, or achieving a negotiated settlement through compromise.

"You could then pass that plan on to Mr. Ayliff, who may well agree to it, and you will have helped to end the war in a noble way."

Ellenberger hopes he has planted a seed of compromise toward settlement on the colonial side. He is confident, too, that another seed of settlement has been planted on the top of the mountain. And he desperately hopes the two will find their way to meet somewhere in the middle.

❧

Moorosi's first wife, MaSakale, is perturbed. She might be older than all the women on the mountain, but she can set them all an example when it comes to prodding their husbands to fight for their nation. If she detests anything, it is to see a man who is vacillating, weak and subservient.

"Why have you set up a white flag behind the stone walls?" she asks as she walks up to a group of advisers sitting around Moorosi.

"Have we not fought off the enemy? Have we not killed many of them? Have we not shown them to be weak fighters?

"And now you want to surrender?

"Could we have done more? Could we have fought harder? Could we have killed more of the enemy? What kind of man are you that you want to give up?"

Moorosi looks around at his advisers and realizes they are probably asking similar questions. He turns back to MaSakale. "We are not surrendering. Our men have performed well. We have scored many victories for our people. I am very happy with what they have done."

"Well, why then, have you put out the white flag?"

"Listen to what I say to my people and you will learn."

He pauses, making clear that it is important that MaSakale, his other wives and his advisers all understand what he is about to say to them.

"As you know, the coming of winter has reduced the amount of food available to our people," Moorosi continues. "Our supplies of grain are being reduced and it is becoming harder to replenish them."

During harvest, Moorosi says, the Baphuthi men were able to sneak down from the mountain on to unguarded grain fields and supplement their supplies.

"But now, as you know, there is no grain left to be harvested. The only supplies we can obtain are those stored in villages, but those supplies have been reduced by the flight of people. Our Baphuthi people hiding in caves along the river valleys also need grain to keep alive. They cannot give it all to us. As you have seen, too, the colonial forces have stepped up their patrols and have increased the number of men on picket duty. It is harder now for us to leave and return with food supplies.

"We also have eaten many cattle and goats. Others have died from the cold at the top of the mountain. We have fewer left."

Already, Moorosi continues, he has asked about 200 of the Baphuthi men and about the same number of women and children to leave the mountain under cover of night and to shelter in caves where they can find food more easily and from where they will emerge to take back the country once the colonial forces accept defeat.

"My son Lehana is with them," he adds.

"You 300 men who remain on the mountain are, like you Maketa, among our best shots and our strongest warriors. There are enough of us here to defend the mountain stronghold. But those of us who remain have to be careful how we use our food supply to make the best of what we have."

His wife MaSakale nods. "We have been working to enable the supplies to last as long as possible. The women have developed clever ways of providing food." One of the ways is to take a few of the hides set aside to provide clothing and convert them into fragments that are ground, like corn, between two stones and boiled to form a nourishing soup. "It is good. I drink it every day. Look at me. Am I not strong? Am I not healthy?"

"Yes, I am proud of what you women have done," says Moorosi. "But last night, when it was dark, a messenger from the missionary Ellenberger came to talk with me. He says we must talk peace with the white fighters. We must be willing to make some concessions so there can be peace. He says if we are suffering so are the white people. And I know that to be so. We have had reports from Mfengu who have heard the white soldiers saying they are unhappy. They want to go home; they do not like the cold weather.

"We would like to see an end to the war. So would they.

"So, Reverend Ellenberger says, we must look for a way to meet them halfway and they will also want to look for a way to meet us halfway. We meet in the middle and there you have peace. Is that not a good thing?"

Moorosi says the colonial forces have been thwarted twice in their attempts to take the mountain. They must be frustrated. Surely, he reasons, they will not be foolish enough to attack a third time. They will not be satisfied with guarding his mountain month after month. They are looking for a way out.

"I will talk with them," he tells MaSakale, "and perhaps we can get an end to this war and bring about peace."

"But you have put up a white flag," MaSakale replies. "To the white people that means we want to surrender. We cannot give up now. We are winning. We are not losing. Only losers surrender."

Moorosi is about to respond when a messenger runs up. "The white chiefs are calling for you," he says.

Moorosi walks down the path toward the pole with the piece of white material fluttering at the top. He recalls how he had found the white cloth among the supplies taken months ago from Thomas's Shop. How long ago that now seems.

Across the plateau he sees three men — all dressed in the finery that marks them as senior officers — standing and looking toward him.

"Are you ready to surrender?" an officer shouts.

"I want to talk about peace," Moorosi replies.

20

Quthing — Tuesday, July 8, 1879

Brabant, accompanied by Colonel Southey and Captain Tainton, who will act as interpreter, stand below the stone walls.

"I am confident that Moorosi would not raise a white flag or say he wants peace under false pretences," he says, "but I have to be careful that it is not a clever decoy and so I have given instructions for a group of troopers to stand guard. You never know how sly these savages can be, do you? To them, lying and deception come naturally."

"I want to talk peace," Moorosi repeats.

After a brief parley with Brabant, Tainton turns up to face Moorosi. "Are you then willing to give up your arms, come off the mountain and surrender?" he asks.

"I want you to promise that, if I come down off my mountain and do not fight against you, you will not punish me for anything you say I've done," Moorosi says.

Tainton speaks briefly once more with Brabant and Southey before replying. "We cannot promise you that. You have broken the law and you must be punished for that. You have rebelled against the Cape colonial rule and we cannot allow you to go unpunished."

Moorosi is insistent. "No, I want peace. I am giving in. I will not fight you any longer. I will not send my people out to attack you. But I do not want you to punish me. I want to live in any village that you choose for me."

The three officers hold a short discussion after which Tainton shouts back, "Come down off the mountain and we can sit down and talk about the terms of your surrender."

Now it is Moorosi's turn to suspect trickery and deceit.

"I and my mountain are one," he says. "Why do you want me to come off my mountain? I have told you that I have given in if you agree not to attack me. Now it is time for you to say what you will do.

"I want peace. You say that I am a child of the government and that the government is my father. So now I have given in to my father. I swear before the great God that I have given in. Why must I come down? I want peace. What more do you want from me?"

The colonial officers hold another discussion at the base of the wall.

"He says he has given in and we must not attack him, but he wants to go unpunished, live in a village, and presumably continue to be the chief. It doesn't make sense."

Brabant agrees. "This is typical of the way these people think. He raises a white flag. He tells us we have won. He tells us he has surrendered. That seems clear to me. But does he want to come off the mountain? No. What, then, does a surrender mean? How can we have won if he does not want to leave the mountain?"

Tainton offers his explanation. "I think he is trying to say that he will not fight against us any longer if we do not fight against him any longer."

"But that is not a surrender," counters Brabant.

"No," replies Tainton. "He did not use the word surrender. He is telling us that we have won, but I think he also believes that he has won. In other words, it is a stalemate. Sentiments such as these do not always come across correctly in translation.

"As he keeps repeating, he wants peace. He is asking us to be benevolent to him, as a father is to his child. He says he has already been punished. Now he wants peace and he does not want us to punish him any longer. He wants to be free to live in any village we choose for him. He wants us to meet him halfway."

"I have no authority to debate the issue," Brabant says. "The only authority I have is to accept an unconditional surrender."

The words of Ellenberger that Moorosi would likely offer a compromise return to him. But he deems such a suggestion impractical. How can he be certain that Moorosi will honour such a peace and not continue fighting? He remembers what happened with Bowker.

Tainton moves away from the officers, takes a step toward the wall, and looks up at Moorosi, patiently waiting alongside the white flag.

"We will accept nothing but the unconditional surrender of you and all the men on the mountain," he says. "Colonel Brabant says he has no power to decide on anything else, but he will report to the government."

MaSakale's words ring in Moorosi's ears. "Only losers surrender."

He realizes these men do not want compromise as Ellenberger said they might. They want to defeat him. What they want is for him to give up, to hand himself, his land and his people over to the white government. Not satisfied only with that, they will want to punish him, too, and take away their arms so they will never be able to defend themselves again. They will be like slaves to the whites.

If that is what he has to do to achieve peace, he does not want it. Even death would be better than to surrender and be oppressed by the government. But Ellenberger said he should talk to the government about achieving peace through compromise. So he will present his part of the bargain one more time.

"I want to stop the fighting," Moorosi says. "I want peace."

But Brabant has no intention of talking any further.

"I will give you half an hour to get back to the top of the mountain. At that time, the white flag must be taken down," Brabant says.

The white officers walk back to their camp.

"I think we are close to winning this battle," Brabant says. "Clearly the man is suffering. His people are hurting, their food supplies are dwindling. He wants all this to end. When he says he wants peace he really is saying, I want to surrender. But surrender on his terms. He is only halfway there. He cannot take that full step of surrender. But, as he suffers even more, he will realize that full surrender is the only way to prevent further suffering and eventual defeat. It is all a matter of time."

꧁꧂

As Moorosi makes his way back up the path to the mountain top, Maketa runs up to ask him what has happened. When he hears, he is pleased. "I am glad you did

Contemporary photograph shows government headquarters camp at the mountain.

not surrender," he says. "We will win. I will go and take down the flag."

"No, leave it there," Moorosi replies. "I want to show them that I am ready to talk peace, but they are the ones who want to talk war and only of defeating me and my people."

Quthing — Tuesday, July 29, 1879

The white flag, tattered and torn from the harsh winter and the winds that blow restlessly across the mountain, continues to fly in its spot behind the stone wall, as it has done for three weeks now.

Brabant's task is becoming more challenging each day. Six months since colonial troops first arrived to oust Moorosi from his mountain fortress, and two failed attacks later, the siege of the mountain is stalled, leading to growing dissension among the volunteers who are tired of enduring the monotonous, cold and dreary duty at the mountain, which seems to be achieving nothing.

Some of the men have been at the mountain for six months. Their boots have broken apart from the constant walking on the rocks, but they are unable to buy boots at the camp and have not been issued new footwear. Blankets had been discarded on the way up to the mountain in the summer so that the horses would not be too heavily weighed down. Now the men, who never anticipated being here in the winter, need them on the cold nights and don't have them.

Food is scarce, although the soldiers are able to sustain themselves with meal and meat bought by government agents in the Orange Free State and sent to them. Coffee and tea also have run out and sugar is a luxury.

"I cannot stand this any longer," Douglas Sampson, a volunteer, tells Alex Granville.

"The boredom is punishment enough, but in addition we have to survive this winter without the benefit of a house warmed against the cold by a roaring fire. To endure such conditions for a day is not much to ask, for a week it becomes arduous. But for weeks on end, it is simply not worth it."

"That is only part of the problem," Granville replies. "I think another problem is that you volunteers are good men, but you are not well organized. I have noticed many volunteers showing bad discipline. And not even that is their fault. You are simply badly led and I cannot blame you for feeling bored. You need the discipline to feel you are performing a useful role in this war."

The men also have no guarantees they will be compensated for wounds or disabling injuries. In case of death, they do not know whether provision will be made for their widows and children.

As a result, some volunteers are quietly drifting off and returning to their homes in the Cape Colony.

The dissension has spread to the Cape Mounted Riflemen, some of whom are applying for discharge, asserting their time of service has expired. But Brabant has refused them permission to leave.

Brome decides the time has come to join the others wishing to leave, but, wary of the consequences and of being called a coward, he does not want to sneak off. He approaches Brabant and requests a discharge.

"I cannot allow you to leave," Brabant says. "You are to serve out your term as a proud member of the Cape Mounted Riflemen as the other 500 members of the CMR are doing. When you joined up you must have known what it would involve."

"Yes, sir, but we were told we would be policemen, not soldiers. And since I have been here I have realized that we are not protecting anything of ours. The Baphuthi have no intention of invading my farm and our colonial land. They are bent only on preserving what they have.

"I have changed my attitude toward them. I see them now as good, brave people, fighting for what is their own just as I thought I would be fighting for what is my own when I signed up.

"Now I realize they have no evil intentions against us; we have evil intentions against them."

Brabant scowls. He grabs Brome by the collar and shakes him.

"We are not evil people, soldier," he says sternly. "I will not have you say that. The rebels on that mountain over there are the evil people.

"We are noble people advancing a noble cause. We are fighting for our country, for our fellow countrymen and ultimately for the Queen we love and respect. She is not evil and we are not evil. Anyone who thinks we are evil deserves to be thrown into an insane asylum.

"You should be whipped for speaking like this."

As Brabant grabs the other side of his collar with his other hand and shakes him even more vigorously, Brome realizes he has gone too far.

"I am merely giving my reasons as to why I would like to be released from my duties, sir. I should not have used the word evil, sir. If you say I cannot leave and that I must stay, I will perform the duties to which I am assigned, sir."

Brabant releases his grip on Brome's collar.

"Very well. But be warned if I find you to be rebellious, you will be severely punished. I will not tolerate this sort of dissent within my ranks.

"I refuse your request for discharge. You get back there and fight in the way you are instructed to fight. I will not tolerate any insubordination. Do you hear me?"

"Yes, sir."

Cape Town — Tuesday, August 26, 1879

Anxious to extricate the government from the morass into which the war against Moorosi has thrust it and hearing little of meaningful progress from the mountain, Prime Minister Gordon Sprigg is taking a more active role in trying to end the war. He has asked Major F. W. Nixon, a British military officer and an engineer, and Colonel Jarvis, the commandant-general of colonial troops, to travel to the mountain.

Between them, Sprigg hopes, they will devise some way to end Moorosi's rebellion.

Transkei, Thursday, September 4, 1879

"Look at what is happening in Basutoland," Hamilton Hope tells Mhlonthlo, the paramount chief of the Mpondomise, in whose territory he serves as magistrate. "Chief Moorosi has opposed colonial rule and now he is finding himself at war with the government. He has had some victories, but he cannot win this war. The government will eventually conquer him and destroy Moorosi and his people.

"This is what happens when native people will not listen to the government, when they are not obedient and they try to say they, and not the magistrate, are in control of the people.

"Moorosi wouldn't listen to me. I warned him many times he would pay a high price for not accepting government rule over his people. Now he's paying that price. I hope you take this as a lesson for you and your people. Listen to me, accept that the government comes first and you come second and you will enjoy peace."

Mhlonthlo is unimpressed with Hope's thinking, but will cooperate. For now.

Quthing — Monday, September 8, 1879

Major F. W. Nixon, armed with a budget of £200 and accompanied by two royal engineers and eight mining experts, arrives at the mountain today to meet with Brabant, who returned last night from a patrol into the surrounding hills.

"I have been sent here by the prime minister," Nixon tells Brabant, "to devise a military strategy in which Moorosi's Mountain fortress can be taken, probably using mining methods."

Brabant is sceptical. He is aware that Nixon served in the ninth frontier war as an officer in the most professionally trained corps in the British Army, but he is not in the mood for far-fetched suggestions.

"I have heard some unusual ideas about how this war should be waged," Brabant

tells Nixon. "Apparently some planner offered to blow up the mountain so that its
mighty mass should fall into the gorge at the junction of the Quthing and Orange
rivers.

"The planner claims that this colossal scheme has the great recommendation of
utility, for the waters of the rivers thus dammed up would form a mighty reservoir
from which the neighbouring country could be well irrigated."

"I have heard of that plan," Nixon says. "I agree that it is somewhat outrageous,
but I will look at a less spectacular way in which we can blow up at least part of the
mountain."

Accompanied by Brabant, Nixon examines the fortress from all angles, occasionally using an opera glass. He takes notes. He talks with men in the camp, learning of
slack discipline, inadequate training and low morale among the volunteers. He hears
how Moorosi has successfully supplemented his grain and cattle on the mountain
with regular forays that take the colonial troops by surprise.

He is told, too, that the attacks on the stone walls were ineffective because the
men were not prepared to risk their lives in running in a group across the open space
between the saddle and the walls.

Nixon learns, too, of the abortive attempt by Scott to hurl cannon balls behind
the stone walls and of the dynamite attacks by Brabant on some of the occupied
caves he encountered on his patrols.

He instructs the mining experts to look at the feasibility of using dynamite to dig
a tunnel under the mountain and gain access to the walls in that way.

By evening, the engineers have reached several conclusions. They meet with Nixon.
"We could hew a gallery from the cave at the north-western base of the mountain
in such a direction as to place a mine under the first schanz," one of the mining
engineers says. "The resulting blast would blow a huge hole in the wall."

"I agree," responds Nixon. "That blast would certainly succeed in driving off the
defenders and our men could scramble up the side of the mountain unchallenged
and make their way over the collapsed wall. The moral effect of firing such a mine
successfully would be great."

"But would it materially assist the attack?"

"I would imagine that the blast would make the slope steeper and therefore make it
even harder to climb. And the difficulty of the attack would only have begun because
the lines of the second and third schanzes are above. Could those be blasted away?"

"We could not get near enough to them," the miner says.

Further discussion reveals the engineers have no other suggestions.

"So what you are saying is that mining operations would not help much," Nixon says.

The men agree.

Nixon walks to Brabant's tent and summarizes his conclusions.

"Mining operations will be of no avail," he says.

"What do you think we should do then?" Brabant asks.

"My view is that the first action you should take is that the first schanz should be
breached by a couple of guns of moderate calibre, say 9 or 12 pounders."

"That is what we did in the last attack," Brabant responds. "The problem is that no sooner do we blast away the structure than they rebuild it."

"I understand you had some success last time when you consistently blasted away at the walls for many hours," Nixon counters.

"Yes, that is true, but —"

"The pounding by the guns should be followed by a force of 500 men," Nixon continues. "They could be positioned under the ridge and near the cave on the north eastern side before advancing on the wall in a determined attack.

"This might lead to the certain sacrifice of perhaps a tenth of their number.

"For such an attack well disciplined men, accustomed to act together and ready to follow where they are led are absolutely necessary, for the advance from each schanz in succession would have to be made under fire up a steep ascent."

"That is your conclusion?" Brabant asks. "Essentially we throw 500 men at the walls, assume that 50 will be killed and thereby take the mountain?"

"It is. But I must add that your officers agree that the colonial forces, as at present organized and disciplined, are not to be depended on for such an attack."

Quthing — Friday, September 12, 1879

For the first time, Whitehead has been assigned night picket duty. It is a pleasant change; not only will it relieve the boredom, but it will give him an insight into life on the saddle at night.

Picket guarding saddle [*The Graphic*, 1879]

He reports for duty and is told the officer in charge has not yet arrived. "I'm not really sure when he arrives," a soldier says, "as I am often asleep by that time."

"Asleep? Aren't you supposed to be keeping watch?"

"We take turns to keep watch. Nothing much happens during the night."

Whitehead soon determines that none of the men has his rifle loaded. "What would happen if the Baphuthi were to suddenly surprise you?" he asks. The men grunt in reply. Whitehead cannot make out what they are saying.

Soon most lie down behind the sandbags that form the first line of defence and fall asleep, leaving two men to keep a lookout.

Whitehead decides he will

remain on guard behind the breastworks, keep his rifle loaded and not succumb to the malaise of the others. Ahead he can see, reflected against the lower stone walls, the flickering light of a Baphuthi fire.

⁂

Lemena is hungry. He has been sitting around the fire behind the stone wall, his gun at his side, for many hours, but has not received the meal that he was promised.

"I am going to get the food myself," he says. As he climbs the path to the summit, he pulls his blanket around him to ward off the evening chill. At the mountain summit, he searches for food in his hut.

The noise awakens Moorosi. "Why have you left your post?" he asks.

"I am hungry. No one brought me my meal."

"Don't worry about food. You can eat later. Get back to your post. What if the government men attack us? Is your stomach more important than our lives?"

Lemena turns and heads down the path to the stone walls.

"I will shoot you if you do this again," Moorosi shouts after him.

"I have enemies everywhere," Lemena grumbles, throwing up his hands in the air. "The whites want to shoot me. The Mfengu fighting with the government want to shoot me. And now my own king wants to shoot me."

⁂

About an hour after Whitehead takes up his picket position, a man arrives who identifies himself as the officer in charge, a corporal named Ben Masoopie. Whitehead soon warms to the man's friendly spirit and sense of humour.

"Are you trying to see men over there?" Masoopie asks.

"Yes, but all I can see are the reflection of the fires."

The two peer across the shadowy plateau, their eyes concentrating on the walls and the fires behind them.

"I think I see something moving there," Masoopie says, pointing to the bottom of the first stone wall. "Yes, yes. I see three Baphuthi men moving toward us!"

He grabs his rifle, takes aim and fires. Whitehead fires as well. Although he cannot see any movement, he assumes that Masoopie's vision is better than his.

⁂

A still hungry Lemena arrives back at his post in time to hear a rapid succession of fire emanate from the saddle. He hunkers down behind the stone wall.

"What are they firing at?" he asks.

"We're not sure," a man responds. "But we are firing back."

"They're firing at nothing," laughs Lemena. "The darkness makes the white men's eyes work backwards. When we send men down to fight them, they don't see them. But when we are not sending men to fight them, then they see them."

⁂

As the Baphuthi bullets whistle toward them, the men on picket duty suddenly spring awake. "Stand to your arms," Masoopie shouts, standing straight up, with his bayonet in one hand and folding his arms. His wide hat, blue serge jacket, leggings and pose remind Whitehead of Napoleon.

The men, woken from their sleep, raise their rifles and fire toward the stone walls.

The Baphuthi hold their fire, preferring to save their ammunition. After a while the pickets stop firing and the mountain quiet returns. After a short time, most of the men wrap themselves in their blankets and fall asleep.

"At least that gave them something to do," says Masoopie.

༺ঙ্গ༻

The Baphuthi retain their vigilance, fearful that the colonial soldiers could launch another attack at any time. But, his attempt at a settlement having failed, Moorosi feels the need to do more than wait for another assault on his fortress. He must break the stalemate and go on the attack.

He sits down with his leading advisers. "We must do something," he says. "We cannot sit here and wait for them to attack us again. And all the time they are building up their forces. It is time for us to go on the attack ourselves."

Assisted by his advisers, the king devises a radical plan of action aimed at swinging the war in his favour.

Masitise, Sunday September 14, 1879

The number of refugees gathered around the Masitise mission station grows as the war drags on. Some have come because they are unwilling to fight whereas others have been brought here after being wounded. All find a place to stay.

The mission station is a neutral site that neither side would dare attack. So Ellenberger does not question whether the wounded and asylum seekers are anti-government, pro-government or innocent Baphuthi caught up in the battle. Here he protects them, provides for them, and prays for them.

Among those who have gathered today in the crowded church is a young Baphuthi man whose right lung was pierced by a bullet. For seven weeks, Ellenberger tended to the wound and saved the man's life.

Sitting alongside him is a 5-year-old grandson of Moorosi whose left humerus was shattered by a bullet. The missionary extracted six pieces of bone from the wound, dressed it regularly and bandaged the arm in such a way that the boy recovered its use. Ellenberger closed the wound, now quite clean, by grafting skin on it.

The result has been higher attendance at church services and a growing interest in Ellenberger's message.

"I am delighted to tell you that a revival has broken out here at Masitise," he tells the congregation in today's service. "You have come here to seek peace from war and you have found the Prince of Peace. In the past few weeks we have added 90 new converts. I am pleased that, in this painful chapter in our history, we have found the One who would have us never fight any more wars, the One who would have the whole world be at peace with one another, as we are in Masitise today."

Quthing — Tuesday, September 16, 1879

The men have been asleep for less than an hour when they are awakened by fire from the direction of the saddle.

"It is just the pickets proving they're there before they sleep," laughs Granville, who is sharing a tent with James Corfield.

"It sounds more serious than that," Corfield replies, jumping out of his bed and leaving the tent.

Granville stays to tie his laces and, by the time he leaves the tent, cannot see in the darkness where Corfield has gone, but realizes that the exchange of fire between the saddle and the mountain is more intense than usual.

Kneeling behind the earthworks that guard the camp, his rifle at the ready, he can see a mass of men around the saddle, but holds off firing as he is unsure in the darkness whose side they are on.

The scene is one of utter confusion.

⚜

The plan devised by Moorosi and his advisers appeared to be a sound one. Relayed by a messenger to loyal Baphuthi in the surrounding countryside, it was for 180 warriors, accompanied by 20 pack horses, to leave the caves in which they were living, to travel to the base of the mountain and, from there, launch an attack on the colonial forces in the dark, taking them by surprise in the early hours of the morning.

The government men could be expected to be ready for an attack from the mountain, they reasoned, but not from the surrounding countryside.

Once the attack began and the government soldiers were diverted, Moorosi would send his men down the mountain. Together the two forces could kill large numbers of soldiers sleeping in their tents, just as they had done in the attack on the Chiappini camp.

Late yesterday, the outlying warriors left their caves. They timed their move so that they would arrive at the mountain at night when they would camp in the dark at the bottom of the cliffs on the northern face, unseen by the colonial forces. From there, in the early hours of the morning, the plan was that they were to launch an attack on the colonial encampment.

But as they arrive in the darkness early today, creeping quietly along under a cliff, they walk into a group of Mfengu dressed in distinctive white blankets given them by the colonial forces.

The Baphuthi are nonplussed.

No one was supposed to be camped here; the messenger from Moorosi was clear about that.

True, no one was — until 300 Mfengu relief forces from the Cape Colony arrived yesterday and moved here under orders from Brabant.

When the Mfengu, sleeping in the open, see the Baphuthi, they open fire.

⚜

Corfield awakens amidst an eruption of gunfire. Opening his tent flap, he stares into the darkness, making out the forms of men on the plateau. The firing in intense.

Grabbing his carbine, he runs up the hill toward the plateau. "What's going on?" he yells. "A group of Baphuthi are trying to get up the mountain," a soldier shouts in reply. "The Mfengu have caught them. They're firing on them and so are we."

Night attack at Mount Moorosi [*Illustrated London News* 1879]. Sketch, drawn from the western side of the mountain, shows the saddle on the left and the neck in the middle.

As he readies to fire, he asks, "How do you know who is who?"

"The Mfengu are the ones in the white blankets," the soldier says. "Don't fire at them. Fire at anyone else who is black."

The darkness and movement of the men render the shooting on all sides less than accurate.

Nevertheless, some of the Mfengu bullets find their target and a few of the thousands of rounds fired randomly by the colonial troops find their quarry. Soon several Baphuthi lie dead on the mountain slopes.

But the gains are not all on the Mfengu and colonial sides.

A Baphuthi charges a Mfengu and stabs him in his arm with his spear. The Mfengu falls. The Baphuthi grabs his blanket and pulls it around him. Others follow his lead, stabbing the Mfengu, who drop their blankets in the confusion as bullets whizz around them.

The chaotic firing and stabbing continues until a bank of mist rises from the Orange River and wafts across the plateau, reducing visibility to zero.

The fighting stops.

The Baphuthi escape up a path to the top of the mountain.

⚜

Moorosi walks down the path to greet the arriving warriors.

They tell him seven men are dead and several wounded, but most of the men and the horses they brought with them have made it through enemy lines.

"Why are you wearing white blankets?" Moorosi asks. "Our people do not wear white blankets."

"Let me tell you," says one. "These blankets, they are bullet proof."

Quthing, Thursday September 18, 1879

After a week's stay in camp, Colonel Jarvis sets off on his return journey to King William's Town.

The week he spent at Moorosi's mountain has been a revealing one for the man who heads the colony's defence operations.

Little progress to end the war is being made and morale at the camp is extremely low. He has few solutions to suggest to the prime minister, including looking for a new commander at the mountain with a bolder plan of action.

Maseru — Wednesday, October 1, 1879

Monitoring Moorosi's war from his post in Maseru, Griffith is developing a new concern. He is worried that the war will spread to the rest of Basutoland as a result of growing anger over disarmament.

When the policy was first mooted, the Basotho were led to believe that if they fought on the side of the government they would be allowed to keep their arms. Now it is clear from the way the measure is being implemented that the Cape authorities are determined to disarm all black people under their jurisdiction, whether they assist the government or not. Many Basotho now fear they will soon be in the same position.

Griffith believes that the disarmament policy is a recipe for disaster in Basutoland and is afraid that if Moorosi's war is not concluded soon all of Basutoland will follow his example and be at war with the colony.

He will write to Sprigg to warn him how serious matters have become.

Cape Town — Monday, October 6, 1879

Griffith's warning letter and increasing pressure from Parliament convince Prime Minister Sprigg he needs to do even more to end the war against Moorosi.

"It is imperative that we devise a solution to end the war," Sprigg tells Ayliff. "You know, as I do, that we cannot allow events to continue as they are driving our colony more into debt and drifting into a wider conflict in that territory. We need to end this costly escapade."

Ayliff nods in agreement.

"Right now the war is our top priority. We must bring it to a conclusion. Once we have done that, we can start implementing the policy of disarmament in the territory to make such rebellious acts as this by Moorosi impossible in the future.

"Some three months ago we were told that Moorosi was hurting and had offered to talk with us about ending the war. But he is still on his mountain, defying our best forces to come and get him.

"I believe we should replace Colonel Brabant — who, like Colonel Griffith, has failed to oust Moorosi from his mountain — with a new commander who will be under orders to turn the Cape Mounted Riflemen into a force that can take the mountain. I welcome suggestions for the new commander.

"I believe, too, that now also is the time for me to enter the fray, not just in giving orders, but in person. I plan to travel to the mountain in the next few weeks, observe the situation at first hand and, I hope, talk to Moorosi personally.

"I believe that a lot of the chief's inspiration to rebel came from the Zulus. If the Zulus could defeat the white men, he must have reasoned, he could do so, too. But now that the Zulus have been defeated, he must be having second thoughts. I'll tell him it is useless trying to defy the strength of the government. We will win in the end.

"Should my talks for some reason fail, I will hand over charge of our troops to a new commander and instruct him to implement the Nixon plan to attack the mountain with a force of 500 men.

"But before I visit the battlefield I will stop over in Maseru and talk to the chiefs and the people there. Bearing in mind Griffith's concerns about the people opposing disarmament, I will explain the law to them in terms they can understand and tell them disarmament is in their own best interests. I am sure that they will hand in their arms voluntarily after I talk with them."

Quthing — Wednesday, October 8, 1879

Although his plan to attack the colonial troops failed, Moorosi remains convinced he needs to take the offensive in the war. He must not be content simply to watch the white troops camped around his mountain. He must drive them off, sending them back across the Telle River into the Cape Colony.

So it is that, since the end of September, he has called in all remaining fighting men from the cave hideouts along the rivers. Lehana is back on the mountain, ready to lead attacks when called upon by his father to do so.

"Now that the good weather has arrived, it is time for us to move," Moorosi tells his sons Lehana and Letuka. "We must not just sit back and wait for the government to attack us again. We must go out and attack them. We must frighten them and drive them away from the mountain. Then perhaps they will be prepared to talk to us about peace.

"They have sent one of their big guns away; our men have learned through spies among the Mfengu that it has been sent away to be repaired. Soon it will return. Before that happens, we must attack them.

"Our people here on the mountain are still strong. We have cattle and grain supplies. Our ammunition supplies are plentiful. We must start with a big attack. We must launch it while the government soldiers are asleep."

Letuka reminds his father of the great victory they achieved in the attack on the camp at the junction of the rivers where the whites were killed in their tents.

"Let us do that again," Moorosi says. "They have set up another camp there. Although it is better guarded, we can attack it again. Let's go and attack it tonight, my son. You can lead the attack again, the way you did before. That will frighten them and when we threaten more attacks they will run away from the mountain."

Quthing — Thursday, October 9, 1879

Letuka returns with his band of fighters to the mountain in the early hours of the morning. "We fired on the men at the camp where the rivers meet," he reports to Moorosi. "We could see the white tents even though it was dark.

"They fired back, but it was too dark for them to see us.

"Then suddenly, from behind us, the Mfengu came and fired on us. They were right behind us before we knew it and took us by surprise. We were forced to run away and return to the mountain."

"Very well," Moorosi says. "We must do better next time. We cannot allow the

Mfengu fighters to stop us again. This is the second time they have ruined our plan.

"But perhaps we can achieve our aims without killing any soldiers. We will do so by approaching the other camps around the mountain in a strong force at night when the government's rifles are of no help to them as they cannot see us well enough to shoot at us. We will creep up on them without them even knowing we are there and show them that we are able to attack them and kill them if we want to do so. We don't have to kill any of them, just frighten them.

"When we have them afraid we will tell them they must talk to us about a settlement or else next time we will kill them before they know what is happening."

Quthing — Friday, October 10, 1879

Quietly, their bare feet making no noise on the rocky ground, 50 Baphuthi slip off the mountain at 1 a.m. They elude the colonial pickets, who have no idea they are there, and move around the sleeping soldiers' tents. Unseen, they steal sticks of dynamite from the ammunition dump.

Quietly, they creep back up the mountain, leaving only their footprints — and less dynamite — as evidence of their silent demonstration of power.

"We found their tracks this morning," Brabant tells his senior soldiers. "I am amazed they did not try to shoot at us. We can only assume that this was a practice for a larger attack, which could come any day now.

"Clearly these men are capable of creeping up on our tents at night without us being aware of their presence until they are right on top of us. They are likely to do so again, and we must be ready for them. So I want you all to sleep dressed in your uniforms, with your firearms at the ready for any emergency.

"On the positive front, I am pleased to say that I am expecting the 12-pounder gun, which has been repaired in Aliwal North, to arrive here tomorrow and two mortars and plentiful supplies of food will follow in a few days."

As the Cape Mounted Riflemen wander off to their tents after Brabant's talk, they air their complaints. It is all very well, they say, for Brabant to talk about sleeping in their uniforms, but, after almost eight months at the mountain, their uniforms are a bit the worse for wear.

"No new clothes for three months now," Whitehead says to Granville. "Look at us. Look at our uniforms."

He tugs at his breeches, which are torn in numerous places and into which he has sewn part of a blanket, and at his black velvet corduroy shirt, which has buttons missing and which he has sewn up where it was torn at the elbows.

"Our boots are damaged from continually walking over the stones and rough ground. I have started wearing my socks over my boots to protect my feet."

He pushes his foot forward to display his socks covering his boots. The others laugh.

"Me, too," says one, pushing his foot forward.

"Have any of you had bad dreams?" asks Whitehead. "I had one in which I dreamed

I came face-to-face with Moorosi and I was fighting with him."

"Who won?" asks Granville.

"It was a tie. I screamed at him and woke myself up."

"I also had a dream about confronting the chief," offers John Brown of No. 4 Troop. "I dreamed I saw Moorosi, and he objected to be captured, so I laid forcible hands on him. Then I was awoken by Booty, who shares my tent, who was returning my blows with vigour."

The men laugh. "Did Booty say anything to you about it?" asks one.

"Yes. He objected to my having a loaded carbine alongside me at night."

Maseru — Thursday, October 16, 1879

The Basotho start arriving early in the morning, assembling on a gently sloping hill above the colonial government headquarters in Maseru, where they have been told the leader of the Cape Colony will address them at the annual *pitso*. By 10 a.m. some 8,000 have assembled. Many carry brightly coloured umbrellas to shield them from the summer sun. Others sit or stand alongside their horses.

"This body of cavalry is almost as numerous as that which Marlborough had at Blenheim," Sprigg tells Griffith as he walks to the spot at which he is to speak.

After a missionary, the Rev. A. Mabille, says a prayer, Griffith introduces Sprigg, telling them he has travelled all the way from Cape Town to tell them of his plans for the future of the Basotho people.

Mojela reads a translation of a message from Letsie, who, clearly believing this meeting is important enough for him to attend, is seated in front of his people. The message diplomatically praises the government and, harking back to the reason the

Contemporary painting depicts a *pitso* near Maseru.

British took over the running of Basutoland in the first place, talks of the "peaceful protection of Her Majesty."

After saying the government is pleased that the Basotho "have taken no part with the rebel Chief Moorosi," Sprigg tells them that the hut tax will be doubled next year. Instead of paying 10 shillings, they will now pay one pound.

Not a way to win over your audience. Nor does it help when Sprigg suggests that "the proposals that the government is making are not for its own advantage, but simply for the advantage of the people here, and that every penny that is raised by taxation amongst you will be spent for your own good and your own advantage." Already, the Basotho people are aware that a greater proportion of the hut tax leaves Basutoland for use by the government elsewhere — including its use in the war against Moorosi. They simply do not believe what Sprigg is saying.

But the remarks that Sprigg makes next really get his audience fired up.

The government has decided that the Basotho people need to surrender their arms, he tells them. "This is not a harsh, or unjust, or unkind measure on the part of the government; it is done simply for the good of the people themselves.

"I would ask you, the Basothos, what use you have for guns in this country? Can you in ordinary times do any good with them? I feel sure that you will admit that you cannot do any good in ordinary times; but then I would ask you, can you do any harm with the guns, not only to the white man but to yourselves?

"I need only point you to what is going on in Moorosi's district and at his mountain; and I would ask you now whether you do not think it would have been a good thing if all Moorosi's people had been disarmed a year ago?

"It is the belief of the government that if Moorosi and his people had not possessed guns they would never have gone into rebellion; they could not have held the mountain against our forces for half an hour.

"The government feels that, like the rest of the natives in South Africa, you possess very much the character of children, and the government knows that children cannot at all times trust even themselves; that they are led away by excitement, and that when the war fever is abroad in the land, the natives often become infected by it, and without the slightest intention of going into rebellion they are drawn into it, and then they use these guns, which they had no intention of using, for the purpose of fighting against the government and their fellow creatures."

The looks on the faces of his audience should warn Sprigg that his words are not being well received. But he continues, speaking of establishing a small Basotho militia force that would be armed and would put down any disturbances.

"The government wants you to become like the white man, and not to regard it as a proof of manhood that you possess guns.

"I ask you to believe that the government knows better than yourselves what is good for you, and when the order is given by the government that the guns shall be surrendered, I ask you to render cheerful obedience to that order, believing that it will work for your ultimate good and tend to your prosperity as a people."

After warning the men about the dangers of brandy and declaring that the government will do all it can to prevent its introduction in Basutoland, Sprigg ends with an invitation to the people to speak out and not be quiet.

Letsie and the senior chiefs are silent. For them, it is expedient not to speak — by a custom all Basotho understand, they will leave the initial sentiments to be expressed by the junior chiefs and they will speak later.

Mabusetsa: "With regard to the hut tax all I have got to say is it is a difficult order to obey. Most of the people will be too poor to pay it; you might order us to pay two or three pounds instead of one pound, but we still would not have the money to pay it."

Tsita Mofoka: "I am only sorry that I am black today; I think that being black is a very great misfortune. The reason I say it is a misfortune is that although you may be following the government ever so faithfully, it turns round upon you and says, you do not belong to me, just because you have a black skin."

Tsekelo Moshoeshoe, a brother of Letsie: "We are to be disarmed, not because we have done any evil, but just because our colour is black. To take away our arms would be to tear our hearts from inside our bosoms. Perhaps it is true as Mr. Upington said in Parliament we are the natural enemies of the white man because we are black."

With the junior chiefs having had their say, the responsibility moves up the line to Letsie's son Lerothodi: "This matter of the hut tax is a very serious one to some of us poor Basotho. I am a poor man, and I have now ten wives; that will make ten pounds that I have to pay. The ten-shilling hut tax has already hurt Moorosi. What is the one-pound hut tax going to do to us? Are we going to rebel like Moorosi?

"We have guns now and we never have done any harm with them. We have used them for good. When the government called on us to use our weapons to keep order in our country, we have always obeyed.

"When Mr. Griffith asked me to assemble my people to wage war for the government, we agreed to do so. In just the past few months, I led two thousand of my men in the war against King Moorosi.

"We drove him and the Baphuthi people back to their mountain stronghold. We helped in the siege against his mountain. You were pleased to use us then. Now you want to take away our weapons so we can never use them again in the service of the government.

"How do you expect us to keep law and order in this country if we are turned into women by being deprived of our arms?"

Sprigg waits for the interpreter to complete the translation, then replies in typically political fashion by ignoring Lerothodi's main complaint.

"I want to thank you, chief, for your help against Moorosi. He is acting like a naughty child and needs to be taught a lesson. We will defeat him and we will take away his weapons when we have defeated him so he cannot defy us again. I will be making this clear to him after I leave here."

Quthing — Friday, October 19, 1879

The test set by Moorosi early today is for a band of Baphuthi to see whether they can evade the Queenstown and Mfengu pickets on the Quthing River side of the mountain. They climb down the hidden path on the south-eastern side of the mountain, unnoticed by the pickets, and begin to walk around the mountain.

But minutes later, shots are fired their way. They return and report to Moorosi that it seems that the pickets are becoming more vigilant, but they still believe an attack on the men sleeping in the tents is feasible.

"I have shown them we can attack them and cause many to die if we want to do so," Moorosi tells his advisers. "Now I must talk to them again about a settlement of this war. Perhaps they will listen to me this time."

Quthing — Monday, October 20, 1879

Brabant takes comfort in knowing that, although the Baphuthi have made sorties into their ranks, they have not yet launched their anticipated all-out attack on the headquarters camp. He is determined to be patient and put on as strong a face as he can, particularly as Sprigg is due to arrive soon.

"I need hardly remind you that the last thing we need is a successful attack by Moorosi on our forces while he is here," he says. "They are increasing their incursions into our camps, but we are becoming better prepared for them.

"Last night several of the enemy tried to pass our lines and were fired at. I would like to remind you — "

Brabant is interrupted by shouts from sentries closer to the mountain.

"Moorosi has put up a white flag on the lower schanz," a man yells.

"We have seen the flag before," says Brabant. "But we will send an interpreter up there immediately to find out what it is he wants now."

21

Quthing — Tuesday, October 21, 1879

Brabant prepares to send a translator to find out why Moorosi has put out another white flag. But he is pre-empted by the Baphuthi themselves, who send two men with the flag across the plateau to the headquarters camp. In the front, carrying the flag, is a short man dressed in a red nightcap and a white blanket, likely taken from the Mfengu in the recent clash. Behind him strides a tall man who identifies himself as the youngest son of Moorosi.

Through an interpreter, they say they have shown great restraint in not attacking the colonial forces, even though they have demonstrated their ability to infiltrate their ranks. But, they say, Moorosi would like Brabant to talk with him personally about peace.

After much parleying, Brabant goes up to the first stone wall.

"I would like to talk to you again about reaching a peace accord with you," Moorosi tells Brabant, with Tainton once again interpreting. "But I am afraid of you killing me and my people if we do so. I want an assurance that we will be able to live in peace on our land if we do agree to a peace treaty."

"I have already made it clear to you that we require nothing but your unconditional surrender," Brabant replies. "But the prime minister, the man who runs the government in Cape Town, will be here soon. He might agree to talk with you."

Moorosi agrees to wait until Sprigg arrives.

Quthing — Friday, October 24, 1879

The troops in the camps around Moorosi's Mountain have never been as organized and as obedient as today. Their sudden devotion to duty springs from one source. The prime minister is here, having arrived yesterday in an eight-horse omnibus after a journey from Maseru, accompanied by Griffith, Austen and Barkly.

With Sprigg, too, is 38-year-old Colonel Zachary Stanley Bayly, appointed earlier this year as commander of a unit of the Cape Mounted Riflemen. He is a rising star in the new defence department set up at Frere's prodding last year. Although a newcomer to the military and better known as the owner of the Pig and Whistle tavern in Kimberley, Bayly was in charge of a unit of men who repulsed a Gcaleka attack at Holland's Shop during the Ninth Frontier War two years ago. He also commanded a victorious battle at Umzintzani in Natal Colony.

Sprigg's avowed purpose in visiting the battlefield is to see the scene of operations for himself, hold talks with Brabant, other senior officers, and, if it can be arranged, Moorosi. While he is here he will appoint Bayly as the new commander of the colonial troops, in place of Brabant.

The troops believe their future at the mountain will be determined by these talks,

311

which could lead to either a peace treaty or a resumption of hostilities.

Sprigg asks Brabant about the feasibility of another assault.

"I do not think it's advisable," Brabant replies. "My men are disheartened and very weak in numbers. The volunteer burghers are useless for an assault."

"You have no special plan to oust Moorosi?"

"Not right now. The only suggestion anyone has come up with is to storm the mountain with hundreds of men who are willing to die if necessary. That is essentially Nixon's plan. But even if I am given the additional men willing to undertake the task, I do not think I would be justified in risking a certain loss of life and possible failure for my own glorification."

"How would you feel if I replaced you with Colonel Bayly, whom I have asked to join me here?"

"I think that, if he can get his regiment together and bring it here with him, he will have a much better chance of success," Brabant replies.

"Very well, that is settled then. Colonel Bayly will take over the command of the troops. But before he does, I would like you to arrange a meeting for me with Moorosi, similar to the one you told me you held with him earlier. He is expecting me to talk with him, is he not?"

"Indeed, he is, Mr. Prime Minister."

"I am confident he will listen to reason, as the Basotho people did when I addressed them recently in Maseru, and that he will surrender. Then we can settle this war without having to call on Colonel Bayly."

Brabant dispatches a messenger to take a white flag to the mountain and tell Moorosi that the prime minister would like to talk with him.

About 30 minutes later, the two men who earlier brought Moorosi's white flag from the mountain arrive. The king, they say, wants Sprigg to meet with him on the mountain.

"No. It is better if the chief comes down from the mountain and meets with the prime minister here," Brabant says.

The men return to the mountain, confer with Moorosi, and march back across the plateau once more.

"King Moorosi says that he is a dog and the prime minister is a lion and the dog objects to talking with the lion in the lion's territory," the man who identifies himself as Moorosi's son reports.

Sprigg and Brabant assure the men that Moorosi will be safe if he comes down from the mountain to talk to them. The messengers return to the mountain, but return with the same message: The prime minister must come to the mountain, this time adding that old age is also a factor in Moorosi's plea.

"Very well," Sprigg says. "I will go to the mountain."

A look of concern flashes across Brabant's face. "With all respect, sir, you are putting yourself in the path of danger," he says. "You must understand that these men are ruthless. They are masters of deceit and trickery. You would be risking your life by going on to the mountain. I can give you some protection, but the mountain is filled with armed men ready to shoot at a moment's notice.

"Once up there you will be absolutely in his power. He can murder your whole party without any fear of immediate retaliation."

"But did you not go up to the mountain to talk with him?" asks Sprigg.

"Yes, sir, but I am paid to take such risks. It is part of my duty to run such risks. It cannot reasonably be said to be part of your duty."

"Thank you for your concern, colonel," Sprigg replies. "But I will go to the mountain. Please arrange for me to meet with Moorosi tomorrow morning."

This mountain path is close to the meeting place. The mountain opposite is on the other side of the saddle and the neck.

Quthing — Saturday, October 25, 1879

In all his years of leading men in battle, Brabant never has been this anxious. As he walks alongside Sprigg across the plateau to the mountain, he half expects a shot to ring out and to hit one of them. Accompanied by Colonel Bayly, Captain O'Connor, two senior officers and a translator, they comprise a small group and make easy targets; as part of the agreement, Moorosi has stipulated that if any other government men should go beyond the saddle "they will be shot like dogs."

Brabant does not breathe any more easily as they walk along a path that leads behind the first stone wall to the point where the white flag was first raised. This is the appointed place at which Sprigg is to talk with Moorosi. And here, Brabant shudders to think, they could be attacked and brutally murdered and no one could help them.

The meeting place is set between a rock, the point where the first and second stone-wall tiers meet at an angle and the mountainside. Here, Moorosi, dressed in his cloak and hat and accompanied by 15 of his senior advisers, takes a seat on a box. Sprigg, Brabant and Bayly sit on chairs that have been carried for them by the senior officers. Moorosi's son Letuka, an adviser to Moorosi named Qhamane, and two other men sit on rocks opposite them.

None of the men on either side is armed. Moorosi has learned how sensitive the white men can be to the carrying of arms and he wants to make it clear that he is sincere about discussing peace. He is pleased to see that Sprigg, for his part, instructed none of his group to bear weapons.

After an exchange of pleasantries, Sprigg, through an interpreter, tells Moorosi that he might not be aware yet, but the Zulus have been conquered.

"They have been completely suppressed," he says. "Cetshwayo has been captured and he is in jail in Cape Town. I saw him there before I came here."

Moorosi shows no reaction. He already knows.

"Also, your own Basotho people are against you. They have been assisting the colonial forces and there are even some Basotho left in the colonial camp where they are ready to fight against you."

Again, Moorosi is little moved. He knows how much support he has received from the Basotho people and how few are against him. Only a few weeks ago his people were able to supplement their supplies, including more ammunition, with the help of Basotho. Moorosi also knows the few Basotho left in the colonial camp are not eager to fight him.

"You cannot hold out much longer, chief," Sprigg continues. "You are isolated, alone and cannot summon help from anywhere. We will continue to surround this mountain and make it impossible for you to obtain food, water or wood."

Moorosi knows he is isolated, but not as isolated as Sprigg thinks he is. He also is confident that his people are better armed — and better marksmen — than the Zulus. He has a mountain fortress that the Zulus did not have. He has held out for six months and can hold out much longer. In addition, he has the means to win this war. Already, he has shown the government how easy it would be to attack the soldiers at night.

"So now I am giving you the opportunity to surrender to my government and to that of Letsie, your king," Sprigg adds.

"I am interested in hearing how we are to surrender," Moorosi replies. "But I must ask you why you refer to me surrendering to Chief Letsie. I am surprised you say that he is my king because I am the king of the Baphuthi, whereas Letsie, he is the king of the Basotho."

Sprigg ignores Moorosi's assertion.

"We want to offer you the opportunity to surrender. You must not take false hope in the attack you made on May 29th when your people ruthlessly killed 21 of our government's soldiers. That attack is not going to help you win this war."

Moorosi is angered at Sprigg's attitude.

"I did not ask for this war," he says. "It is you who have sent men here to kill me and my people. We attacked the men in the tents at the meeting of the rivers because you attacked us in our caves. We could have attacked many more of your soldiers in their tents, but we didn't do so.

"If you will take your soldiers away everything will be peaceful again. You said we were going to discuss peace, so please tell me why you are sitting here and telling me these things about me killing your people. You sent men here to kill my people; I am only defending my people."

"I am saying that if you and your people continue to kill our soldiers by hiding on the mountain, we shall send in additional soldiers and punish you. There is no way that you can avoid dying a painful death."

"I kill your soldiers only because they are attacking me," Moorosi reiterates. "Now I am asking you to give me your opinion on how I should surrender. I am asking you how we can go back to having peace in my country. But you are not talking to me as a leader. You must remember that I am a king, too, just as you are. The way you are talking is not the way to talk to a person who might conquer you. You are talking to me like a child not as a leader equal to you."

"You are not a leader equal to me," Sprigg responds, sitting straight up as his anger rises. "I am the Prime Minister of the Cape Colony and no chief is equal to me.

"You ask how you should surrender. I will tell you. You should surrender to me and the government will do whatever it wants to do to you. That is what surrender means. Give in now and you will no longer be subject to bombardment from our guns, you will no longer have to suffer here on the mountain, trying to obtain enough food to keep you alive.

"Surrender comes with a price. You cannot surrender and expect the government to allow you to go free and continue your rebellious ways. You have done wrong and must hand yourself over completely to the government or else face the consequences. That is what surrender means. It means you give up and we declare victory."

"I will never surrender to you on those terms," Moorosi says. "I will fight you and I will defeat you."

The two men debate for three hours. But they make no headway.

The talks stall.

Finally, Sprigg says, "I will give you one more chance, Moorosi. Will you offer your complete surrender?"

Moorosi is adamant. "Not if it is on your terms. It is no good us talking any longer. You do not want to discuss a way in which we can live peacefully together. You want me to hand myself over to you like a slave."

Moorosi stands. "I am leaving now. We will continue to defend ourselves against the people you sent here to kill us. We will do so until you realize you cannot defeat us. The people you sent to kill us will themselves be killed. Those who do not die will be so afraid that they will run away, like a dog with his tail between his legs."

Sprigg also stands. "I am warning you, Moorosi. You are choosing death. What you choose is what you will get. And it will not be long before you get it. I am appointing Captain Bayly here to be in charge of our soldiers. The day he starts to attack you it will be the end of you, your arrogance and your tiny nation. Your necks will be broken on this mountain. Even though you think you are invincible, we will conquer you."

"I will face the consequences," Moorosi replies as he starts to walk away. "I will rather die on this mountain than surrender to you on your terms."

Moorosi turns and makes his way back up the mountain.

"I will give you one more chance," Sprigg says as the Baphuthi leader walks off.

Moorosi stops and turns to face him.

"I will give you and your people until nightfall to surrender unconditionally. Every man who comes down from the mountain before the sun sets tonight will be regarded as one who has surrendered."

Sprigg leads his contingent down the mountain path to the camps below. Moorosi leads his group to the mountain top.

Each leader returns to his people to tell them the result.

The sun sets with no Baphuthi coming down from the mountain. The talks are over. The war goes on.

Quthing — Sunday, October 26, 1879

At 11 a.m., as Bayly formally takes over command of the troops from Brabant, the soldiers turn out to see a display of colonial bravado aimed at sending a message to Moorosi. A shell fired from the 12-pounder incredibly falls right into the spot where the parley was held yesterday. Three other shots are fired. They are less accurate, but succeed in hitting the stone walls near the meeting spot.

Quthing — Tuesday, October 28, 1879

Sprigg hands Bayly a copy of Nixon's report and points out the main suggestion — that a body of well disciplined and well trained men make the assault on the mountain.

Bayly agrees. "With your permission, I would like the three yeomanry regiments to leave when Brabant leaves. Also, let the burghers go home. I have seen enough of them in the short time I have been here. We have no need for those untrained complaining volunteers who scare at the sight of a sheep.

"And most of the Basotho who are still left here can leave, too. Their hearts are not in this war and, from what I've gathered in the few days I've been here, as many of them side with Moorosi as are against him.

"But I do need more Cape Mounted Riflemen. I need a larger force to do an effective job. I will also need an improved supply of food and supplies for my men and for their horses. We do not want them to go hungry or have inadequate clothing and boots.

"Finally, I need a few weeks to train these men properly and to ensure that this time we do not have any laggards or cowards among them. They will risk their lives, but they will do so in the service of their country.

"With the weather improving every day, we should be in a good position to mount a solid attack that will bring the chief and his followers to their knees."

Sprigg is impressed with Bayly's professional approach and determination.

"Your requests are approved," he says. "You can start moving out the men you do not want immediately and training those you do want. I will leave tomorrow for Cape Town, knowing this command is in good hands. I expect to be able to report to the next session of Parliament that we defeated the Baphuthi and are in control of their land."

"I am confident you will be able to do so, Prime Minister."

Brabant enters the tent. "I am leaving now, Prime Minister," he says. Trying to avoid any intimation of the bitterness he feels, he turns to Bayly. "When you have been a month here, colonel, and know the mountain as I know it, and if you find you are unable to achieve anything, I will come up again and relieve you."

"Farewell, colonel," Bayly responds. "I will bear your words in mind."

Sprigg's party leaves camp for Thomas's Shop, where he will stay before returning to Cape Town. The troopers relax in their tents surrounding the mountain. The tension has noticeably lessened.

Following Bayly's orders, the volunteers still in the camp prepare to leave for home. The full-time soldiers have been told they will undergo strict training in the next month before launching another assault on the mountain. For now, they are happy to enjoy themselves. They open their rations of whisky and soon the sounds of their revelling echo across the mountains.

As the party continues into the night, the pickets are eager to join. Some take off early. After all, who will know? All the senior officers are with Sprigg at Thomas's Shop, now named Fort Hartley in honour of the doctor who established the hospital there. A few of the pickets remain on duty, with the promise that they will be relieved a little later so they can join in the revelry, too.

Moorosi has abandoned his plan for an all-out attack on the colonial soldiers. The response to his latest attempt to infiltrate the camp has persuaded him that the soldiers are guarding themselves better, meaning that an assault on them could lead to large losses among the Baphuthi. He does not want to risk such a setback. Instead, he will launch smaller surprise raids on the soldiers even as he guards the mountain and replenishes his supplies.

So it is that, as midnight approaches, a number of Baphuthi climb down the mountain and steal through the bush at its base in a wide semi-circle to approach the pickets from behind the saddle. The full moon helps them find their way easily and the noise of the soldiers' shouting and singing covers any sounds they make.

They creep behind the sentries, load their rifles and fire on the men on the rocky promontory above them.

The few pickets still on duty fire back and a couple run to the noisy camp ground to summon help.

By the time help arrives the fighting is in full swing as white soldiers, their backs toward the mountain, fire on their black attackers who are behind the saddle. In a short lull, a picket turns and sees movement on the moonlit mountain.

"They are doing it again," he shouts. "They are moving cattle up the mountain. Scores of them."

The pickets turn their fire toward the mountain, but are forced to watch their backs, too, as the Baphuthi behind them continue to fire. Soon spears are being flung toward them from behind the saddle.

As more men arrive from the camps, the Baphuthi retreat.

But the attack has served its purpose. The cattle disappear behind the rocks at the top of the mountain.

Moorosi is delighted at his new wealth. "Forty-seven," he shouts. "Let that white chief tell us we cannot survive for much longer. We will show him he is wrong."

Quthing — Tuesday, November 4, 1879

The wagons that rumble into camp are loaded with a five-and-a-half-inch mortar, 16-pound shells and other supplies. Granville, who by now has developed expertise with mortars, assists Captain William Bourne to off-load the mortar. Bourne — among those who arrived with Bayly — was a leader during the Ninth Frontier War two years ago.

Granville remarks that morale in the camp has improved since Bayly took command a little more than a week ago. New life seems infused into the men by cricket matches, athletic sports and shooting contests.

"You should have been here earlier," he tells Bourne. "Morale was all but absent. The men thought the war could not be won without the loss of many lives and even then they were not sure it could be won at all. The volunteers' heart was not in it. Now, with the volunteers leaving, the mood has changed. You don't hear as much about it being impossible to take the mountain."

The men are instructed to check out the mortar and place it in position with the other guns on the south-western side of the mountain, 1,000 yards from the stone walls.

"Look how old it is," Granville says to Bourne. He points to the inscription on the gun: G.R. 1806 for George Rex, or King George III. "It's 71 years old."

Bourne nods. "One of the men told me it has performed service at Cape Town for many years. It stood outside the museum."

Granville laughs. "So we attack the enemy with a museum piece do we? Let's check the fuses that came with it."

When the men find the fuses that came with the gun do not work, they spend several hours transforming 7-pounder fuses. They work. Problem solved.

Next they place iron bands around the carriage so that it will stand up to steady use over many days. "Don't want the old girl falling apart on us," Granville says.

Granville and Bourne return to assist with the off-loading of the wagons. It is starting to rain and the rest of the supplies have to be put under shelter.

In the wagon load are 25 scaling ladders, each 10 feet in length, 24 inches wide and with sides one and half inches deep. Built in Aliwal North, they are equipped with iron sockets two inches long at each end to link the sections. Ropes to tie them together are included.

Granville wonders how the officers can even think the ladders and ropes can help them scale the walls in the face of Baphuthi firing. "Fat lot of use these will be," he says to Bourne as they carry the ladders to a new stone building in which they will be stored along with the ammunition. "If you ask me, these are suicide devices. Want to die? Place one of these against the walls and climb. You'll get your wish.

"Also, they're badly made. Well designed, but not put together very well. To make them stronger, we're going to have to tie two of them together."

"Well, let's try them out anyway," Bourne replies. The men link two of the ladders together and place them against a nearby ledge. They collapse before anyone can stand on them. Other ladders 15 feet long that they find in the wagon are stronger.

As they are working out how the ladders can be put together, Lieutenant Springer walks up, offering to be of assistance. "We might be able to get these to work," he says. Assisted by Bourne and Granville, he cuts the wider ladders to half their width, removing the iron joints, and tying them up with raw ox hide.

"Why didn't they build them like that in the first place?" Granville asks.

Bourne is silent. He is in deep thought. He looks at the ladders.

"Don't you agree?" Granville asks; clearly Bourne's thoughts are elsewhere.

Granville continues, trying to attract Bourne's interest once more. "I still don't know how useful those ladders will be, even though they are stronger now. They will serve only to expose us more to the enemy. Must we prove again that storming the mountain doesn't work?"

Bourne remains silent.

"Don't you agree?"

Bourne recovers from his thoughts. "Yes, yes. I understand what you are saying," he says. "But I have an idea that I must pass on to the colonel."

"What is it?"

Bourne walks off without replying.

Quthing — Sunday, November 9, 1879

Normally Sunday is like any other day at the mountain. But not today. On cleared ground near the camp stands a man in the light rain, dressed in a black shiny robe down to his feet with baggy "lawn" sleeves tied with a black ribbon at the wrist, from which a white ruffle projects. He wears a crimson doctor's hood.

Dr. Webb, bishop of Bloemfontein, leads the men in a hymn and prayer and delivers a short sermon. Webb prays for the men's safety and success at war and leaves them with a number of hymn books. The men, ordered by Bayly to attend, appear moved by the service.

In the evening, the sound of hymn singing wafts from several tents. But while the other men sing or simply talk together, Brome sits alone in his tent. The service has had a strong impact on him, but perhaps not in the way Webb intended. Months ago, when he signed up to join the Cape Mounted Riflemen, he believed it was his patriotic duty to defend his family and his property against those who would take it away from him. Fighting against heathen people was the right Christian thing to do.

But the harsh reality of the battlefield has focused his thoughts in ways he did not expect. Brome wonders how Webb can pray for the white soldiers' safety when they are setting out to kill other people also made in the image of God. In praying for the whites, he was, in effect, praying for blacks to be killed, wasn't he?

Is that what Christians are supposed to do?

Quthing — Thursday, November 13, 1879

The Rev. Ellenberger has cancelled all his plans for today. Emma is giving birth to their tenth child and the fifth to be born in the Masitise cave house. With Ellenberger's expert medical assistance, the birth is uncomplicated. As Emma holds the newborn in her arms, Frederic sits alongside her.

"We will call him Victor," Emma says. "And we will always remember that he has been born not far from the sound of gunfire."

"Indeed," Ellenberger replies. "Let us pray he will grow into a peaceful world where men will realize that to do good to one another rather than harm helps us all be better people."

Quthing — Sunday, November 16, 1879

The yeomanry and the other volunteers have almost all gone. Convinced the mountain is impregnable and having no desire to add their lives to the 90 who have died trying to achieve the impossible, they were pleased to agree with Bayly's order to leave. Now only 50 of these minimally trained militia men remain.

Bayly is pleased to see them go. Taking Moorosi's mountain is a job for professional soldiers. The new commander has assembled a force of 275 members of the Cape Mounted Riflemen, 40 Border Guard volunteers — the best he could find among the hundreds who had been at the mountain — and 460 black soldiers, whom he will use as a back-up. The black soldiers include 260 Thembu and 150 Mfengu from the Cape Colony. Only 50 of the 2,000 Basotho under Lerothodi remain. The others have either been dismissed or have drifted away.

Bayly announces the mountain will be stormed in four days — on Thursday, November 20. To prepare the way, he orders a constant bombardment.

"Starting tomorrow morning, I want the mortar to be kept in action day and night for the next four days," he tells Bourne and Granville. "We will use it in conjunction with the other cannon, which will also be kept in constant action. During the day we will punch into those stone walls with the 7-pounders and lob shells into the trenches behind them with the five-and-a-half pounder. At night, the 7-pounders will fire star shells that will light up the mountain. I want to give those damned barbarians no rest. By the time we are ready to attack they will be tired and disoriented and will lack the spirit to fight back."

Quthing — Wednesday, November 19, 1879

It is not only the screaming of the shells and mortars every three or four minutes throughout the day. It is not only the explosions and the shaking of the ground.

It is not only the star shells that repeatedly light up the night. It is not only the damage being done to the walls, which constantly have to be repaired. It is not only the clouds of smoke from the gunfire that blanket the mountain and the pungent smell of gunpowder that accompanies it. It is not only the danger to the Baphuthi themselves, several of whom have been injured and a number killed.

It is the combination of all these factors that is unnerving Moorosi's warriors.

For three days now, it has been difficult to relax during the day and is hard to sleep at night. They lie awake, anticipating the next blast, hoping each will be the last so they can sleep. Eventually they succeed in sleeping for a few hours. But with each passing day they are becoming more sleep deprived and disoriented.

The extent of this gunfire also is greater. Because the government forces have moved the mortar closer to the mountain, they are able to reach farther than the crest of the mountain. Some of the shells are landing in the living area on the flat mountaintop. The men have moved the cattle to parts of the mountaintop that are safe behind rocky outcrops and have learned how to avoid the worst of the shelling.

Moorosi, however, is finding it increasingly difficult to persuade his men of the necessity to hold on. The bombing, he tells them, eventually will stop. The whites will run out of ammunition and will become tired of firing the guns all the time. But Moorosi's men continue to leave the mountain in a steady trickle. More than half the 500 who were guarding the mountain when the war started have left, finding refuge in caves or villages deep in Baphuthi territory or in Kornet Spruit.

Those who are left are his best fighters and his finest marksmen and Moorosi remains convinced they can defeat the white forces. He does not need a large army, as the whites seem to do. All he needs is a courageous force, one that can fire with pinpoint accuracy, anticipate the movements of the whites and outwit them. He still has such a force.

"The whites' big guns can reach a little distance beyond the crest of the mountain," Moorosi points out in a evening talk with his men. "The rest of the area is safe. If you move away, you will find that the guns are only noise and cannot hurt you.

"When you go down to the walls to defend us, keep using the ox hides that I have given you. Hold them over your heads and they will protect you from the pieces of shell that explode against the rock behind you and in the air. It is working well and saving lives.

"We need to keep defending the mountain. The whites will become tired of firing the guns at us. If they try to storm our walls again, we will defeat them.

"They will be the ones to surrender. Not us."

Moorosi stands, prompting his listeners also to stand.

"Come, Lemena, show us we are not afraid."

Lemena raises his spear, brandishing it in the air.

"You, Moorosi, great and mighty king!" he chants. "You, who have an army."

He turns to face the rest of the men who also raise their spears.

"Griffith sent his forces," he shouts.

Beating time with their feet and waving their spears, the men chant a responsive chorus: "We destroyed them!"

"The soldiers came."

"We destroyed them."

"The burghers came."

"We destroyed them."

Soon the men are dancing from side to side across the mountain top. Their singing grows louder.

"The big guns came."

"We destroyed them."

"Brabant sent his forces."

"We destroyed them."

"The mounted police came."

"We destroyed them."

Lemena turns to face Moorosi once more. "You, the great and mighty king! You, who have an army! When will they dare to repeat their attack?"

"We will destroy them! We will destroy them! We will destroy them!"

As the sound of their final shouts echo across the valley, and the men sit down, the artillery fire stops. The men wait, bracing themselves for the next firing. It takes a while. After 15 minutes, another blast rocks the mountain. They wait again; this time even longer. After a while it stops altogether. Says Lemena with a broad smile, "They must have heard our war song and have given up."

⚜

Granville shakes the mortar from side to side on its carriage as though that will fix it. But the firing mechanism appears to have failed. He has no idea how to repair it.

He has kept a careful count of the firings since they put the museum piece to use three days ago. The gun has fired 367 times, an average of once every 10 minutes during the daylight hours. Although old, it has been the most effective of the large guns. But now the mortar's work appears to be over.

"I think this old lady has finally succumbed," Granville says to Bourne.

"But it has been effective," Bourne replies.

"Yes, we have achieved what Bayly wanted," replies Granville.

A bugle sounds: The men are to assemble at the parade grounds for an important address by Colonel Bayly.

Bayly stands on a slight rise, looking down on the 500 men assembled below.

"For some weeks now, we have been developing our plan to take the mountain," Bayly tells them. "We have reconnoitred every part of it. We have examined every gully, every rock and every bush. We received a plan of action suggested by Major Nixon who also spent some time examining the mountain. I also was assisted by Captain Bourne, who had an idea for an attack that I have incorporated in our plans. You'll hear about that later."

Bourne looks across at Granville and smiles.

"Those of you who wish to have them will be issued with long Sniders and bayonets in place of the carbines you have been carrying up to now. I think you will find those more effective against the enemy, who appear to have newer and more efficient weapons than we have had.

"Now the time has come to implement our plans. Moorosi's Mountain will be taken tomorrow by the Cape Mounted Riflemen!"

The men dutifully cheer. At least Bayly seems confident.

"Five parties will storm the mountain," Bayly continues. "One will assault the mountain from the front, crossing the saddle and attacking the stone walls. That party will consist of 25 members of the Wodehouse Border Guard, who are among the few remaining volunteers. Eighty Mfengu under the command of Lieutenant Muhlenbeck will storm the mountain from the ridge on the east of the plateau.

"You will take up your positions about 350 yards from the first row of stone walls in the darkness and will launch your attack at dawn tomorrow. The firing of a rocket over the mountain will be your signal for attack. You will proceed under the element of surprise as most of the Baphuthi are likely still to be asleep, recovering from the massive fire power we directed their way.

"You will storm the walls, ascend them and overpower the enemy."

The men are quiet. Members of the guard cast ominous glances at one another, aware of the casualties that took place on the two previous assaults — and with a force that numbered considerably more. They wonder why they have been singled out for this attack. Bayly has made it clear that the Cape Mounted Riflemen are his elite troops, yet they — the few volunteers left in the camp and the Mfengu fighters — are being chosen to storm the mountain.

Sensing the men's unease, Bayly continues.

"You have the option of obeying these orders or leaving camp at once," he says. "I will not tolerate anyone taking part in the storming party who is not wholly committed to the task at hand. We have no room for the craven and chicken-hearted."

The men maintain, at least outwardly, a calm determination that helps one to bolster the other. They have come so far, endured so much, that now they are willing to risk almost anything to end this war.

Bayly repeats his offer, allowing the men time to move if they wish to do so.

Silence. No one moves.

"Thank you. I know you will do your duty.

"But, although it will be the main one, these men will not be our only storming party," he continues. "And the same options apply to all of you. Either you are with me or you are against me. If you are not prepared to take part in this mission, leave now. I want only the men committed to doing their duty to God and country."

Brome stays frozen in place. He rephrases Bayly's words in his mind, "We want only those men committed to doing their duty to God *or* country."

Now is his chance to opt out. Now is his chance to choose God above country.

But he cannot do it. His legs will not move. He is unwilling to fight, but more afraid to stand alone and say so. The pressure from Bayly, the officers as well as his colleagues form a powerful force that overrides the conviction that following these orders is morally wrong. He will go with the crowd. He will choose country.

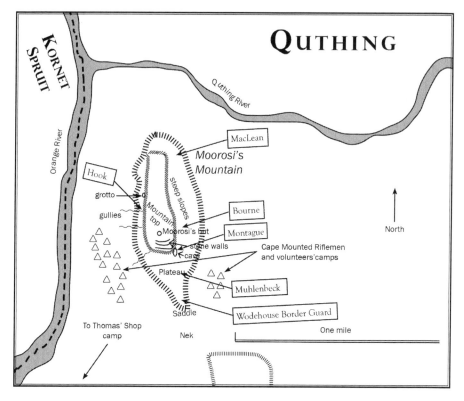

Whitehead and Granville, for their part, realize this is a desperate engagement. They are being called upon to put their lives on the line.

The men are all silent. No one wants to be seen as a coward. They look at one another. They stay where they are.

"Very well. Four other parties will ascend the mountain from the sides, on the east and west, in a large circle from right to left around the mountain. These parties will move off when the moon sets at midnight tonight, which is in a few hours. The darkness will give them the opportunity to take up their positions unseen by the enemy. Once in their positions, they will wait for daybreak before attacking. When the rocket is fired to signal the advance, they, too, will swing into action.

"Two parties will attack on the eastern side of the mountain. Each will consist of two troops of Cape Mounted Riflemen. You know who you are.

"One party will be under the command of Captain Montague. It will consist of 181 officers and men. They will ascend the mountain from the cave in which men under Captain Grant hid before ascending the mountain in a previous assault. It is now known as the commandant's cave or Grant's Cave.

"The other party, 100 yards farther down the mountain, will climb up a fissure on the eastern side of the mountain called Bourne's Crack, a low piece of rock in a krantz, 100 yards to the right of the cave. It will be led by Captain Bourne, who will be assisted by Lieutenant Springer, Lieutenant Sutherland and Lieutenant Hatton.

It will consist of 174 officers and men.

"Each man will carry 70 rounds of ammunition slung around his neck. Your rifles will be equipped with bayonets. You will be given fuller instructions later tonight.

"Another party will be headed by Lieutenant Allen MacLean and will consist of those Mfengu who are not in the first party. They are to scale the mountain up a path at the back, or north-east of the mountain, at the area known as 'the spring,' a fountain at the back of the mountain. We believe this footpath is used by the Baphuthi to move to and from the mountain and was used in the attack on the Chiappini camp. It is steep, but we hope to use the element of surprise strongly here and when you attack, as I have mentioned, we expect most of the Baphuthi to be asleep.

"As in the case of the first party, I expect absolute devotion to duty. You too, have the option of following orders or leaving at once."

No one moves.

"The final party, consisting of Mfengu, Thembu and Basotho, will attack up the gully on the southwest front of the mountain and will be led by Captain Hook."

"Now return to your camps. You are free to talk among one another and make a noise this evening if you wish. The enemy will think we have forgotten about them. But once it is midnight, and the moon has set, I want you to move about as silently as possible by placing your socks over your boots. Let the enemy think you are asleep.

"As your arrival on the top awakens the Baphuthi, they will come running down the paths that lead to the stone walls, thinking that will still be our main point of attack. But you'll be attacking from behind. Use your new Sniders to the best of your ability. Dress as you wish, but every man must carry a rifle, a revolver and ammunition.

"I am expecting every one of you to show no quarter to the men on the mountain. Should you come across any women or children, you are not to molest them in any way. But you are to do your utmost to oust Moorosi and his band of rebels from their mountain stronghold. Do not hold back in any way. If you must shoot, then shoot. We will not win this battle by talking; we have tried that. We will not win it by taking prisoners; we have taken a number already.

"We will win this war only by using our fire power. I am relying on each of you to give it his all.

"With that in mind, I am offering tonight a reward of 200 pounds for the capture of Moorosi. Dead or alive. The same for Lehana. Two hundred pounds. Dead or alive. A reward of 25 pounds, with promotion, goes to the first man on the top of the mountain. There will be other rewards for meritorious acts. Now go and enjoy yourselves for a couple of hours. It will not be long before the Cape Mounted Riflemen take Moorosi's Mountain."

The men dutifully cheer and move off.

Moorosi is tempted to let his guard drop. The bombing has stopped and nothing has happened. His men's morale has been sapped, they are tired from lack of sleep and they are demoralized because many have left the mountain.

As Moorosi walks slowly around the mountaintop, he peers down on the camps where he can see the men moving around like ants finding a new food source. They appear agitated and excited. For the last few weeks they have trained more vigorously.

The whites attacked before after one or two days of sustained bombing. Now they will do so again. There are fewer of them, but they seem better prepared. He recalls Sprigg's words, "I am warning you, Moorosi. You are choosing death…Your necks will be broken on this mountain. Even though you think you are invincible, we will conquer you."

Such is the white men's bravado. They think they are more clever than anyone else. They are convinced their soldiers, marching up and down to nowhere, are the best. They consider their military strategy to be superior.

Moorosi has proven over and over that the white soldiers can be beaten. His warriors have defeated government raids on their caves. They have repulsed two attacks on the mountain. His people have smuggled men, food, oxen and water on to the mountain by outwitting the white commanders. His men have used guile to outwit the whites' grandiosity. They have shown that the whites can act without thinking and are easily distracted.

Yet he cannot shake the sense that this attack will be different. For one thing, the bombing was more intense. Also Bayly seems more determined and the soldiers appear to be more organized and more active. He assigns more sentries than usual to guard the stone walls.

"Be aware that they probably will attack in the early morning," he says. "That is what they did before. They will not attack after the moon has set tonight, because they will be unable to see what they are doing, but they might attack once the sun begins to rise tomorrow."

He tells most of his men to sleep tonight in the trenches behind the stone walls. He wants them to be ready, he says, whenever the attack might come.

The men assigned to the guard agree, even though it is a tough task to peer into a quiet dark motionless world for hours and stay awake.

❧

Bayly has forbidden the sale of liquor at the colonial camp for several days, but a few of the men have brandy and whisky that they stored away earlier, which they share with their colleagues.

A gallows humour helps the men prepare for the morning's challenge, particularly those who have been assigned to the frontal assault.

"What are you going to drink?" asks one. "It had better be a stiff one, if you can find one, while you have the chance. One of Moorosi's men may stop you from enjoying another for some time to come."

A number of the men, unable to sleep, are writing letters to be taken in the next post, many fearing it is their last word home. The married men write messages that, should they die, will be sent to their wives. In the quiet of the night, the men are all too aware that tomorrow could be the last day of their lives.

22

Quthing — Thursday, November 20, 1879

The moon sets just after midnight and the stars are all that remain to bathe the bush around them in a soft, eerie light. The sergeant-majors move from tent to tent, waking the men who have fallen asleep and alerting the others.

"Now then, fall in quickly and make as little noise as you can," Bourne says as Granville tumbles out of his bed.

"Seems like I had no sleep at all," Granville says.

Dark forms glide about the camp as the men assemble, as instructed, at the parade ground, where a roll call is taken, one of the quietest Granville has ever heard.

"Left turn, slow march ahead," a sergeant major instructs them under his breath. In single file, they creep along the side of the mountain. Hardly a sound breaks the stillness of the night except for the stealthy tread of the men or the clatter of a pebble, dislodged accidentally, as it bounds over the rocks. All are concerned not to tip off the Baphuthi, whom, they hope, are all asleep.

Bourne instructs Granville to follow right behind him. At his side are Lieutenants Springer, Sutherland and Hatton as well as Whitehead.

"We will make our way along the eastern side of the mountain," Bourne explains. "Fifty Basotho will carry ladders for us as we make our way to the bottom of the two ways to the top. Two Basotho will carry each ladder, one at each end. Twelve ladders will be assigned to our group, who will climb up the one fissure, and 12 to Montague's group, who will climb up the other path, the one from the cave. We have one ladder to use as a spare.

"Once we reach the bottom of our path, we will place our ladders against the mountainside and use them to climb a series of six natural giant rock steps that ascend the mountain. I have identified these steps as a way of scaling the mountain.

"But we can't get up them without the use of the ladders as each giant rock step is six to eight or possibly even 10 feet high; we can't tell for sure until we get there."

Granville glances at Bourne. So this was his plan. Why could he not have told him of it?

"By using two ladders roped together," Bourne continues, "we will be able to climb up to the top of the first step. More ladders will be handed up to the men who have made it on to the step. They will rope those ladders together and place them on the next step. Once the ladders are in place, they will climb to the top of the second step.

"And so we will go until we reach the top of the sixth step.

"Once there, we will have put in place a series of ladders that will take us to the top.

"Montague's group, on the left of us, will use their ladders to try to scale their path. They do not have the benefit of natural steps as we do, so they likely will have a harder task.

"When the ladders are in place and we are poised unseen on them one behind the other, we will wait until dawn when a rocket is fired. That will be the signal for the three other parties to storm the mountain from the front and sides. The enemy will rush to the walls to fire at the attackers in the way they did in the previous two assaults.

"At that point, we will be climbing on to the mountaintop from our positions on the ladders. Once on the top, we will assemble and move across the mountaintop to attack the enemy from behind.

"If the other group — the troop on our left — is successful in reaching the top, both of our groups will reach the top at the same time, establishing a large force up there.

"Right, men, let's go."

The men set off, making their way across the mountain slope toward the attack points, steadily climbing higher up the mountainside. In the darkness, they trip over rocks and stumble into holes. Every now and then one tries to stifle his scream of pain as he slips on a rock and twists his ankle.

The outline of the mountain, which the men can just make out, looms alongside.

Granville cannot resist breaking the silence. He moves forward along the line of soldiers to walk alongside Bourne.

"Why," he asks him in a whisper, "didn't you tell me of your plan to attack up the giant steps?"

"Colonel Bayly asked me not to tell anyone," Bourne replies. "He has heard that plans like these have a way of getting out and reaching Moorosi. We have to realize, he said, that there are spies among the black people and that we are not always careful when we speak in front of them. We tend to act as though they're not there.

"Also, he said, if the Wodehouse Border Guard and the Mfengu know that their storming of the walls from the front is only a diversionary tactic, they will not do it well. It has to seem like the real thing.

"That is why Bayly acted as though the ladders would be used by the main storming party to climb the stone walls. Truth is they are all being used by us and the main storming party will have none."

"But you could have told me," Granville protests, his voice rising. "I would not have told anyone."

"Shhh," Bourne replies, realizing he is speaking too much and placing his finger on his lips. "Strict silence," he whispers. "Our voices carry in the quiet mountain air."

Granville nods.

After traversing the mountainside for about 30 minutes, they reach an overhanging ledge. Here, they stop for a few minutes' rest.

"Where are the natives carrying the ladders?" asks Bourne. He instructs Whitehead and Springer to find out.

As they double back, the men hear a clattering noise and shouts from the Basotho who have dumped the ladders, ropes and ammunition on the ground and are shouting to the Baphuthi on the mountain.

"Stop the shouting," Whitehead says as they reach the Basotho. "If you do not want to help us, don't. But stop warning the Baphuthi."

As the Basotho continue shouting, Whitehead and Springer raise their Sniders. Whitehead fires a warning shot.

The men are quiet as they stare into the barrels of the guns.

"That's better," says Whitehead.

"Now do as you were told. Pick up the ladders."

The Basotho run off down the mountain into the dark of the night. Whitehead fires another shot in their direction.

"Don't waste your ammunition," Springer says.

"What do we do now?" asks Whitehead.

"Let's take one of the ladders up to the ledge and tell Bourne what happened."

Bourne is unmoved. "We continue as before. We are well rid of those turncoats. We will still climb the mountain.

"Even though the Baphuthi have been warned that we are on this side of the mountain, they might not be aware of what we plan to do.

"And, even if they are aware," Bourne continues, "there are no defences on this side of the mountain. No stone walls to overcome. When we climb to the top we will step on to level ground. We might have lost some of the element of surprise, but we can still succeed in making it to the top of the mountain, which proved impossible on the front face."

Bourne turns to face the men. "Our mission continues as planned with only one difference. I want volunteers to pick up the ladders, rope and ammunition and carry them to the bottom of the paths. The rest of us will continue on."

⁂

Hook's group is making its way up the first stretch of a steep gully on the western side of the front face of the mountain at 1 a.m. when the commander hears whispering among the Thembu and Mfengu fighters assigned to his command. Their attitude to his orders and some of the words he overhears lead him to believe that a number will refuse to fight and might even turn their Sniders on the Cape Mounted Riflemen.

He selects 50 Mfengu whom he is confident are loyal and orders the rest to move away from the mountain. It is better to lose their potential help than to risk their treachery, particularly as his assignment is largely a diversionary tactic.

⁂

Alerted by the Basotho who had been carrying the ladders, Raisa is taking command of the Baphuthi on the mountaintop. He reports to Moorosi.

"It's another attempt to distract us," Moorosi says. "Just as they did before, when they tried to attack us on the other side, they want us to move away from the front walls and concentrate our attention here. They won't be able to climb up these sides of the mountain. "If you see them approaching the top, those who are here can throw down rocks on them and shoot at them if necessary to stop them, but we must concentrate our attention on the front walls."

⁂

Fifty members of the Cape Mounted Riflemen scramble down the western side of the mountain, pick up the ladders abandoned by the Basotho and carry them

Gully on the western side of the mountain climbed by Hook's group.

Eastern face of mountain, showing likely area of "Bourne's Crack".

to the point at which they are to start scaling the mountain.

It has taken them 90 minutes from the camp to reach this point, far longer than planned. They are tired from lack of sleep and carrying the ladders. Soon, the rocket will be fired to signal the start of the attack and they have not yet set the ladders in place, let alone climbed on to them. But it is still dark and they have time if they work as fast as they can.

❧

The men under Bourne are able to assemble the ladders and place them on the first slopes. But as they climb up, they find that the ladders collapse easily. With four men on them, they bend and break apart. In addition, some ladders are shorter than others, making it more difficult to join them. The only solution, they find, is to tie them together, overlapping one ladder with another so they are not as long but are stronger.

Lashing the ladders slows them down, but within 45 minutes the men are making good progress. So far, the men whisper to one another, the Baphuthi are quiet.

"They don't know what we're doing," Whitehead says to Bourne. "They probably didn't hear the Basotho warning them."

❧

The soldiers above the commandant's cave, led by Montague, make faster progress than Bourne's men.

But progress has its downside. By the time they have set the third set of ladders in place and are readying the fourth set, they come close enough to be seen by Baphuthi, peering over the edge above them.

The Baphuthi hurl down stones and boulders, as well as stone-filled hides, forcing the soldiers to duck for cover.

As a Baphuthi peers over the edge above them, one of the Cape Mounted Riflemen raises his Snider and shoots. His aim is true. The warrior falls forward and his body falls down the mountainside, hitting against the rock cliff.

The soldiers, stunned by the incident, watch for more heads to appear above them. None do, but the reality of their task is starting to hit home. This is indeed a matter of life and death, of shoot or be shot, as Bayly had said it would be.

Brome, assigned to the group under Montague, assists his fellow soldiers in placing the ladders, secretly hoping the plan will not succeed and he will be able to turn around and go back to his tent.

As the men continue to place the ladders, the stone and rock attack from above gains in intensity.

A large rock crashes down, striking a boulder just above a group of men before bounding over their heads and splintering on the rocks below. A fragment hits a Mfengu on scouting duty, sending him, doubled up as a ball, down the hillside.

Hit by another rock, a ladder spirals down the mountain slope, clattering to the ground below. As a replacement ladder is handed up to them, the soldiers realize they are now one ladder short and might not make it all the way. Suddenly the mission is looking a lot more difficult.

When the Baphuthi push a dead cow over the edge, narrowly missing one of the men, but striking another ladder and sending it, too, tumbling down the mountainside, the troopers call on their leader, Montague, to abandon the climb. He agrees. The venture has become too risky.

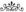

"They are going back down," Raisa says. "We have stopped them. The white soldiers' tactic to divert our attention didn't work.

"We must go and help to guard the front walls because they will soon attack us there."

The frontal assault of the stone walls appears to the men assigned the task to be an invitation to almost certain death. At least they are to storm the mountain while it is still fairly dark, giving them some hope they can avoid the Baphuthi bullets.

Shortly after 2 a.m., the 25 members of the volunteer Wodehouse Border Guard file two by two up to the saddle. Here they join the 80 Mfengu fighters who are to attack up the "spring" path on the right of the mountain under Capt. MacLean.

As the group under MacLean move off, Captain Muhlenbeck addresses the men under his command who are to attack from the front.

"You are to wait here until ordered to move," he says.

"As soon as I give the order you are to storm the mountain and make as much noise as you can. Shout, scream, yell. In that way, we will encourage one another.

"Obviously the enemy will concentrate their attention on us. But — although we will attack when it is just starting to become light so we can see where we are going — the darkness will prevent the enemy from seeing you effectively.

"You are to run to the walls, climb them and attack the Baphuthi as they stand behind the schanzes.

"Does everyone understand our task?"

The men respond in chorus, "Yes, captain," with little enthusiasm.

With no light more than the starry skies above, and ordered not to talk but simply to wait until ordered to move, the men become drowsy.

By 3 a.m. many have drifted off to sleep.

⁂

With the men under Montague abandoning their assault, the task of reaching the summit falls on those under Bourne.

Bourne whispers, "I believe they might be thinking that our only attack is the one Montague is leading," he says. "I don't think they have seen us here. Keep working as quickly and as quietly as you can. Pass the word along, but don't raise your voices."

He scrambles down to the other group. "You must continue. I do not want you to stop," he tells Montague.

"But," Montague protests, pointing up the gully. "It has become extremely dangerous up there. We don't have the benefit of the giant steps that you do and they can see us more easily than they can see you."

"No matter. You need to make it appear that you are still climbing," Bourne says. "The Baphuthi seem to think that you're the only ones placing ladders on this side of the mountain. Let's keep it that way. If my group can avoid being seen, we can creep up and surprise them."

Montague instructs his men to continue.

Their cessation of the climb, however, has given the Baphuthi the impression that the soldiers have abandoned their plans to try to ascend the mountain at that point. Most turn away and return to the front stone walls.

Bourne returns to his group, who have almost completed placing the ladders on the giant steps that form "Bourne's Crack."

After tying them together and putting them in place, they climb the ladders and gather in groups on the ledges at the top of each step, waiting for the signal from Bourne to get on to the ladders and climb to the top.

When the last ladder is readied for its placement on the final step, Springer volunteers to go first.

"I will go up and place the final ladder. It will fall a little short," Springer tells the men. "But I am taller than all of you and I will be able to clamber up the remaining distance more quickly."

"As soon as Springer starts climbing up the last ladder, you should follow him," Bourne tells the men. "When we're on top, the plan is to fix bayonets and march in formation to the south-east and take the enemy from behind.

"You should take the lead from Springer. Follow what he tells you to do.

"Remember, there is a big reward for the man who captures or shoots Moorosi."

Able now to see his way more clearly in the morning light creeping across the mountain, Springer clambers his way up the ladder over the final stretch of rock.

Behind him, the men, aware that Springer is likely to receive the reward for being the first on the top of the mountain, are eager to be right behind him and among the first on the top of the mountain, perhaps even beating Springer to it.

They bunch on the ladders, threatening to break them. But, although they bend under the weight, the lashed-together ladders hold.

⁂

The rocket signalling the start of the attack on all fronts is fired at 4 a.m. Springer finds hand holes in the 15 feet of rock above the top ladder and pulls himself up. At the top of the last rock step, he reaches up to a narrow ledge to his left about four feet from the top of the mountain. He pulls himself up.

But Springer has come within view of the Baphuthi, who cannot see down this fissure from the edge of the mountain, but can see the ledge.

Springer looks up and sees two Baphuthi men, both with raised rifles in their hands, above him.

One cocks his rifle and points it at Springer's head.

"Don't come up here or I will shoot you," the man says.

"Well, fancy seeing you here," replies Springer, reaching down for his revolver. "I would not shoot if I were you, because I might shoot you first."

Before Springer can lift his gun, however, the Baphuthi fires.

⁂

When the rocket is fired to signal the advance, Muhlenbeck orders the men under him to move away from behind the saddle and to storm the walls from the ridge on the right of the plateau.

Still groggy from their sleep, the volunteers find the fear of death suddenly overtaking the fear of disobeying a command. None moves forward.

"You go first," one says, rising to his feet.

"I would prefer it if you went first."

"I said advance!" Muhlenbeck shouts, frustrated by the men's failure to move. He was told he was getting the best trained and most courageous men available, even though they might be volunteers.

Now they simply stand there.

"Advance!" he screams. "I am instructing you to advance! Now, damn you, Now!"

The men stay where they are.

⁂

The soldiers gathered just below Springer watch in horror as the Baphuthi warrior takes aim at their lead man and pulls the trigger.

The crack of the rifle is followed by a puff of white smoke that drifts into the air above them.

The bullet penetrates Springer's shirt. But it only grazes his shoulder.

Stunned, Springer hesitates.

The second Baphuthi fires. This time the shot is off its mark and hits a nearby rock. Springer raises his revolver and, before either of the two Baphuthi can fire again, shoots one, hitting him in the heart. The other Baphuthi, unaware of the presence of the men on the ladders below, runs off.

The body of the struck Baphuthi falls to the ledge alongside Springer, bounces off and rolls down the mountainside. It hits and breaks two ladders tied together lower down the mountain and knocks the men off them. The soldiers tumble down the mountain alongside the body of the Baphuthi warrior.

They pick themselves up and find they have suffered only minor injuries. "It's as well we were near the bottom and did not have far to fall," comments one.

Ignoring the body lying in the bushes, the men gather two more ladders, rope them together and put them in place.

By the time they are done, the men ahead of them are following Springer, climbing to the top of the mountain.

Angered and frustrated at his men's refusal to follow his orders to storm the mountain from the front, Muhlenbeck wonders how he can get them to move. As every minute passes, the sky is becoming lighter, making it easier for the Baphuthi to aim.

"Very well. I will show you the way," Muhlenbeck shouts, believing that, given the lead, the men will follow.

Muhlenbeck sets off on the 350-yard stretch of open plateau.

James Corfield, carrying a carbine, with his water bottle and bag at his side and extra cartridges slung around his neck, follows him. He and Muhlenbeck are alone.

As shots ring out from the stone walls, Corfield trips over a rock, landing behind a small ledge. But it provides little shelter and he stands up and sprints ahead once more.

The sound of the 12-pounder fired from behind him frightens him. He seeks shelter behind a nearby rock about 120 yards from the base of the stone walls.

The men following Springer pull themselves up to the ledge and on to the mountaintop, encountering little resistance from the Baphuthi.

Within five minutes, scores of Cape Mounted Riflemen are on the top of the mountain. The rest scramble up the ladders, but in their eagerness, too many men climb on them and the ladders break. Nevertheless, using the broken ladder steps, and pulling themselves up the mountainside, the men make it up.

The men in Montague's group abandon their attempts to reach the top by their path and climb up the broken ladders behind Bourne's group. In spite of his reluctance, Brome joins his fellow soldiers in clambering to the top of the mountain, joining 200 already there.

Bayly's plan is working. Only about 30 of the Baphuthi are on the mountaintop. The rest are behind the stone walls defending against an attack from the front.

The Baphuthi on the mountaintop find shelter behind a stone wall originally built near the crest of the mountain to counter an attack from the front. They squat behind it to fire from the other side on an enemy attacking them from the rear.

When they realize what is happening, scores of Baphuthi leave the trenches behind

Remnants of the stone wall on the mountaintop behind which the Baphuthi sheltered.

the front walls and climb to the crest of the mountain where they join their compatriots behind the stone wall.

Bourne, taking command of all the colonial soldiers on the mountaintop, shouts, "Remember your orders! Get into formation!"

The soldiers form a line, their bayonets at the ready.

"At the order, forward march."

The men wait.

"Forward march!"

They are all here now. Granville, Whitehead, Bourne, Springer, Brome and the rest of the Cape Mounted Riflemen.

They are joined by MacLean's group who climbed the path at the spring. With them, too, are the men under Hook who climbed the gully on the western side.

The colonial soldiers, numbering almost 400, form a long line around the edge of the mountaintop.

As they move forward, the soldiers set fire to the thatch covering the huts. Soon huge flames light up the mountaintop with an orange glow.

The Cape Mounted Riflemen cheer as they march toward the Baphuthi hiding behind the stone wall, holding their bayonet-tipped rifles before them.

Brome, caught up in the fervour, marches with them. Farther down the line, Whitehead and Bourne stride purposefully forward.

❧

When the soldiers on the mountaintop are 50 yards from the wall, Raisa moves forward, raising his hands in a gesture of surrender. The soldiers pause. The firing stops and an eerie silence settles over the scene as the Baphuthi and the soldiers alike are unsure how to react.

"Take two paces forward," Bourne says in his best military voice. Raisa does not respond. He shrugs his shoulders, indicating he does not understand.

"I said take two paces forward."

Raisa responds by raising his hands in the air as high as he can. His palms reflect the glow of the fires destroying the huts.

The soldiers, unwilling to let any Baphuthi escape punishment, yell, "Give no quarter! Bayly said to give no quarter!" For weeks, they have recalled the time when the severed head of King was displayed behind the front stone wall, how the men in the Chiappini camp were slaughtered, how the Baphuthi killed the pickets guarding the saddle, and ways in which they were repeatedly embarrassed by men who have outwitted and outfought them.

"Give no quarter," they were told. And no quarter will be given.

Without warning, a soldier fires. Raisa, shot in the chest, screams and collapses. The Cape Mounted Riflemen rush forward with even more determination.

Caught up in the frenzy, they lose any constraints they might have had to play by the rules of organized warfare, firing furiously and with abandon in their eagerness to extract vengeance and pour hatred on these "savages."

The organized march turns into a chaotic contest to determine who can extract the most carnage in their rush forward.

No quarter will be given.

Lemena emerges from behind the stone wall on the mountain crest, runs forward and flings his spear toward Brome. As the spear tears a superficial wound in his leg, Brome feels a rush of anger fired by intense fear surge through his body. He must kill or be killed.

Before the Baphuthi man can fully recover his balance, Brome runs at him with his bayonet. Lemena turns in an attempt to avoid the blow. Brome feels the resistance as the sharp steel point enters Lemena's side, just below his heart. He watches as Lemena's face reflects the pain. With blood oozing from the wound, Lemena buckles over and falls.

As Brome withdraws his bayonet from Lemena's body, he gasps at the blood covering it, and then looks down to see the man he has bayoneted bleeding profusely. He recognizes Lemena. The awful realization of what he has just done strikes him.

He has killed a man.

Not just any man. The intelligent man with the cheeky sense of humour that they all liked, even though he was the enemy, even though he was regarded as a savage. The man of justice. The man of pride in his people.

For a moment, as Brome stands affixed, looking at Lemena's lifeless body, he no longer hears the noise of the battlefield.

In his senses, the players in the deadly drama around him pause in mid-action. Life stands still.

He has killed a man.

A man who did him no personal wrong. A man who deserved to live.

As the fighting continues to rage, no one notices Brome standing transfixed, staring in disbelief at his blood-covered bayonet and the man who lies unmoving on the ground below him.

He has killed a man.

Bourne is of a different mind. Thrilled with the knowledge that his "six-steps" plan of attack worked, he fires at the Baphuthi, now fleeing from behind the wall. He has no doubt now that the Cape Mounted Riflemen have won this war, and because of him more than anyone else.

He savours the sweet smell of victory in this do-or-die game.

Whitehead, too, is indulging in the high-risk high-adventure thrill of battle. He narrowly avoids a bullet, then smiles with satisfaction as he watches the Baphuthi scatter. Never before has the adrenalin pumped through his body as it is right now.

Screaming in fear, Baphuthi run down the mountain toward the stone walls that form the front tiers, hoping the edifices will provide some protection.

Some, panic stricken, jump over the side of the mountain, falling to their deaths on the rocks below.

Two dozen Baphuthi succeed in escaping the fighting and jump down the edges of rocks, hiding in small groups under the edges where they plan to stay until they can slide down a gully when the soldiers have left.

Others incredibly make it down the mountain, slipping and sliding down the gullies on the western side.

The rest continue to fire from behind the walls at the crest of the mountain, determined to resist to the end, even as the soldiers descend on them and surround them.

Soon Baphuthi bodies lie everywhere as the Cape Mounted Riflemen continue their mass killing spree

The few women and children left on the mountain, spared by the rampaging soldiers, stand in a huddle, begging for mercy and wailing uncontrollably as they watch their fathers, husbands, brothers and sons bayoneted and gunned down.

Bourne and Whitehead find themselves caught up in the contagious spirit to destroy.

They are true soldiers now. Any last vestige of compassion has left them. Their conscience that would insist that killing another person is wrong is silenced.

The commanders have lost control and are unable to devise any sort of Baphuthi surrender, even if they wanted to do so. The mountain has been commandeered by an out-of-control group of white desperadoes who have been sent to kill and destroy and now are determined to do so with gusto.

No quarter will be given.

A hut in which the Baphuthi had stored ammunition explodes in a huge ball of flame, sending fragments of wood, stone and bullets into the air.

The colonial soldiers, who duck as the fragments fly around them, succeed in avoiding most of the shrapnel. For a while the explosion disorients everyone on the mountain, but soon the killing resumes, the bodies pile up and the chaos continues.

❧

Down on the plateau, all is quiet. Corfield huddles behind the rock, wondering how long he will be stuck here. He hunkers down as the firing on the top of the mountain intensifies. He waits for the bullets to fly around him.

There are none.

As the firing continues, he raises his rifle and gingerly looks out. He looks toward the mountain. There, just below the crown, Lieutenant McMullen is waving the Cape Mounted Riflemen's flag and a surge of relief flows through his body. Somehow they have taken the mountain.

A minute or two later he has joined Muhlenbeck near the base of the stone walls. "The firing is not coming from the Baphuthi, but from our men firing into the schanzes from the top," Corfield says in amazement. "How did they get there?"

"They used scaling ladders to climb up the steep sides of the mountain," Muhlenbeck explains. Our task in storming the walls was to act as a feint, to divert the Baphuthi attention away from the gullies. I couldn't tell you that earlier because we wanted our attack to look genuine."

"Feint, my eye," says Corfield. "The volunteers fainted, is what happened. Fat lot of good they were. As it was they did absolutely nothing."

Muhlenbeck is silent. He hopes the men's failure to follow his command and his lead will be overlooked in light of the tremendous victory.

❧

The Baphuthi still alive behind the walls on the mountaintop, surrounded on all sides, fight back furiously. Confused by the sudden onslaught that seems to have come from nowhere, they try desperately to hold their ground, flinging their spears and firing toward the colonial troops as they attack them.

They are hopelessly outnumbered.

Soon the trenches behind the stone walls are awash in blood. Bodies lie everywhere.

❧

Less than an hour after the attack began the firing on the mountaintop dies down.

Smoke continues to pour from the smouldering huts, covering the mountain in a thick black cloud.

Strewn across the mountain top, scores of Baphuthi bodies lie at angles and pointing in haphazard directions, some piled on top of one another, some in groups, others alone, gunned down or bayoneted as they tried to run to safety.

Some bear begging looks on their faces, their hands raised in a desperate last-minute plea for mercy. The bodies of a few women and children, killed by flying shrapnel, lie among those of the men. Dead and dying cattle are strewn across the mountain top.

Two bodies lie inside a torched hut, burned beyond recognition.

Whitehead glimpses a white object in the ruins of the ammunition hut. As the smoke starts to clear, he sees it is a skull built into the side, placed there, he assumes, to act as a talisman to protect them against the white soldiers. He shivers as he realizes it is probably the skull of his friend William King.

The top of the mountain, now fully lit by the morning sun, has mostly fallen silent, but the talking and laughter of the colonial soldiers, delighting in their victory, can be heard as they tour the remains of Moorosi's village.

They pick up pieces of earthenware pots blown apart in the fighting.

They shiver at the site of the body of a vicious dog, snarling its teeth in a post-mortem threat.

They wonder at the way the Baphuthi survived for so long on the mountain.

In a shallow cave on the mountain top, they etch the date and their names into the rock with the tips of their bayonets as a lasting testimony to their prowess.

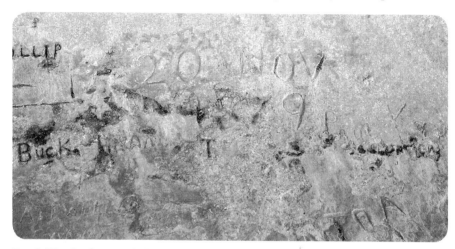

Top: Soldiers' etchings in shallow cave on mountaintop near "Bourne's Crack." Note date: "20 Nov" and below it "1879." Below, left: The cave. Right: View over valley from cave.

The men are joined by Bayly, dressed in a deer-stalking hat, cardigan jacket and yellow riding cords tucked into his socks, standing next to the Union Jack erected alongside the mountain's crown. Bayly beams with delight, proud that his plan worked and that the colonial troops have suffered so few casualties.

Before long, Bayly and most of the soldiers clamber down the mountain, ready to celebrate.

But first Bayly must tell the world of his success. In his tent, he pens a message for onward transmission to Cape Town: "I assaulted the mountain on the 20th inst. from five different positions, all parties leaving camp for their respective positions at the dip of the moon. The mountain was ours at a quarter past four o'clock a.m.... Moorosi at present not turned up."

⚜

In a rocky outcrop on the north-western side of the mountaintop, three Baphuthi men, who escaped the battle scene as the fighting erupted and have been watching the carnage from a distance, head toward the mountain's northern edge.

One, a lot older, is slower than the others. A son walks in front and the other son behind him. They vied for the right to be heir to the kingdom. Now, with their lives and the existence of their people in the balance, that dispute is forgotten as the three seek a hideout where they will not be found by the soldiers.

Their people have been decimated. Most of what they fought for has been lost. But they are still alive, and while they are still alive their nation is still alive.

⚜

Lieutenant McMullen seizes a Baphuthi, one of few taken prisoner in the capture of the mountaintop. "Where is your chief?" he asks him angrily. "Where is Moorosi?"

The man fails to answer. He wants to say he does not know where his king is, but he is afraid he might make the soldier even more angry if he does.

McMullen places his carbine under the man's chin.

"Tell me, where is Moorosi? You must know where he is. Tell me!"

No response.

"I will shoot you if you don't tell me!"

The man remains silent, frozen with fear.

McMullen fires his carbine, blowing the prisoner's head to pieces.

No quarter will be given.

⚜

Concerned that Baphuthi who fled at the outbreak of the fighting might still be hiding on the mountaintop, Whitehead decides not to join the other soldiers leaving the mountain. He will search the rocky outcrop on the north-western side of the mountain for stragglers.

As Whitehead draws closer to the outcrop, he spots a couple of Baphuthi sticking their heads out from behind a rock. He is right. Not all the enemy are dead. Not all have fled. Is the war then really over?

"What has happened to Moorosi?" he wonders. "Has someone claimed the £200 reward for his capture? As he is pondering these questions, he hears gunfire from the rocks where he saw the Baphuthi. Running across the uneven ground toward the noise, he follows a path through the outcrop, where he finds Private Thomas Swash lying on his side behind a rock. "Three natives fired at me," he says. "One of the shots hit me." He points to a growing patch of blood on his thigh. "They went down that path."

The war is not yet over.

Two soldiers, also attracted by the sound of gunfire, arrive at the scene.

"You go down the path," one says to Whitehead. "We'll carry Private Swash to a place where he will be safer. But be careful. We heard that the natives dropped a charge of dynamite over the ledge. They might try to set it off at any time."

Along the narrow path, Whitehead sees the three Baphuthi heading for a protruding rock. He raises his carbine and fires. The man at the back falls — "like a slain ox," Whitehead thinks to himself.

Moving past the body, Whitehead follows the path, which twists around large rocks, narrowing as it winds its way along the western side of the mountain. Around a corner, on the north-western corner of the mountaintop, Whitehead comes to a shallow grotto, about 10 feet high, near the edge of the cliff that plunges a sheer 1,500 feet to the valley at the confluence of the Orange and Quthing rivers.

He stops. A man he suspects is Lehana kneels at the grotto, his rifle at the ready. He is looking away, down to the valley below, and has not seen him.

Whitehead creeps quietly forward and sees a grey-haired man sitting in the grotto. He raises his rifle. Aiming at the man's chest, he pulls the trigger. The old man reels backward. Whitehead reloads his rifle.

At the sound of the shot, Lehana wheels around. Seeing Whitehead, he loads his rifle. But, before Lehana can fire, Whitehead fires again, this time sending the bullet into the old man's neck. The man rolls forward, slumping to the ground.

Lehana fires moments after Whitehead's second shot. Whitehead ducks. The shot, which would have struck him in the face had he not moved, pierces the badge on Whitehead's cap, splitting it in two as it knocks his cap off his head.

Lehana shoots at Whitehead [*The Graphic*, 1879]

Remains of ammunition storage hut, found at the end of the war to contain four tons of gunpowder.

When Whitehead raises his rifle to return Lehana's fire, the warrior jumps up and takes off on the path, back toward the mountaintop. Whitehead follows. In a short time, he draws close to him and the two exchange shots. Lehana runs off once more and Whitehead tries to follow him further, but loses the trail.

He is returning along the path through the rocks, on the edge of the mountain, when the dynamite that the soldiers warned him had been dropped over the edge explodes on his right, a few yards ahead of him.

The blast causes Whitehead to lose his footing and sends him reeling backward. He falls and finds himself rolling down a slope. He makes a desperate attempt to grab hold of bushes and grass to stop his slide, but is unable to cling to them for any length of time; some slip through his hands, others pull out from the soil by the roots as he grabs on to them.

He continues to slip 30 yards downhill without being able to appreciably stop, sliding toward the edge of a sheer cliff edge. He stares down in fear. He is about to careen over the edge and plunge to his death on the rocks 1,500 feet below.

✦

As the colonial soldiers reach the lower slopes of the mountain and look back on where they have been, they break out into cheering and laughing,

"When I look at the way we came up, I cannot believe we actually did it," says Robert Kennan.

"I was confident we could make it up the crack — and we did," says Bourne.

Brome walks quietly alone. He is not proud of what he did.

It is true no one can call him a coward. No one can accuse him of failing to perform his duty. He has been a gallant soldier, serving his country. But a profound sense of guilt is tearing at his soul. He served his country, but he fears he did not serve God.

He killed a man.

He plunged his bayonet into him, robbing him of his life. A man who did him no wrong. Nothing now can bring that man back to life. He cannot go back in time to reverse his action. This deed — this wrong deed, this evil deed, this murderous deed — will haunt him forever.

He killed a man.

Walking slightly behind Brome, Granville is looking forward with eager antici-pation to returning home now that the war is over. He is ready to return to dull boring England once more. He wonders who won the reward for capturing or killing Moorosi — a prize that had been forgotten during the intense fighting at the top of the mountain.

Suddenly it strikes him. No one has spoken of the Baphuthi king. Where is Moorosi? Was he captured during the fighting? Did he die? Granville is not alone in his thoughts. Around him, men are picking through the bodies, searching for anyone who looks as old as the king. Now and then one picks up a body and carries it down the mountain to Bayly, hoping they will earn the reward.

Whitehead stops his slide by digging his boots into the ground and against a rock just before reaching the cliff edge. He lies there clutching the mountain, panting. He can feel his heart pumping. Stunned, but only slightly hurt, he regains his footing and climbs carefully up the slope to the trail.

Although most of the white soldiers have left the mountain, Whitehead is not convinced that the battle is over. Lehana —assuming it were him — is still at large. A number of Baphuthi are likely also still on the mountain and could be hiding until the colonial forces leave, enabling them to retake the mountain.

Whitehead continues to scout the mountaintop. Eventually the troopers leave and Whitehead suspects he is alone — except for the few remaining Baphuthi.

It is party time at the camp ground and the liquor, banned by Bayly for the last few days, is now flowing freely. They are alive. They won. The threat has gone. They will soon be going home. Could the situation possibly be any better?

But not all the men are accounted for. Bourne still has not found his friend. He hopes Whitehead survived the battle in good shape.

Whitehead has been keeping guard on the mountaintop for some hours, but has caught only occasional glimpses of Baphuthi. When he fires at them, they disappear and he is unable to find them.

It is 4 p.m. when a sentry arrives. "You have been reported missing," the sentry says. "All the rest of the men have been accounted for. Our forces have only two seriously injured. I'm told Private Swash was wounded and is not expected to survive. Private Corfield was hit in the shoulder joint. One Mfengu is dead. We wondered whether you had been injured, or even killed, but I am pleased I found you here unhurt. You can go back down to the camp; I'll take over the guard duty here."

Whitehead, tired and relieved to escape the pungent odour of the carcasses of cattle, horses and heaps of human bodies, walks down the mountain path.

The scene on the way down is as sickening as that on the top. Baphuthi bodies lie strewn behind the stone walls.

In the trench behind the lowest wall a Baphuthi with white hair and a colourless face is among a dozen bodies. He lies at a grotesque angle, making his body look even more strange and out of place. Whitehead realizes this is the albino who many said was such a good shot. He will shoot no more now.

Whitehead feels a twinge of emotion. This man did his best for his people, as he saw it. He defended them with his ability to shoot. One who would have been an outcast in many societies, he served people who cared for him. Now all he did has come to nothing. In the end, all that mattered was he was on the side that lost.

At the camp, Whitehead walks to Bayly's tent and asks to see the colonel.

"What do you want with me?" asks Bayly.

"Beg your pardon, colonel. I am wondering if anyone has found Moorosi," Whitehead says.

"No, a number of people have brought me bodies, but none of them was Moorosi. We assume he died on the mountain, but no one has claimed the reward."

Whitehead tells Bayly how he stayed at the top of the mountain, keeping the remaining Baphuthi at bay. "I did not realize it at the time, but I suspect now that a man I shot up there might have been Moorosi, lying in a shallow cave. I did not get a chance to look properly at him because I was shot at by a man guarding him."

Out of the corner of his eye, Whitehead sees that James Neville, of the Wodehouse Guards, is standing outside listening. Neville leaves, calling a few Mfengu soldiers to accompany him.

Whitehead continues his report to Bayly, but he is interrupted by a spate of gunfire from the mountaintop. The men leave the tent and look toward the mountain gullies. They see a group of Baphuthi jump down the edge of the mountain, clambering down what remains of the ladders, and run off toward the river.

"Those were the men I saw on the mountain," Whitehead says. "The sentry let them get away."

"I am sure one of those men was Lehana," says the Quthing magistrate Austen who has been at the mountain since the attack began. "The one who started it all appears to have escaped. But I'm told that almost all of Moorosi's other sons have been killed as well as most of his followers."

He adds that he climbed the mountain earlier and, knowing the men involved, identified the bodies of Letuka, who was lying on a path toward a rocky ledge, Motsapi, a son of Moorosi who was reputed to be a splendid shot, Masepuli, a nephew of the chief, and Thladi, a grandson of Moorosi and one of the prisoners who was forcibly released from the prison at the residency.

"I also know that Muntsu, who hid for a long time in a cave before joining the rest on the mountain, was killed, as was Lemena. Indeed, Moorosi's whole family appears to have been wiped out, except for Lehana.

"But I have no idea where Moorosi himself is. I did not see him or his body."

A Mfengu man carries a body of an old Baphuthi man. He lays it down before Bayly. "This is Moorosi," he says.

"No, I am afraid it is not," Bayly replies. "He is an old Thembu chief."

Angry at not qualifying for the reward, the Mfengu man dashes the lifeless head to pieces with a thick fighting stick that he carries.

Later that afternoon, Neville — the man who had been listening at Bayly's tent when Whitehead was reporting — arrives with the body of an old man, which Mfengu have helped him carry down from the mountain. Whitehead follows them to the tent.

"How did you get this body?" Bayly asks.

"After the fighting had died down, I realized there were Baphuthi left on the mountain," Neville says. "So I went back up to the mountain. As I arrived at the top, I saw a native drop over a ledge of rock and run round a narrow footpath, about a foot or two wide. I fired at him. He ran toward a shallow cave.

"I was joined by a Mfengu policeman and we ran toward the cave, but the cave was protected by three or four armed people. They fired at us and the Mfengu was wounded in the hip. Another Mfengu arrived and told the Baphuthi to come out in their language, but they did not respond.

"We moved away from the cave.

"Later Sergeant Paterson of Yeomanry joined me. He had dynamite with him, which we threw toward the cave entrance. The Baphuthi moved off and we entered the cave where we found this body with wounds on the neck and the ribs. He had crawled in there to die. We thought it looked as though it could be Moorosi's body."

"Yes, that indeed is the chief," Bayly says. "Well done, Private Neville, you will receive the 200-pound reward."

Whitehead, convinced Neville's story was a fabrication, is quick to protest.

"I am sure I shot that man while I was guarding the mountain after everyone left," he says. "He looked like this man, old, short and wrinkled, but with fine, almost European features. He bore himself with dignity, even when he was shot.

"Now Private Neville, who heard me talking, has gone up to the top of the mountain, found the body and claims the reward."

"I cannot give you the reward based simply on a story like that," Bayly tells Whitehead. "The reward must go to the man who brought me the body."

"But that is the man I shot," counters Whitehead.

"I shot Moorosi."

Neville protests. "*I* shot Moorosi. I brought down his body," he insists.

Bayly is more convinced by Whitehead's explanation than that of Neville. He realizes, too, that Neville made no mention of shooting the Baphuthi leader until Whitehead claimed he had done so. But he has made his ruling. The man who brought him the body will get the reward.

Nevertheless, he hands Whitehead 25 pounds.

"Here is compensation for you. The important thing is we defeated the wily old chief. He won't be around any longer to defy the law.

"You can be proud of that."

Bayly instructs the men to move away and to take Moorosi's body with them.

"I do not want it lying here," he says.

⁂

At the top of the mountain, the thatch roof of the hut that Moorosi occupied is charred and the top layers of rock that form the hut itself is blackened. It is deserted now and likely will be forever.

On the ground, unaffected by the fire, alongside a group of charred amulets, lies the Bible given to the chief by Ellenberger. A large rectangular hut is found to contain six to seven tons of gunpowder. Other huts contain a plentiful supply of corn and other food. Clearly, the soldiers conclude, the Baphuthi could have held out for a long time.

⁂

Moorosi's body is carried out of Bayly's tent by a group of soldiers. They laugh as they parade the king's body around the camp. As they return from their parade, a soldier shouts, "Cut off his head the way they cut off King's head."

⁂

Bayly sends an updated report to Cape Town:

"Moorosi turned up; was shot through the neck at the first assault, and managed to creep into a cave where he was found about three hours after, dead. The whole affair is over; it only requires a few natives, assisted by a small party of the Europeans, to patrol the country."

Speaking to his senior officers, Bayly outlines his victory.

"By our count, 70 of the chief's warriors died in the fighting. A considerable number, possibly 120, fled down all sides of the hill in the deficient light when they saw the war was over, but every man of importance, except for Lehana, is now believed to be dead.

"Moorosi lost 16 sons and nine grandsons. In addition, 12 men and seven or eight women have been taken prisoner.

"These people will not be giving us any trouble any more.

"Like Moorosi, the Baphuthi tribe has been decapitated. It will disappear into the sands of history.

"I have given instructions that tomorrow the stone walls should all be dynamited so that the stones and earth cover the bodies of the dead Baphuthi in the trenches. Bodies lying on the top of the mountain should be dynamited. I want no trace to remain of the defences or of the bodies.

"The Cape Mounted Riflemen have done us and themselves proud in helping us to bring down an uncivilized rebellious barbaric leader who dared defy the colonial government.

"Springer was named a captain the moment he stepped on the top of the mountain. Captain Bourne, who was in charge of the storming party, will be gazetted for a brevet majorship.

"I hope this will be a lesson to those who are insane enough to rebel against a constituted authority of the British government. Our colonial forces will always prove a safeguard of peace in the exact proportion of their ability to strike terror and destruction to any misguided tribe. God save the Queen."

Queenstown — Monday November 24, 1879

Early today, four days after the end of the battle, the body of Private John Brome, Cape Mounted Riflemen, is found in a bed at Queenstown Hospital where he had been taken after complaining he was ill on his return from Moorosi's Mountain. He committed suicide by shooting himself.

Quthing — Saturday, November 28, 1879

For a week, colonial soldiers, working in 24-hour shifts, dismantle the stone walls and clear the mountain. It is unpleasant work. Cattle, dead and dying, immense quantities of bones and human bodies have to be removed. A powder magazine containing six or seven tons of gunpowder is blown up.

The men successfully complete the task. "It looks quite decent and respectable," Granville says as the colonial soldiers are discharged.

302

Colonial Office, March 8, 1880.

THE following Despatch, with its Enclosures, has been received from the Right Honourable Sir H. B E. Frere, G.C.B., &c., Governor of the Cape Colony :—

Government House, Cape Town,
SIR,   *February 9, 1880.*

WITH reference to my Despatch of the 17th ultimo, I have the honour to transmit the accompanying supplementary return of casualties which have occurred in the colonial forces during the months of November and December, 1879.

I have, &c.,
H. B. E. FRERE, Governor.
The Right Hon. the Secretary of State,
Colonial Office.

Supplementary Return of Casualties which have occurred in the Auxiliary Forces of the Cape of Good Hope during the months of November and December, 1879.

Private John Brome, C.M.R., committed suicide at Queenstown Hospital, by shooting himself with a revolver, 24th November, Queenstown Hospital ; nearest relative, Mrs. John Brome, Komgha.

Private Thomas Swash, C.M R., fatally wounded at attack on Morosi's Mountain, 11th December, Thomas' Shop Hospital, Basutoland ; nearest relative, Mrs. Swash, 48, New Weston-street, Long-lane, London. Shown in November return as wounded.

Private John Leonard, C.M.R., died of disease of liver and stomach, 22nd December, Thomas' Shop Hospital, Basutoland ; nearest relative Mr. J Leonard, Lunatic Asylum, Fort England, Grahamstown.

W. F. D. COCHRANE, Captain,
A. A.-G. Colonial Forces.
January 27, 1880.

But the soldiers themselves look far from respectable as today they start straggling back to the colony through the mountains. As nearly all their horses died during the campaign, they are forced to ride on bullocks, wagons or even walk. Their clothing is tattered and their boots are falling apart. Some have part of their blankets sewn into their breeches. "A fine crew we look," Whitehead says.

"Our clothing is only one aspect of the bad way we were treated," says Granville. "I think it would have been a gracious act, which I would have valued, if they had offered me something to acknowledge the service I rendered. Bayly called on us to give the attack everything we had and that our country would be proud of us. Well, we did give it our all. Now we are left with no thanks. But I'm sure Bayly will get his praise."

"At least I received 25 pounds for my trouble," says Whitehead, "although I spent it all on drinks for everyone in camp on Thursday night."

EPILOGUE

By February 1880, hundreds of Baphuthi who surrendered or were captured during the nine-month war, and who are able to handle pickaxes and spades, are employed at the magistracy and on the public roads. Among them is Mafetudi, Moorosi's chief messenger, who surrendered before the end of the war.

Those Baphuthi who found sanctuary with the Ellenbergers remain at Masitise. The rest, defeated and disillusioned and their numbers decimated, abandon their ancestral homeland, finding new homes in the isolated mountains of Basutoland where they teeter on the edge of survival as a nation.

Lehana, putative heir to the kingdom, is the only one of the Baphuthi leaders known to have escaped uninjured at the end of the final assault and, following a brief return to the mountain, is reported to have left Quthing for Matatiele.

After an outcry by missionaries, Moorosi's head, which was sent to King William's Town, is returned to the Baphuthi for burial with his body.

The highest medal of honour that a British or colonial soldier can earn — is awarded to three colonial soldiers.

• Peter Brown for his actions in carrying water to two wounded men sheltering behind a rock in the first attack on Moorosi's mountain.

• Robert George Scott for his action in volunteering for the dangerous assignment of throwing shells behind the enemy lines.

• Dr. Edmund Baron Hartley for bravery and devotion to duty in attending to the wounded under fire and carrying Corporal A. P. Jones to safety.

They are presented with little fanfare, partly because the medals were won in the first two failed attempts to oust Moorosi from his fortress and partly because of growing public disillusionment with the war itself.

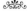

Many settlers conclude the destructive war against Moorosi and the Baphuthi people achieved nothing of value or honour for the colony. Moorosi was not only a valiant warrior but an outstanding military strategist and an engineer of great merit, they add.

Indeed, rather than averting further conflict, it is not long before the Cape Colony's victory creates new, more widespread, strife. The wider conflict is sparked when the colonial government draws up plans to sell much of the conquered land in Quthing to white colonists. The government argues that selling the land will recover a portion of the costs of the war and will show other black nations that rebellion will not go unpunished. The Basotho are furious; Letsie sends a petition to the

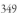

Cape Parliament on May 14, 1880 strongly opposing the plan for white settlement.

Ellenberger supports Letsie, pointing out to the colonial government that the confiscation of Quthing land is contrary to Moshoeshoe's original arrangement with the British. Other missionaries join the opposition to the plan. But the protests fall on deaf ears; the missionaries' appeals merely serve to anger Governor Sir Bartle Frere and the Cape Colony government who press on with their plans.

Basotho anger over the white-settlement plan is intensified by opposition to the disarmament act, which the colony moves to enforce in Basutoland.

In September 1880 the new Liberal British government — led by William Gladstone, which ousted the Conservatives under Benjamin Disraeli in April, 1880 — recalls Sir Bartle Frere to England, citing strong differences with his policies. But even the removal of the architect of the disarmament act and the white settlement plan fails to deter the colony.

When in December 1880 the Cape government appoints a commission to inspect Quthing with a view to dividing it up for white settlement, the Gladstone government in Britain steps in and instructs the colony to abandon the plan. The colonial government reluctantly complies.

But the damage has been done. Fuelled by the white-settlement plans, attempted implementation of the disarmament act, and growing fear that the colony will turn on them as it did on Moorosi, rebellion grows among the Basotho.

⚜

The growing unrest in Basutoland reaches into the Transkei — to Hamilton Hope, the first magistrate in Quthing and now the magistrate at Qumbu.

On October 23, 1880, at Sulenkama, near Qumbu, Hope prepares for a meeting with leaders of the Mpondomise people at which he will insist that the people help him to fight Basotho rebels in the north, even though Mhlonthlo, their king, has said he cannot do so now as his wife, a daughter of Sarhili, has just died.

Charles Brownlee, chief magistrate of Griqualand East, warns Hope his move is risky. Mhlonthlo, he says, has a "treacherous and unreliable disposition" and "could side with the rebels rather than cooperate with Hope."

In response, Hope says he will be true to the chivalrous traditions of his family and name and will proceed. "I believe I can perform an important service to my country and I am prepared to incur any risk in accomplishing this end," he says. "My opinion is that as in a game of cards, having led my king of trumps, if anybody in the game holds the ace, I lose the trick, and, if not, my king wins."

The meeting is attended by four white officials — Hope, his clerk A. Davis, and two young officials Charles Henman and Robert Warren — and 900 Mpondomise.

Mhlonthlo invites Hope and the officials to sit in a circle. Even though he will not lead his people, he is prepared, he says, to hand them over for Hope's final orders on sending an armed force against the Basotho rebels.

"I am now putting you in Mr. Hope's hands," Mhlonthlo tells his people. "He will tell you what to do and you must obey him."

Mhlonthlo takes Davis by the hand and leads him away, saying he wishes to speak with him.

At this prearranged signal, a Mpondomise man named Mahlangeni plays the ace of trumps. He seizes Hope's long beard from behind and, pulling up his head, stabs him in the breast. He also stabs Henman and Warren.

The three die in minutes.

Hope's clerk, Davis, is spared as his father and brother serve as missionaries to the Mpondomise and Mhlonthlo's fight is only with the white government and, in particular, its magistrate, Hamilton Hope.

Hope's death certificate is signed by Emile Rolland "brother of widow Emma Cecile Hope."

⁂

Hope's successor also does not escape the growing turbulence in Basutoland.

In January 1881, John Austen, still serving as the colonial magistrate in Quthing, is called upon to deal with an anti-government group who have crossed into the territory. The group includes a small number of Baphuthi living in the mountains, bent on revenge against the colony for the Moorosi war.

Austen mismanages the ensuing battle and is killed in a clash on a plateau just south of Moorosi's mountain. A Baphuthi decapitates Austen in retribution for the mutilation of Moorosi's body. He sends the severed head to Letsie.

⁂

Growing unrest in Basutoland turns into the "Gun War" against the Cape Colony.

On August 25, 1881, Griffith, unwilling to implement the colonial policy on disarmament, is given a year's leave prior to retirement. Maitin, working for the colony in Maseru, is obliged to resign in January 1882 to escape an unacceptable transfer that he believes is victimization for his political views.

⁂

Faced with an uprising across Basutoland it cannot put down, the Cape Colony, on March 18, 1884, formally withdraws from Basutoland, which reverts to its earlier status as a British protectorate.

The Basotho achieve the only successful revolt by any indigenous people against the Cape Colony.

In the end the colony loses everything for which it fought against Moorosi — and more. It not only loses Quthing, but also the entire country of Basutoland, which never becomes part of the Cape Colony, nor of South Africa. Today it is the independent kingdom of Lesotho.

⁂

In spite of the conflict, Frederic Ellenberger, the man of peace, continues his work at Masitise, living in the cave house and conducting services at his 400-seat church. In later years he expands his outstations from three to 12 and many Basotho who move into Quthing become Christians under his and Emma's ministry before he retires after 45 years on the mission field.

View bonus items, express your opinion, and learn more at www.sent-to-kill.com

Made in the USA
Charleston, SC
12 July 2014